WEB DATABAS

WEB DATABASE SYSTEMS

Barry Eaglestone and Mick Ridley

McGRAW–HILL BOOK COMPANY
London▫New York▫St Louis▫San Francisco▫Auckland▫Bogota
Caracas▫Lisbon▫Madrid▫Mexico▫Milan▫Montreal
New Delhi▫Panama▫Paris▫San Juan▫São Paulo
Singapore▫Sydney▫Tokyo▫Toronto

Published by
McGRAW–HILL Book Company Europe
Shoppenhangers Road, Maidenhead, Berkshire, SL6 2QL, England
Telephone 01628 502500
Fax 01628 770224

British Library Cataloguing in Publication Data
The CIP data of this title in available from the British Library, UK

Library of Congress Cataloging–in–Publication Data
The CIP data of this title in available from the Library of Congress, Washington DC, USA

1 2 3 4 5 BB 5 4 3 2 1

Typeset by Barry Eaglestone and Mick Ridley
Printed and bound in Malta by Interprint Limited

_____CONTENTS_____

PREFACE   xi

1 INTRODUCTION TO WEB DATABASE SYSTEMS   1

1.1 Database technology   3
   Database basics   3
   The organisation   4
   An organisation's information system   7
   The database approach to information systems   10
   The database management system   14
   Summary   19
1.2 The Internet and the Web   20
   Migration from the computer room to the work place   20
   Computer networks   21
   The Internet   22
   The Web   24
       Hypermedia   25
       HTML   26
       URL and HTTP   29
       Gateways   30
   Summary   30
1.3 Web Databases   31
   Web applications   31
   Web enhanced database systems   33
   Database enhancement of Web systems   35
   Summary—When to use Web databases   36
1.4 Summary   36
Exercises   38

PART I DATABASES   43

2 DATA MODELS AND RELATIONAL DATABASES   45

2.1 What is a data model?   45
2.2 Relational databases   47
   SQL   47
   The structural part   49
       Domains   52
       Keys   52
   SQL schema definition language (SDL)   54
       Creating a new database   55
       Creating a new base relation   55
       Definition of domains   57
       Changing the schema contents   57
   The manipulative part   58

Operators of the relational algebra   59
    Cut operations   59
    Paste operations   61
    Set operations   64
SQL implementation of the manipulative part   65
    Retrieval of columns from a single table   67
    Retrieval of selected rows from a single table   69
    Computation   77
    Retrieval from more than one table   80
    Nested selects   84
    Set operations on tables   88
    Changing values in the database   90
The integrity part   93
    SQL integrity features   94
Views   97
Other features of the relational data model and SQL   99
2.3 Summary   100
Exercises   101

3 NEW DATABASE TECHNOLOGIES   107
  3.1 Limitations of relational databases   108
  3.2 Object databases   112
  ODMG object database standards   113
  UML   117
  The structural part of the object data model   118
    ODMG object definition language (ODL)   129
    Example ODL schema   129
    General features of an ODL schema   132
    ODL type definitions   133
    ODL class and interface definitions   134
    Type properties   134
    State properties   135
    Operations   136
    Structured and collection types   137
    Type definitions   138
    Literals   139
  The manipulative part of the object data model   140
    Object database manipulations   142
    OQL   143
    OQL pick and mix operations   149
    Selecting objects from a collection   151
    Processing the selected objects   154
    Processing a collection of many types of object 156
    Creating structured objects   158
    Conversion of an object from one type to another 160
    Operator composition   161
  3.3 Object-relational databases   163
  Large data objects   164
  Triggers   165

Object-oriented features   165
   UDT   166
      Distinct UDT   167
      Structured UDT 168
      Operations on UDT 169
   Object identifiers   170
   Subtype/supertype relationships   171
   UDT encapsulation   172
   UDT operations   173
   UDT polymorphism   175
   UDT summary   176
   Parameterised types   177
   SQL:1999 tables   177
3.4 Persistent programming languages   179
3.5 Summary   180
Exercises   180

PART II THE WEB   187

4   WEB TECHNOLOGY   189
4.1 The Web—basic concepts   190
   What is the Web   192
   The Web and the Internet   193
      TCP/IP   193
      IP addresses   195
   The Web as an Internet application 197
      Servers and clients 197
      Browsers   198
      Search engines 200
   The Uniform Resource Locator (URL) 201
   HTTP   204
   The history of the world wide web 206
4.2 How does a user put information on the Web   208
   Web servers   209
   The structure of web sites   210
   Representing information on the Web 212
   Hyperlinks   212
4.3 An HTML tutorial   213
   How to create HTML documents   213
   A very simple HTML example   214
      Common errors —overlapping tag pairs 215
      Common errors — repeated singular tags 216
   Validity and invalidity   216
   Adding content to HTML   217
      Headings and paragraphs 217
   Links   219
      Absolute, partial and relative links 220
      Links to different types of server or resource 222
   Lists   223

Tables	224
Images	226
HTML forms	226
Structure and presentation	228
Some more advanced features	229
Writing good HTML	231
HTML validation	231
4.4 Presentation and processing of Web pages	232
Cascading style sheets	232
DOM: the document object model	234
Web caching	235
Browser caches	235
Proxy caches	236
4.5 Dynamic Web pages	237
CGI	238
Java	240
JavaScript	242
When to use JavaScript	243
4.6 New developments	244
XML	245
4.7 Summary	247
Exercises	250

PART III WEB DATABASES 257

5 WEB DATABASE DESIGN	259
5.1 The Web database design process	259
Conventional database design methods	260
Web database design	262
5.2 Data Analysis	266
Types and occurrences	267
Entities, attributes and relationships	267
Entity relationship modelling	268
Data analysis methods	271
Bottom-up data analysis	272
Top-down logical data analysis	279
5.3 Conceptual Modelling of Web pages	284
Extending ER modelling for Web data modelling	285
Web data analysis	288
Web data extraction	289
Web database connectivity analysis	293
5.4. Data design	295
Normalisation	300
First normal form (1NF)	302
Keys and functional dependencies	302
Keys	302
Functional dependencies	303
Second normal form (2NF)	304
Third normal form (3NF)	307

	Summary definition of 1NF, 2NF and 3NF	309
	A final note on normal forms	309
5.5	Web data design	310
	Logical web page schemas	310
5.6	Summary	318
	Exercises	319

6 IMPLEMENTATION OF WEB DATABASES   327

6.1	Physical database design	328
	Storage structures	331
	Heap files and serial search	332
	Access keys	334
	Sorted files	335
	Hash files	336
	Indexes	339
	Multi-level indexes	341
	Indexed Sequential Access Method	341
	B-trees	342
	Clustering	345
	Changes to the logical database design	346
	Physical database design—summary	346
6.2	Web database connectivity	348
	The web architecture revisited	348
	Client side approach	350
	Server side approach	351
	Implementation choices—client or server	352
6.3	Client processing	358
	Browser extensions	359
	External applications	359
6.4	Server processing	359
	Server side scripting	360
	ASP (Active server pages)	362
	JSP (Java server pages)	363
	PHP	363
	Server side JavaScript	365
	SSI (Server side Include)	365
	ColdFusion	369
	Other	370
	Server side scripting—summary	370
	Common Gateway Interface (CGI)	371
	Perl	372
	Ingres-Ice	376
	O2-O2Web	379
	Problems of CGI	381
	Extending the server functionality using its API	382
6.5	Java	384
	JDBC (Java database connectivity)	385
	Java applets	386
	Java servlets	387

Java CGI	391
Alternatives to JDBC	394
SQLJ	395
ODMG Java binding	396
6.6 Web database implementation choices	397
Client side processing: Java or JavaScript	397
Appearance	397
Database connection	398
Data validation	399
Graceful degradation	400
Browser detection	401
Feature bloat	401
User interfaces and the Web	402
User interfaces and the intranet	402
User interfaces and control	403
6.7 State and transactions	404
Transactions	404
Incomplete or abandoned transactions	405
Interference between transactions	406
Locking and deadlock avoidance	409
Two-phase locking	410
Deadlock	410
Two-phase commit	412
Web database transactions	412
Hidden variables	415
URL rewriting	416
Cookies	417
User authentication	418
Session tracking techniques - summary	418
6.8 Security, privacy and identity	419
Web security	420
Client security	421
Database security	422
Malicious code	425
Efficiency vs security	427
6.9 A Web site in a database	428
6.10 Summary	430
Exercises	435
EPILOGUE	445
BIBLIOGRAPHY	447
INDEX	453

PREFACE

The book is intended to be suitable for an undergraduate course. Accordingly, it should not be necessary for students to have undertaken prior courses on database or Web technology. We have tried to present the material in an accessible way, avoiding excessive use of mathematical notions and including realistic and familiar examples.

Much of the book is tutorial in style—many of the issues, are presented through a progressive series of examples. This material is reinforced by exercises at the end of each chapter. Where possible readers are encouraged to implement examples and their solutions to exercises using a suitable DBMS and Web server.

The content is organised in three parts following a general introduction in Chapter 1:

- Part I introduces databases moving from the theoretical notions of data models through to their implementation via relational, object or object-relational systems.
- Part II introduces the basic concepts of the World Wide Web.
- Part III shows how databases and the Web can be combined and considers the design and implementation issues that must be tackled when building Web database systems.

When we completed this book, in late 2000, we used the most up to date information we had on a number of standards. Since this is a very dynamic area, changes in standards are still underway and later usage may differ from the versions available to us.

We intend to maintain a Web page for the book at

http://www.staff.comp.brad.ac.uk/~mick/wdb/

This will include
- links to the Web resources listed in the bibliography, updated if necessary .
- notes of any errors etc.
- access to teaching material which is available on application from the authors.

1

INTRODUCTION TO WEB DATABASE SYSTEMS

This book is about two powerful computer technologies—database technology and the World Wide Web, usually referred to simply as the WWW or the Web (the latter is used in this book). It describes how an even more powerful technology can be created when these two are used together. Database technology is important because it allows large collections of data of all types (text, numbers, pictures, sounds, etc.) to be stored on computers and used efficiently and without duplication by relevant applications. The Web is important because it provides a cheap and simple way to store and access information and execute computer programs stored on computers the world over. These two technologies can be used together to enable many computers, possibly in different parts of the world and with their own databases, to work together to provide solutions to single and often complex problems.

This introductory chapter is structured to answer the following questions:
- What is the database approach?
- What is the Web?
- What are the characteristics of Web database applications?
- Why and when is it advantageous to link a database to the Web?

The chapter introduces basic notions of databases, the Web, and the characteristics of Web database systems, in which both the Web and database technology are used. These notions are illustrated using many examples, including Web databases that are used in systems for buying and selling using the Web. This form of Web-based commercial activity is an example of e-commerce (or electronic commerce). The same example Web database applications will be developed in subsequent chapters to illustrate more detailed material.

In our treatment of this material we focus on the important principles and features. A wide variety of technologies are currently used in both database and Web systems, and can be used in Web database systems. We will survey what we think are the most significant and relevant technologies in both areas. A consequence is that the book cannot be a complete reference for the technologies covered, i.e. SQL, HTML, Perl, Java, JavaScript etc. In many cases such reference material can be found on the Web itself or in printed material and we will make reference to such material for those interested in more detail. Examples in programming languages will, we hope, be instructive to readers even if they are not too familiar with the detailed syntax of the particular languages used. To aid in this and for clarity we will often simplify some programming examples to emphasise the relevant points at the expense of a more complete example.

We will attempt to use recognised standards throughout. This is always important in computing but especially so with Web applications where interaction between computer systems is an essential. The issue of standards is a complex one. Standards range from internationally agreed and recognised ones, such as those from ISO, e.g. SQL:1999, through important *de facto* standards e.g. ODMG. On the Web, particularly since it is such a fast developing technology, there are very few standards with the permanence and standing of ISO standards. Many "standards" in fact only have the status of recommendations, such as the current HTML 4 from the W3C. The Internet has a history of such recommendations, or RFCs (Recommendations for Comment), that have no legal or binding status but are widely adopted. In practice RFCs must be adhered to if systems are to communicate with one another. Other standards, such as HTML 3.2, were only *post-hoc* recognition of a common subset of practice developed and accepted by different proprietary browsers. This followed the failure, in adoption at least, of HTML 3.0. Some "standards", such as cookies or Java, originate with one company, then gain wider acceptance and are clearly en route to some sort of standardisation, even if that is not entirely formalised. Clearly it is good practice to adhere to standard (normal) use of these technologies whatever their formal position on the road to standard recognition. For example, we will not be using non-standard extensions to HTML. Some are widely implemented (i.e. by current Netscape and Internet Explorer versions) but there is often little formal specification of these features and a strong chance that an application that relies on them will be unusable by other browsers (or even future versions of those browsers).

This chapter is structured as follows. Sections 1.1 and 1.2 respectively introduce database and Web technologies. Web database systems, in which both are used, are described in section 1.3. These topics are respectively described in greater detail in Parts 1, 2 and 3 of this book. The chapter concludes with a summary and exercises.

1.1 DATABASE TECHNOLOGY

This section introduces the basic concepts of database systems and overviews the most important technologies. We therefore focus on two types of database technology, relational and object databases.

DATABASE BASICS

Computers, often connected to other computers, people and machines, are now a part of everyday life. For example, we use one or more computers whenever we borrow a book from a public library, pay for groceries at a supermarket checkout, withdraw money from a cash machine, drive a car or use a washing machine.

In general, computer programs assist people and machines to carry out many of the activities that enable organisations of all types to operate effectively. To do this, application programs will usually have to access stored information about the organisation and the environment within which it must operate. For example, a program that produces pay slips for employees of a commercial organisation must access information about employees, pay scales, pension schemes, and the taxation rules within which the company must operate.

Computers usually represent information about an organisation and its environment as data, which are stored as data files on storage devices, such as disk and CD-ROM. A database management system (DBMS) is a particular type of computer program that is used by application programs to manage and provide access to the stored data. The collection of data managed by a DBMS is called a database, and the database and DBMS, together with the application programs that use the database, are collectively called a database system.

DBMS are now a standard component of all types of computer systems, ranging from large mainframes to small personal computers (PCs). Also, it is usual for computers to be connected to other computers, so that they can solve problems together and exchange information. For example, many people own low-cost PCs, which include a DBMS, such as Microsoft Access, and which can connect to and communicate with other computers via the conventional telephone system, for example, using the Internet (see 1.2). Consequently, it is no longer unusual for a computer system to be created by combining many inter-linked computer systems, many of which will support a database system. For example, when we withdraw money from a cash machine using a credit card, the transaction will involve access to many inter-linked computers, including the one that controls the cash machine and those that store data about the accounts of credit card holders.

Though many DBMS are now easy to use, it is important to understand the ideas upon which they are based in order to use them most effectively. In this section we therefore explain the database approach as a preliminary to an overview of how it can be implemented using the main types of database technology.

THE ORGANISATION

To understand the database approach, we must first appreciate the relationship between a database and the organisation within which it operates. A database system exists to provide an organisation with the information necessary for it to carry out its activities. An organisation is a very general term which refers to "any organised body or system or society" [Concise Oxford Dictionary], and the database approach is applicable to organisations in general. Database systems are used in all walks of life, including manufacturing industry, businesses, service industries, education, government, scientific research, and for domestic use. In this sub-section this diversity of application is illustrated by examples of database systems.

In the early days of database technology, i.e. the 1960s and early 1970s, the installation of a database system represented a major investment for large organisations, such as big business and government, and accordingly the scope and importance of the database system to the organisation had to be significant. The aim was often to create a single collection of data relevant to the operation of the organisation, which the different application programs could then share. A database of this type is called a corporate database and is illustrated in Example 1.1.

EXAMPLE 1.1

Bruddersfield Books is a large publishing company organised to produce and sell its books at a profit. A DBMS is used by the company to store data that represents information concerned with the running of the business. For example, the data represents information about employees, customers, sales and purchase orders, print runs, and books held in stock. The database applications include financial control, management planning, inventory management, production management, commissioning and developing publications, and sales order processing.

The costs of hardware and software needed to implement a database system are now relatively small, as is the cost of computer network facilities needed to allow one computer to access databases stored on other computers. Consequently, DBMS are now used by all sizes and types of organisation, not just the large ones, and are often used to build database systems for individual applications. Example 1.2 illustrates a very small-scale database system, which is now feasible because of the availability of database software as a standard feature of low cost PCs.

EXAMPLE 1.2

The Eaglestone family household is an example of a small organisation. The family is a society that is organised, at least sufficiently to ensure that members are housed, fed, and clothed. The family uses a DBMS and spreadsheet on a PC in order to assist in managing the family's finances. The database system is used to represent information about financial commitments, such as mortgage payments, insurance premiums, taxation dues, and investments. The database applications include generating the financial statements that assist in tasks such as buying a new car, or filling in tax returns.

Computer networks can provide wider access to computer systems and the services they provide. There are a number of ways in which a set of interconnected databases can be organised (see [Sheth 90]). Example 1.3 illustrates one form of distributed database system, called a multidatabase system.

EXAMPLE 1.3

A national museum is organised for the maintenance and study of collections of historically interesting artefacts, such as Stone Age axes, and fossil collections. The museum uses a number of DBMS, each of which stores data to represent details of artefact collections held by a particular department in the museum. The databases hold textual descriptions and also images of individual artefacts. Database applications are used for museum administrative activities, such as accession, preservation, dating and loan of the artefacts, and also to support historical research, by allowing academics to access the information represented. Network facilities within the museum (a local area network or LAN) make it possible to access the data held in any department from any of the museum's computers. The museum's network is also connected to an international computer network (the Internet), which allows researchers outside of the museum, possibly in other countries, to study its contents by remotely accessing the museum's databases.

Databases have traditionally been used to represent information as numbers and text. However, modern database technology now supports representation of many different forms of information, including sounds, images and video. Examples 1.3 and 1.4 illustrate this capability. Both systems store images as well as numbers and text. Example 1.4 also illustrates the use of a database system as an embedded component of a machine.

EXAMPLE 1.4

Part of a ship's navigation system is organised to help ensure that the ship gets from port to port without mishap. This system uses a DBMS to store data that represents information about the ship's surroundings. This information is input from the ship's radar system, and is used by applications programs that control other components of the ship's navigation system. For example one of the database applications is an identification system which analyses radar images, and identifies ships and other vessels detected on the radar.

Finally, Example 1.5 is included to illustrate an application of database technology in which video and photographs are stored and information about time and space is important.

EXAMPLE 1.5
A group of archaeologists maintain a database system to represent and organise information gained during an excavation of historical sites. The database is used to record photographs and video records of artefacts unearthed during the excavation. The database must also record maps and diagrams of the excavation site and information about the times and location associated with the artefacts.

The above five example organisations are each very different in terms of how they are organised and what they do, but have important similarities when analysed from a database perspective. These similarities are explained in the following sub-sections.

AN ORGANISATION'S INFORMATION SYSTEM
One way of viewing an organisation is as a system of **activities**. The activities take place within the organisation in order for it to fulfil its function. Each of the above example database applications (Examples 1.1 to 1.5) can be analysed in this way. For example, Bruddersfield Books (Example 1.1) must commission and develop books, buy materials and print the books, sell and deliver them, and collect and bank the remittances. It must perform these activities in order to achieve its objective of selling books at a profit.

The activities of an organisation do not operate at random or in isolation. They must be co-ordinated by a flow of information within the organisation and between the organisation and the outside world. Bruddersfield Books, for example, prints books on the basis of information concerning sales orders placed by customers, market research, sales forecasts, printing capacity, and the availability of materials required for printing.

There is therefore an underlying system of information activities concerned with maintaining the flow of information necessary for an organisation to function. This underlying system is called the organisation's information system, and is concerned with capturing, storing, and transmitting the required information. The information system of Bruddersfield Books (Example 1.1), for example, includes activities for financial control, management planning, production management, inventory management, commissioning and development, and sales order processing. These activities provide the information necessary to manage activities such as purchasing raw materials, and printing, pricing, storing, and selling products.

Information flow between activities within an organisation can be formal or informal. Formal information flow is a consequence of predetermined procedures for recording and communicating information. For example, when the museum (Example 1.3) acquires a new artefact, the accession procedures require that details of the artefact are recorded by filling in special forms and filing them. These forms are used in subsequent museum procedures in which the dating and preservation of artefacts take place. At Bruddersfield Books a salesperson will record orders placed by customers on special order forms which will be filed and processed so as to ensure that ordered products are produced, delivered, and paid for. Automated systems (such as the navigation subsystem (Example 1.4)) rely exclusively on formal information flow, since all information is automatically captured, stored, and used by the computer programs. Formal procedures for communicating information are essential in large organisations, such as big businesses, where the work of many people must be managed and co-ordinated.

In addition to the information that flows formally as a consequence of an organisation's procedures, other information flows informally, for example, as a consequence of observing other activities taking place or by word of mouth. Informal information flow becomes more important in small organisations involving just a few people. For instance, the Eaglestone family (Example 1.2) will rely almost exclusively on informal information flow between members (it is unusual for a family to operate within a set of rigidly prescribed procedures). However, the family also benefits from the formal information flow from other organisations, such as bank statements, tax demands, bills, and receipts.

The formal flow of information can take place only if the information can be expressed and communicated in some tangible form. However, information is an abstract commodity; you cannot touch information, but can gain information by touching something. Database technology is concerned with one particular form of information representation within a computer system, i.e. as data. Data consists of symbols recorded on some recording medium, such as paper, disk, or CD-ROM, to represent facts, concepts, or instructions in a formal manner so that they can be interpreted or processed by humans or machines. Information is the meaning that the human observer assigns to the data by means of the known conventions used in the representation.

EXAMPLE 1.6

The museum (Example 1.3) represents the date an artefact was acquired by entering 010895 in the appropriate field of a form. This number is data and is intended to convey the meaning "first day of August in 1995". This information is conveyed only if observers know the convention used. An American, for example, may misinterpret the data as meaning "eighth day of the first month of 1995" by assuming a different convention for representing a date.

In practice, computers will have a single internal representation for a particular type of data, but produce multiple representations in print or displayed to conform to conventions understood by different users. For example, data storage systems will typically include a date datatype that will allow you to enter dates in a number of formats such as 1st Aug 1995 or 1/8/95. The dates will be stored in an internal format hidden from the user and it will be possible to query or alter this information with an understanding of what a date means. In general, the numbers and text on an organisation's records are its data, and the information is the meaning assigned to those numbers and text.

Information represented as data is retained within an organisation for as long as the information is of potential use. For example, the museum (Example 1.3) will retain data describing a particular historical artefact at least for as long as the museum owns that artefact. Bruddersfield Books (Example 1.1) will retain details of an order placed by a customer at least until the order has been delivered and the remittance has been paid. The total collection of data stored within an organisation at any particular time is referred to as the organisation's database. This data may be stored in various forms, such as paper records and magnetic disks. However, the term database usually refers only to the information recorded as data and stored on computer storage devices.

THE DATABASE APPROACH TO INFORMATION SYSTEMS

An organisation's database is often stored as a collection of data files, usually stored on magnetic disk, and the application programs which access the database are often written to do this by directly reading and writing the records stored in these files. Alternatively, a database management system (DBMS) may be used to store, maintain, and access the database. In this sub-section we contrast these two approaches, and identify advantages of the latter.

The traditional (pre-database technology) approach is to design computer programs to support specific information activities, and data files that provide the application programs with the data they need. In such systems the database exists as a collection of files. This approach is centred on the application, rather than the data that must be processed.

EXAMPLE 1.7

A file-oriented sales order processing system at Bruddersfield Books would typically include programs and files shown in Figure 1.1. The files record details of customers, products, and outstanding sales orders. The sales order processing system is a program (or possibly a set of programs) which inputs data detailing new sales orders, checks that the new data is valid, and updates the appropriate files. It also produces the documents needed to ensure that the ordered products are produced and delivered.

Example 1.7 illustrates a number of characteristics that are typical of file-oriented systems.

1) Each file represents a particular phenomenon, or entity, which we are interested in. The three files in the example form a part of the organisation's database and each represents entities of a particular type, i.e. customers, products, and sales orders. Each record of a file represents an occurrence of an entity. For example, records in the customer details file represent the customers of the organisation. The fields of the records represent facts about the entities. For instance, a record in the customer details file will record the customer's name, address, credit rating, etc. These are the attributes of a customer.

2) Relationships between entities are represented by duplicating data. For example, a sales order is related to the customer who placed that order, and so the value of the customer's identification number is

stored in both the sales order file record that represents the order and also the customer details file record that represents the customer.

3) Applications share data. Many applications may require access to the same information, and so may share the same data. For example, the Production Control system and the Inventory Control system will also require access to data stored in the Product Stock file.

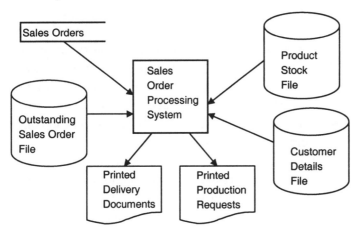

Figure 1.1 Example file-oriented computer system

The above characteristics are a consequence of the function of the data, i.e. representation of information about the entities relevant to the organisation. It is therefore necessary to use the data structures available to model the entities, their properties, and relationships between them.

A weakness of the file-oriented approach is that whereas files are structures for storing data such that it can be accessed efficiently, different programs may have different data access requirements. There are therefore two additional characteristics of file-oriented systems:

4) Data files are organised for the convenience of specific programs.
5) Programs must have built into them knowledge of how files are organised, the ways in which records can be accessed, and the meaning of the data.

These characteristics have two undesirable consequences:

1) Many file-oriented computer systems are likely to be unstable. This is because their design is based on the ways tasks are performed, rather than the structure of the information used in performing those tasks. Ways of doing things can and do change frequently within organisations. New systems must be developed and existing systems must be modified to accommodate these changes. However, changes to a file–oriented computer system can be expensive, because the data collected for applications may not be in an appropriate form for the new or altered applications. Data may therefore have to be duplicated and reorganised, or some compromise reorganisation of existing files may be necessary, so that the files can be accessed by both old and new applications. Modification to the structure of existing files will also require modifications to the existing programs that access them. Consequently, neither the investment in collecting data or in developing programs is preserved.

2) Management of data can be difficult. Data may be distributed across a number of files to be accessed by different application programs, and the duplicated data may be stored in different forms for the different programs. This makes it difficult to ensure that the data is consistent, up-to-date, correct, and secure.

The above two problems can be overcome using database technology. The database approach to computerising information activities is to treat an organisation's data, i.e. its database, as a resource that is shared by all relevant application programs. The data is made shareable by structuring it so that it has the same structure as the information that it represents. Application programs can then be programmed to access the logical structures of the information that is processed, rather than the structure of the files that are used to store the data that represents it. This means that programs that require access to the same information can access the same parts of the database.

A general objective of the database approach is therefore:

> *A database should be a natural representation of information as data, with few imposed restrictions, capable of use by all relevant applications (including the ones not thought of yet) without duplication.*

In general, information may be thought of as being about inter-related entities. For example, the publisher (Example 1.1) will record information about customers, products, and employees, some of whom are salespersons. These are inter-related; for example, products are related to the customers who place the orders for them and the salespersons through whom the orders are taken. The database approach is to store information as data in such a way that the data is structured to represent the entities (there will be collections of data to represent each salesperson, each product, and each customer). The data must also be linked in some way to represent the relationships between the entities represented (the data for a product will be linked to the data that represents the customers who have ordered it).

Consequently, the database approach is centred on the data, rather than on the processes applied to the data (see Figure 1.2).

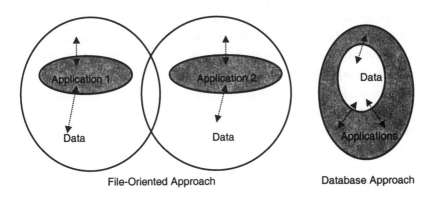

File-Oriented Approach   Database Approach

Figure 1.2 File-oriented vs. database approach

The extent to which a database and the programs that use it are maintained as independent resources depends on the nature of the organisation that the database is designed to serve. Where a database is designed to solve a very specific problem, as is the case in the navigation system (Example 1.4), the database and the programs that use it are very closely connected. In such cases the database is embedded within the system and is only accessible by operating the system. Alternatively, the database may be designed to store data for a wide range of applications (as is the case for the publishing organisation (Example 1.1)). In such cases, the database exists as a resource in its own right, and is managed and administered by a specialist group or person, called the database administrator (DBA).

THE DATABASE MANAGEMENT SYSTEM

A database management system (DBMS) enables an organisation to implement the database approach. It does this by supporting descriptions of data, both in terms of how it is physically stored and in terms of the logical structure of the data. The physical structure of the data is to do with how the data is represented on storage devices such as disks, i.e. the file structures and the methods used to access data. The logical structure of the data is to do with how it appears to the users of the database. The logical structure of the data determines the ways in which the data values are combined and inter-linked, and the ways in which they can be accessed and modified. An advantage of this separation between logical and physical structures is that users of a DBMS can define logical data structures that are the same as the structures of the information represented. At the same time, users can define physical data structures that implement the logical structures in such a way that the data can be used efficiently. In this way, a DBMS makes possible a natural representation of information as data by shielding the user from the physical data structures. The user sees only the data that is structured in a way that models the structure of the information it represents, and not the ways in which it is stored (see Figure 1.3).

The descriptions of the data structures are called schemas. The database has two parts: the database intension, which is the set of schemas which define the structure of the database, and the database extension, which is the data values themselves, contained in the database. Schemas are conventionally organised into three levels (see Figure 1.4): the internal, logical, and external levels. The internal model describes how data is physically represented, the logical model describes the logical structure of the database and the external models describe logical data structures that have been defined for specific applications.

The feature by which the logical view of the database is made independent of the way the data is actually stored is called data independence, and is the source of many of the benefits gained from using database technology.

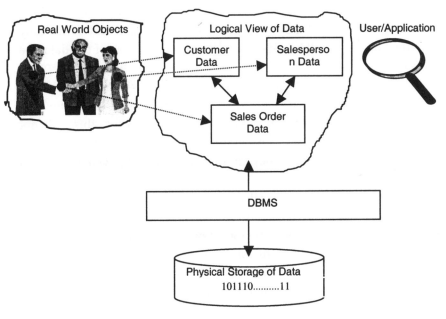

Figure 1.3 The DBMS and the world

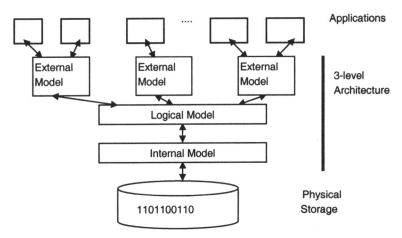

Figure 1.4   3-level database architecture

Data independence provides the following advantages:

1)   The database may be tuned without it affecting the users. For
     instance, in order to make a database system run faster, hashing

algorithms may be changed, new indexes may be introduced, or methods of linking related records may be altered. None of these changes will affect the logical structure of the data, and so the only effect on users will be a change in the speed and size of the database system.

2) The database may evolve without upsetting existing applications. The database may be changed to represent information about new entity types, relationships, and attributes. However, this will not affect an existing user, providing those entities, attributes, and relationships that are relevant to his or her application are still represented.

3) Data may be shared by applications, including future ones. Since the users of the data are only concerned with its logical properties, there is no need to re-organise data for a new application.

4) Greater productivity is possible. In general it is easier and faster to create applications programs in a database environment than it is in a conventional file-oriented environment. Programs are simpler because there is no need to include details of how data is physically stored; and a database system typically includes tools to automatically generate applications programs from descriptions of what they must do, rather than how they must do it.

In addition to the above advantages that stem specifically from data independence, there are other advantages that are a consequence of maintaining data as a separate and integrated resource.

5) Greater security and integrity control are possible. When the database approach is applied, data is treated as a central resource that must be managed. This management is done by the DBA. The responsibilities of the DBA are the design, maintenance, and evolution of the database. The DBA must also ensure the integrity and security of the data in the database, but this job is made easier because the data is collected together within a single integrated structure.

Two important benefits result from these advantages: firstly, investment in developing applications is preserved. It will not be necessary to change applications programs when the database is changed to be more efficient, or to accommodate new applications. Secondly, investment in storing data is preserved. Data will not have to be re-stored in some other form for new applications.

There are also costs incurred when applying the database approach:

1) Additional software is required to support the database approach. This will include the DBMS itself, software to extend programming languages so that they may access the database, special database languages and tools for building database applications, and various special programs for database organisation and maintenance.
2) For large-scale database applications (such as Examples 1.1 and 1.3), organisational changes will be necessary. A DBA must be established to manage the database. The DBA is responsible for database design and administrative tasks. The latter include authorising access to the database, monitoring and co-ordinating database usage and security, and ensuring adequate response times. Programmers, analysts, and users will have to be trained.

The above expenses may be prohibitive for certain applications which are relatively independent of other applications and which process small amounts of data.

Some DBMS may be better suited than others for specific types of applications. DBMS differ according to the types of logical data structures they support for representing information as data and the operations that are supported by the DBMS languages. A collection of logical data structures from which databases can be constructed, together with the set of operations that can be used to manipulate databases and the rules that ensure that databases are plausible, is called a data model. Different DBMS can be classified according to the data model they implement. (Data models are explained and discussed in Part 1.)

Most up-to-date DBMS are of a type called relational DBMS (RDBMS) (see Chapter 2). RDBMS are based upon the simple idea that information can be represented as tables of values. For example, a business could use an RDBMS to represent information about its employees as a table in which the columns contain employees' names, addresses and national insurance numbers (see Figure 1.5(a)). An RDBMS will also support facilities for querying and manipulating the tables of data. The international standard language for this is called SQL, an example of which is given in Figure 1.5(b) (an extended SQL tutorial is given in Chapter 2).

Employee

Name	Address	NI Number
Barry Eaglestone	Huddersfield	YB123456
Mick Ridley	Bradford	YS654321
Jenny Eaglestone	Huddersfield	XL132435

Figure 1.5(a) Example table in a relational database

```
SELECT Name, NI_Number
FROM    Employee
WHERE Address = "Huddersfield";
```

Name	NI Number
Barry Eaglestone	YB123456
Jenny Eaglestone	XL132435

Figure 1.5(b) Example query on the relational database in Figure 1.5(a) and the resulting table

In general, all operations on a relational database produce a table, which will either be a new table containing the results of a query or an updated version of one of the tables stored in the database.

RDBMS are powerful and often easy to operate. They have been used successfully in many types of organisation, e.g. in business, manufacturing, and service industries, education, government, and scientific research (see [Eaglestone 91] for a comprehensive explanation of relational database technology). However, there are also many applications for which RDBMS provide a poor solution. In particular, RDBMS are poor at representing information about entities with complex structure and where modifications to data involve complex operations. For example, an RDBMS is not an appropriate tool for representing information about electronic circuits in a system for designing VLSI chips. This is because the circuits can have complex structures; they can be composed of many inter-linked components each of which may also have a complex structure. Also, modification to the data representing an electronic circuit is complex because it is necessary to compute the electrical effects of the component modification on the circuit as a whole.

A new generation of database technology is now emerging which can overcome many of the limitations of relational database technology. This new generation primarily supports two types of database, called Object Databases and Object-Relational Databases (see Chapter 3 also, see [Eaglestone 98] for a comprehensive explanation of object database technology). Object database management systems (ODBMS) and Object-Relational database management systems (O-RDBMS) are based on features of object-oriented programming languages. Examples of such languages are Java, C++ and Smalltalk. The combination of object-oriented programming capabilities and conventional DBMS facilities provided by object and object-relational database technologies has produced a powerful environment for representing and making use of information about an organisation.

An advantage of object and object-relational database technology over relational database technology is that it can represent both complex information structures as data, and also complex processes associated with the information represented. An important use of this facility is to represent types of data, other than text and numbers. For example, new database technology can be used for multimedia applications in which information is stored as images, sounds and video (as in Example 1.5).

SUMMARY
In this section we have introduced the basic concepts of database technology.

Central to the notion of a database is the information system of an organisation. This is a system of information activities which capture, store and transmit the information necessary for an organisation to function. The organisation's database is the collection of data that represents that information and is retained within the organisation.

The database approach is to store and access this data, such that the data has the same structure as the information that it represents. This is made possible using a database management system. The main database technologies are relational, in which data is stored in logical tables, and object and object-relational databases, in which object-oriented facilities are used to store both data and the processes associated with the data.

1.2 THE INTERNET AND THE WEB

In this section we introduce the Internet and the Web. These are developments within the large and complex area of data communications and computer networks. A technical treatment is beyond the scope of this book. Instead, the area is discussed in terms of the capabilities of the technologies and their importance in designing and implementing information systems.

The section first discusses two milestones in the evolutions of computer technology—the migration of computers out of the computer room into the workplace, and the inter-connection of computers for electronic interchange of information. The Internet is a network that links together computer networks situated across the world. This is introduced as a development in computer network technology. Finally, we introduce the Web, which is an Internet application that allows a wide range of information and services to be stored and accessed on the Internet. Computer networks, and the Internet and the Web in particular, are important because they allow computers to support activities of an organisation's information system in a natural way. This and the previous section are preliminary to Section 1.3, in which we introduce the benefits of systems in which both database and Web technologies are used.

MIGRATION FROM THE COMPUTER ROOM TO THE WORK PLACE

Resilient, low-cost and powerful computers are now widely available. For example, it is not unusual for individuals to own powerful PCs, costing £100s, rather than £1,000s, for use within the home. This contrasts with computers of the 1960s and early 1970s, which were literally large and heavy, a major investment for large organisations, and required a special controlled environment within which to operate, i.e. the computer room, and teams of specialists to supply them with data and to program and operate them. This evolution has changed the role of computers in information systems. Computers are now placed where the activities that they support take place and are used directly by person(s) and machine(s) that perform those activities. For example, a salesperson may carry with her a laptop computer to retrieve details of products in stock and customers, and to record sales transactions when visiting customers. In general, it is usual for employees involved in information tasks to have a desktop computer to assist in those activities. This contrasts with the previous situation, where computers provided remote data processing services to and from which the data and processed data had to be ferried. Consequently, support for information activities can now be seamlessly integrated into the organisation's structure, and the role of a separate "data processing" department has largely disappeared.

In addition, the fall in cost and increase in power of computers have extended the range of applications that are economically viable to all forms of activity within an organisation—the computer is now a standard piece of equipment within the home, office, shop floor, etc.

COMPUTER NETWORKS

Information must flow between the activities of an information system, such that they can share and communicate information about the organisation and its environment (see Section 1.1 An Organisation's Information System). For example, accounting activities within Bruddersfield Books (Example 1.1) require information generated by sales order processing activities concerning sales transactions. Communication of information can take various forms, such as passing written or printed paper reports, verbal communications such as telephone conversations, or the exchange of electronically recorded data, for example, on disk or CD-ROM.

Computer networks provide the most direct means of information flow between computers that support information activities. Computer networks provide connections between computers for direct computer-to-computer transmissions of information in a digital form, via electronic links, such as wires, optical fibre, radio, microwave, or satellite. For example, computer(s) used for sales order processing may be situated in a sales office, linked by a local area network to computers in the accounts office, and the warehouses, thus enabling each computer system to access relevant information stored at the other sites.

An organisation must also interact with its environment. For example, Bruddersfield Books (Example 1.1) must interact with its customers, suppliers, Inland Revenue, transportation companies, etc. Computer networks therefore often support communication between organisations. Organisations may create their own private network to allow them to co-operate more effectively. For example, such a network may be used to link Bruddersfield with its larger customers and suppliers, so that data, such as purchase and sales orders, can be communicated electronically between computers in the respective organisations.

Also, organisations may communicate with other organisations and individuals, via public and community computer networks. For example, the authors of this book communicate via JANET, the UK's academic and research network. JANET, which is funded by UK government bodies, links universities, colleges of higher education, research council establishments and organisations that work in collaboration with the academic and research community.

The information flow within an information system and between the system and its environment may be formal or informal (see 1.1). Computer networks support both types of communication. Computer-to-computer communications can be used formally to execute pre-determined communications procedures. For example, Bruddersfield Books has procedures for transmitting sales orders directly from the salespersons' laptop computers to the Sales Office computer. Computer-to-computer communications can also be used informally, for example, for sending *ad hoc* messages between members of staff within an organisation.

THE INTERNET

The Internet implements a mechanism for linking together computer networks. It can be viewed as the "glue" which sticks together existing computer networks the world over, to form a single worldwide computer network. This facility is comparable with the integration of national telephone networks, which now enable people to telephone to and from anywhere in the world. The spread of the Internet has brought about a dramatic increase in the availability and use of computer networks both for communication within and between organisations.

The Internet achieves this integration of computer networks by implementing standard communications protocols by which computer networks can communicate. A communication protocol is a set of rules by which communications between computers takes place. These rules specify the ways in which messages are encoded, and determine the types of messages that can be sent and the messages that must be sent in response. Different computer networks often use different protocols. However, the Internet implements a standard set of protocols, called TCP/IP (Transmission Control Protocol/Internet Protocol) (see Ch 4 The Web and the Internet) that allow different computer networks to communicate with each other.

A node of the Internet is typically a computer, which is part of a network that connects together workstations or PCs located within a small area, such as a department or office of an organisation. Small computer networks communicate with larger networks to form a hierarchical structure. For example, an office network may communicate with the network for its department, which in turn may communicate with a company wide network, which may communicate with a national network, and so on.

Each computer on the Internet has a unique address, called its IP (Internet Protocol) address. This has a numeric form. A computer on the Internet also has a symbolic name.

EXAMPLE 1.8

At the time of writing this book, the address of the University of Bradford Department of Computing's Web server is 143.53.28.200 and it is known as www.comp.brad.ac.uk.

IP addresses are used to enable computers to communicate with other computers via the Internet. In practice, communication between two computers will involve messages being passed via intermediate computers in many different inter-linked networks operating different protocols. However, this mechanism is invisible to the sender and receiver computers, in the same way that when we talk on the telephone, we are unaware of the mechanisms by which our voices are transmitted.

The Internet has become a worldwide network of computers that provide access to networks the world over, and thus connects the individual computers in those networks. In 1999 the Internet linked over 60,000,000 node computers in over 800 countries, to provide a single integrated facility for communicating information, and is still expanding rapidly. The Internet can create a connection between any two computers connected into the Internet, providing the sender of information knows the Internet address of the receiver. Access to, and use of the Internet is currently low cost, and often free to users. Certain computer networks and services that are accessible using the Internet charge their users, but otherwise, the cost of using the Internet is often that of making the connection to the Internet, for example, using a public telephone line.

The Internet is therefore important because it provides a ready made, low-cost, global infrastructure for communicating, both within and between organisations. The best known and most widely used Internet application, electronic mail (or email) illustrates its extent and power. Using email, a message can be sent to users of any computer connected by the Internet, providing the Internet address, by which the user is identified, is known to the sender. For example, the preparation of this book has been made possible only through extensive use of email on the Internet. The authors work in universities in different parts of the UK and frequently travel overseas. Email has been used to discuss and work together on the preparation, regardless of where they are located at any particular time.

The same techniques as are used by the Internet, e.g. the TCP/IP protocols, are often used within an organisation to implement its own private networks. These are called Intranets. Also, different organisations will often create a private network for inter-organisation communications, again using Internet technologies. These are called Extranets.

THE WEB
The Web is an application of the Internet. It provides a simple way of accessing information and running programs stored on computers connected by the Internet. In addition, the Web has a memory within which information can be represented, stored and accessed. This stored information can be inter-linked across the Internet.

This brief introduction to the Web restricts itself to a few important characteristics and capabilities. Greater detail is given in Part 2 of this book. Also, we try to avoid introducing an excess of Internet jargon. The concepts introduced here are:
- Hypermedia—the form in which information is stored on the Web
- HTML— the language for coding hypermedia information

- URL—the addresses used to access Web resources such as hypermedia documents and programs.
- HTTP— the protocol used to access Web resources
- Gateways— a means by which other environments, such as database systems, are accessed from the Web.

HYPERMEDIA

Information is stored on the Web as inter-linked hypermedia documents that are stored on the computers connected by the Internet.

- These documents are called -media documents because they can contain not only text, but also other media, such as images, sound and video. A document can also contain executable programs, which may for example, dynamically create animated images or other documents.
- The documents are hyper- because they can have complex structures. Web documents are made of inter-linked parts, each of which can comprise a diversity of media. Embedded within each part can be links to other parts of the document, and to parts of other documents. The linked parts can be stored on the same or on different computers. Readers of documents can move from one part to another, or read other referenced documents by following the links. The links between the parts of documents are called hyperlinks.

EXAMPLE 1.9

Figure 1.6 illustrates a hypermedia document stored on the Web, as displayed in a Web browser. Note the use of both text and images. Note als, the highlighted text and icons which are the links to other documents and services. For example, the user can retrieve the document pr-010499.html (see Figure 1.8) by "clicking" on the text "news". They can also invoke an email client by "clicking" on the mailbox icon or the "Eagleley Webmaster" text. The structure of the example document is shown in Figure 1.7.

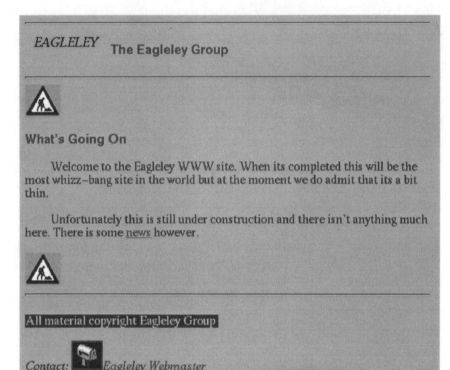

Figure 1.6 Eagleley Home Page (under construction version)

The Web is unlike previous information storage and communications facilities in the following respects:

- There is no notion of a centralised information store that is managed by professional information management staff. Any organisation or individual connected to the Web can create and store their own hypermedia documents on the Web. Anyone can reference any other Web document.
- The geographical location of documents is unambiguously determined by their Web addresses.
- The Web has a simple and uniform user interface, regardless of the computers being used. This provides a natural way of reading and navigating between Web documents. It hides from users the different representations of data in the local systems and the mechanisms by which data is brought to their client computers.

HTML

Web multimedia documents are written using **HTML** (Hyper-Text Mark-up Language). An example is given in Figure 1.8 which is the HTML source of the document shown in Figure 1.6. Alternatively, a derivation or extension of HTML may be used (HTML and other related languages are described in Chapter 4).

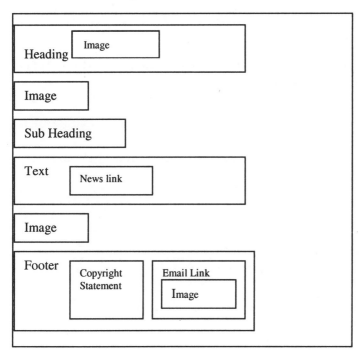

Figure 1.7 Structure of the Eagleley Home Page

Figure 1.8 Eagleley Home Page source code (under construction version)

```
<!DOCTYPE    HTML    PUBLIC    "-//W3C//DTD    HTML    4.0
Transitional//EN">

<HTML>

<HEAD>
<LINK REL=Stylesheet HREF="house.css" TYPE="text/css" MEDIA
=screen>
<TITLE>Eagleley Group</TITLE>
</HEAD>
```

Figure 1.8 Eagleley Home Page source code (under construction version)—continued

```
<BODY>

<HR>
<IMG SRC="eagleley_trans.gif" ALT="EAGLELEY." ALIGN = left>
<H1> The Eagleley Group</H1>
<HR>

<!--- comments-->
<IMG SRC="construction.gif" ALT="Construction work ahead.">
<BR>

<H2> What's Going On</H2>

<P CLASS=LIT>
Welcome to the Eagleley WWW site. When its completed this will
be the most whizz-bang site in the world but at the moment we do
admit that its a bit thin.
</P>
<P CLASS=LIT>
Unfortunately this is still under construction and there isn't
anything much here. There is <EMP>some</EMP>
<A HREF="pr-010499.html">news</A> however.
</P>

<IMG SRC="construction.gif" ALT="Sorry for any delay." >
<BR>
<HR>

<P CLASS=REV>
All material copyright Eagleley Group
</P>
```

Figure 1.8 Eagleley Home Page source code (under construction version)—continued

```
<ADDRESS>
Contact: <A HREF="mailto:info@Eagleley.com">

<IMG SRC="mailbox.gif" ALT="">Eagleley Webmaster</A>
</ADDRESS>

</BODY>
</HTML>
```

Figure 1.8 Eagleley Home Page source code (under construction version)—concluded

A mark-up language describes the contents of documents by including codes (in HTML called tags) within the document, usually before and after the parts that they describe. HTML therefore is used as follows— Web documents have only a little predetermined structure, within the <BODY>...</BODY> section the content of the document many sorts of headings, text, images, links, etc. may be used. Their contents can be described with HTML code. For example,

```
<ADDRESS>
Contact: <A HREF="mailto:info@Eagleley.com">
<IMG SRC="mailbox.gif" ALT="">Eagleley
Webmaster</A>
</ADDRESS>
```

declares that this fragment of HTML is an address. It is contained within <ADDRESS>...</ADDRESS>, a side effect of this is that it is displayed in italics in many browsers. Within the address itself we also have a hyperlink and an image.

URL AND HTTP
The Web's system for addressing the hypermedia documents, and their parts, is similar to the use of IP addresses to address Internet nodes. Each Web resource is addressed by a unique URL (Uniform Resource Locator). The protocol by which a connection between a browser and a

client is established and used is called HTTP (HyperText Transfer Protocol) (see Chapter 4). The URL names the protocol by which the resource is accessed, the computer on which the resource is located (the server), and the address of the resource itself.

```
http://www.staff.comp.brad.ac.uk/~mick/
```

     protocol   server   address

GATEWAYS

The Web is based on the idea that certain computers play the role of client, i.e. they request services, such as access to specific hypermedia documents, and other computers play the role of server, i.e. they provide the requested services. A program for viewing and accessing Web resources, called a browser, implements a client. Widely used Web browsers include Microsoft Internet Explorer and Netscape Navigator.

Web servers can also provide a client with access to other environments, such as database systems, by running programs called gateways. A gateway can be programmed in any of a variety of programming languages and is also identified by a URL. The address part may be more complex than the example above and may include parameters to be passed. In many cases the result of accessing such a URL is that a hypermedia document is created dynamically. The mechanism by which a Web server accesses a gateway is called the Common Gateway Interface (CGI). (Gateways and other ways of accessing database systems are described in Chapter 6.)

SUMMARY

In this section we have given an informal and non-technical overview of developments in data communications and computer networks. In particular, we have overviewed the Internet and the Web and their impact on information systems.

From this perspective, the Internet is important because it provides a low cost, ready-made infrastructure for information interchange between computers. This allows computers that support information activities to be placed where those activities take place and to be operated directly by those involved. It allows the information required by those activities to be implemented, at least partly, by computer-to-computer communications. Also, it allows the required information flow with other organisations to be, at least partly, by computer-to-computer communication. Consequently, information systems can be implemented in a natural way, with seamless integration of computer and communications technology within the activities and information flows that they support.

The above capabilities have led to a trend for modern computing systems to be distributed, i.e.

- The system's activities are supported, possibly by different computers, located where the activity takes place, and accessed directly by the people or machines involved in those activities.
- The computers that implement the system are linked to allow computer-to-computer transmission of information in a digital form.

The Web also allows a computer system to interact with other systems in the environment within which its organisation operates. This has led, for example, to the use of the Web for buying and selling to customers the world over.

1.3 WEB DATABASES

In this penultimate section, we consider the types of system that can be created by bringing together the power of database technology (see Section 1.1) and the Web (Section 1.2). First, we discuss current uses of the Web. We then discuss Web database systems from two perspectives—how the use of a DBMS can enhance Web applications, and how a connection to the Web can enhance database systems.

WEB APPLICATIONS

The Web was originally envisaged as a mechanism for storing and providing access to documents. This remains a major Web activity.

- **Web Publications**—This is using Web documents to publicise and disseminate information. For example, information about this book is accessible as Web documents maintained by McGraw-Hill (see http://www.mcgraw-hill.co.uk). Also, most academics have their own Web pages (see http://www.staff.comp.brad.ac.uk/~mick/). Publication on the Web is unregulated and is for the main part *ad hoc*, and of widely varying quality, validity and integrity. However, there are now many large and valuable information sources published on the Web, such as searchable libraries of documents, reports and journals. For example, the UK National Health Service maintains on the Web digital libraries of health-related publications. Many journals and conference proceedings are published on the Web. Some electronic journals (e.g. Information Research Journal) exist only as Web publications.

The publication applications have a significant impact, because of the low cost and wide accessibility of the Web. However, the scope and role of the Web now extends beyond that of publicity. Users of the Web can now access a wide and rapidly expanding range of services, which can involve executing programs and accessing and updating multimedia data stored both on the Web and in other environments. Other types of Web application are as follows:

- e-commerce (or electronic-commerce)—This is now one of the major uses of the Web. e-commerce is more than just buying and selling using the Internet. e-commerce embraces the use of electronic communications for all business processes — advertising, initiating business deals, buying and selling, services before and after sales, transactions between organisations, financial transactions, etc. In some cases the product itself is delivered digitally, for example, when buying and selling software. e-commerce can be business-to-customer, business-to-business, customer-to-administration, and business-to-administration.

- Group activities—The ability to both store and update information and to communicate with other users across the Web has led to a range of applications that support group work. These include support for discussion groups; for example, these are used in education to enable groups of students to work on joint exercises. Also, many special interest groups have created discussion groups. Computer-Supported Co-operative Work (CSCW) systems provide support for projects involving teams. This technology has been used to provide shared group storage, for example for working documents, and facilities for the control and co-ordination of the group's activities. Workflow Management systems provide specialised tools to manage business processes in which many individuals are involved.

- Embedded systems—Computer systems that are components of a construction, such as a car, a ship, industrial equipment, etc. may use the Internet to access and update relevant information, such as weather conditions, locations ...

The availability of the Web for communication within, and between, organisations has also brought about changes to the organisations, themselves:

- Removal of boundaries within organisations—Organisations used to be constrained by physical boundaries due to their geographical positions. The Web goes some way to making those boundaries less restrictive. For example, employees can work from home and communicate with the employee organisation via the Web, organisations and teams within them can be geographically dispersed, and yet work closely together using the Web.
- Removal of boundaries between organisations—Organisations can co-operate more closely. This has led, for example, to outsourcing. Outsourcing is the practice of taking some key activity within an organisation and delegating it to some other organisation. For example, a manufacturing organisation may delegate financial management to a bank.

The above list of applications is illustrative of how the Web is currently being used, but it is not exhaustive. One of the most powerful features is the ability to include programs within hypermedia documents, which can be executed from client computers. This capacity means that only programmers' imaginations and skills limit the range of potential Web applications.

WEB ENHANCED DATABASE SYSTEMS

The Internet and the Web can extend the capabilities of database systems in two respects:

- Wider access: By connecting a system to the Internet, the potential population of users is extended across the world.
- More services: The Internet can link together different database systems to provide new services.

Example 1.10 illustrates one of the ways the Internet and the Web have made possible wider access to existing database systems and have also made it possible to combine database systems to provide comprehensive services.

EXAMPLE 1.10

Eagleley EuroHotelBooking is a Web service for booking accommodation in a number of European cities. This service can be accessed by anyone using the Web. It utilises a number of database systems in order to provide a comprehensive service for booking hotel accommodation and for arranging transport between the city airports and hotels. The service maintains its own database within which it records information about bookings made. It also accesses, via the Web, database systems of the hotels that may be booked in order to ascertain room availability and to place booking with specific hotels. Similarly, airport taxi database systems are accessed via the Web to book transport between booked hotels and the relevant airport.

Database systems can be connected to the Internet for use via the Web simply to allow remote access, but the connection can also be used to integrate with other systems. The following types of connection are possible:

- Remote connections: A database system, which is accessible via the Web, can be used from anywhere in the world.
- Client-server architectures: It is common place for database applications programs and the database itself to run on different computers. These can communicate via the Internet. The advantage is that computers can be configured for their specific roles, e.g. data storage, graphics, computation, etc.
- Distributed databases: Some DBMS have facilities that allow different parts of a database to be stored on different computers. Data is distributed in such a way that users are made unaware of this. The advantage of this is that data can be stored where it is used.
- Multidatabases: There is also an emerging database technology called Multidatabase technology which allows a number of independently managed databases to be combined to provide integrated access to the data stored. Example 1.10 illustrates this.

In general it is beneficial to connect an existing database system to the Web to provide wider access, to facilitate distribution of the database, or to make it available to be used in conjunction with other systems also available on the Web.

DATABASE ENHANCEMENT OF WEB SYSTEMS

The alternative perspective is to consider how using a DBMS can enhance a Web application. The Web has its own persistent store for hypermedia documents, and is therefore comparable to databases. However, there are significant differences.

- Regular formats: Hypermedia documents stored on the Web are described individually, using a mark-up language, HTML. A mark-up language is used to describe the contents of documents with no imposed structure. Terms are inserted to identify the nature of the parts and the ways in which they should be treated. This contrasts with a database, where the format of data of different types is predefined by the database description, called the schema.

- Large volumes: A database system typically handles large volumes of data. It can do this because all data of the same type has the same format. This allows special techniques to be used to efficiently find relevant data. The Web, on the other hand, does not impose a uniform structure for similar data, and accordingly, lacks the facilities for sophisticated retrieval of data.

- Administration: A database is designed to store data as a managed resource. Accordingly, it provides a range of facilities to maintain the integrity of the data and to support multiple concurrent use. The Web, on the other hand, does not support any data administration. It is left to the individual how best to manage their Web pages. The Web does not support any notion of data correctness or consistency.

Consequently, there are situations when it is appropriate to use a DBMS to manage the data of a particular Web application. This is particularly important for Web applications that allow users to access large amounts of data, such as on-line banking services, where the customers require access to account details. A DBMS will provide sophisticated data retrieval and manipulation facilities, optimised for specific databases, together with enhanced security and integrity facilities.

A Web application can be given greater flexibility by storing its data in a database, rather than in Web documents. The latter are fixed, whereas, data can be retrieved from a database to construct new Web documents, as they are needed. The latter are called dynamic (as opposed to static) Web pages.

Note, however, when a DBMS is used specifically to store information to be presented in dynamic Web pages, the database approach has less relevance. Rather than aiming to use the database to provide "a direct representation of information as data, shareable by all relevant applications" (see 1.1 Database Technology), the database may be seen as a means of providing efficient storage and access to the data associated with each of the Web pages that can be displayed. In such cases, efficient operation of the Web application becomes more important than representing the meaning of the data stored.

SUMMARY—WHEN TO USE WEB DATABASES
The use of both database and Web technologies within a single system is advantageous in the following situations:

- Wider access to a database—by connecting a database system to the Web we make possible worldwide access to the database.
- System distribution—the Web allows a database and its applications to be distributed. Data can be stored where it is used and/or applications can be located where the activities they support take place. An advantage is the ability to configure computers for specific tasks.
- Better querying, manipulation and administration of Web data— DBMS provide sophisticated facilities for data querying, manipulation and administration. Web applications that must utilise large volumes of data will therefore benefit from using a DBMS to store their data.

1.4 SUMMARY

An **organisation** can be viewed as a system of activities co-ordinated by a flow of information. The **information system** is the underlying system concerned with maintaining this information flow.

Formally communicated information is represented as **data**. An organisation's **database** is the set of data that is recorded within the organisation at any one time. Database usually refers specifically to the data that is stored on computers.

The conventional **file-oriented approach** is to build computer systems to support specific activities, or applications. This approach is unstable because of the changing nature of activities, the need to share data, and the dependence of the programs on the structure of the files.

The **database approach** is to treat the database as an entity in its own right, and to design it to model the organisation. A special program called a **database management system (DBMS)** is used to manage and provide access to the database. Selective logical views are defined for each application. The **database administrator (DBA)** is responsible for managing the database.

The advantages of the database approach are independence of applications from changes in the representation of the database, or its evolution. Also, central control of data provides better data security and integrity.

Its data model defines the ways in which data can be structured and manipulated by a database. Most databases implement the **relational data model**, which allows data to be stored within sets of tables. There is also an emerging generation, of **object** and **object-relational systems**. These are based upon object-oriented features that allow complex structures and complex behaviours to be implemented, for example, to store multimedia information.

Two important milestones in the evolution of computer systems are the migration of computers out of the computer room to the workplace, and the use of computer networks to allow computers to communicate, within and between organisations. The **Internet** now takes these developments a large step further by linking together computer networks the world over, using **TCP/IP** protocols. **Intranets** and **Extranets** respectively use Internet technology to create private networks for communications within and between organisations.

The **Web** provides a simple uniform interface to the Internet and a facility for storing and retrieving inter-linked **hypermedia** documents. Hypermedia documents are coded using a mark-up language called **HTML**, or a derivation of it, and are addressed by **URLs**. Programs called **gateways** on the Web server computers provide access to other environments. Gateways are accessed using the **Common Gateway Interface (CGI)**. Users access Web resources from client computers using

browser programs. Links between clients and servers are established using a protocol called **HTTP**. Web applications include publishing, e-commerce, support for group activities, and embedded systems.

Web database systems are systems in which both Web and database technologies are used. These provide wider access to database systems, ways of distributing systems and more services through integration of systems.

EXERCISES:

(1.1) Web databases bring together database and Web technologies. Explain what each of these contributes to a Web database.

(1.2) Distinguish between the terms data, database, database management system (DBMS) and database system.

(1.3) Explain the relationship between an organisation, its activities, and its database.

(1.4) Describe four database applications, in addition to those in Examples 1.1 to 1.5, given in this chapter. These should respectively illustrate the use of a database as a corporate database, as a multimedia resource, as a small scale embedded component of a system, and as part of a distributed database system.

(1.5) Using one of the example database applications you have given in your answer to (1.4), show how the associated organisation can be viewed as a system of activities.

(1.6) A manufacturing organisation buys and sells secondhand cars. Identify some of the information activities of this organisation and the flow of information between them (Hint: the organisation will have to record all of its transactions and its current stock of cars).

(1.7) Give an example of formal information flow between a bank and its customers.

(1.8) A small business comprising a potter, a salesman, and a secretary makes and sells china pots. Give examples of the informal and formal information flow that may occur within this organisation.

(1.9) Explain the term database and how it relates to an organisation's information system.

(1.10)   Identify problems that may occur when a small business implements its information system in a file-based fashion.

(1.11)   Consider the Bruddersfield Books case study (Example 1.1). Describe how programs and files might be used in this organisation to record the hours worked by staff and to produce pay slips. What are the entities, facts about them and relationships between them, that must be represented in the files?

(1.12)   Identify two weaknesses of storing a database as a collection of files. Illustrate undesirable consequences of these weaknesses, using as an example scenario, the cost of implementing changes to a payroll system when changes to taxation laws require existing information about employees to be recorded in a different way and new information also to be recorded.

(1.13)   Keywords in the definition of the database approach are natural, shareable, and duplication. Explain the significance of each of these words in this definition.

(1.14)   Give examples of the entities, attributes, and relationships that the pottery business in Exercise 1.8 would wish to represent within a database.

(1.15)   Explain how applying the database approach should result in preservation of investment in both applications and data.

(1.16)   What is the role of the database administrator?

(1.17)   A database has an intension and an extension. Explain these terms. What will be stored in each of them?

(1.18)   What is the purpose of a schema within a database system?

(1.19)   Distinguish between logical and physical data structures.

(1.20)   What is the role of a database management system (DBMS) with respect to the logical and physical representation of information as data?

(1.21)   Explain the concept of data independence. What are the benefits of data independence?

(1.22)   Explain how the 3-level database architecture in Figure 1.4 supports data independence.

(1.23)   With reference to Examples 1.1 to 1.5 explain if a database administrator is required and what her role should be.

(1.24)   What are the costs of moving from a file-oriented system to using a DBMS?

(1.25)   What is a data model?

(1.26) How is information stored in a relational database system?

(1.27) Give an example of an application for which a relational DBMS is unsuitable.

(1.28) Explain two advantages of object and object-relational databases over relational databases. Also, what are the advantages of relational databases over object and object-relational databases?

(1.29) The directors of a small engineering company currently store all of their data in files. You have been asked to advise them on the desirability of using a database management system. Write a short report setting out the potential advantages and disadvantages of changing to database technology.

(1.30) How does the migration of networked computers into the workplace provide more natural support for information systems?

(1.31) Give examples of how it is advantageous for an organisation, e.g. a bank, to use networks to communicate electronically between its departments, and also with other organisations.

(1.32) Give examples of formal and informal electronic communication that is possible using networks, both within and between organisations.

(1.33) Computer networks existed before the Internet. Why then was the Internet so important? What added facilities did it bring?

(1.34) What is the purpose of a communications protocol? What is the significance of the communications protocols set called TCP/IP?

(1.35) The Internet can be said to be at the top of a hierarchical structure of networks. Explain what this means.

(1.36) What is an IP address? What is it used for?

(1.37) How many computers are currently linked to the Internet? (Hint: this information may be found by searching the Web.)

(1.38) Email is the best known Internet application. Using this as an example, explain the power of the Internet, both for communication within and between organisations.

(1.39) Distinguish between the terms Internet, Intranet and Extranet. Give examples of where each would be used.

(1.40) In broad terms, what is the relationship between the Internet and the Web.

(1.41) What is the role, with respect to the Web, of the following: hypermedia, HTML, URL, HTTP and gateways.

(1.42) Hypermedia has two component terms, hyper- and media. Explain the significance of each of these.

(1.43) What is the role of a hyperlink with respect to the Web? Give an example of where one should be used.

(1.44) Give an example of how hypermedia could be used in the Museum database system in Example 1.4.

(1.45) In what respects is the Web unlike previous information storage and communications facilities.

(1.46) HTML is a markup language. How does a markup language differ from a schema language? How is HTML used on the Web?

(1.47) Sketch a Web page that represents a digital photograph image of you, text giving your cv, and a link to a Web page that describes other members of your family. Outline the structure of the page, as in Figure 1.7.

(1.48) What is a URL? What is it used for?

(1.49) With reference to the example Web page in (1.47), explain how URLs are used.

(1.50) What is HTTP?

(1.51) The Web is based upon a clients and servers. Explain their specific roles.

(1.52) Distinguish between the terms client and browser. Give examples of widely used browsers.

(1.53) What is the purpose of a gateway on the Web? Give an example application of a gateway.

(1.54) Give an example of how the Web can remove boundaries between organisations through outsourcing.

(1.55) You have been asked to advise the directors of a small engineering company on the desirability of using the Web for communications within the company and with their major suppliers. Write a short report explaining the features of the Internet and the Web, and setting out the potential advantages and disadvantages of using the Web as proposed.

(1.56) Web databases use facilities of the Web and of DBMS. Explain their respective roles, and give three example Web database applications, in addition to those listed in Section 1.3 Web Databases, Web Applications.

(1.57) Give an example of how the Web can remove boundaries within a retail organisation.

(1.58)   Two scenarios within which Web and database technologies can be brought together are Web-enhanced database systems and database-enhanced Web systems. For each, give an example application and discuss the advantages of combining the technologies.

(1.59)   Distinguish between the following ways of accessing databases via the Web, remote connections, client-server architectures, distributed databases and multidatabases. Give examples where each could be useful.

(1.60)   Databases and the Web both store data, but have different capabilities. Discuss the features of a database that distinguish it from data stored on the Web, and *vice versa*. Give examples of when each is appropriate.

(1.61)   Illustrate with examples three advantages of Web databases, i.e. wider access, system distribution and better querying, manipulation and administration of Web data.

(1.62)   You have been asked to advise the directors of a small engineering company on the desirability of using a relational DBMS to improve the facilities of their Web-accessible catalogue of products, and also of making it possible for customers to place orders, via the Web. Write a short report setting out the characteristics of Web databases and the advantages that these offer if applied to the proposed applications.

Part I

DATABASES

In this part we look at database technology in greater depth. This builds on the first chapter, in which the two ingredients of Web databases, i.e. database and Web technologies, were introduced. Specifically, the chapters set out to answer the following:

- What is a data model?
- What is a relational database?
- What is an object database?
- What is an object-relational database?
- What is a persistent programming language?

2

DATA MODELS AND RELATIONAL DATABASES

This chapter sets out to answer the following:
- What is a data model?
- What is a relational database?

Data models are described because they are the basis of database technology. A data model is a set of structures with which a database can be constructed, operations that can be used to manipulate databases, and rules that ensure that databases are at least plausible. DBMS differ according to the data model they support for representing and manipulating information as data. This chapter explains the concept of a data model, and then describes the current mainstream database technology, i.e. relational. Newer database technologies, i.e. object and object-relational, are described in Chapter 3. Relational database technology is based upon the relational data model. In our description of relational databases, we also describe the international standard relational database language, SQL. Care is taken to provide a thorough, tutorial style, description of SQL, as this is the database language that most Web database system implementers are likely to encounter.

Section 2.1 explains the concept of a data model. Relational databases are then described in Section 2.2. This section describes each part of the relational data model, i.e. its structure, operations and integrity constraints, and how each is implemented in SQL. The chapter concludes with a summary and exercises.

2.1 WHAT IS A DATA MODEL?
The database approach is to maintain a database that is a natural representation of information as data (see 1.1 Database Technology: The

Database Approach to Information Systems). Database systems achieve this by storing and manipulating data in structures that correspond to the structure of the information represented by the data. For example, data about books would be grouped into structures that represented authors, titles, publishers and the relationships between them. This is made possible because a DBMS will support a particular data model.

A data model is a theoretical model of databases, because with it one can create sets of formulas that represent or model database systems. Theoretical models are used in all branches of science. They are used to categorise and possibly simplify or approximate the phenomena that are being studied. For example, weather forecasters use theoretical models to describe and predict the weather conditions. A theoretical model is a set of concepts, operations and rules, often expressed mathematically, that behave in a way that mimics the behaviour of that which is being modelled.

A data model therefore has at least three parts relating to the way information is modelled as data:

1) a structural part, that is a collection of the types of structures, i.e. the building blocks, with which a database can be constructed;
2) a manipulative part, that is a collection of the operations that can be applied to the database, including operations for retrieving and updating data, and for changing the structure of the database;
3) an integrity part, that is a set of rules that all valid databases must obey.

The two important roles of a data model are:
• A DBMS implements the structures, operations and rules defined in its data model;
• Database designers and researchers can use a data model to reason about database systems, without actually having to build them.

The quality of a theoretical model can be judged by how accurate and complete a representation it provides of the things it models, and the extent to which its predictions correspond to what actually happens. For example, an economic model that predicts inflation when in fact there is deflation is a poor model. Similarly, the quality of a data model must be judged on how well it can model information and its behaviour. In this respect the data models on which mainstream database technology is based, i.e. relational, object and object-relational, have respective strengths and weaknesses. These are discussed in the following sections of this chapter and in the following chapter, in which each of the above data models and the associated technology are described.

2.2 RELATIONAL DATABASES

Most up-to-date DBMS are currently based upon a data model called the relational model. The relational model was first published in 1970 by Edgar F. Codd who was then a researcher at IBM's San Jose laboratories in California, USA, as a theoretical model for large shared databanks.

The relational model was the first widely accepted formally defined data model. Its advantages include:

- Logical—The relational model describes a logical view of data, i.e. the way in which it appears to the user. This contrasts with previous data models that were not formally defined, and were complicated by details relating to the physical representation of data, i.e. how data is stored and accessed on storage devices.
- Simplicity—As will be seen in the following description, the model has only one simple storage structure, the table, and uses straight forward "cut and paste" operations to retrieve and manipulate data.
- Mathematical rigour—The relational model is mathematically defined. This makes it suitable as a basis for database theory, as well as actual database system.
- Set-oriented—The operations of the relational model operates upon large chunks of the database at a time. This contrasts with previous data models that had operations only to access one record at a time.

SQL

The international standard relational database language is called SQL. SQL is an acronym for Structured Query Language and is sometimes pronounced sequel. SQL was invented in the IBM San Jose Research Laboratory by D. Chamberlin and others. The prototype IBM RDBMS System R, built at San Jose, used SQL as its language, and System R later became the basis of IBM RDBMS products DB2 and SQL/DS. SQL and SQL-like languages have now been universally implemented by leading

RDBMS suppliers. SQL is now an official standard, having been adopted by many standards organisations, including ANSI, ISO and BSI.

SQL instructions can be used to define the structures of the relational data model in order to implement specific databases, and to retrieve and manipulate databases. As with other database languages, there are two parts of SQL:

- The Schema Definition Language (SDL) is for defining the database structures. SDL includes facilities for defining database structures and integrity constraints, for specifying the ways in which relations are to be physically stored, for defining the external models (see 1.1), and for authorising users to access the database;
- The Data Manipulation Language (DML) is for using the data stored in the database.

SQL is used in three contexts.

1) As a stand-alone database language—Using stand-alone SQL, complete database applications may be expressed purely in SQL statements. These applications may be executed interactively, statement by statement, or alternatively, sequences of SQL statements may be stored and executed as programs.
2) As an embedded database language—Embedded SQL statements may be included within computer programs written in other conventional programming languages, such as COBOL, C++ or Java.
3) Integrated into Fourth Generation Languages (4GLs), system generation applications and "wizards"—A number of products integrate SQL into their 4GL environment tools, making it possible, for example, for SQL instructions to be executed from within a report generator, spreadsheet or graphics generator.

The SQL standard has now undergone two major updates.
- SQL—The original standard was published in 1986, with minor modifications and corrections in 1989. The most significant modification in 1989 was support for referential integrity (see SQL Integrity Features later). This first version is usually called SQL, SQL1 or SQL-89.
- SQL2—The first major update was in 1992, usually referred to as SQL-92 or SQL2. SQL2 extended the language to support many more

features of the relational data model and also to support a richer set of data types.

- SQL:1999 or SQL3—This is sometimes called object-oriented SQL, because most notably it extends SQL to include features normally associated with object-oriented systems (see Chapter 3). SQL:1999 was so called because it was due to be adopted as a standard in the latter part of 1999.

RDBMS implement the SQL standards to different extents. Accordingly, three levels are defined. These classify systems according to the level of support they provide for SQL.

1) Entry SQL—This is similar to SQL1.
2) Intermediate SQL—This also contains features of SQL2 that are of greatest use in actual database systems.
3) Full SQL—As the name suggests, this is the complete SQL language.

Systems are evolving towards full SQL through the addition of features. They have also anticipated new features that will be introduced by SQL:1999. However, a consequence of anticipating a standard is that there are variations in the ways in which the features are implemented in different systems.

The following subsections describe the three parts of the relational model and also describe how SQL can be used to implement the structures, operations and rules of those parts, to create actual database systems. The SQL introduced will be mainly Entry SQL, i.e. SQL1. Where the more advanced features of SQL2 are used, these will be identified. The new features introduced in SQL:1999 will be described in a later chapter, when object-relational databases are described (see Chapter 3).

THE STRUCTURAL PART

Structurally, relational databases are the simplest form of database. The relational model represents all information as tables of data values. Using the terms of the relational model, the tables are called relations, their columns are called attributes, the column headings are called attribute names, and the values in the columns, attribute values. The rows are called n-tuples or more usually just tuples. These structures are illustrated in the simple example database in Example 2.1.

EXAMPLE 2.1

The four tables in Figure 2.1 depict a small relational database. The database represents (simplified) information about hotels, hotel chains, customers and hotel bookings that they have made. These entities are represented as follows:

- *Each hotel described (in Hotel) is described by an identification number (HotelNo), address (Address) and the number of rooms (Rooms).*
- *Each customer (in Customer) has an identification number (CustNo) and a name (CName).*
- *Hotel chains (in HotelChain) also have identification numbers (ChainNo) and names (HCName).*
- *The relationship between a hotel and the hotel chain that owns it is represented by storing the chain number (ChainNo) in the Hotel table.*
- *Relationships between a customer and the hotels in which they have a reservation are described by the rows of the Booking table, each of which contains a customer number (CustNo) and a hotel number (HotelNo), together with details of the booking, i.e. the room class (Class) and the reservation dates (Period). Each booking also has an identifier (BkNo).*

An alternative explanation of the relational data model is in terms of conventional files, each with just one type of record. A file corresponds to a relation, fields to attributes and records to tuples (see Table 2.1).

Relational terminology	Tables	Files
Relation	Table	File
Tuple	Row	Record
Attribute	Column	Field
Attribute name	Column heading	Field name
Attribute value	Table entry	Data item

Table 2.1 Relational structures

An important difference between a relation and a table or file is that the relation has no ordering. The attributes and tuples have no ordering—there is no first or last attribute or tuple. A second difference is that there can be no duplicate attributes or rows. Each attribute name must have a unique name within its relation and no two tuples within a relation can be identical.

In this book we will mainly use the informal but widely used terminology, referring to relations as tables, attributes as columns, and tuples as rows.

The database approach is to represent data so that it has the same structure as the information it represents (see 1.1). In a relational database, this is done by defining each table to represent some type of real world entity (e.g. hotel, customer and hotel chain), or a type of relationship between entities (e.g. booking). A column of a table represents a property or attribute of the entity or relationship (e.g. name or number). A value in a row therefore represents properties of a particular occurrence of an entity or relationship (e.g. an hotel, an hotel chain, a customer, and the relationship between a customer and a hotel for which they have made a booking).

Hotel

HotelNo	Address	Rooms	ChainNo
H1	The Grand, Honley	1320	HC1
H2	Great Western, Barnsley	500	HC2
H3	Luxury Heights, Ljubljana	620	HC1
H4	The Independent, Sheffield	620	⊥

Customer

CustNo	CName
C1	M. Ridley
C2	B. Eaglestone

HotelChain

ChainNo	HCName
HC1	Happy Days
HC2	Hampton Hotels

Booking

BkNo	CustNo	HotelNo	Class	Period
B1	C1	H3	3	1 Jan 2000 : 8 Jan 2000
B7	C2	H3	3	1 Jan 2000 : 8 Jan 2000
B9	C2	H1	1	2 Feb 2000 : 4 Feb 2000

Figure 2.1 Example Relational Database

Two other important features of relational structures are domains and keys. Both are to do with the meaning of the data structures, i.e. they are semantic features.

DOMAINS

A table in a database is used to describe real world entities or relationships between them. Column values represent facts about those entities or relationships. A domain may be thought of as the set of facts of a particular type that may be represented in the database. Each column is therefore defined on a domain, i.e. the set of all possible values that can occur within that column. For example, the CName column of the Customer table in Figure 2.1 is defined on the domain of all possible customer names. Similarly, the CustNo column is defined on the domain of all possible customer numbers. Every value of a database must be a member of some domain. Thus the domains on which a database is defined can be viewed as the database's vocabulary, and therefore determine all the things that can be said about the world from within the database.

In the original relational model domain values had to be single-valued, i.e. a value in a domain cannot be split up. Formally, this means that domain values must be atomic. This restriction is called first normal form, and has been relaxed in more recent versions of the relational model, where, for instance, each column value can be an array of values.

Domains are important because they make it possible to represent relationships between entities. A relationship is modelled by representing the same fact more than once within the database. For example, the hotel number, H1, is represented both in the HotelNo column of the Hotel table, and also the HotelNo column of the Booking table. This represents the relationship between The Grand, Honley and the customer, C2, who has booking a room in that hotel. The value H1 represents the same fact wherever it occurs in those two columns because they are both defined on the same domain, i.e. hotel identification numbers.

KEYS

Keys are also to do with the meaning of data. Keys are used to represent the names of the entities and relationships represented in a database. A key is one or more columns of a table, where their values will always be different for each row in the table. Also, every column of a key must be necessary for its values to be unique for every row—if three columns together form a key, then it is not possible to form a key from just two of them.

EXAMPLE 2.2

The keys of the tables in the Figure 2.1 database are identified in Table 2.2. These respectively identify the entities or relationships represented, i.e. hotel, hotel chain, customer, and booking. Note that,

- *a table can have more than one key—HotelChain has two, ChainNo and Name, since both the hotel chain identification number and name of the chain are unique for each hotel chain.*
- *a key may comprise more than one attribute—Booking has two keys. The booking number, BkNo, is one of them. The other is made up of all of the other columns, since a customer may make different bookings for different periods at the same hotel, or for different classes of room at the same hotel and for the same period.*

Table	Keys
Hotel	Hotelno, Address
Customer	Custno
Hotelchain	Chainno, Hcname
Booking	Bkno, (Custno, Hotelno, Roomclass, Period)

Table 2.2 Keys in the database in Example 2.1

A table may have many keys. These are called candidate keys. For any table, one candidate key will be selected as the primary key. Those not selected are called alternate keys. A primary key is selected so that we can guarantee that each row has some unique value, since a primary key is not allowed to have a null value (null represents the absence of a value). Primary keys are used to cross-reference between rows in order to represent relationships between the entities modelled by those rows. Columns used to cross-reference primary keys are called foreign keys.Primary key columns are often specially created within an organisation for identification purposes, e.g. identification numbers for hotels, customers, or hotel chains.

Note that in the relational data model all information is visible as data. Relationships between the entities represented by different rows are represented by storing the same value in each of the related rows. For this reason, the relational model is called a value-based model. For example, the relationship between a hotel and the hotel chain that owns it is represented by storing the relevant hotel chain number (ChainNo) in both the Hotel and HotelChain tables. The relational structures are summarised in Figure 2.2.

SQL SCHEMA DEFINITION LANGUAGE (SDL)

SQL SDL includes statements with which to define or modify the structure and characteristics of a database system. These are stored in a part of a database called the database schema. The other part is the database itself in which the data is stored. The schema and the part of the database in which the data is stored are respectively called the database intension and extension.

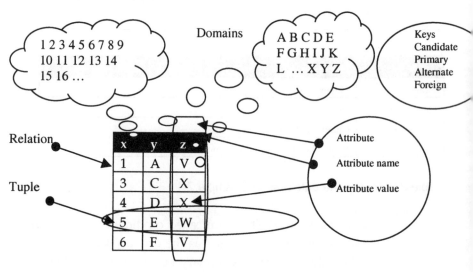

Figure 2.2 The structural part of the relational model

A multi-level database systems architecture was described in Chapter 1. This architecture consists of external, logical and internal models. Descriptions of these models are stored in the sub-schemas, schema and storage schema, respectively. However in a RDBMS there is typically a single schema in which all descriptions of the database structures are stored. A relational database schema describes the logical structures and properties of database tables. In addition the schema describes details concerning the implementation and use of the tables, such as how relations are physically implemented and users' privileges. In this chapter we describe only the features concerning the logical properties of a database (other SQL features are covered later (see Chapter 5)).

The relational database itself is the set of tables that the user sees as tables of data values. From the user's point of view the schema of a relational database exists as the data dictionary, sometimes called the system catalogue. The data dictionary is usually also stored as a set of tables and is also accessible using SQL.

CREATING A NEW DATABASE

Before a user is able to create tables and populate them with data, a schema must be created within which the description of the database may reside. The following example illustrates the SQL instruction for achieving this.

```
CREATE SCHEMA Eagleley AUTHORISATION Eaglestone
```

The above SQL creates a new schema, named Eagleley. The owner of the schema is specified as Eaglestone. If either the schema name or owner name is omitted, it is by default assumed to be the name of the user who issued the command. In addition, descriptions of the elements of the database can be specified in a "CREATE SCHEMA" instruction. These are simply appended to the instruction. However, it would not be unusual to create an empty schema and subsequently populate it with element descriptions.

CREATING A NEW BASE RELATION

The following SQL example, when executed, will create the Booking table shown immediately below it. The statement adds an empty table to the database and adds its description to the schema.

```
CREATE TABLE   Booking
(
    BkNo       CHAR(5)     PRIMARY KEY,
    CustNo     CHAR(5)     NOT NULL,
    HotelNo    CHAR(4)     NOT NULL,
```

```
Class         SMALLINT    DEFAULT 3,
PeriodINTERVAL YEAR TO DAY
NOT NULL,
UNIQUE (CustNo,HotelNo,Class,Period)
)
```

Booking

BkNo	CustNo	HotelNo	Class	Period

This statement includes examples of all the features of the SQL "CREATE TABLE":

- The new empty table is given a name, Booking in the example.
- Each column of the table is defined. A column is given a name and a type. In the example, three types have been used, CHAR (character), SMALLINT (small integer) and INTERVAL (time interval).
- Optionally certain integrity constraints may be defined These can be used to constrain combinations of values within a table. The example illustrates the three types of integrity constraint that can be specified:
  - "PRIMARY KEY" signifies that the BkNo column is the primary key and therefore must have unique non-null values in each row;
  - "NOT NULL" indicates that the CustNo, HotelNo and Period columns may not have null values.
  - "UNIQUE" ensures that the values of the columns CustNo, HotelNo, Class and Periód are unique for each row The "UNIQUE" constraint in the example also illustrates how constraints that effect a combination of columns are specified at the end of the table specification.
- Optionally, columns may also be given default values. For example, when a new row is inserted, the example statement specifies that the value in the Class column will be 3 if it is not specified.

In addition to the integrity constraints on column values within a table, it is also possible to specify within a "CREATE TABLE" statement constraints which constrain combinations of values across more than one table. These are covered later (see SQL INTEGRTY FEATURES).

DEFINITION OF DOMAINS

In the above example "CREATE TABLE" instruction, columns are defined on standard predefined types. The standard predefined types include NUMERIC, DECIMAL, SMALLINT (small integer), FLOAT (floating point), REAL, and DOUBLE PRECISION. These are data types that one would expect to be supported by any programming language. Note that we use the term data type rather than domain. The distinction is that a data type defines a range of values that a column may have and the operators that may be applied to them, but a domain is to do with the meaning of those values. For example, in the above example "CREATE TABLE" statement, both BkNo and CustNo have the same type, i.e. CHAR(5), but are defined on different domains, since they represent different facts. However, SQL2 does also allow the database implementer to define "domains" that represent more of the meaning of the data and which can be used instead of the predefined data types. This facility is illustrated in the following SQL example.

```
CREATE DOMAIN CustomerNumber AS CHAR(5)
DEFAULT VALUE "        "
NOT NULL
```

Note that the "CREATE DOMAIN" statement allows the implementer to define a named domain (CustomerNumber in the example). The domain has a data type. This may be a predefined data type, such as CHAR or SMALLINT, or another user defined domain. In addition, optionally, the specification may specify a default value and integrity constraints.

CHANGING THE SCHEMA CONTENTS

The SQL SDL includes statements for removing or altering specifications in the schema.

The following SQL statement will remove from the database the table Booking, created by a previous example.

```
DROP TABLE Booking;
```

The drop instruction can be used to remove any type of element specified in the schema. For example, "DROP SCHEMA Eagleley" would remove the entire schema. Obviously "DROP" has a rather dramatic effect. Later in this chapter we will describe statements for restricting its use.

SQL also allows existing specifications to be modified, using the "ALTER" statement. For example, columns may be added to or removed from a table, or the definition of a domain may be changed. This feature is illustrated in the following SQL statement, which will add an extra column, named Discount, of type integer, to the table Booking.

```
ALTER TABLE Booking
ADD Discount INTEGER
```

The values of this new column will be initialised to NULL for every existing row of the relation. Integrity constraints, "NOT NULL" or "UNIQUE", cannot therefore be specified for the new columns.

THE MANIPULATIVE PART

The manipulative part of the relational data model defines the set of things that can be done to a relational database. This is described mathematically. Using the mathematical definitions, expressions can be defined to model database retrieval and manipulation operations that a database system must perform. The mathematical definition takes the form of relational algebra. In the algebra, a table in a relational database is modelled by a structure called a mathematical relation, and operators define new relations when applied to them.

Relational algebra is to relational tables what conventional algebra is to numbers. In conventional algebra we can write expressions with variables, constants and arithmetic operators. When numbers are assigned to the variables, the expression will return a number as its value. Similarly, an expression in relational algebra has variables, constants and operators. However, the constants are tables, the values assigned to the variables are tables, and the value returned by the expression is also a table. This is illustrated in the following example expression in relational algebra:

Customer **union** {<C3, "Jenny Eaglestone">}

Here we have a variable, Customer. This is a variable because it names a table, the value of which can change overtime. There is also a constant, [<C3, "Jenny Eaglestone">] which is a table with just one row. The operator in the expression is union. The value returned is a table that includes all the rows of the Customer table with the addition of the row specified by the constant. In this way this expression represents the insertion of a new row into a table.

The relational algebra serves two purposes. Firstly, it provides a formal tool for describing relational databases and applications. This can be used for research purposes, for example, to seek better database design methods and query optimisation techniques. Secondly, it prescribes what it should be possible to do using a relational database query language, such as SQL.

It is not necessary to understand relational algebra to design, implement or use a relational database system. However, the following brief and informal overview will give the readers an appreciation of the types of operations it is possible to perform using a relational query language, such as SQL.

OPERATORS OF THE RELATIONAL ALGEBRA
In general the operators of the relational algebra can be thought of as providing "cut and paste" operations with which rows and columns can be "cut" out of tables, and can be combined, or "pasted" together, to form new tables. They provide the equivalent to scissors with which columns and rows can be cut out of tables, and paste for sticking the cuttings together to form new tables.

CUT OPERATIONS
There are two operators for "cutting" out rows and columns. These are respectively called restrict and project.

Restrict selects rows from a table where some specified condition is true. For example, the following expression will define a table with only those rows of Hotel for which the value of the column named HotelChain is 'HC1'.

restrict Hotel **WHERE** ChainNo = 'HC1'

Given the example database in Figure 2.1, the value of this expression will be the following table:

HotelNo	Address	Rooms	ChainNo
H1	The Grand, Honley	1320	HC1
H3	Luxury Heights, Ljubljana	620	HC1

Project defines a table created from specified columns of a table. For example, the following expression will define a table with just two columns, HotelNo and ChainNo, projected from the Hotel table.

project Hotel **over** HotelNo, ChainNo

Given the Figure 2.1 database, the value of this expression will be the following table:

HotelNo	ChainNo
H1	HC1
H2	HC2
H3	HC1
H4	⊥

Note that using the above two operators, we can represent database queries, such as "describe the hotels owed by the Happy Days hotel chain " and "who are the customers with current hotel bookings".

Like operators in conventional algebra, those of relational algebra may be used in conjunction. For example, the query, "what are the addresses of hotels owned by the Happy Days hotel chain (HC1)." is represented by restricting the rows of Hotel and then projecting out the address column, as follows:

project (restrict Hotel **where** ChainNo = 'HC1') **over** Address

Given the Figure 2.1 database, this expression defines the following table:

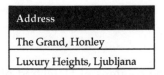

Address
The Grand, Honley
Luxury Heights, Ljubljana

PASTE OPERATIONS

There are also two "paste" operations. These are used to define tables that are constructed by combining data from two tables. The two operators are cartesian product and join.

Cartesian product (denoted times) is a binary operator, i.e. it operates upon two tables. The value is a table in which the rows are formed by combining a row from the first with a row from the second argument table. The result will include all possible combinations. An example relational algebra expression in which the cartesian product is used is as follows:

Customer **times** HotelChain

Given the database shown in Figure 2.1, the above expression defines the following table:

CustNo	CName	ChainNo	HCName
C1	M. Ridley	HC1	Happy Days
C2	B. Eaglestone	HC1	Happy Days
C1	M. Ridley	HC2	Hampton Hotels
C2	B. Eaglestone	HC2	Hampton Hotels

Note that the table defined by the above expression has rows that are formed from all possible combinations of a row from the Customer table and a row from the HotelChain table.

The other "paste" operation is the join. This is similar to cartesian product, with the added advantage that the rows in the table defined are restricted to those that satisfy some condition. There are various forms of join. The simplest is called the natural join. This combines the rows of two tables when the values in the columns that are common to them are the same. An example natural join expression in the relational algebra is as follows:

Hotel **join** HotelChain

The table defined will have the columns of Hotel and of Customer. As with the cartesian product, each row will be formed from one row of Hotel and one row of Customer. However, the result will only include combinations where the common columns have the same value. In this case, the common attribute is called HotelNo. Given the database in Figure 2.1 the table defined by the above expression is as follows:

HotelNo	Address	Rooms	ChainNo	HCName
H1	The Grand, Honley	1320	HC1	Happy Days
H3	Great Western, Barnsley	500	HC1	Happy Days
H2	Luxury Heights, Ljubljana	620	HC2	Hampton Hotels

The above expression models the query "retrieve details of hotels and the hotel chains that they are part of". Note that the common column, ChainNo, only occurs once since it represents the same types of fact in the two tables. Note also that any row in one of the argument tables that does not have a matching row in the other does not occur in the defined table, i.e. it is lost. For example, the data for "The Independent, Sheffield" does not occur, since it is not part of a hotel chain.

Variations on the natural join allow specification of the condition that associates the joined tables and retrieval also of the unmatched rows. These variations are illustrated as expressions on the following tables:

X

A	B	C
1	5	9
1	4	9
2	3	6

Y

A	E	F
1	5	7
1	4	8
2	3	9

The condition that associates the tables can be specified in a **theta-join**. The following example illustrates this.

X **join** Y **where** X.A > Y.A

The example defines a table with rows from X and Y combined where the value in the A column of X is greater than the value in the A column of Y, as shown below:

Y.A	B	C	Y.A	E	F
2	3	6	1	5	7
2	3	6	1	4	8

Note that the result table includes all the columns of X and of Y. The A column occurs twice, qualified by the respective table names. The term "theta" in theta-join refers to the comparison operator used. This example is therefore a greater than-join. Other comparison operators can also be used. Such as < or =. The equi-join (i.e. where the test is for equal values) is the most useful form, since this can describe associations between rows that describe the same entity.

Note also, that both of the above join operations will lose unmatched rows. A third type of join operation retains unmatched rows. They are included in the resulting table with null values where the values of the matched row would otherwise go. This type of join is called the outer join. For example,

Hotel **outer join** HotelChain

defines the following table:

HotelNo	Address	Rooms	ChainNo	HCName
H1	The Grand, Honley	1320	HC1	Happy Days
H3	Great Western, Barnsley	500	HC1	Happy Days
H2	Luxury Heights, Ljubljana	620	HC2	Hampton Hotels
H4	The Independent, Sheffield	620	⊥	⊥

Note that an extra row is included in which is stored the row of Hotel for hotel H4, but since this is not part of a hotel chain, values from HotelChain are null. There are also variations on the outer join. The left outer join retains unmatched rows of the first argument table, the right outer join retains unmatched·rows of the second and the full outer join will retain unmatched rows from both tables.

SET OPERATIONS

Finally, there are the operators that construct tables from the rows of two similar tables. The operators in this group, i.e. union, intersection and difference (denoted minus), will be well known to those familiar with set theory. To illustrate the set operations, consider the following two tables, which respectively represent customers who are bad debtors and those who currently have a reservation on a hotel room.

BadDebtor

CustNo	Cname
C1	M. Ridley
C9	M.Smith

Active_Customer

CustNo	Cname
C9	M. Smith
C2	B.Eaglestone

The union operator defines a table with all of the rows of both of the argument tables. For example, given the above two tables,

   BadDebtor **union** ActiveCustomer

defines the following table:

CustNo	Cname
C1	M.Ridley
C9	M.Smith
C2	B.Eaglestone

The intersection operator defines a table with only those rows that occur in both of the argument tables. For example,

   BadDebtor **intersect** ActiveCustomer

defines the following table:

CustNo	CName
C9	M.Smith

Finally, the difference operator (minus) defines a table with only those rows of the first argument table that do not occur in the second. For example,

BadDebtor **minus** ActiveCustomer

defines the following table:

CustNo	CName
C1	M.Ridley

SQL IMPLEMENTATION OF THE MANIPULATIVE PART

For the database systems implementers and users, the operators of the relational algebra are implemented by SQL instructions. These can be used to retrieve and manipulate data and are collectively called the SQL Data Manipulation Language (DML). However, it is more usual for higher level software tools and applications programs to be used to generate and execute the SQL, since these allow implementers and users to describe their requirements in a simpler and more direct way. For example, using these, the implementer can create a database system mainly by filling in forms or by giving examples of the queries they wish to make.

Like relational algebra, DML statements operate on tables and define new tables derived from them. In fact all the statements that may be expressed in the relational algebra may also be expressed as SQL DML statements. A language with the ability to express that which can be expressed in relational algebra is said to be relationally complete.

The SQL DML is illustrated in the following subsection as a progressive tutorial. SQL examples are applied to the Figure 2.1 database. Readers are encouraged to implement and execute these examples using an actual relational DBMS as they work through the tutorial in order to gain practical familiarity with the language.

The basic structure of a DML statement is

```
SELECT target_list
FROM list_of_tables
```

```
WHERE condition;
```

The meaning of this form of statement is

"retrieve a table containing the columns specified in the target_list, by **selecting** values **from** those combinations of rows in the tables specified in the list_of_tables, **where** the condition is true".

The target_list may simply be a list of column names, or it may indicate that various computations are to be applied to the retrieved values.

In general the above type of SQL statement is evaluated in the following way:
1) The cartesian product of the tables in list_of_tables is created.
2) The table created in 1) above is restricted so as to include only the rows for which the condition is true.
3) The columns specified in the target_list are projected from the relation created in 2).

The following example illustrates the evaluation of this basic type of SQL statement.

```
SELECT A, B, C
FROM X, Y
WHERE D = E;
```

We now evaluate the above expression for the following X and Y tables.

X

A	B	D
1	2	3
1	3	2

Y

C	E	F
1	2	3
9	2	3

1) The cartesian product of the tables in the list_of_tables is formed. The cartesian product, X **times** Y, is the table containing all possible pairs of rows, one from X and one from Y.

X **times** Y

A	B	D	C	E	F
1	2	3	1	2	3
1	2	3	9	2	3
1	3	2	1	2	3
1	3	2	9	2	3

2) Rows are then restricted to those for which the condition, $D = E$, is true, giving

restrict (X **times** Y) **where** D = E

A	B	D	C	E	F
1	3	2	1	2	3
1	3	2	9	2	3

3) The A, B and C columns, i.e. those in the target_list, are then projected out, giving

project (**restrict** (X **times** Y) **where** D = E) **over** A,B,C

A	B	C
1	3	1
1	3	9

We now have the result table.

RETRIEVAL OF COLUMNS FROM A SINGLE TABLE

The following SQL retrieves a single column table. The column of the resulting table is named Class and its values are all the values of the Class column in the table, Booking.

```
SELECT Class
FROM Booking;
```

Given the Figure 2.1 instance of the Booking table, i.e.

Booking

BkNo	CustNo	HotelNo	Class	Period
B1	C1	H3	3	1 Jan 2000 : 8 Jan 2000
B7	C2	H3	3	1 Jan 2000 : 8 Jan 2000
B9	C2	H1	1	2 Feb 2000 : 4 Feb 2000

the above SQL retrieves the following table

Class
3
3
1

Note that the resulting table includes duplicate values, though of course there can be no duplicate rows in the database table it represents (see above). There are two "3"rows in the table because there are two rows in Booking for which the Class column value is "3". It is often desirable to keep these duplicates within the result table. For example, the user may actually wish to know if there is more than one "class 3" booking. Also, it takes additional processing time to remove duplicates and the user may want speedy results.

It is possible to remove duplicate rows from the table that represents the result of the SQL instruction, by using the DISTINCT option. For example,

```
SELECT DISTINCT Class
FROM Booking
```

produces the following table

Class
3
1

The above examples are equivalent to the relational algebra expression

project Booking **over** Class

It is possible to project on more than one column. For example,

```
SELECT DISTINCT CustNo, Class
FROM Booking
```

retrieves the following table

CustNo	Class
C1	3
C2	3
C2	1

SQL allows "*" to be used as a shorthand way of specifying that all columns are to be retrieved, as in:

```
SELECT   *
FROM Booking
```

This will retrieve the following table

BkNo	CustNo	HotelNo	Class	Period
B1	C1	H3	3	1 Jan 2000 : 8 Jan 2000
B7	C2	H3	3	1 Jan 2000 : 8 Jan 2000
B9	C2	H1	1	2 Feb 2000 : 4 Feb 2000

RETRIEVAL OF SELECTED ROWS FROM A SINGLE TABLE

The SQL SELECT instruction may be used to express the function of the restrict operator in the relational algebra (see CUT OPERATIONS above). For example,

```
SELECT *
FROM Booking
WHERE Class = 3;
```

has the same effect as the relational algebra expression

restrict Booking **where** Class = 3

Given the above instance of the Booking table, the SQL will retrieve the following table

BkNo	CustNo	HotelNo	Class	Period
B1	C1	H3	3	1 Jan 2000 : 8 Jan 2000
B7	C2	H3	3	1 Jan 2000 : 8 Jan 2000

The "WHERE" condition clause in an SQL SELECT can be complex and that gives the SQL "SELECT" much of its power. The components of a "WHERE" condition are as follows.

- The condition, or predicate, is constructed from terms, each of which may be true or false or unknown for any given row. Examples of terms are Class = 3, BkNo = 'B7', and CustNo = 'C1'.
- Terms may be combined using the usual logic operators, i.e. and, or and not. The effect of the logical operators is shown in the truth table in Table 2.3.
- Brackets may also be used to specify how a condition is to be evaluated.

X	Y	X and Y	X or Y	Not X
true	true	true	true	false
true	false	false	true	false
true	unknown	unknown	true	false
false	true	false	true	true
false	false	false	false	true
false	unknown	False	unknown	true
unknown	true	Unknown	true	unknown
unknown	false	False	unknown	unknown
unknown	unknown	Unknown	unknown	unknown

(The rows of this truth table show the values of the expressions "X and Y", "X or Y" and "not X" for given values of X and Y. For instance, the first row shows that when X and Y are both true, then "X and Y" and "X or Y" are both true, but "not X" is false.)

Table 2.3 The Logical Operators

The following SQL includes all of the above components.

```
SELECT *
FROM Booking
 WHERE NOT (Class = 3) AND
 (HotelNo = 'H1' OR Name = 'H3')
```

The effect of this SQL is to select all the rows of Booking which describe either booking at hotel H1 or H3, but excluding those for class 3 rooms. Given the above instance of Booking, execution of the SQL statement will produce the following table.

BkNo	CustNo	HotelNo	Class	Period
B9	C2	H1	1	2 Feb 2000 : 4 Feb 2000

The rules for evaluating a condition expression against a row are:
- an expression is evaluated from left to right;
- sub-expressions in brackets are evaluated first;
- "NOT"s are evaluated before "AND"s and "OR"s.

Example 2.3 illustrates the application of the above "WHERE" condition evaluation rules.

EXAMPLE 2.3.
In this example, the condition,

```
NOT(Class = 3) AND
(HotelNo = 'H1' OR HotelNo = 'H3')
```

is evaluated against the row,

BkNo	CustNo	HotelNo	Class	Period
B9	C2	H1	1	2 Feb 2000 : 4 Feb 2000

The expressions in brackets are evaluated first (left to right).

```
(Class = 3)  is false
```

To evaluate the sub-expression (HotelNo = 'H1' OR HotelNo = 'H3') *we first evaluate the terms.*

```
HotelNo = 'H1' is true
HotelNo = 'H3' is false
```

This sub-expression therefore becomes

```
(true OR false)
```

which has the value true (see line 4 of the Table 2.1 truth table). Having evaluated the expressions in brackets the condition therefore becomes

```
NOT false AND true
```

The"NOT"s are evaluated before "AND"s and "OR"s.

"NOT false" *has the value true*

(see line 1 or 2 or 3 of the truth table above). The condition therefore becomes

"true AND true"

which returns the value true (see line 1 of the truth table above). Thus the condition returns the value true.

In general the meanings of the logical operators, "and", "or" and "not", are similar to their meanings in the English language. However, care should be taken. For instance, the Eagleley marketing manager may ask for "details of class 1 and class 2 hotel bookings" meaning that she requires details of bookings for class 1 rooms and bookings for class 2. However, the stated request is ambiguous. A valid interpretation is "retrieve details of bookings for rooms which are both class 1 and class 2", which is not what the requester meant. Though there is no such ambiguity in logic, it is common for users who are new to SQL to use "and" in the same ambiguous way that they use it in speech. It would not be unusual for instance for a novice user to express the above query using the following SQL

```
SELECT *
FROM Booking
WHERE Class = 1 AND Class = 2;
```

This SQL does not correctly express the intended query, and will always retrieve an empty table; there cannot be a row of Booking where the value of Class has two values! The correct SQL is

```
SELECT *
FROM Booking
WHERE Class = 1 OR Class = 2;
```

As well as equality, "=", the other usual comparison operators may be used in a "WHERE" condition. The condition may include, != (not equal), < (less than), > (greater than), <= (less than or equal to), and >= (greater than or equal to). For example,

```
SELECT *
FROM Hotel
WHERE Rooms > 1000
```

will retrieve details of hotels with over 1000 rooms, i.e. those rows of the Hotel tables in which the value in the Rooms column contains a value greater than 1000.

It is also possible to select on the basis of a value being within or not within a specific range. For example the following SQL expression,

```
SELECT *
FROM Hotel
WHERE Rooms NOT BETWEEN 100 AND 200
```

will select details of hotels where the number of rooms is not between 100 and 200.

In cases where retrieval is based upon specific values, rather than a range, the "in" comparison may be used. This tests for membership of a set of values. The set may be explicitly stated, as in the example below, or it may be retrieved from the database using a "nested SELECT" instruction (see below). This feature is illustrated in the following SQL.

```
SELECT *
FROM Booking
WHERE CustNo IN ('C1', 'C2', 'C3') AND
HotelNo NOT IN ('H1', 'H5')
```

The above SQL selects bookings details made by customers, C1, C2 and C3, but not for hotels H1 or H5. Given the above instance of Booking this will return the following table

BkNo	CustNo	HotelNo	Class	Period
B1	C1	H3	3	1 Jan 2000 : 8 Jan 2000
B7	C2	H3	3	1 Jan 2000 : 8 Jan 2000

Another common requirement, particularly where text is stored, as is the case in many Web database applications, is to perform "fuzzy" searches for certain character strings. That is, values are matched to find those that are similar in some aspect, but not necessarily exactly alike. The "LIKE" comparison is used for this purpose. The following SQL give an example of fuzzy string matching.

```
SELECT *
FROM Hotel
WHERE Address LIKE 'The%';
```

The above SQL selects details of hotels where the address starts with the letters "The". The right hand-side of the comparison expression defines a character pattern. The expression is true for a particular row if that pattern exists in the left-hand side attribute value. In the example, the pattern is represented by the characters "The", followed by character "%". The latter represents "any character string". "The%" therefore represents the letters "The" followed by anything. Therefore, given the following instance of Hotel

Hotel

HotelNo	Address	Rooms	ChainNo
H1	The Grand, Honley	1320	HC1
H2	Great Western, Barnsley	500	HC2
H3	Luxury Heights, Ljubljana	620	HC1
H4	The Independent, Sheffield	620	⊥

the example SQL statement will retrieve the following table

HotelNo	Address	Rooms	ChainNo
H1	The Grand, Honley	1320	HC1
H4	The Independent, Sheffield	620	⊥

A pattern definition consists of a character string which may include a number of characters with special meaning.

- % represents an arbitrary string, i.e. any string of characters. In the example, S% represents S followed by any other characters, e.g. Smith, Small, ...
- _ represents a single arbitrary character, e.g. B_OWN represents BROWN, BLOWN, BOOWN, ...

- [ ] square brackets may contain any number of letters, each of which is tested individually in the specified position. For example, B[RLO]OWN represents either BROWN or BLOWN or BOOWN.

To select details of all hotels whose addresses begin "T", followed by something, followed by "Hon", and then the rest, we would use the following SQL expression

```
SELECT *
FROM Hotel
WHERE Address LIKE 'T%Hon%'
```

Given the above instance of Hotel, this example SQL statement will retrieve the following table.

HotelNo	Address	Rooms	ChainNo
H1	The Grand, Honley	1320	HC1

The next two examples illustrate the use of square brackets for specifying sets of characters that may occur in a specified position.

```
SELECT * FROM Hotel
WHERE Address LIKE '[LT]%'
```

The above retrieves rows where the address starts with either "L" or "T". Given the above Hotel table, this retrieves the following table

HotelNo	Address	Rooms	ChainNo
H1	The Grand, Honley	1320	HC1
H3	Luxury Heights, Ljubljana	620	HC1
H4	The Independent, Sheffield	620	⊥

The next SQL example specifies a range of characters which may be the first character of the value of Address.

```
SELECT * FROM Hotel
WHERE Address LIKE '[K-M]%'
```

The above will retrieve rows where the address started with any letter in the range "K" to "M". In the case of the above Hotel table, this will retrieve:

HotelNo	Address	Rooms	ChainNo
H3	Luxury Heights, Ljubljana	620	HC1

In some cases we wish to retrieve rows in which a special character such as "%" or "_" actually occur. To specify this, a method of saying that in this case "%" and "_" are to be themselves and not special characters is required. This can be done with the use of ESCAPE characters, as in the following example SQL.

```
SELECT *
FROM Hotel
WHERE Address LIKE 'S/_/%%' ESCAPE /;
```

The above SQL specifies such a retrieval. In it the slash (/) character has been nominated as the escape character. In the pattern definition any character that is preceded by / is taken as itself and not as some special character. The above SQL will retrieve an empty table, since there are no addresses that begin with the characters "S_%" in the example Hotel table.

Finally, in this subsection, we consider retrieval where null values (represented by "⊥") are stored. A row of a table is used to represent information about some entity and the column values represent facts about that entity. However, sometimes facts about a particular entity are unknown or not applicable. When this is the case, a null value is stored. Nulls are not the same as spaces or zeros. A null represents the fact that no value has been specified, where as spaces or zeros are specific values.

SQL includes facilities for selecting rows where specified column values are null, as illustrated in the following SQL.

```
SELECT *
FROM Hotel
WHERE ChainNo IS NULL AND Rooms IS NOT NULL;
```

The above SQL will retrieve details of hotels for which no hotel chain has been represented but the number of rooms is specified. Give the above Hotel table, the SQL statement will retrieve the following table.

HotelNo	Address	Rooms	ChainNo
H4	The Independent, Sheffield	620	⊥

Note, the above SQL is not the same as

```
SELECT *
FROM Hotel
WHERE ChainNo   = '       '  AND Rooms != 0;
```

The latter selects hotel details for which the hotel chain number has been recorded as spaces and the number of rooms is not zero, and would therefore retrieve an empty table.

COMPUTATION

Using SQL, it is possible to retrieve values computed from the values of a table. This is done by specifying formulae in the target_list of the "SELECT" statement, as illustrated in the following SQL.

```
SELECT  Invoice_No = BkNo, ItemNo, Quantity,
Value = Price * Quantity
FROM    InvoiceLine;
```

Given the following InvoiceLine table

InvoiceLine

BkNo	ItemNo	Quantity	Price
B1	I5	4	55.00
B1	I8	1	24.50
B2	I5	5	55.00
B2	I12	5	12.00

the above SQL will retrieve the following table

Invoice No	ItemNo	Quantitiy	Value
B1	I5	4	220.00
B1	I8	1	24.50
B2	I5	5	275.00
B2	I12	5	60.00

Note that the fourth column, named "Value", of the result table contains values computed from values within the database. Also, the column of booking numbers has been named "InvoiceNo". Normally, a column in the result table takes its name from the column(s) of the database table(s) from which it has been retrieved, but any column may be renamed in the manner illustrated in the above example.

The usual arithmetic operators may be used within the formula, i.e. +, −, * (multiply), /, ** (to the power of). Some RDBMS also provide mathematical functions, for example, for use in statistical and graphical applications.

The other form of computation that might be required is on columns rather than rows of tables. Using SQL this is possible by applying summarising functions. The following set functions are supported in standard SQL, but some systems also support many more.
- AVG is used to average the values of an attribute.
- MAX returns the largest value of an attribute.
- MIN returns the minimum value of an attribute.
- SUM returns the total of the values of an attribute.
- COUNT returns the number of values in a column or the number of rows in a table.

The use of these is illustrated by the following SQL

```
SELECT Ave = AVG (Price), High = MAX(Price),
   Low = MIN(Price), Prices = COUNT (*),
   Prices = COUNT (DISTINCT Price)
FROM InvoiceLine;
```

When applied to the above InvoiceLine table, the above SQL will retrieve the average, highest and lowest price and the number of rows in the table and the number of different values in the Price column. The results would have been NULL rather than zero if there were no values to summarise. Given the example InvoiceLine table, the SQL will return the result below

Ave	High	Low	Prices	Prices
36.625	55.00	12.00	4	3

Once again, note how the result columns have been renamed to make the names meaningful, and the use of the term "distinct" to remove duplicate values from the calculation.

In some cases it is also important to apply computations not to all values in a column, but to groups of related rows. This is achieved in SQL using the "group by" clause. This may be thought of as creating a number of tables, one for each distinct value of the column specified. The select statement is then applied to each of these sub-tables to create the rows of the result table. For example, the following SQL,

```
SELECT Invoice = BkNo, Items = SUM (Quantity)
FROM InvoiceLine
GROUP BY BkNo;
```

will produce the total price for each booking. The resulting table, given the above example InvoiceLine table, is

Invoice	Items
B1	5
B2	10

The "group by" clause may be qualified by the "having" clause which states additional conditions that rows of a sub-relation must satisfy. For example, the SQL,

```
SELECT  Invoice = BkNo, Items = SUM (QUANTITY)
FROM InvoiceLine
GROUP BY BkNo
HAVING COUNT (*) > 1 AND  SUM (Quantity) > 5;
```

will report only those invoices with more than one line, and which are for a total of more than 5 items. The result will therefore include only the second line of the above table.

Finally, in this subsection, we consider presentation of the result table. We have already seen how meaningful names can be given to columns, as illustrated in the previous SQL examples. Also, though the rows and columns of a table in a relational database have no ordering, it is often more meaningful for the rows of the table to be displayed or printed in sequence. For example

```
SELECT *
FROM Booking
ORDER BY BkNo,Class DESC;
```

will retrieve a table which represents the rows of the Booking table in descending numerical order of Class within ascending alphabetical order of BkNo, i.e. their ordering in Figure 2.1. If there is no "order by" clause, the order of the rows of the resulting table will depend upon how the query is evaluated, and how the queried tables are physically stored.

RETRIEVAL FROM MORE THAN ONE TABLE

The join operator of the relational algebra makes it possible to define a table that is made up of data taken from more than one table. This is an important facility, because it makes it possible to extract information about related entities. For example, a join may be used to define a table representing information about customers and also the hotel reservations they have made, even when customer and bookings information is stored in different tables. In this subsection we describe how join operations are expressed in SQL.

In general, two or more tables are combined by identifying them in the "FROM" clause and by specifying the joining condition in the "WHERE" clause of a "SELECT statement". The columns of the resulting table are specified as usual in the "SELECT" clause. This is illustrated in the following SQL.

```
SELECT Customer.*, Booking.*
FROM Customer, Booking
WHERE Customer.CustNo = Booking.CustNo;
```

The above SQL will retrieve a table that has all the columns of the Customer table and also all the columns of the Booking table. Each row in this result table will comprise the values of one row in Customer and the values of one row in Booking. The two component rows will be combined and included in the result table when the condition in the "WHERE" clause is true, i.e. the values of the CustNo columns in the two rows will be equal. Executing the above SQL with the following two tables

Customer

CustNo	Cname
C1	M.Ridley
C2	B.Eaglestone
C3	J.Brown

Booking

BkNo	CustNo	HotelNo	Class	Period
B1	C1	H3	3	1 Jan 2000:8 Jan 2000
B7	C2	H3	3	1 Jan 2000:8 Jan 2000
B9	C2	H1	1	2 Feb 2000:4 Feb 2000

gives the result table below

CustNo	Customer. CName	BkNo	Booking.CustNo	HotelNo	Class	Period
C1	M.Ridley	B1	C1	H3	3	1Jan2000: 8Jan 2000
C2	B.Eaglestone	B7	C2	H3	3	1Jan2000: 8Jan2000
C2	B.Eaglestone	B9	C2	H1	1	2Feb2000: 4Feb2000

Note the following:
• The "FROM" clause must list the names of all tables accessed in order to retrieve the specified table. It must even list those tables accessed, but whose data is not included in the resulting table.
• Sometimes the same column name will occur in two or more tables, e.g. CustNo occurs in both Customer and Booking. In such cases, it is therefore necessary to qualify column names used in the SQL by preceding them with the appropriate table name. This avoids any ambiguity. That is why CustNo is prefixed by either Customer or Booking in the above example.

- Not all rows of Customer occur in the result. For example, the row, <C3, J.Brown> does not occur because there are no bookings for that customer.

The above SQL is equivalent to an equi-join in the relational algebra (see Paste Operations above).

It is desirable that table names should be chosen so as to be meaningful. However, where a table name is long it is often convenient to be able to use some alternative shorter name. It is possible to do this by specifying correlation names in the "FROM" clause. For example, the above SQL could be rewritten as

```
SELECT C.*, B.*
FROM Customer C, Booking B
WHERE C.CustNo = B.CustNo;
```

In the "FROM" clause above, both tables accessed are named and also assigned correlation names, C and B respectively. The correlation names may then be used instead of the full table names. Note however, the correlation names are only valid within the SQL statement in which they are declared.

Correlation names are sometimes not just a convenience (to avoid excessive typing) but are necessary. This is the case when a table is joined with itself. For example, we could retrieve details of hotels that are larger than Luxury Heights, Ljubljana, as follows.

```
SELECT H.*
FROM Hotel L, Hotel H
WHERE L.Address = 'Luxury Heights, Ljubljana'
  and H.Rooms > L.Rooms;
```

Below is the table that the above SQL will return when executed with the instance of the Hotel table in the Figure 2.1 example database

HotelNo	Address	Rooms	ChainNo
H1	The Grand, Honley	1320	HC1

In general, all of the join operations (with the exception of the outer join), described in the summary of relational algebra, can be expressed by specifying appropriate "SELECT" and "WHERE" clauses. Also, if the "WHERE" clause is omitted, the effect is to form the cartesian product, since there is then no restriction of the rows that can be combined in the result table.

As a further example, the following SQL executes the natural join, Hotel join HotelChain

```
SELECT H.*, HC.HCName
FROM Hotel H, HotelChain HC
WHERE H.ChainNo = HC.ChainNo
```

Note that in the above SQL it was necessary to specify the columns of the result relation to exclude two ChainNo columns, since the natural join includes only one column for each column name, even when it occurs in both argument tables.

SQL2 also supports explicit join operations. The advantage is that the join condition is not complicated by also having to include any restrict conditions, and *vice versa*. This feature is illustrated by the following SQL, which joins Hotel and HotelChain, selects details of hotels with under 800 rooms, and displays the address and hotel chain of the selected hotels.

```
SELECT H.Address, HC.CName
FROM Hotel AS H INNER JOIN HotelChain AS HC
        ON H.ChainNo = HC.ChainNo
WHERE H.Rooms < 800
```

In this SQL-2 syntax, the natural and theta-joins are called inner joins, to distinguish them from outer joins. The main difference between inner and outer joins is that an inner join loses unmatched rows, whereas an outer join retains them. As well as specifying "inner join" it is also possible, using this notation, to specify "left join", "right join", and "full join". These respectively specify a left outer join, a right outer join and a (full) outer join. For example, the following SQL will retrieve also the addresses of hotels with fewer than 800 rooms, but that are not part of a hotel chain.

```
SELECT H.Address, HC.HCName
FROM Hotel AS H LEFT JOIN HotelChain AS HC
        ON H.ChainNo = HC.ChainNo
WHERE H.Rooms < 800
```

The respective result tables for the above two SQL statements are given below

Address	HCName
Great Western, Barnsley	Happy Days
Luxury Heights, Ljubljana	Hampton Hotels

Address	HCName
Great Western, Barnsley	Happy Days
Luxury Heights, Ljubljana	Hampton Hotels
The Independent, Sheffield	$\perp$

Though the above SQL examples operate upon either one or two tables, it is possible for SQL instructions to operate upon more than two tables, as in the next example.

```
SELECT CName
FROM Customer C, Booking B, Hotel H
WHERE C.CustNo = B.CustNo AND
        B.HotelNo = H.HotelNo AND
        H.Address = 'Great Western, Barnsley';
```

The above SQL will return the names of customers with a booking to stay at the Great Western, Barnsley. Note that although only data from the Customer table is retrieved, all of three tables accessed must be listed in the "FROM" clause.

NESTED SELECTS
Much of the expressive power of SQL is a consequence of the facility by which "SELECT" statements may be included within the "WHERE"

clause of another "SELECT" statement. This nesting is illustrated in the following example.

Consider the following query: "Determine the address and size of all hotels in the Happy Days hotel chain". This query could be expressed in SQL as follows, using features already described.

```
SELECT Address, Rooms
FROM HotelChain HC, Hotel H
WHERE HC.ChainNo = H.ChainNo AND
      HC.CName = 'Happy Days';
```

Given the Hotel and HotelChain tables in Figure 2.1, this returns,

Address	Rooms
The Grand, Honley	1320
Luxury Heights, Ljubljana	620

However, the use of nested selects offers an alternative "step by step" way of forming an equivalent query, as follows.

1) First find out the chain number of the Happy Days hotel chain. This may be expressed using

```
SELECT ChainNo
FROM HotelChain
WHERE CName = 'Happy Days';
```

This query may be input and tested. The table produced is

ChainNo
HC1

2) The results of the above SQL may now be used to SELECT the required details of the hotels in chain HC1, as follows

```
SELECT Address, Rooms
FROM Hotel
WHERE ChainNo IN
```

```
(SELECT ChainNo
 FROM HotelChain
 WHERE CName = 'Happy Days');
```

Note the use of "in" within the condition. This tests if a hotel chain number is contained in the set of hotel chain numbers retrieved by the nested select.

The above SQL example of a nested select has the following form

```
SELECT target_list_1
FROM   list_of_relations_1
WHERE  attribute IN
       (SELECT target_list_2
        FROM list_of_relations-2
        WHERE condition)
```

The inner select retrieves a set of values, and the outer select retrieves rows where specific column values are members of that set. The outer select tests the results of the inner select using the "in" operator. This compares column values with those in a set defined either explicitly or by the nested select (as above). The "in" operator means " is equal to any member of the set". At times however, the user may wish to test for other relationships, such as "is greater than all members of the set" or "is less than some member of the set". This is possible using qualified comparison, as illustrated in the following examples.

```
SELECT * FROM Hotel
WHERE ChainNo != 'HC1' AND Rooms > ALL
      (SELECT Rooms FROM Hotel
       WHERE ChainNo = 'HC1');
```

The above SQL will retrieve details of hotels larger than all of the hotels owned by the hotel chain, HC1. "ALL" qualifies the operator ">" so that it has to be true for every value in the set retrieved by the inner select. Given the following Hotel table the above SQL will return an empty table, since there are no hotels with more that 1320 rooms.

Hotel

HotelNo	Address	Rooms	ChainNo
H1	The Grand, Honley	1320	HC1
H2	Great Western, Barnsley	500	HC2
H3	Luxury Heights, Ljubljana	620	HC1
H4	The Independent, Sheffield	620	⊥

Alternatively, comparison operators may be qualified by "any" in order to specify that the operator must hold for at least one value of the set (standard SQL allows "some" to be used instead of "any"). The example below illustrates this facility.

```
SELECT *
FROM Hotel
WHERE ChainNo != 'HC1' and Rooms > ANY
      (SELECT Rooms
       FROM Hotel
       WHERE ChainNo = 'HC1');
```

In this case, the SQL will retrieve details of the Great Western and The Independent, since both have more rooms than the Luxury Heights.

The operator "in" has been used in previous examples to select details associated with values in a set. Some SQL select instructions will always retrieve a single value. This is the case, for example, when the "WHERE" condition tests for a particular primary key value. In such cases the comparison operators that operate upon single values may be used. These operators are: =, <, >, < >, <=, >=. For instance, a previous SQL example could be rewritten as follows, and still have the same effect.

```
SELECT Address, Rooms
FROM Hotel
WHERE ChainNo =
      (SELECT ChainNo
       FROM HotelChain
       WHERE CName = 'Happy Days');
```

This is because hotel chain name is unique for each hotel chain, and the inner select will therefore always retrieve a single-column table with a single value.

Sometimes, we are concerned with the presence or absence of values in the table retrieved by an inner select, rather than the values themselves. In such cases we must test to see if the table returned by the inner select is an empty set. This is done using the "exists" operator. To illustrate this facility, consider the database query "are there any customers who have not made a booking?". This query can be expressed in SQL as follows

```
SELECT * FROM Customer C
WHERE NOT EXISTS
      (SELECT *
      FROM Booking B
      WHERE C.CustNo = B.CustNo);
```

The above will retrieve details of each customer where there are no bookings recorded in the Booking table. It operates as follows. The inner select defines the set of Booking rows that have the same customer number as some customer row. If there are no Booking rows corresponding to a particular customer row then this set is empty and the "not exists" condition is true.

Note the use of the correlation names in the condition of the inner select. These provide a means of communication between the inner and outer selects.

SET OPERATIONS ON TABLES
SQL includes facilities for applying the set operators—union, intersect and difference. (Note that most systems support UNION, but intersect and difference are SQL2 features.). These SQL operators are illustrated using the following BadDebtor and ActiveCustomer tables.

BadDebtor

CustNo	Cname
C1	M. Ridley
C9	M.Smith

ActiveCustomer

CustNo	CName
C9	M.Smith
C2	B.Eaglestone

The union operator combines the elements of two sets into a single set. In SQL it brings together rows of two tables into a single table. Like the UNION operator in relational algebra, the SQL "UNION" operator defines a table with all of the rows of both of the argument tables, as illustrated in the following example SQL.

```
SELECT * FROM BadDebtor
UNION
SELECT * FROM ActiveCustomer
```

The table returned by the above SQL is as follows

CustNo	CName
C1	M. Ridley
C9	M.Smith
C2	B.Eaglestone

The intersect operator retrieves a table with rows that occur in both of the argument tables, as illustrated in the following SQL.

```
SELECT * FROM BadDebtor
INTERSECT
SELECT *
FROM ActiveCustomer
```

The above will retrieve the following table

CustNo	CName
C9	M.Smith

Finally, the difference operator denoted "minus" or "except" will return rows that are in the first but not the second of the argument tables. For example,

```
SELECT * FROM BadDebtor
MINUS
SELECT * FROM ActiveCustomer
```

CustNo	CName
C1	M. Ridley

The SQL set operators combines results from two "SELECT" statements. Also, there is a constraint that the arguments of "SELECT" statements must return tables in which corresponding columns have the same type, i.e. they must be union compatible. The above will remove duplicate rows, i.e. those which occur in both of the argument tables. If the duplicate rows are required, the operator "UNION all" should be used.

CHANGING VALUES IN THE DATABASE
SQL includes "update", "delete" and "insert" commands for altering the contents of tables. Like the "SELECT", previously described, these commands operate on sets of rows. In certain forms they include embedded "SELECT" statements.

Hotel

HotelNo	Address	Rooms	ChainNo
H1	The Grand, Honley	1320	HC1
H2	Great Western, Barnsley	500	HC2
H3	Luxury Heights, Ljubljana	620	HC1
H4	The Independent, Sheffield	620	⊥

The following sequence of SQL examples illustrate the facilities for altering the values in rows of database tables. The examples are illustrated by showing the result of executing them with the Hotel table, given above.

The following SQL will change the ChainNo value from null to 'HC4', and increase the Rooms value by 5, for the row that describes "The Independent, Sheffield".

```
UPDATE Hotel
SET ChainNo = 'HC4', Rooms = Rooms + 5
WHERE HotelNo = 'H4';
```

The result of the above SQL is to modify the Hotel table as shown below.

Hotel

HotelNo	Address	Rooms	ChainNo
H1	The Grand, Honley	1320	HC1
H2	Great Western, Barnsley	500	HC2
H3	Luxury Heights, Ljubljana	620	HC1
H4	The Independent, Sheffield	625	HC4

The "UPDATE" instruction updates a single relation at a time, but may alter many rows, i.e. all those that satisfy the "WHERE" condition. Note also that new values may be computed. They may in fact be computed using any of the expressions that may be used in the target_list of a "SELECT" statement.

SQL includes an "insert" command for adding new rows to a table. The new rows may be specified by sets of values, or may be created from values already stored in the database. The two examples given below illustrate these two facilities.

The following SQL illustrates the facility for inserting a new row into a table, where the values of the new row are specified.

```
INSERT INTO Hotel (HotelNo, Address,Rooms,
ChainNo)
VALUES ('H5', 'The Lodge, Emley', 512);
```

When applied to the above (unupdated) example instance of the Hotel table, the above "insert" instruction will produce the modified Hotel table, as shown below.

Hotel

HotelNo	Address	Rooms	ChainNo
H1	The Grand, Honley	1320	HC1
H2	Great Western, Barnsley	500	HC2
H3	Luxury Heights, Ljubljana	620	HC1
H4	The Independent, Sheffield	620	⊥
H5	The Lodge, Emley	512	⊥

Note that the new row includes a null value in the ChainNo column. This is because the value is not specified in the "insert". An RDBMS that does not support nulls would place a default value in ChainNo, usually, spaces for character fields and zero for numeric fields. Also, a default will be inserted if it is specified for that column when the table or domain was specified (see CREATING A NEW BASE RELATION above).

The following example illustrates the SQL facility for inserting new rows that are constructed from values already stored in the database. First, we create a new table for storing details of hotels with fewer than 501.

```
CREATE TABLE SmallHotel
(
        HotelNo       CHAR(5)       PRIMARY KEY,
        Address       CHAR (30),
        Rooms SMALLINT
);
```

We now create rows from the values in the Hotel table. The rows in which we are interested are those where the condition, Rooms < 501, is true, and it is only the HotelNo, Address and Rooms columns that are required for the new rows. The new rows are created by the following SQL

```
INSERT   INTO   SmallHotel(SmallHotelNo,   Address,
Rooms)
SELECT HotelNo, Address, Rooms
FROM Hotel
WHERE Rooms < 501;
```

When applied to the above (unupdated) Hotel table, the above "INSERT" creates the following SmallHotel table

SmallHotel

SmallHotelNo	Address	Rooms
H2	Great Western, Barnsley	500

Note, the use of an embedded "SELECT" instruction to retrieve the set of rows to be inserted. Also, the column names of the table into which the rows are to be inserted need not be the same as those of the tables from which the rows are retrieved.

Finally, in this subsection, SQL includes a "delete" command with which sets of rows may be deleted from a table. The following SQL will remove from the Hotel table all rows describing hotels in the HC1 hotel chain.

```
DELETE FROM Hotel
    WHERE ChainNo = 'HC1';
```

The effect when applied to the original Hotel table is as follows

Hotel

HotelNo	Address	Rooms	ChainNo
H2	Great Western, Barnsley	500	HC2
H4	The Independent, Sheffield	620	⊥

The power of this delete facility is that it may be used to delete individual rows, by specifying the primary key value in the "WHERE" condition, or it may be used to delete sets of related rows, as in the above example.

THE INTEGRITY PART

The integrity part of the Relational Data Model is the set of rules that all databases must satisfy. These rules are defined to ensure that a database is at least plausible. The relational model has just two integrity rules called entity and referential integrity.

1) Entity integrity—This rule requires all primary keys to have only non-null values. This is a necessary restriction to ensure that every row can be uniquely identified by the name of the entity it represents.

2) Referential integrity—This rule requires each foreign key to have either a value that occurs elsewhere as a primary key, or a null value. This rule prohibits cross-references to entities that are not described in the database.

These constraints are illustrated in the following database, in which both are violated. Entity integrity is violated by the second row of Hotel, since the primary key, HotelNo, has a null value. Referential integrity is violated by the third row of Hotel, since the ChainNo value is HC6, but this does not occur as a primary key in the HotelChain table.

Hotel

HotelNo	Address	Rooms	ChainNo
H1	The Grand, Honley	1320	HC1
⊥	The Royal, Halifax	200	HC2
H5	Grimble Towers, Emley	200	HC6
H2	Great Western, Barnsley	500	HC2
H3	Luxury Heights, Ljubljana	620	HC1
H4	The Independent, Sheffield	620	⊥

HotelChain

ChainNo	HCName
HC1	Happy Days
HC2	Hampton Hotels

In addition, there may be application-specific integrity rules. For example, though the Rooms column of the Hotel table in Figure 2.1 is neither a key or a foreign key, it still does not make sense to describe a hotel without any rooms, and so a "NOT NULL" integrity constraint would be appropriate for that column.

SQL INTEGRITY FEATURES

Using SQL, we can ensure that entity integrity is enforced by declaring the primary key columns in the "CREATE TABLE" statement. The primary key values are then constrained such that they cannot have null values and must be unique within the table. A table may have many keys, but only one primary key. Also, the primary key may comprise either a single column or many columns. The two ways in which primary keys can be declared is illustrated below in the example SQL.

```
CREATE TABLE  Hotel
(
        HotelNo      CHAR(4)       PRIMARY KEY,
        Address      CHAR(30)      NOT NULL,
        Rooms        SMALLINT      NOT NULL,
        ChainNo      CHAR(4)
        REFERENCE    HotelChain.ChainNo
        ON DELETE SET NULL
        ON UPDATE CASCADE
)

CREATE TABLE HotelChain
(
        ChainNo      CHAR(4),
        CName        CHAR(30)      UNIQUE
        NOT NULL,
        PRIMARY KEY (ChainNo)
)
```

Note that the HotelNo column in Hotel is specified as "PRIMARY KEY". Also, in HotelChain the alternative syntax is used, in which the primary key is specified after the columns have been specified. The latter is necessary in cases where the primary key comprises many columns.

The above example SQL also illustrates how referential integrity can be enforced by declaring the foreign key columns of a table and identifying the corresponding primary keys. There are two ways of specifying foreign keys in a "CREATE TABLE" statement. The method illustrated is to specify the foreign key column as a "reference" and identify the corresponding columns that are referenced. Alternatively, the foreign key columns can be identified after the table columns have been specified, as "foreign key" columns. The example illustrates the former syntax.

If referential integrity is enforced, this poses the problem of what to do if a referenced row is deleted or updated. SQL allows the following actions to be specified:

- "set null"—the foreign key is set to null when the referenced row is deleted or updated such that the value of the foreign key no longer exists in the cross-referenced column.
- "cascade"——If the cross-referenced row is updated, the foreign key value is changed to the new value of the row that it cross-references. If the cross-referenced row is deleted, then so are the rows that reference it.
- "set default"—the value of a foreign key is reset to a default value, if it ceases to be valid because the row it cross-references has been updated or deleted.
- "no action"—any update or delete operation that would violate referential integrity is rejected.

The above example "CREATE TABLE" statements illustrate how the first two of the above operations are specified for a foreign key (ChainNo), respectively on delete and update. Other operations are specified in a similar way.

Application-specific integrity constraints can also be specified using SQL. Previous examples have already illustrated how columns can be constrained to be "NOT NULL" and/or "UNIQUE". In addition, "checks" can be specified for columns to ensure that they are plausible. These are specific conditions that the values of a column must satisfy, and can be based upon other values in the database. In fact, the conditions can be any of those that can occur in the "WHERE" clause of a "SELECT" statement. The two forms of SQL "checks" are illustrated in the following SQL.

```
CREATE TABLE LARGEHotel
(
        HotelNo      CHAR(4)
        CHECK (500 > (SELECT Rooms
            FROM Hotel H
            WHERE HotelNo = H.HotelNo)
)
```

```
CREATE ASSERTION  AllwaysOneHotel
CHECK ( 1 <= (SELECT count (*) FROM Hotel))
```

Note that the first of the above examples is specific to a particular row of a table, and checks that the hotel identified is described in the Hotel table as having more than 500 rooms. The second example creates an assertion. Assertions exist separate from the table specifications, and need not be associated with a single column. For example, an assertion can constrain one or more tables. The example assertion ensures that the Hotel table will always include at least one row.

VIEWS

SQL allows the above structural, manipulative and integrity features to be used to present applications with the illusion that special tables, called views, exist. These tables contain only the data needed for an application and are presented in a suitable form for that application. Views are used to create external models (see Section 1.1 Database Technology: The Database Management System) for specific applications. Requiring an application to access a database via a view can be likened to putting blinkers on a horse; so as to remove from sight all irrelevancies and distractions. Thus life becomes simpler.

- The use of views becomes very desirable where a database becomes large and complex because the view hides the complexity of the database as a whole from the application.
- Also, views can be used to shield programs from some of the effects of changes to the structure of a database.
- A third advantage is that by hiding irrelevant information from a program the chance of information being inadvertently or maliciously accessed and perhaps modified is reduced.

A view defines a virtual table, i.e. a table that appears to the user and the programmer to exist but does not actually exist. Instead, it is derived from base tables (i.e. tables stored in the database) and from other virtual tables by executing a query on them. This query is stored as part of the view definition using the database querying facilities already described. Queries on the view are then converted into queries on the base table by the DBMS's query manager.

This concept of virtual tables should become clearer with the aid of an example. Below are the Hotel and HotelChain tables used in previous examples. Consider an application which provides a hotel booking service exclusively for hotels in the Happy Days chain. This application could be greatly simplified if it could access a single table that describes only hotels in that chain. It is simple to retrieve this table using the SQL querying features previously described. The query and the retrieved table are shown immediately following the Hotel and HotelChain tables, below.

Hotel

HotelNo	Address	Rooms	ChainNo
H1	The Grand, Honley	1320	HC1
⊥	The Royal, Halifax	200	HC2
H5	Grimble Towers, Emley	200	HC6
H2	Great Western, Barnsley	500	HC2
H3	Luxury Heights, Ljubljana	620	HC1
H4	The Independent, Sheffield	620	⊥

HotelChain

ChainNo	HCName
HC1	Happy Days
HC2	Hampton Hotels

```
SELECT H.HotelNo, Address, Rooms
FROM Hotel H, HotelChain HC
WHERE H.ChainNo = HC.ChainNo
      AND HC.HCName = 'Happy Days';
```

HotelNo	Address	Rooms
H1	The Grand, Honley	1320
H3	Luxury Heights, Ljubljana	620

The above result relation does not exist as a base table but is derived from base tables. A view mechanism makes it possible to create the illusion for a user or application program that the above table does actually exist in the same way that base tables exist. A table such as this which is so derived is a virtual table.

In SQL, the above table could be created as a virtual table by the following instruction.

```
CREATE VIEW HappyDaysHotel AS
    SELECT H.HotelNo, Address, Rooms
    FROM Hotel H, HotelChain HC
    WHERE H.ChainNo = HC.ChainNo
        AND HC.HCName = 'Happy Days';
```

The result of executing the above SQL is that a user or application may then access HappyDaysHotel, a virtual table, in much the same way that it would access a base table such as Hotel or HotelChain. In fact, the RDBMS will provide this facility by modifying SQL instructions which access HappyDaysHotel so that they instead perform the appropriate access to the tables, HotelChain and Hotel, from which it is derived.

Even though views can be accessed in the same way as base tables, not all views can be updated. This is because there is not always a one-to-one relationship between values in a view and the corresponding values in the base tables. A change to the data in the view can therefore be ambiguous or undefined. In general, views that are derived from a single table and that include the primary key are updatable. Others are not.

The rules in standard SQL2 are that a view is updatabase only if the following constraints apply:
• DISTINCT is not specified
• Every column of the view is a column of a base table (rather than a function or constant)
• The FROM clause specifies only one table
• The WHERE clause does not include nested selects
• There is no GROUP BY or HAVING clause in the view definition.

OTHER FEATURES OF THE RELATIONAL DATA MODEL AND SQL
In the above section we have described the relational data model and the way it is implemented using SQL, the standard relational database language.

There are other features of standard SQL that will be covered later in this book. Some are to do with the physical implementation and administration of the database. For example, these specify the file structures used to store tables and the access and security mechanisms.

2.3 SUMMARY

A **data model** describes ways in which data can be structured, manipulated and the rules for ensuring that the data is plausible. It will therefore have **structural**, **manipulative** and **integrity** parts. A DBMS will implement a specific data model.

Most up-to-date DBMS implement the **relational data model**. The structural part of the relational data model comprises only one simple structure, the table. A relational database is simply a collection of tables. The data is stored as values within those tables. The manipulative part is defined as a mathematics for defining tables from the contents of other tables. This mathematics is called the **relational algebra**. The capabilities of relational algebra are made available to relational database users in the form of **SQL**, the international standard relational database language.

A description of the structure of a database is called its **schema**. The schema of a relational database defines a set of tables. A schema and tables within a schema are defined in SQL by the "**CREATE schema**" and "**CREATE TABLE**" instructions.

Data manipulation can be modeled by the operators of the relational algebra and can be thought of as cut and paste operations on tables. These can be implemented in SQL using "**SELECT**", "**update, **"**delete**" and "**insert**" instructions.

The integrity part of the relational model is a set of two rules that ensure that a relational database is plausible. The **entity integrity** rule ensures that all entities represented have unique names, by prohibiting null valued keys. **Referential integrity** ensures that cross-referenced entities are also described within the database, by prohibiting foreign key values that do not also occur as key values. In SQL these are respectively specified by specifying primary and foreign keys in the "CREATE TABLE" instruction. In addition, application-specific constraints can be specified using "NOT NULL", "UNIQUE" and "check", either within the table specifications or as assertions.

Views allow the presentation of data in appropriate forms for specific applications. Views are virtual tables defined by stored queries on base tables.

EXERCISES

(2.1)   What is a data model and what is its purpose?

(2.2)   A data model is a theoretical model of databases. Explain, and give examples of theoretical models used in other areas.

(2.3)   What are the three parts of a data model?

(2.4)   Explain two important roles of a data model.

(2.5)   The quality of a theoretical model can be judged by how accurate and complete a representation it provides. Specifically, how do you judge the quality of a data model?

(2.6)   From where and whom did the relational data model originate?

(2.7)   Identify four advantages of the relational data model.

(2.8)   What are the two parts of SQL and what are their respective functions?

(2.9)   Describe three contexts within which SQL can be used.

(2.10)   SQL has now gone through a number of revisions. Outline what these are.

(2.11)   Explain what is meant by Entry SQL, Intermediate SQL and Full SQL.

(2.12)   What is the purpose of the structural part of the relational data model?

(2.13)   The technical terms for the structures of the relational model are relation, attribute, and tuple. Explain what these mean, using terms relating to tables.

(2.14)   Structures in a relational database are represented as tables. What constraints does a relational database impose on the contents of a table?

(2.15)   Explain the concept of a domain. Why is it important for achieving a natural representation of information as data?

(2.16)   What is a key of a table? What is the relationship between a table key and the entity represented by the table?

(2.17)   What restriction does first normal form place on the content of a table? Why is it imposed on relational databases?

(2.18)   Distinguish between candidate key, primary key, alternative key and foreign key.

(2.19)   Why is the relational model said to be value-based?

(2.20)   Sketch a relational database to store information about books in a library, the borrowers, and loans. Identify the tables, attributes, domains and the different types of key in your sketch.

(2.21)   What is a schema and what is its purpose?

(2.22)   What is a data dictionary or catalogue and what is its purpose? Using the SQL SDL, create the following database structures:

(2.23)   Create a schema called Library, giving Ridley authorisation.

(2.24)   Within the schema create a table called Book with columns, BookNo, Title, Publisher, ISBN and NumberCopies. BookNo is the primary key and all of the columns must be not null, with the exception of ISBN. The latter must be unique. NumberCopies must default to 1.

(2.25)   Create a table called Author with columns AuthorName and BookNo. The combination of AuthorName and BookNo form the primary key.

(2.26)   Create a table called Borrower with columns BorrowerNo, Name, Address, Telephone, and DateRegistered.

(2.27)   Create a domain, LoanNo, comprising five characters.

(2.28)   Create a table called Temp, with columns X, Y and Z, the colums should be of types integer, float and string respectively.

(2.29)   Add an additional integer column to the Temp table, called Extra then remove the table.

(2.30)   Create a table called Loan, with columns LoanNo (primary key), BorrowerNo, BookNo and DateOfLoan.

(2.31)   On completion of exercises 2.23 to 2.30 you will have created a schema for the database in Figure 2.3 and associated empty tables. Using SQL, insert sample data including that shown in the Figure.

(2.32)   Explain the functions of the manipulative part of the relational model.

(2.33)   What is relational algebra? Write relational algebra expressions to represent the following queries on the Book, Author, Borrower and Loan tables created in the previous exercises (Figure 2.3).

(2.34)   Define a table containing details of the borrower number U1.

(2.35)   Define a table containing the borrower numbers and names of all borrowers described in the Borrower table. Define a table containing the borrower numbers and names of all borrowers registered after 1st April 1990, described in the Borrower table.

(2.36)   Define a table containing details of all possible combinations of a book and a borrower.

(2.37)   Define a table where each row contains details of a book and one of its authors, using the natural join operator.

(2.38)   Define a table containing details of all books for which there are more than one copy, and which are currently on loan to a borrower.

Book

BooklNo	Title	Publisher	ISBN	NumberCopies
B1	Object Databases	McGraw-Hill	0077093542	5
B2	Web Database Systems	McGraw-Hill	0077096002	10
B3	Relational Databases	Thornes	0748711767	2
B4	Weaving the Web	Orion	0752820907	3

Author

AuthorName	BookNo
B Eaglestone	B2
M Ridley	B2
B Eaglestone	B3
B Eaglestone	B1
M Ridley	B1
T Berners-Lee	B4

Loan

LoanNo	BorrowerNo	BookNo	DateOfLoan
L0001	U1	B2	19/09/1999
L0002	U2	B1	14/02/2000

Borrower

BorrowerNo	Name	Address	Telephone	DateRegistered
U1	Joe Bloggs	1 High St	273 6587	01/01/1990
U2	Joe South	3 Low Rd	273 8809	25/12/1999
U7	Joe Brown	5 The Close		01/01/2000
U9	James Brown		274 1111	01/05/1949

Figure 2.3 Example Relational Database

(2.41)   Define a table of borrower details and the book number of the books on loan to them. The book number should be null if a borrower does not have any loans. (Hint: use the outer join)

(2.42)   What does relationally complete mean, with respect to a database language.

(2.43)   Is SQL relationally complete?

Answers to the remaining questions should be expressed as SQL queries on the database in Figure 2.3.

(2.44)   Retrieve the Borrower table.

(2.45)   Retrieve Borrower numbers of all borrowers.

(2.46)   Retrieve Borrower numbers and names of all borrowers.

(2.47)   Retrieve the names of all Authors (remove any duplicates).

(2.48)   Retrieve details of Borrower with borrower number U2.

(2.49)   Retrieve details of the books not published by McGraw-Hill and of which the library holds more than one copy.

(2.50)   Retrieve details of the books not published by McGraw-Hill and of which the library holds more than one copy, but which do not have a null ISBN, ignoring books B1, B2 and B3.

(2.51)   Retrieve details of books of which the library has between 5 and 10 copies.

(2.52)   Retrieve details of books, excluding those of which the library has between 1 and 3 copies and between 6 and 10 copies.

(2.53)   Retrieve details of authors of books with numbers in the following list, B1, B3, B9 and B10, but not with authors in the following list, B Eaglestone, M Ridley

(2.54)   Retrieve details of books with titles that start with "An Introduction to".

(2.55)   Retrieve details of books the title of which includes the word "organisation" or "organization".

(2.56)   Retrieve the numbers of books written by an author whose name contains a hyphen followed by any three letters.

(2.57)   Retrieve book titles which include the characters "%" or "_".

(2.58)   Retrieve details of borrowers without a telephone number (this is indicated by a null value), who do have a known address.

(2.59)   The average weight of each book in the library is estimated to be 500 grams. Retrieve and estimate the total weight of the books in the library. Remember there may be multiple copies.

(2.60) Retrieve the maximum, minimum and average number of copies of books in the library.

(2.61) How many books are there in the library when none are on loan?

(2.62) How many authors does each book have? (Hint: use GROUP BY).

(2.63) How many authors does each book have, in the list, B1, B2, B6, B7 andB10?

(2.64) Retrieve details of books in ascending book number order.

(2.65) Retrieve details of loans in descending date of loan order within ascending book number order.

(2.66) Retrieve the names of the authors of the book called "Object Databases".

(2.67) Retrieve the title and publisher of books written by B Eaglestone or by M Ridley, but not by both authors.

(2.68) Retrieve the authors of books on loan to Joe Bloggs.

(2.69) Use the inner join to retrieve details of books and their authors.

(2.70) Retrieve details of borrowers and the numbers of the books on loan to them. Where a borrower does not have any books on loan, include a null in the book number column.

(2.71) Retrieve the authors and titles of books on loan to Joe Bloggs. Do as an exercise in the use of nested selects (do not include more than one table name in each nested "FROM" clause.)

(2.72) List details of books which are held in a quantity greater than all of the books on loan to Joe Bloggs.

(2.73) Using nested selects, retrieve details of borrowers who do not have any books on loan.

(2.74) Create two tables, OldBorrower and NewBorrower to respectively represent details of borrowers who were registered before and after 1st April 1990.

(2.75) Increase the number of all books written by one author by 5.

(2.76) Create a new table called BooksOnLoan with the same columns as the Book table, plus an additional column for the BorrowerNo. Insert data to describe books on loan, using the "INSERT...SELECT..." instruction.

(2.77) Delete rows from Borrower for all borrowers who registered before the year 1950.

(2.78) Explain the two integrity rules of the relational model.

(2.79) Use SQL to create integrity constraints that will maintain referential and entity integrity for the example Library database.

(2.80) Create an assertion to ensure that the number of copies for any one book is between 1 and 20.

(2.81) Express the queries in 2.3 in SQL to operate on the database in Figure 2.3.

(2.82) What are the advantages of defining views for an application, as opposed to directly processing the base tables?

(2.83) Define a view on the database in Figure 2.3 with columns of the loan table and also the borrower details in the Borrower table. Is the view updateable?

(2.84) Define a view containing details of loans that have been made before 1st January 1999. Is the view updateable?

3

NEW DATABASE TECHNOLOGIES

A new generation of database technologies has been emerging since the mid-1980, and is likely to replace current mainstream relational database technology, described in Chapter 2. This new generation incorporates many of the ideas associated with object-oriented programming languages in order to overcome limitations of relational databases. This chapter overviews the three main database technologies that are part of this new generation. Accordingly, it aims to answer the following questions.

- What is an object database?
- What is an object-relational database?
- What is a persistent programming language?

First, in section 3.1 limitations of relational databases (see Chapter 2: 2.2 Relational Databases) are explored in order to establish why a new generation of databases is needed. We then describe the two technologies that are emerging as the core of third generation database technology. These are object and object-relational database technologies. Object databases are described in section 3.2. In it the main features of object databases are described and contrasted with relational databases. The parts of the object data model are then described in greater detail, as is their implementation using the ODMG Object Database Standards. These are the *de facto* object database standards. Section 3.3 describes object-relational databases and the newest version of SQL, SQL:1999, which implements them. Object-relational databases are based upon the relational data model, but extended to incorporate features of object-oriented systems. Finally, section 3.4 briefly describes persistent programming languages. These can be viewed as an alternative to using database technology. Persistent programming languages are conventional programming languages that have been extended to store and access persistent data, i.e. data that remains after the program that created it has terminated, thus providing database-like facilities. The chapter concludes with a summary and exercises.

3.1 LIMITATIONS OF RELATIONAL DATABASES

Though relational databases remain the most widely used database technology for Web database systems, they do have limitations. Object and object-relational database technologies are two of a number of responses to those shortcomings. Since its introduction in 1970, the relational data model has been the dominant focus for both researchers and software providers, resulting in a sophisticated theory and technology. After an initial experimental period, relational databases have served as the mainstream state-of-the-art database technology since the 1980s. The adoption of International Standards for relational database languages has been a key factor in the technology's widespread adoption—the SQL relational database language (see Chapter 2: 2.2 Relational Databases) and its counterpart for remote access to databases, RDA (Remote Database Access) are defined by ANSI and ISO.

The main strengths of the relational data model are:

1) Simplicity—All information is visible as values in tables. There are no implementation-type features visible, such as file structures and access methods. The relational algebra and query languages, such as SQL, which implement it, support simple "cut and paste" operations on tables.
2) Rigour—The relational data model has been defined with theoretical rigour and provides a mathematical basis for researching issues such as database design, database languages, and query optimisation.
3) Practicality and generality—RDBMS have provided efficient implementations of the relational data model, and have been successfully used for a wide range of areas of applications (in business, industry, scientific research, engineering, etc.).

In spite of these strengths, relational technology has limitations and is inappropriate for certain classes of application. The gap between relational theory and actual implementations of RDBMS has been cited as an explanation of these shortcomings [Codd 90]. Edgar Codd, the inventor of the relational data model, published twelve rules [Codd 85] in an attempt to establish the requirements for a true implementation of the relational data model and to rectify misunderstandings which were giving rise to this under-performance of relational technology. In summary, the rules are:

1) All information must be represented as values in tables.
2) Each data item must be accessible by the combination of table name, key value and column name.
3) The RDBMS must support null values for representing missing or inapplicable information in a systematic way.
4) The database description (the schemas) must be represented at the logical level as values in tables.
5) At least one relational database language should be expressible as strings of characters and have a well-defined syntax. It should be usable interactively or within applications programs, and should support data definition, view definition, data manipulation, integrity constraints, authorisations and transactions.
6) Where possible, views should be updateable (a view is a derived table, and is defined by storing the query which returns it within the database).
7) Insertion/update/deletion operations should operate on tables and should handle a set of rows at a time.
8) Database users and applications should be unaffected by changes to the ways in which tables are stored.
9) Applications should be unaffected by changes to tables which do not destroy the information they access.
10) Integrity constraints should be specifiable in the relational database language and be stored in the database, not the programs.
11) Applications and users should be unaffected if the database is distributed over a number of computers networked together.
12) A low-level database language should still be constrained by the integrity constraints.

These rules are all based upon the underlying principle (rule 0) that all database management should be possible entirely through features of the relational data model.

Codd's twelve rules expand the scope of the relational data model to embrace practical data management issues. This broadening of scope was later consolidated by Codd, when he published version two of the relational model (RM/2) [Codd 90]. RM/2 comprised the original structural, manipulative and integrity parts, but also additional parts concerning aspects of database management, such as authorisations, the data dictionary, views, attribute naming and data types [Codd 90].

Implementation of the above rules and extended definition of relational database technology provides improved data management features of RDBMS. However, they do not address a major weakness of relational databases, i.e. their limited capacity to represent the structure, behaviour and the meaning of data. This results in a **semantic gap** between the conceptual model produced during the data analysis phase of designing a database, i.e. what the designer wishes to represent in the database, and the logical model produced by the data design phase, which is actually implemented using the DBMS, what the designer actually represents (see Figure 3.1) (see also Chapter 5, which describes database design in detail).

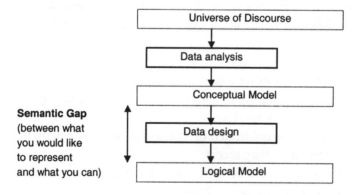

Figure 3.1 The Semantic Gap in the Database Design Process

Consequently, there are two specific classes of application for which relational databases are particularly inappropriate.

1) Object intensive applications, e.g. design applications, multimedia and office systems, in which entities have complex structures and behaviour.

2) Rule intensive applications, e.g. expert systems, which require access to both facts and also the logical rules which apply.

The representational weaknesses of the relational data model stem from the following limitations:

1) Inability to represent structurally complex and behaviourally complex entities—In a relational database a complex entity must be represented as values in many tables associated by common values.
2) Lack of semantic features—The relational model provides a language with which to structure and manipulate data, but does not represent any interpretation for the structures or manipulations in terms of their real world meaning
3) Inability to represent knowledge, other than simple facts—There is no natural way to store general rules in the database. Only limited forms of rule such as integrity constraints can be stored in the database itself, other rules have to be embedded in the code of applications programs rather than in the database.

These four limitations are part of the motivation for the third generation of database technology, in preference to a relational database technology with enhanced data management. Both object and object-relational databases have been developed to represent entities with complex structures and behaviour, such as exist in many scientific and engineering applications, office applications, and multimedia and graphical information systems.

Both object and object-relational technologies achieve greater expressiveness using object-oriented features. These provide extensible type systems. That is, in addition to the built-in types, such as integer and character, users can define new types to represent other sorts of data. In addition, new complex types, such as sets, lists, arrays and structures, can be constructed from simpler types. An extensible type system can therefore be used to represent structurally and behaviourally complex entities.

The ability to define new types has changed the nature of much database research and development. The limitations of the relational data model previously meant that it was necessary to extend the model itself to increase its capabilities, whereas the expressiveness of a data model with an extensible type system can be increased simply by defining new types. This latter approach has been used, for example, to better handle multimedia data. Increasingly application or media specific facilities are made available to users in the form of pre-programmed libraries of types that they can re-use and if necessary specialised for specific applications.

Object and object-relational databases are now described in the following two sections.

3.2 OBJECT DATABASES

Object databases are a relatively new type of database system. (For a full description of Object Databases, see [Eaglestone 98].) They were introduced in the mid-1980s and are now emerging as part of the new generation of database technology that is likely to supersede relational databases (see Chapter 2). This new generation is the third generation of database technology. Relational databases are the second, and network and hierarchical databases are the first.

Object databases evolved in response to a need for more sophisticated ways of managing, administering and using data. In particular, the object data model, upon which object databases are based, captures more of the meaning of the information represented.

The first two generations of data models were concerned mainly with representing the meaning of data in terms of the structure of the information represented. The third generation of data models, in addition, represented the meaning of data in terms of the behaviour associated with the information represented.

Structural meaning of data is concerned with the entities it represents and the ways in which they are inter-related. For example, information that the Eagleley Hotels database system must describe includes hotels, hotel chains, customers and hotel bookings placed by those customers. This sort of knowledge can be represented by combining and linking data values in ways that correspond to the structure of this information. The structure of the information represented by a database is called its structural semantics.

Information can also be analysed in terms of behaviour, i.e. the things that can happen to the entities. For example, information about Eagleley Hotels must also describe the placing of bookings by, and receiving payments from customers. The behaviour of an entity that is represented by procedures associated with a particular data structure is called its behavioural semantics.

First and second generation data models are concerned solely with representing the meaning of data in terms of the structure of the information represented, i.e. the structural semantics; the behavioural semantics must be represented within the programs that use the data. In fact, the relational model is even poor at representing structural semantics. In a relational database there is only one logical data structure, the table, and so there is no discrimination between the different types of information represented. For example, entities and relationships between entities are both represented in the same way, i.e. as tables. These limitations are overcome to a large extent by object database technology. Object databases provide a richer representation of the structure of the information represented by the data than is possible using first or second generation models. Also, object databases provide facilities for representing within the database the behaviour of the information represented by the data (see Figure 3.1). This is made possible by using concepts taken from conventional database technology, and also from object-oriented programming languages, such as Java, C++ and Smalltalk. Like object-oriented programming languages, object database systems allow users to extend the type system to include new types specially tailored to their applications. For example, a designer of a hotel booking database can create types to represent information about hotels and customers, in addition to the basic built–in types, such as integer and character.

ODMG OBJECT DATABASE STANDARDS
The object data model has existed in a confusing variety of forms, with different and sometimes contradictory terminologies and definitions [Nelson 91]. This is a consequence of the newness of the technology, and the fact that object database concepts have evolved from a variety of object-oriented programming languages, rather than from a single theoretical model, as was the case with relational databases. Object databases are still the focus of much research and continue to evolve.

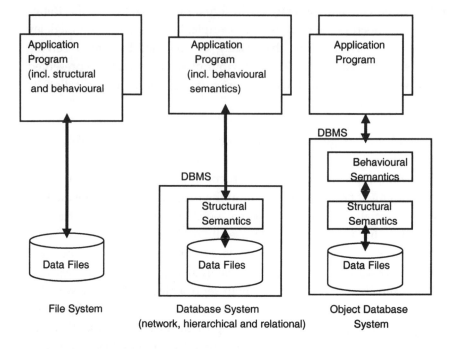

Figure 3.2 The Evolution of Data Models

Though there is as yet no official object database standard, clear definitions of the object data model are now emerging.

The "Object Oriented Database System Manifesto" [Atkinson 90] was an early attempt to clarify what an object database is. More recently, object database system vendors have attempted to introduce some conformity by forming themselves into a standards group called the Object Data Management Group (ODMG). This group has proposed the ODMG standards for an object data model and object database languages [Cattell 00]. Though ODMG standards currently have no official status, their influence is likely to be considerable. This is because the members represent a significant portion of the object database systems market, and are committed to producing "ODMG compliant" products. The ODMG standards are therefore likely to dominate the object database market, in the same way that SQL dominates the relational database market, and have become a *de facto* standard.

The ODMG Object Database standards define a number of computer languages to implement different aspects of object database systems. The language for defining interfaces to the object database structures is called the Object Definition Language or ODL, and is a data definition language for object database systems. In addition, an ODMG-compliant ODBMS will support a data manipulation language called the Object Query Language (OQL) which can be used as a stand–alone query language. ODMG has also specified bindings between ODL and OQL, and other programming languages, i.e. Java, C++ and SmallTalk, so that ODL and OQL can be integrated into computer programs to implement the object database structures and to implement the object database applications.

The role of ODL is summarised in Figure 3.3. Note that ODL code is sandwiched between the applications programs and the object database—ODL can be thought of as providing programs with a window into object databases. As with relational databases, a data definition language description of all or part of an object database is called a **schema** and defines metadata, i.e. data about the data stored, whereas the applications, written using OQL, manipulate the data itself.

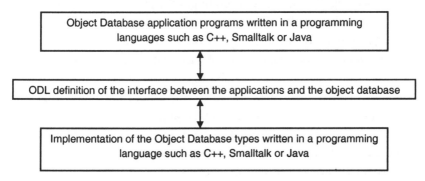

Figure 3.3 The relationship between ODL and other programming languages

Figure 3.4 shows the division of functions between the programming language and ODL. ODL supplies the object database with metadata, which is stored using the structures of the object data model (in the same way that a relational database schema is stored as tables). The ODL also supplies applications programs written in other programming languages with interfaces to the object database structures that they must access and manipulate.

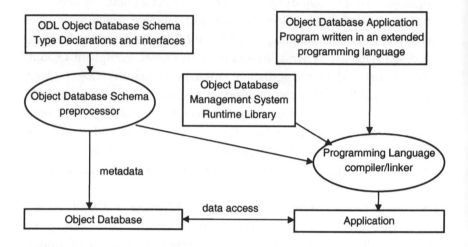

Figure 3.4 The relationship of ODL to an object database schema and applications

The facility whereby ODL, OQL and a particular programming language can be used together is called a binding. ODL/OQL bindings have been defined to enable applications to be created using various programming languages, currently Java, C++, and Smalltalk. An advantage of using different database languages to implement different aspects of an object database system is that object databases can be defined in a way which is independent of the languages used to implement the object types and applications. Different languages may be appropriate for different types of application. For example, image processing applications of a museum object database are best implemented using programming languages with advanced image processing features, whereas other applications in this system require only the features of conventional languages. Two further advantages of the independence of ODL from specific programming languages are, firstly, the ability to port object database systems from one programming environment to another, and secondly, the ability to operate many object database systems together, even when different languages have been used to implement them. This latter point is important if we are to realise the potential for global access to information sources now made possible through the Internet and the Web.

The ability to define interfaces to objects in a way that is independent of the languages that are used to implement or utilise them has a general use in distributed object-oriented environments. This ability makes it possible for many applications to share and utilise objects which provide general services. The Object Management Group (OMG) (not to be confused with the Object Data Management Group (ODMG)) has defined standards that address this general requirement. The OMG standards include an architecture for object request brokers (the Common Object Request Broker Architecture (CORBA)) [OMG 91] and an object interface definition language called IDL. An object request broker acts like a telephone exchange via which messages can be passed to and between objects stored in a distributed environment. The ODL builds upon the standards defined by the OMG—ODL is an extension of IDL. The CORBA architecture has also been implemented to support a number of Web applications.

UML

Further standardisation is provided by the acceptance of the Unified Modeling Language (UML) [Booch 99, Jacobson 99, Rumbaugh 99, Rational] as the *de facto* standard notation for designing object-oriented systems. UML has been defined as a common notation for the leading design methodologies for object-oriented systems, i.e. the methods associated with Booch [Booch 94] (the Booch method), Rumbaugh [Rumbaugh 91] (OMT) and Jacobson [Jacobson 92] (OOSE). These methods, as well as the notation are now being merged [Jacobson 99].

The above methods were developed independently and had different names for similar concepts and different ways of representing comparable parts of the design process in diagrams. As of 1996 a process of unifying these methods and notations was underway to produce what was first known as the Unified Method (UM) and is now called the UML. It is planned that UML will be submitted to the OMG as the basis for a standard in this area. UML does not prescribe the design process, but instead provides a diagrammatical language for representing the analysis and design of an object-oriented system. If widely accepted as a standard, UML will provide a single terminology and diagrammatical language for expressing and communicating design ideas for object-oriented systems.

The description in this section follows the UML and ODMG standards. UML is used to diagrammatically represent object database structures in subsections that describe the parts of the object data model. Each description is followed by an overview of how the part is implemented using the relevant ODMG object database languages.

THE STRUCTURAL PART OF THE OBJECT DATA MODEL

Like the relation data model, the object data model has only one type of structure, the object. An object database is a collection of objects, each of which represents an entity that is of interest to the organisation that the database serves. An object approximately corresponds to a row of a table in a relational database. However, an object can represent more of the meaning of the entity it represents than is possible in a row. The characteristics of an object are:

1) identity—a unique and unalterable object identifier assigned to the object. This models the fact that entities represented by objects are uniquely identifiable (this serves the purpose that the primary key serves for a row of a relational table).
2) state—the state of an object is the set of values that it contains. The values represent facts about the entity represented by the object, including facts about associations with other entities (the state corresponds to column values that form a row of a relational table).
3) behaviour—the behaviour of an object is the set of operations that can be applied to it. These operations are designed to model ways in which the entity represents can behave. The procedure that implements a particular operation on an object is called a method. (Behaviour of entities cannot be represented in a relational database, and so must be coded in the applications.)

EXAMPLE 3.1

The object that represents the Eagleley Hotels customer, M.Ridley, will have an object identifier, which was automatically assigned when it was created. This identifier distinguishes that object from all other objects. The object will have a state that comprises values that represent facts, such as the customer's name, address and telephone number. It will have a behaviour which consists of a set of operations that can be applied to the object to model activities such as making a hotel reservation and paying the bill.

The state of an object includes attribute values that represent facts about the entity represented. An attribute exists only as part of an object and is not an object in its own right. An attribute therefore has no object identifier—it can be referred to only by first referring to the object that contains it.

Optionally, certain attributes can be designated as object keys. The values of an object key will distinguish each object from other similar objects, even when the values of all other properties are the same. Often there is an obvious choice of key, since certain properties represent the names or identifying numbers of the entities modeled by the objects. For example, the customer number attribute is an obvious choice of key for the objects that represent customers. Key values must be explicitly specified and maintained by the end-user of an object database system, but object identifiers are automatically assigned and maintained.

The entity and object in Example 3.1 are depicted using UML notation in Figure 3.5. The object is represented as a box. The name of the type of object, Customer, is given in the top half. This name is underlined to show that the box represents an actual object rather than properties of many objects. The values contained by the object, i.e. its state, are listed in the bottom half.

Figure 3.5 Object Diagram for Mick Ridley

An object's state may also include relationships. A relationship represents an association between the entity represented by that object and entities represented by other objects. Each relationship is given one or two descriptive names and has a value. The first name labels the relationship path from the object to the associated object(s), and the optional second name labels the inverse relationship path, from the associated object(s) to the object. The value of a relationship comprises the object identifiers of the associated objects.

EXAMPLE 3.2

A customer is associated with the booking she places. The state of the object that represents a customer will therefore include a relationship that associates it with the relevant booking objects. The relationship value in the state of the customer object will comprise the identifier of an object that contains all of the objects that represent bookings placed by that customer, and the inverse relationship value of each of those booking objects will contain the object identifier of the customer object. The relationship path from the customer object to the booking objects, and the inverse relationship path from the booking objects to the customer object will both have a name, HasMade and MadeBy, for example.

A relationship (like an attribute) is not an object in its own right. It does not have an object identifier, and can be referred to only by first referring to the object that contains it.

The object identifier is separate from the object's state and is not visible to the user or database programmer. It provides a means of referencing objects within the system. Object identity is an important property, since it means that an object remains the same object, even when its state takes a completely new set of values. Conversely, since an object's identity is independent of its state, it is possible to represent different entities that have the same properties.

EXAMPLE 3.3

Suppose an object is created to represent an employee who has just been recruited by Eagleley Hotels, and the object state comprises the employee's name and address. Later the employee marries and moves to a new house. Both the name and the address are therefore altered, but the object is still the same object—its identity remains the same. This is consistent with the changes to the real world entity that is represented by the object. Though the recorded state of the entity has changed completely, it is still the same entity.

Object identifiers can be used to represent associations between objects. In particular, objects can represent entities comprising many parts, possibly with shared components.

EXAMPLE 3.4

Two objects represent different Eagleley Hotels' holiday packages to India, respectively, for a long weekend and a two week tour. A third object represents an afternoon excursion from New Delhi to the Taj Mahal in Agra, which is a part of both tours. Both of the product objects therefore include the value of the Taj Mahal excursion object identifier as part of their respective states to indicate that they have a component in common (see Figure 3.6).

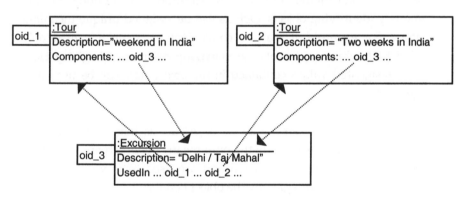

Figure 3.6 This diagram represents how object identifiers can be used to represent entities with a shared component. The objects represent the entities in Example 3.5. The diagram represents the objects as boxes, each with a unique identifier, oid_1, oid_2 and oid_3. Note that the object identifiers of related objects are contained in the object states.

The fact that an object's identity is distinct from its state means that concepts of object equivalence and object equality are different. Two objects are equivalent if they have the same object identity (that is, they are equivalent if they are the same object), but are equal if they have the same state values (but possibly different identities). We can also distinguish between shallow and deep equality—objects have shallow equality if their states contain the same values (when we exclude references to other objects); objects have deep equality if their states contain the same values and also the corresponding objects to which they are related contain the same values. This contrasts with the relational data model, where equality of rows is based purely on the column values.

EXAMPLE 3.5

*Two objects record the names of two different salespersons. However, since both employees are called James Last, the states of the two objects are the same. The objects are therefore **equal**, but are not **equivalent** since they have different object identifiers. The customer objects are related to other objects that represent the hotel bookings they have each made. Since they are related to different sets of booking objects, with different state values, the customer objects have **shallow equality** but not **deep equality**.*

The object data model supports two additional but optional means of uniquely identifying objects. Objects can be assigned unique meaningful names. For example, it may be convenient to create a named object, called MD, which represents the managing director of Eagleley Hotels. Also, designated values contained in the object state can be used as the object keys.

The procedures associated with an object act as that object's interface. The object operations provide the only means by which an object's state can be accessed and manipulated and are used to model the ways in which the entity represented by the object behaves.

EXAMPLE 3.6

The behaviour of an object that represents a customer comprises a set of operations which model the ways in which a customer behaves. For example, the behaviour will be defined by operations which access, and possibly modify, the state of the customer object to represent what happens when the customer makes a booking or pays the bill.

The facility by which data and procedures are integrated within an object is called encapsulation. Encapsulation achieves two things. Firstly, it provides a representation of the meaning of data contained in the object database, both in terms of the structure and behaviour of the entities modelled. Secondly, encapsulation ensures that data is used only in ways that are consistent with its meaning. The operations provide the interface to the object, and so the state can only be accessed and manipulated by executing appropriate operations. The operations therefore act like a "suit of armour"—they protect the data from being accessed or altered in ways that are contradictory to the behaviour of the entity represented by the object.

When executed, an operation can receive certain objects as parameter values and will return an object as the operation value. For example, a promote operation on an object which represents an employee may take, as a parameter value, a character string literal which describes the new post to which the employee has been promoted, and will return a Boolean literal (i.e. one which takes the value true or false) which indicates whether the operation has executed successfully or not.

The behaviour and state of an object are closely related. The operations which define the behaviour of an object are to do with

1) Retrieval operations—These derive information from the state in a convenient form. For example, an operation on an employee object may extract the age of the employee represented, by performing a computation on the employee's date of birth, which is part of the object's state.
2) Update operations—These make changes to the state in order to model changes that happen to the entity represented by the object. For example, a promote operation on an employee object will change the salary value in the object's state, to reflect the new salary of the promoted employee.

The Object Data Model currently does not distinguish between update and retrieval operations and this can cause problems. For example, a side effect of retrieving the value returned by an update operation is that the state of an object is changed, even if the user is interested only in the returned value. This means, for example, that hypothetical questions, such as "what would Ridley's salary be if we promote him to Head of Department?" need to be handled carefully.

As can be seen from the Examples 3.1–3.5, objects are used to represent real world entities relevant to the database system, such as customers, hotel reservations, hotel and hotel chains in the Eagleley Hotels case study. Objects are also used to represent "computer world" entities, such as the database structures, in the same way that tables are used in the data dictionary of a relational database.

Though the Object Data Model has a single abstraction, the object, which is used to represent all information, there is an important difference between objects that represent values and other types of object. The state of an object that represents a value cannot be changed, whereas the state of other types of object can. The former are called literals (or immutable objects) and the latter are called mutable objects, or just objects. A mutable object is an object that can change its own state. A literal is an object that cannot change its own state.

A literal is a container for a fixed value and serves the same purpose as a constant in programming languages, whereas a mutable object is a container for facts about an entity, the properties of which may change over time. A consequence is that the state of a literal also acts as its object identifier. For example, the literal that represents the number 25 is simply referred to as 25. The object data model includes pre-existing literals which represent all of the constants typically available in a programming language.

It is necessary to represent entities (other than values) as mutable objects, since this enables us to modify an object's state so as to model changes which occur to the entity represented.

EXAMPLE 3.7

The object that represents the Eagleley Hotel customer, M. Ridley (in Figure 3.4), must be a mutable object, so that it can be changed to model changes that occur to M. Ridley.This mutable object will contain within its state literals to represent facts about M. Ridley, such as his name, address and telephone numbers. These literals are replaced by other literals when the object's state is changed, for example, to represent a change of name.

Many objects may share the same set of characteristics; their states can take data values from the same set of possible values and they can be manipulated using the same set of operations. Objects with the same characteristics are said to be of the same object type. An object type definition defines the possible states and behaviour of objects of that type. Objects of a particular type are called instances of that type, and the set of instances of a type is called the type's extent.

EXAMPLE 3.9

All customer objects have the same characteristic; they can take state values from the same "pool" of possibilities, and share the same operations. We therefore say, customer objects have the same type. Each customer object is an instance of the customer object type, and the set of all customer objects is the customer object type's extent.

A type can be implemented in many ways. An implemented type is called an implementation class. Since there may be many implementations of a type, there can therefore be many implementation classes with the same type. This facility is useful, particularly when accessing multiple databases, where the same type may be implemented in alternative ways in different object databases.

An object type can be represented graphically using UML as a box, as shown in Figure 3.7.

Customer
customer_no
name
address
telephone_number
place_order (...)
change_address (...)
change_telephone .(...)

Figure 3.7 A graphical representation of an object type

The object type box is subdivided into three: the top part gives the type name and properties; the middle part describes the instance attributes and the bottom part describes the instance operations. (The Figure 3.6 example provides only a sketch of an object type. However, this notation also allows us to include more detailed information, such as the types of the attributes and details of the operation parameters.)

Figure 3.9 illustrates how the types and classes of an object database are represented in UML. The Figure is a type diagram for a simplified

Eagleley Hotels bookings system object database. Each box represents an object type, and the connecting lines represent relationships between object types. The graphical representation is used primarily in the design of object databases.

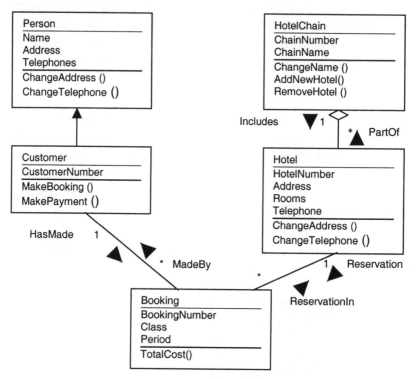

Figure 3.8 Type Diagram for the (simplified) Hotel Booking System

When designing an object database we compose diagrams like this in order to create a model of the part of the world that is relevant to the application; each type represents a sort of entity that is of interest. The name of each type describes the entities represented and is the first name in each icon—Customer, Hotel, etc. Under each type name is the list of attributes (which are part of the state), and a list of operations, which are the behaviour. Relationships between objects are represented by the lines that connect the type icons. The numbers and asterisks (an asterisk means many) at each end of each connecting line shows how many objects can be involved in an instance of the relationship. Connecting lines are also annotated with names and arrows. These are the names of the relationship paths in the direction of the arrow. The arrow from

Person to Customer denotes a special type of relationship—a customer is a specialised type of person.

EXAMPLE 3.9

A booking is related to the customer who made it and the hotel within which rooms are booked. These relationships are represented in Figure 3.7 by lines connecting the Customer icon to the Booking icon, and the Booking icon to the Hotel icon. The line from Customer to Booking has a name, HasMade. This is the path name of the relationship from Customer to Booking objects (the direction of the path is shown by the arrow head). This line is also annotated with 1 and *. This indicates that each occurrence of the HasMade relationship associates 1 Customer object with possible many (*) Booking objects. Similarly, the line from Booking to Hotel is annotated to show that each occurrence of the ReservationIn relationship associates one Hotel object to possibly many Booking objects.

In addition to those properties and operations defined by the object database designer, there are others which are built into the Object Data Model. For example, there are built-in operations to provide general services for all objects (to delete objects, or test for object equivalence), attributes (to assign and retrieve the attribute values), relationships (to create, delete, modify and traverse relationships) and operations (to execute them and to terminate execution in various ways).

Objects can be combined to model entities with complex structures. This is done by including objects that represent components of an entity within the state of the object that represents the composite entity. Objects composed from other objects are called complex objects. In practice, complex objects are usually implemented by including the object identifiers of the component objects within the complex object.

EXAMPLE 3.10

The state of a complex object that represents a Eagleley Holidays holiday package may contain a collection of objects that represent each of the individual events on that itinerary.

Representation of shared components is possible because each object is uniquely identifiable by an object identifier which is automatically assigned to it when it is first created. Object identifiers can never be altered or re-used to identify other objects. This makes it possible to create objects that are collections of other objects, because the state of one object can include the object identifiers of other objects (or even of itself!).

In general, object identifiers can be included in the state of one object to represent a relationship with other objects. For example, the relationship between a customer and the bookings she makes can be represented by including the customer object's identity in the state of each of the booking objects, and/or by including the set of object identifiers for the customer's sales order objects in the customer object's state.

Objects in an object database can be instances of many types simultaneously. This feature models the fact that real world entities can also be classified in many ways. For example, Barry Eaglestone can be classified as a person, an employee and a mammal. Some of these entity classifications are more general than others. For instance, "Barry Eaglestone is a person" is a more general statement than "Barry Eaglestone is an employee". A consequence is that Barry has the specific properties of an employee, but also inherits all of the properties of a person. Similarly, objects in an object database inherit properties of the general types to which they belong, as well as having properties of the most specific types.

This form of property inheritance is illustrated in the Hotel Booking system example in Figure 3.9. A customer is a special type of person, and so will have all the properties of a person (name, address, telephone number), and also an additional property (customer number). In the Figure 3.9 diagram, the arrow from Customer to Person represents that the type implemented by the Customer class (from which the arrow starts) inherits all of the properties of the type of the Person class (to which the arrow points). We say the Customer object type is a subtype of the Person object type, and the Person type is a supertype of the Customer type. A consequence of this is that all Customer objects are also Person objects (though not all Persons are necessarily Customer objects). A consequence is that all the attributes, relationships and operations defined in the Person type definition are automatically added to the Customer definition, i.e. they are inherited.

In this example, Customer has only one supertype, but it is also possible for real world entities to be special cases of many more general entities. For example, a customer may also be an employee of Eagleley Hotels. The CustomerEmployee object type would then need to inherit properties of both Employee and Customer object types. This situation can be modelled in an object database by multiple inheritance. Many supertypes can be defined in a type definition, and the subtype inherits the properties of all of its supertypes.

Inheritance is considered by many to be the most important feature of object data models. Its importance is that it allows object definitions to be re-used when new object classes are added to the object database. In the above example (Figure 3.9) it is not necessary to redefine the properties of Person objects in the Customer type definition. These are automatically inherited and their implementation is therefore re-used in the Customer class. Furthermore, existing applications programs, written to access Person objects, will automatically access all objects which are instances of the subtypes of Person, including those which were undefined when the application program was first written.

ODMG OBJECT DEFINITION LANGUAGE (ODL)

The structures of an object database are specified for an ODMG-compliant DBMS, using ODL in conjunction with other programming languages, such as Java, C++ or Smalltalk. ODL specifies the interfaces to the database structures and the programming languages are used to implement them. As in a relational database, the definitions of the structures used in the object database are defined in a database schema. The purpose of an ODL schema is to enable application programs and tools to create, access and manipulate the contents of an object database.

EXAMPLE ODL SCHEMA

An example ODL schema is given in Figure 3.9 and is used to illustrate features of the ODL language. The types specified are those previously depicted in UML (see Figure 3.9). Figure 3.9 has been contrived to illustrate key features of ODL that are used to specify the structures in an object database. Lines of code are numbered so that they can be referred to, but that is not part of ODL. We have followed the convention of using upper-case for user-defined names, and bold lower-case for words that are part of ODL.

In the following subsections, we describe those features of ODL that are illustrated in Figure 3.9. Other features, not illustrated but of importance, are then overviewed. Note, however, this is not intended as a detailed course in ODL and its use. Rather, we try to give an appreciation of its capabilities and style.

Figure 3.9 Example Object Database Schema

```
1.   module EagleyHotels
2.   {
3.        const PCodeLength = 5;
4.        const CCodeLength = 6;
5.        const HCodeLength = 6;
6.        const HCCodeLength = 3;
7.
8.        deftype Struct AddressType
9.            {String Street, Town, District, Country, Postcode};
10.
11.       exception NoSuchCustomer
12.       {
13.            String<CCodeLength> CustomerNumber;
14.            String ErrorCode;
15.            String ErrorMessage;
16.       }
17.
18.       interface PersonIF
19.       {
20.            attribute String Name;
21.            attribute AddressTypeAddress;
22.            attribute List<Unsigned Short> Telephones[14];
23.       }
24.
25.       class Customer: PersonIF
26.       ( extent Customers key, CustomerNumber)
27.       {
28.            readonly attribute String<CCodeLength> CustomerNumber;
29.            relationship List<Booking> HasMade
30.                inverse Booking::MadeBy;
31.            Booking MakeBooking (in String<HCodeLength> Hotel,
32.                Unsigned Short Class, Interval Period;)
33.                raise ( HotelDoesntExist );
34.            Money MakePayment (in money Amount,
35.            String<BNumberLength> BookingNumber);
36. }
37.
38.       class HotelChain
39.       ( extent Chains, key ChainNumber )
```

Figure 3.9 Example Object Database Schema—continued

```
40.    {
41.            attribute …. ChainNumber
42.            attribute String ChainName
43.            relationship Set<Hotel> Includes
44.            inverse Hotel::PartOf;
45.            string ChangeName (in String NewName);
46.            void AddNewHotel (in Hotel NewHotel);
47.            void RemoveHotel (in Hotel OldHotel)
48.                raises NoSuchHotel;
49.    }
50.
51.    class Hotel
52.    ( extent Hotels, key HotelNumber)
53.    {
54.            attribute String<HCodeLength> HotelNumber;
55.            attribute AddressType Address;
56.            attribute Unsigned Short Rooms;
57.            attribute List<Unsigned Short> Telephones[14];
58.            relationship HotelChain PartOf
59.                inverse Hotel_Chain::Includes;
60.            relationship Set<Booking> Reservation
61.                inverse Booking::ReservationIn;
62.            Void ChangeAddress(in OldAddress, NewAddress);
63.            Void ChangeTelephone
64.                (in unsigned short OldNumber, NewNumber)
65.                raises (NoSuchTelephoneNumber);
66.    }
67.
68.    class Booking
69.    ( extent BookingS, key BookingNo)
70.    {
71.            attribute String<BNumberLength> BookingNo;
72.            attribute Struct Reservation
73.                {String <HCodeLength> HotelNumber;
74.                Short CLASS; Interval Period};
75.            relationship Customer MadeBy;
76.                inverse Customer::HasMade;
77.            relationship Hotel ReservationIn
78.                inverse Hotel::Reservation;
79.            money TOTAL_COST ( );
80.            }
81. }
```

Figure 3.9 Example Object Database Schema—concluded

GENERAL FEATURES OF AN ODL SCHEMA

First, note the following points concerning the overall structure of an ODL schema.

1) The schema, as a whole, forms a module (denoted by the keyword module) called EagleleyHotels. The purpose of packaging code up into a module is that it enables large sections of code to be referred to by some meaningful name.

2) The main part of the schema (lines 18–81) is a list of interface and class definitions, each of which starts with the keyword interface or class. These declare the object types in the object database.

3) Interface definitions are preceded by a few type (lines 8–9), constant (lines 3–6), and exception (lines 11–16) declarations, which start, respectively, with the keywords, deftype, const and exception. The latter is a procedure that is executed in "exceptional" circumstances, in this case, when a code for a non-existent customer is specified.

As in conventional programming languages, ODL has a block structure whereby things are defined within structures, i.e. within interfaces, classes, exceptions and modules. These structures can be nested one inside another. For example, declarations in Figure 3.9 are nested within class definitions, which are in turn nested within a module.

A name declared within a schema must be unique only within the structure in which it is declared. The part of a schema within which a name is guaranteed to provide a unique reference to the thing it names is called its scope. For example, Figure 3.9 includes two declarations of attributes called Address (lines 21 and 57). Their scopes are the PersonIF interface and the Hotel class definitions, respectively. A name can be ambiguous from outside of its scope. It is therefore often necessary to qualify a name by prefixing it with the name(s) of the structure(s) within which it was declared. For example, we can refer to the two Address attributes as Person::Address and Hotel::Address. If we wish to refer to the Address attributes from a different module we must also prefix the module name in order to assure uniqueness, e.g EagleleyHotels::Hotel::Address. Note the use of the double colon "::" to separate the different scope names.

ODL TYPE DEFINITIONS

Figure 3.9 is a complete schema and specifies the structures previously shown in Figure 3.8. The primary purpose of an object database schema is to define the object types used in the object database. Note that most of the object type definitions in the schema are defined by class definitions (lines 25–37, 39–51, 53–68, 70–82). This is because instances of classes, i.e. objects, can be directly created to populate the object database, when the system is used.

EXAMPLE 3.11

The schema for the Eagleley Hotels object database introduced includes class definitions for object types that represent customers, hotels, hotel chains and bookings, since objects of these types must be created to populate the object database.

In some cases an object type is an abstract type—it has no instances defined on it, but instances are defined on its subtypes. In those situations the object type is defined by an interface definition (lines 18–23). An interface definition defines only the behaviour of an object type —an object type defined as an interface cannot be directly instantiated.

EXAMPLE 3.12

Figure 3.9 includes an interface definition, PersonIF, for an object type which represent people, in general. This is an abstract type, since PersonIF objects will not be directly created, but there will be instances of subtypes of PersonIF, such as Customer.

An interface definition must specify the following information:

1) the name of the object type;
2) the names of the supertypes of the object type;
3) characteristics of objects which are instances of that object type, i.e. attributes, relationships and operations.

A class definition will include the above information and also additional information needed to create new objects:

4) properties of the object type, i.e. the extent, keys and the class that it extends (if any).

ODL CLASS AND INTERFACE DEFINITIONS
The following is an example declaration of an object type taken from the Figure 3.9 ODL schemas.

```
25.    class Customer: Person_IF
26.    ( extent Customers key, CustomerNumber)
27.    {
28.        readonly attribute String<CCodeLength>
29.            CustomerNumber;
30.        relationship List<Booking> HasMade
31.            inverse Booking::MadeBy;
32.        Booking MakeBooking (in String<HCodeLength> Hotel,
33.            Unsigned Short Class, Interval Period;)
34.            raise ( HotelDoesntExist );
35.        Money MakePayment (in money Ammount,
36.            String<BNumberLength> BookingNumber);
37.    }
```

An interface definition (e.g. lines 18–23) has the same form, with the exception that the definition starts with 'interface' rather than 'class'. Also, type properties concerned with the type state, i.e. the extent and keys (line 26), are not specified for an interface, since a type defined by an interface cannot be instantiated.

Note that each type definition has three parts, corresponding to the three parts of a UML type box (see Figure 3.3).

TYPE PROPERTIES
The top part (lines 25–26) of a class or interface definition specified information about the type itself, i.e. the type properties. The following can be specified.
- Type name—Each type is given a name (Customer).
- Extent—Optionally, the extent can be named (Customers). The extent of a type is the collection of all of its instances (specified in classes only).
- Keys—Optionally, a type can have keys (CustomerNumber). These serve the same purpose as keys in a relational database, i.e. they are attributes the values of which uniquely identify the objects of that type (specified in classes only).
- Inherited properties—Optionally, types can be defined, from which the type will inherit characteristics (line 25) (see below).

Object types may inherit the characteristics of other object types in two ways.

1) An interface or class inherits the behaviour of types defined as its supertypes (but not the state, since objects of the type specified by the interface cannot be directly created).
2) A class (but not an interface) may also inherit from no more than one extender classes. This means that it inherits the behaviour and the state of the extender class.

The way in which the extender class and the supertypes are specified in ODL is illustrated in the following example.

EXAMPLE 3.13

One way of representing customers who are also employees is as a CustomerEmployee class. This class is a special type of customer, and so it extends the Customer class. It also has two supertype interfaces, EmployeeIF and AccountHolderIF from which it inherits behaviour. The first lines, i.e. the header, of the ODL class definition for CustomerEmployee must therefore start with the following definitions.

```
class CustomerEmployee
    extends Customer
    : AccountHolderIF, EmployeeIF
```

The name of the extender class is specified in a class definition and is preceded by the keyword extends. The names of an object type's supertype interfaces are listed in a class or interface definition and are separated from the object type name (or the extends declaration) by a colon. If there is no extender class, then extends is omitted. If there are no supertypes, then the colon is omitted.

Note that a class or interface may have many supertypes and these must be interfaces. However, a class may have at most one extender class.

STATE PROPERTIES
The middle part of a class or interface definition (lines 27–29) specified the state properties of instances of the type, i.e. attributes and

relationships The latter are represented in UML by lines connecting the type boxes. The following state properties can be defined.

- Attributes—The values of the attributes represent facts about the entities represented by objects of this type. Each attribute definition specifies the attribute name (CustomerNumber in the example) and type (String<CCodeLength>). Also, attributes can be designated "readonly" (e.g. line 86), thus prohibiting applications that use the schema from changing their values.
- Relationships—Each relationship definition identifies the type of the related objects (Set<Booking>, i.e. an object that contains a set of Booking objects) and the names the path from type instances to the related objects (HasMade), and also the inverse path (MadeBy).

OPERATIONS

The bottom part of a class or interface definition (line 30 on) defines the operators that may be applied to objects of this type. Each operation definition will specify the following.

- Operation name—The declaration specifies an operation name by which it is invoked (MakeBooking and MakePayment).
- Operation type—The operation name is preceded by a specification of the type of value returned by the operation. In the example, MakeBooking and MakePayment respectively return objects of type Booking and money. If an operation does not return a value, this is denoted by "void" (e.g. see Figure 3.9, lines 64-65).
- Parameters—In brackets are specified the type and name of any input (in), output (out) or input and output (inout) parameter. (MakeBooking has three input parameters, respectively called Hotel of type string<HCodeLength>, Class of type Unsigned Short Class, and Period of type Interval.)
- Exceptions—An operation can also be associated with one or more exception objects (e.g. MakeBooking is associated with the exception HotelDoesntExist). An exception object represents an exceptional event that can occur when operations are executed. An operation can terminate by executing one of the operations of the relevant exception object when an exceptional event occurs. Exceptions are typically used to handle error conditions.

The attributes and relationships define the state and the operations define the behaviour. In this way, the type definition defines the ways in

NEW DATABASE TECHNOLOGIES

which objects of that type can be used. However, it is not specified how the type is implemented; a type definition defines only the interface to objects. For a type to be used in an object database, it is also necessary for the database designer to provide an implementation. The implementation will define the representation, i.e. data structures used to implement the state, and procedures to implement each operation. These procedures are called methods.

STRUCTURED AND COLLECTION TYPES
ODL allows objects to be complex, i.e. they can be constructed by combining other objects. This can be done in two ways.

- structure types—The values of objects defined on structure types are combinations of objects of possibly different types, similar to conventional record structures. A structure type is defined using the Struct type generator (e.g. lines 8–9, 74–76). A structure can be thought of as a fixed number of named slots, each of which can contain an object of some specified type.
- collection types—The value of an object defined on a collection type is formed by collecting together many objects of the same type. Objects can be collected using the Set, Bag, List, Array (or Sequence), and Dictionary type generators (e.g. line 22). The ODL for defining collection types requires the type generator and then the type of the elements of the collection, in angular brackets, "< ... >". For example, the state of an object of the type Set<Hotel> comprises a set of Hotel objects.

The collection types are as follows, and are summarised in Figure 3.10 and Table 3.1.
1) A set is an unordered collection of distinct objects—an object can occur only once in a set;
2) A bag is an unordered collection of not necessarily distinct objects— the same object can occur more than once in a bag;
3) A list is an ordered collection of not necessarily distinct objects—a list has a first object, second object, etc., and the same object can occur more than once in a list;
4) An array is a collection of indexed objects—an array can be thought of as a list of object containers which can be referred to by their position in the list. Each container may be empty or may contain an object.

5) A Dictionary–object is basically a lookup table. It is a set of pairs of objects, the first acting as a key by which the second can be accessed. For example, a dictionary-object could represent a telephone directory, using Person/Telephone_number object pairs. A dictionary-object is therefore a special type of set-object, it is a set of structures.

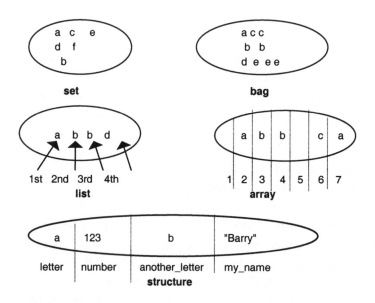

Figure 3.10 Structured Types

Table 3.1: Properties of Structured Types

	Set	Bag	List	Array	Dictionary	Structure
Same type	Yes	Yes	Yes	Yes	Yes	No
Ordered	No	No	Yes	Yes	No	No
Unique	Yes	No	No	No	Yes	No
Indexed	No	No	No	Yes	No	No
Named	No	No	No	No	No	Yes

TYPE DEFINITIONS

Types can be defined and named, and then used in other definitions, using "deftype". For example, in Figure 3.9, the structure type, AddressType is defined (lines 8–9) and then used by name in the PersonIF and Hotel definitions (lines 21 and 57).

Both literals and mutable objects can be structured using either structure or collection types. Also, the type generators for structured types can be used freely to define arbitrarily complex structures, so as to model complex entities as exactly as possible. For example, we could define sets of bags of arrays of structures. However, note that all attributes must be defined on literal types. This means that the lowest level elements of any structured type upon which an attribute is defined must be an atomic literal.

LITERALS

In the Figure 3.9 ODL example, constants are used in the same way that they would be used in a conventional programming language (e.g. lines 3–6). The constants are instances of built-in literal object types. These may be simple or structured. The simple (or atomic) literal types include:

- Integer—these are whole numbers, e.g. 1, 2, -5, -19. (Integer literals may be long or short, signed or unsigned).
- Float—these are decimal numbers, e.g. 1.52, –0.3456, 2.000. (Floating point literals may be single (float) or double (double) precision).
- Boolean—these are the values true and false.
- Char—these are single characters, e.g. a,b,c,d,e,@,#,!.
- String—these are character strings, e.g. "Eaglestone", "Ridley".
- Octet—there are bit stings used to represent "raw" untyped data.

In addition, more complex values types are built-in, created by combining literals defined on the above atomic literal types. These built-in structured literal types includes:

- Date—e.g. 22 03 1995
- Time—e.g. 22:30
- Timestamp—e.g. [22 03 1995, 22:30]
- Interval—e.g. [22:30,23:00].

New literal types can also be defined (other than those based on characters and numbers) using Enumeration (or enum). Enumeration is called a type generator because it is not a type, but can be used to create a new type. This is done by specifying the set of values contained in the new type. For example, the declaration:

```
enumeration Sex {male, female}
```

creates a new type called Sex which can have two instances, i.e. the literals, male and female.

THE MANIPULATIVE PART OF THE OBJECT DATA MODEL

The manipulative part of the ODMG object data model is defined as a set of object database languages that can be used to implement actual object database systems. These are the Object Query Language (OQL) and the object definition and manipulation language (ODL/OML) extensions to programming languages, i.e. Java, C++ and Smalltalk. These manipulate the object databases, defined using the Object Definition Language (ODL) (described in the preceding section).

There is as yet no widely accepted mathematical definition of the manipulative part of the object data model, corresponding to relational algebra. However, there are a number of published object algebras, an example being that of the AQUA object data model [Leung 93, Eaglestone 98]. A major challenge is to establish widely accepted theoretical foundations for the object database technology which is already on the market. This contrasts with relational technology (the previous generation of database technology), where the theoretical relational data model [Codd 70] came first, and the technology that implemented it followed some years later. The absence of formal (mathematical) definitions of object database technology is partly a consequence of its rapid evolution from object-oriented programming languages and earlier generations of database technology. Researchers are currently trying to catch up with the technology.

In this section, we first describe in general terms the ways it should be possible to manipulate an object database, using an object database language, such as OQL. The section then overviews OQL, giving example queries and manipulations. Throughout, the example instance (Figure 3.10) of the object database defined by the ODL schema in Figure 3.9 is used in the examples.

Note that the Customer objects are contained in the extent of the Customer type (named Customers in the Figure 3.10 schema), which is in turn contained in the extent of the PersonIF object type. This is because Customer is a subtype of PersonIF. As a consequence, Customer objects inherit the characteristics of Person objects, and therefore have Name and Address attributes, in addition to the CustomerNumber attribute. Relationships between objects are show by the double-headed arrows.

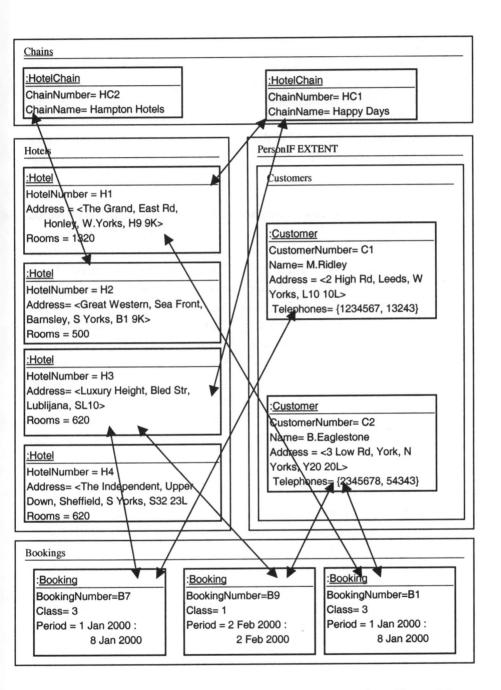

Figure 3.10 An example Eagleley Hotels object database (see Figure 3.9 for the ODL schema)

OBJECT DATABASE MANIPULATIONS

An object database is a collection of objects that represent entities that are interesting to the organisation that it serves. Applications are concerned with creating and maintaining those objects, so as to store information about the current state of the organisations, and to deriving useful information from data held in the objects. Accordingly, the manipulative part of the object data model includes operations to provide the following three facilities.

1) Definition of the objects that are of interest—This facility is provided by what can be thought of as a set of "pick" and "mix" operations. These create collections of "interesting" objects by "mixing" together objects which have been "picked" from existing collections. These operators can represent applications, such as a Travel Agent application that accesses objects which represent relevant customers, hotel chains, hotels and bookings from the extents of the Customer, HotelChain, Hotel and Booking object types.

2) Application of operations to objects of interest—This is necessary in order to modify the states of objects, or to extract interesting information from them. This facility is provided by a set of operators which execute operations, such as the methods that implement the interface operations for the relevant objects. The operators can represent applications, such as in the Travel Agent where it is necessary to execute Customer object operations in order to create objects which represent the associated Bookings.

3) Return of an object which represents the required information—The consequence of querying an object database will be the retrieval of objects which represent the required information. These objects may be newly created or may already exist, and they may be literals or mutable objects. For example, a Travel Agent application may require details of customers with unpaid bills (i.e. a collection of existing (mutable) Customer objects), or the total value of a stay at a particular hotel (i.e. a literal). Accordingly, every OQL query returns an object to represent the required information.

EXAMPLE 3.14

Consider the following problem: "Retrieve the total cost of the bookings made by M.Ridley". The problem can be solved in three steps, corresponding to those identified above.

1) *Definition of the objects that are of interest*—*The above problem is solved firstly, by a "pick" and "mix" operation, in which interesting objects are picked out of the object database. In this case, the interesting objects are those which represent the customer, M.Ridley, and the bookings made by him. These are picked out by searching through the extent of the Customer object type to find the object for which the value of the name attribute is "M.Ridley". This operation corresponds to a restrict operation in the object algebra. Once that object has been located, it is then possible to access the objects which represent the bookings made by M.Ridley.*

2) *Application of operations to objects of interest*—*For each Booking object related to the M.Ridley object, it is now necessary to execute the TotalAmount? operation which calculates the total cost of the planned stay in a hotel, and then to add all of the order values together using a total function.*

3) *Return of an object which contains the required information*—*The result of this query is the total of the booking values computed in the previous step. This is the value of the query and is returned as a single literal.*

OQL

OQL is an object database query language, and is specified as part of the ODMG standards [Cattel 00]. OQL is used to implement the object database manipulation facilities described above. It is a simple query language and does not provide a full programming environment. A particular limitation is that OQL cannot express arbitrarily complex computations, i.e. OQL is not computationally complete. It is therefore necessary to use OQL in conjunction with other computer languages:

1) OQL is used to describe the retrieval and manipulation of objects,
2) the Object Definition Language (ODL) defines interfaces to object types used by the OQL code (see The Structural Part of the Object Model),
3) other programming languages, such as Java, C++ and Smalltalk, are used to implement object operations, i.e. methods,
4) other programming languages (Java, C++ and Smalltalk) are used to implement applications programs, with embedded OQL statements to manipulate the object database.

In case 4), OQL is used as an embedded query language, but it can also be used as a stand–alone query language, i.e. the user can express object database manipulations purely in OQL without having to embed OQL in programs written in other programming languages. Often, ODL and OQL will be automatically created by high level tools and wizards for generating applications.

OQL can be used for both collection-oriented and navigational queries.

1) A collection-oriented query retrieves a collection of objects—the way in which those objects are located is the responsibility of the ODBMS, rather than the application program.
2) Navigational queries access individual objects and use object relationships to navigate from one object to another—it is the responsibility of the applications program within which the OQL is embedded to specify the navigation procedure for accessing all objects of interest.

The designers of OQL have adopted an evolutionary approach. Rather than designing a completely new language, they have based OQL on SQL [Cattell 97, p 83]. Many queries in SQL, sometimes with minor changes, are also valid in OQL and have a similar meaning. However, OQL also extends SQL to deal with object–oriented notions, such as complexly structured objects, object identity, relationships (including subtype/supertype relationships) and operation invocation—none of these features occur within the relational data model. The design of OQL is functional, that is, the results of queries have types which allow them to be queried again, so complex queries can be built up. To allow greater compatibility with SQL, it is also possible, using OQL, to use some *ad hoc* constructions that are valid in SQL. The relationship between SQL and OQL is complicated by the fact that SQL is still evolving (see 3.2 Object-Relational Databases). The ODMG's stated intention is to maintain a degree of compatibility between object database technology and object-relational database technology by integrating features of future versions of SQL within future versions of OQL. However, given the size and complexity of the next generation of SQL (SQL:1999), it is hard to see how this compatibility can be maintained.

In general, OQL has an SQL-like syntax. In fact, most SQL examples in Chapter 2 are also valid OQL expressions. However, SQL and OQL expressions have the following differences in meaning.

1) That which is interpreted as a table name in SQL, is interpreted as a collection–object name in OQL;
2) That which is interpreted as the name of a column of a table in SQL is interpreted as an object characteristic name (an attribute, relationship or operation name) in OQL.

For example, the following SQL expression is also a valid OQL.

```
SELECT HotelNumber
FROM Hotels
WHERE Rooms < 1000;
```

In SQL this expression retrieves a single-column table of values selected from the column called HotelNumber of a table called Hotels where the value of the column called Rooms is less than 1000.

In OQL the above expression retrieves a collection object (rather than a table). In fact it will be a bag-object, since we have not specified that the elements must be "unique". Remember that a bag is like a set, except that in a bag an element can occur many times. Also, Hotels will be collection objects (in the ODL schema in Figure 3.9 Hotels is the name of the extents of the Hotel object types). The where condition compares the characteristic called Rooms of the objects in Hotels (in Figure 3.9, Rooms is defined as an attribute of Hotel) with the literal object, 1000.

Since OQL must operate upon the objects within an object database rather than just the tables of a relational database, it must have a number of features in addition to those of SQL.
• Complexly structured objects—OQL must be able to access objects and their characteristics (i.e. attributes, relationships and operations), even when they are nested within complex structures;

- Navigational access—OQL must be able to access objects using object identities and relationships between objects.
- Object retrieval—OQL must be able to retrieve existing objects within the object database, and also to create new objects;
- Object behaviour—OQL must be able to execute object operations in order to update the state of an object or derive information from its state.
- Inheritance—OQL must be able to utilise the subtype/supertype relationships between object types.

OQL's support for complex types becomes apparent when we consider how it supports the ORDER BY and GROUP BY clauses of standard SQL. These are used respectively to specify the sequence of object in the resulting collection object and the criteria by which objects are grouped, in a manner similar to SQL.

When an "ORDER BY" clause is used, the resulting collection object will be a list-object, since the elements in a set or a bag can have no ordering. This contrasts with SQL, where "ORDER BY" simply specifies how the resulting table is to be displayed. This is illustrated in the first example in Example 3.15.

As in SQL, the OQL query which groups objects from a collection, C, on the basis of the partitioning attributes, P1, P2,... Pn respectively defined on the grouping functions, E1, E2,...En, but excluding those objects for which the condition, F, is *false*, has the form:

```
SELECT *
FROM C
GROUP BY P1 : E1, P2 : E2, ...Pn : En
HAVING F;
```

The resulting object is a collection object, the state of which contains one object for each group. The group objects contain the value of the grouping functions and a collection object that contains the grouped objects. The use of "GROUP BY" and "HAVING" is illustrated in the second and third examples in Example 3.15.

EXAMPLE 3.15

Consider an Employee object type that includes Location and Salary attributes.

1) *The following OQL will return a list-object that contains Employee objects in decreasing order of salary.*

```
SELECT *
FROM EmployeeS e
ORDER BY e.Salary DESC;
```

2) *The following OQL will partition Employee objects in the extent, Employees, such that there are four partitions, respectively containing:*
   - *employees located in Manchester earning over 40,000,*
   - *employees in Manchester earning 40,000 or less,*
   - *employees not in Manchester earning over 40,000*
   - *employees not in Manchester earning 40,000 or less.*

```
SELECT *
FROM EmployeeS e
GROUP BY
        WhichCity? : e.Location = 'Manchester' ,
        Overpaid?: e.Salary > 40000;
```

The above OQL specifies two partition attributes (WhichCity? and Overpaid?), which are defined on partitioning functions (e.Location = "Manchester", and e.Salary > 40000). The partition attributes, WhichCity? and Overpaid?, are of the types of the value returned by their respective partition functions, i.e. they are both Boolean. The objects which are grouped are Employee objects contained in the type's extent, Employees. The type of the result is therefore,

```
SET<STRUCT(WhichCity?:Boolean,
        Overpaid?:BOOLEAN, BAG<Employee>)>
```

This complex structure is a set of structures, each of which contains the value of the grouping expression and a bag containing the grouped objects. This contrasts with the corresponding SQL, which would simply retrieve a table with a row for each group.

3) *The following OQL is equivalent to the previous one, apart from the addition of a "filter" condition (e.Salary > 1000 **and not** (e.Location = "Slough")) which excludes from the groups all objects for which this condition does not return true, i.e. Employees located in Slough earning 1000 or less will be ignored*

```
SELECT e
FROM EmployeeS e
GROUP BY
    WhichCity?:e.Location = 'Manchester' ,
    Overpaid?: e.Salary > 40000
HAVING (e.Salary > 1000 AND
    NOT(e.Location = 'Slough'));
```

The result will be an object of the same type as the result of the previous OQL, but there may be fewer objects in the partitions.

In one respect, OQL improves on SQL. Using OQL it is possible to construct complex queries from simpler ones in a more flexible way than is possible using SQL. An OQL expression is constructed from variables and constants that represent objects, and from operations upon objects. The result returned when an OQL statement is executed is always an object. Also, the type of the resulting object can always be determined by analysing the expression. OQL exploits this property by allowing expressions to be constructed freely from other expressions—an expression can occur within another expression wherever the type of the object it returns is expected (a language with this property is said to be orthogonal). This feature is illustrated in the following example.

EXAMPLE 3.16

The following OQL retrieves a set-object containing a single string literal, "Happy Days".

```
SELECT   c.PartOf->ChainName
FROM   c IN
       SELECT *
       FROM Hotels
```

```
WHERE HotelNumber = 'H1'
```

Note the inclusion of a "SELECT" statement in the "FROM" clause. This is possible in OQL because the object returned is a collection object.

OQL PICK AND MIX OPERATIONS

The first set of OQL features we shall describe are for accessing objects of interest.

In SQL, the simplest form of expression is a "SELECT" statement. In OQL the expressions from which a "SELECT" statement can be formed are also valid expressions. The simplest form of OQL query is therefore an object name—object names are used as entry points into an object database. In the case of a literal, the literal value can be used as the object name.

EXAMPLE 3.17

This example illustrates the use of object names and literal values as queries.

1) *The following OQL query returns the integer literal, 21.*

```
21
```

2) *If the Hotel object for hotel H1 in the Figure 3.10 object database has the object name, MostPopular, it will be returned by the OQL query,*

```
MostPopular
```

3) *Given the Figure 3.10 object database, this next OQL query returns the extent of the Customer object type.*

```
Customers
```

When accessing a mutable object, OQL also allows us to access the value (or state) of that object. To do this, the query must be preceded by an asterisk, "*". This process is called dereferencing and is illustrated in Example 3.18.

EXAMPLE 3.18

Consider a mutable object type, DiaryEntry, which has a single attribute called ENTRY, which is of type string. Two DiaryEntry objects have respectively been assigned the object names, ProjectStart and ProjectEnd. The values of these objects are both "Equinox team meeting".

1) *The following OQL will return false, because ProjectStart and ProjectEnd are the names of different objects.*

```
ProjectStart = ProjectEnd
```

2) *The following query will return true because *ProjectStart and *ProjectEnd will return the values of the respective named objects, and these are the same literal, "Equinox team meeting".*

```
*ProjectStart = *ProjectEnd
```

To allow the parts of complexly structured objects or of related objects to be accessed, OQL allows object and characteristic names to be put together to form a path from a named object to the object or characteristic that we wish to access. The steps in the path are separated by dots, ".", or alternatively by arrows, "->". Dots and arrows are interchangeable in OQL, but we use the convention that dots denote the path from an object to its characteristic, and arrows denote paths from an object to another object via relationships. The next example illustrates access via paths.

EXAMPLE 3.19

The following query assumes that the Hotel object for hotel H1 in the Figure 3.10 object database is named MostPopular.

The value returned by the OQL query,

```
MostPopular.PartOf->ChainName
```

is the string literal, "Happy Days"', since that is the value of the ChainName attribute of the HotelChain object related to the Hotel object called MostPopular via the PartOf relationship.

The orthogonality of OQL means that any OQL query that returns an object of an appropriate type can be used in place of a name. Therefore, note that the components of a path are queries. The objects returned by these queries provide the "stepping stones" by which we eventually reach the required object, attribute, or relationship.

SELECTING OBJECTS FROM A COLLECTION
Often we will require objects that have some common property to be picked from a collection-object, e.g. all customers in a particular area, or all bookings for a particular hotel. In OQL we can implement this type of operations using queries with the same syntax as the SQL queries (see 2.2). All of the SQL facilities described in the previous chapter for retrieving rows from a table can also be used in OQL for reviewing objects from a collection-object. However, OQL is more flexible, because of its orthogonality, in that the where condition can be any expression that returns a Boolean literal, i.e. true or false. Alternatively, the collection-object can be restricted by the expression that forms the "FROM" and/or "SELECT" clauses (see example 3.20).

In addition to the comparison operators of SQL, OQL also supports the following comparisons operators for testing the contents of a collection object:

1) for all—this comparison operator tests if a condition is true for all objects contained in a collection-object. (This operator is called the universal quantifier in predicate logic.)
2) exists—This operator tests if there exists an object within a collection-object for which the specified condition is true. (This operator is called the existential quantifier in predicate logic.)
3) unique—This operator tests to see if there is one and only one object within a collection-object returned by a specified query.
4) in—This tests if a specified object is contained within a collection-object. (One particular use of IN, described in the following subsection, is for testing for characters in a string literal.)
5) some, any and all—These are comparison operator quantifiers, and are used to specify if the comparison is with at least one (SOME or ANY) or all (ALL) of the object in a collection-object. Any of the built-in comparison operators (e.g. !=, <, >, <=, >=) can be qualified in this way.

6) Set inclusion—The comparison operators, <, <= , > and >=, when applied to collection-objects, test if one collection is included in the other.

EXAMPLE 3.20

1) *The following OQL query returns true if all hotels have more than 1000 rooms.*

```
FOR ALL x IN Hotels: x.Rooms > 1000;
```

2) *The next OQL query returns true if at least one of the hotels has more that 1,000 rooms.*

```
EXISTS x IN Hotels: x.Rooms = 1000;
```

3) *An alternative way of expressing the query in 2) is,*

```
EXISTS (SELECT x
   FROM Hotels x
   WHERE x.Rooms > 1000);
```

In its second form, exists, returns true if the collection-object returned by the query is not empty.

4) *If we wish to test if there is one, and only one hotel with more than 1000 rooms, we can use the unique operator, as follows,*

```
UNIQUE (SELECT x
   FROM Hotels x
   WHERE x.Rooms > 1000);
```

5) *The OQL queries in 1) and 2) can also be expressed by qualifying the equals ("=") comparison operator, as in the following two OQL queries.*

```
1000 < ALL (SELECT x.Rooms FROM Hotels x)
1000 < ANY (SELECT x.Rooms FROM Hotels x)
```

6) *This OQL query returns true if the Hotel object named MostPopular is contained in Hotels.*

```
MostPopular IN Hotels;
```

7) *The first two of the next four queries return true if the set-object, Customers includes all of the Customers objects contained in retail–customers. The third and fourth return true, if Customers contains all, but not only the objects in CorporateCustomers.*

```
CorporateCustomers <= Customers
Customers >= CorporateCustomers
CorporateCustomers < Customers
Customers > CorporateCustomers
```

OQL also allows us to access objects contained in ordered collection-objects, i.e. list- and array-objects, by specifying their positions within the collections. This is done in the following ways:

1) first, last—As their names suggest, these operations respectively return the first and the last object contained in a list- or array-object.
2) access by index—Each object contained in a list- or array-object is indexed by a number which indicates the object's positions (the first element is indexed with 0, the next with 1, and so on). OQL queries can access objects contained in a list- or array-object by specifying their index numbers.
3) list (or array) addition—Two or more lists (or arrays) can be combined such that the second becomes a continuation of the first using the conventional addition operator, "+".

EXAMPLE 3.21
The object, HotelList, of type LIST<Hotel>, contains Hotel objects in ascending number of rooms.

1) *The following two OQL queries, respectively, returns the Hotel object for the smallest and the largest hotels.*

```
FIRST(HotelList)
LAST(HotelList)
```

2) *This query returns the Hotel object for the second smallest hotel.*

```
HotelList [1]
```

Note that the index number for the second object in the list is 1, because the numbering is from 0 upwards.

3) *This query returns an object of type list<Hotel> that contains the Hotel objects for the five smallest hotels, in ascending number of rooms sequence.*

```
HotelList [0:4]
```

4) *A second list-object, LuxuryHotels, contains a list of hotels in the luxury range. The following query will return the list-object which contains the objects in HotelList and also the objects in LuxuryHotels as a continuation.*

```
HotelList + LuxuryHotels
```

Objects can be selected from more than one collection object as in SQL, by listing them in the "FROM" clause. Also, as in SQL, the set operators, union, intersection and difference (except) are supported. However, OQL has more flexibility than SQL in this respect, since the collection-objects can be defined by expressions, rather than just names, and also, the expression can navigate between objects using relationships, rather than having to join on the basis of values, as is the case in SQL.

PROCESSING THE SELECTED OBJECTS
Mutable objects are manipulated by executing the operations defined for the respective object types. In fact, this is the only way to change the state of an existing object—OQL does not include any built-in facilities for updating an object database (unlike SQL which has special update, insert and delete instructions).

An instance operation is accessed and executed via a **path**, in the same way that other object characteristics (i.e. attributes and relationships) are accessed. This is done using the dot notation previously described. The only difference is that it is often necessary to provide operations with parameter values—if required, parameter values are appended to the path in brackets.

EXAMPLE 3.22

1) *The following OQL query executes the ChangeAddress operation (declared in the schema in Figure 3.9) with the parameter "Wigan" on the Hotel object named MostPopular.*

```
MostPopular.ChangeAddress ("Wigan")
```

Note that the parameter required by the operation is provided in brackets after the operation name, as when executing a procedure in a conventional programming language, such as Pascal, C or C++. The above query will return a null value, i.e. the value of the operation.

2) *The following query returns a set-object containing the values returned by executing the TotalCost operation on all Booking objects in the extent, Bookings*

```
SELECT DISTINCT
    p.TotalCost
FROM p IN Bookings
```

*Note the use of distinct to remove duplicates from the resulting collection-object. If omitted, the returned object would be a bag, rather than a set. Note also that the **WHERE** clause has been omitted. This is because there is no restrict predicate—we are interested in all objects contained in Bookings.*

The OQL facilities for executing instance operations illustrate one of the less satisfactory features of object database technology. The Object Data Model does not distinguish between retrieval and update operations, and so there is the risk of side effects when an operation is executed simply to access its value—the side effect of retrieving a value can be a change to the object's state. Also, the designer of an ODBMS must take into account and devise strategies for avoiding the problem of inappropriate and multiple executions of an operation upon an object when executing a query. This latter point complicates the problem of optimising the execution of OQL queries.

In addition to the user-defined operations on objects, OQL allows the standard arithmetic operators to be applied to literals . These can be used to construct queries which perform arithmetic computations on numeric literals and which derive new character strings from existing character and string literals. In addition, OQL supports the aggregating functions, that are supported in SQL, i.e. sum, min, max, avg and count.

Of these, the operators for character string manipulations are not covered in the SQL section. These are:

1) Strings are combined using "+" or alternatively, "||". For example, the expression, "Bar" + "ry" (or alternatively "Bar" || "ry") will return the string literal, "Barry".

2) If s is an expression of type string and i an expression of type integer, then s[i] will return the i+1th character in the string (the first character is s[0]). For example, if name has the value "Barry", then name[4] will return the value 'y'.

3) If s is an expression of type string, and low and high are of type integer, then s[low:high] will return the substring starting at the low+1th character of s up to the high+1th character. For example, name[1:3] will return "arr".

EXAMPLE 3.23

The following OQL returns a string literal which comprises the first five letters of the Name attribute, followed by the first three letters of the Town attribute of the Address of each Employee object.

```
SELECT DISTINCT e.Name[0:4] + e.Address.Town[0:2]
FROM Employee e;
```

The result of the OQL will be a literal set-object containing string literals. Note that literals of type character are denoted by single quotes (strings have double quotes). Also, note that the elements of a string (or list or array) are numbered from zero upwards.

PROCESSING A COLLECTION OF MANY TYPES OF OBJECT

An added complexity can occur when executing operations on a collection-object that contains objects of many types. In such situations, there may be multiple implementations of the operation. It is therefore necessary to determine, for each object, which implementation to use. OQL supports two different ways of resolving this problem.

1) Late binding—This mechanism allows general queries to be specialised for each object when the query is executed.
2) class indicators—Class indicators override late binding to ensure that only objects of a specified type are accessed.

EXAMPLE 3.24

Consider a situation where the Customer type has two subtypes, CorporateCustomer and PrivateCustomers, and there are three implementations of the CreateInvoice operation, one for each of the three types. The following OQL exploits late binding in order to execute the most appropriate implementation of CreateInvoice for each Customer object in a collection-object, Customers.

```
SELECT c.CreateInvoice FROM Customers c
```

The late binding mechanism ensures that when the OQL is executed, each object in the collection is considered separately and the most specific implementation of CreateInvoice for that object is applied. For instance, the CorporateCustomer implementation of the CreateInvoice operation will be executed for a Customer object that is also of type CorporateCustomer.

Late binding is a useful mechanism, since it allows operations to be invoked at the most general level, but then executed at the most specific. This simplifies applications programs, since they do not have to take into account differences between subtypes. Late binding also insulates applications programs from many changes to the object database. For instance, if we add a new specialisation of Customer, EmployeeCustomer, and provide a fourth implementation of CreateInvoice for the new subtype, the OQL in Example 3.24 will still be valid, and will operate correctly on collections which also include EmployeeCustomer objects.

Sometimes we may wish to override late binding, and ensure that we process only specific types of object within a collection. This is done using class indicators, as in the following example.

EXAMPLE 3.25

The following OQL will access the DISCOUNT attribute, but only for Customer objects contained in Customers which are also of the subtype, CorporateCustomers.

```
SELECT ((CorporateCustomers)c).DISCOUNT
FROM Customers c
```

OQL which utilises late binding has no special syntax, because late binding automatically takes place, by default.

CREATING STRUCTURED OBJECTS

Structured-literals (i.e. set-, bag-, list-, array-, and structure-literals) can be created using the object constructor operators, STRUCT, SET, BAG, LIST and ARRAY, as illustrated in the following example.

EXAMPLE 3.26

1) *The following OQL returns a bag-literal, containing the characters, 'b' , 'a' , 'r', ',r' and 'y', (note that an element can occur many times in a bag, but all elements must be of the same type),*

   BAG ('b', 'a', 'r', 'r', 'y')

2) *The following OQL returns a set-literal, containing the integer literals, 2, 4, 8 and 16 (note that elements must be distinct in a set, and must be of the same type).*

   ```
   SET (2, 4, 8, 16)
   ```

3) *The following OQL returns a structure-literal, with elements called initials, name and children. Their respective values are the list–literal, {'M','J'}, the string–literal "Ridley", and the integer–literal, 2 (note that elements of a structure are named, and may be of different types)*

   ```
   STRUCT(initials: LIST('M','J'), name: "Ridley",
       children: 2)
   ```

The third OQL query in Example 3.26 again illustrates the way in which queries can be freely constructed from others—the queries includes the query, LIST('M','J'), which, in turn, includes the queries 'M' and 'J'.

Type names are used as constructor operators to create new mutable objects of the specified type.

EXAMPLE 3.27

The following OQL creates a new Hotel object,

```
Hotel (HotelNumber: "H10",
            Address: "The Royal, Sidney")
```

The parameters provide initial values for the properties of the new Hotel object. Properiesy that are not initialised, in this case Rooms, are assigned the null value, nil.

Example 3.27 illustrates how it is possible to create an object by specifying its attribute values. We can also build a new object from existing objects. This is done by including queries on the object database as parameters for the constructor operator, as in the next example.

EXAMPLE 3.28

In this example we assume that the following types have been declared:

```
TYPE HotelSize
ATTRIBUTES
      HotelNumber: INTEGER
      Rooms: SHORT
END_TYPE;
TYPE HotelSizes SET<HotelSize>;
```

The following OQL will create a mutable object of type product_colours

```
HotelSizes (SELECT DISTINCT
      h.HotelNumber, Rooms
      FROM Hotels h);
```

Note the use of the type name, HotelSizes, as an object constructor operator. Note that the value is retrieved from existing Hotel objects. The value returned by the parameter query is a literal collection-object, the elements of which are structures containing a HotelNumber value and a Rooms value from a Hotel object. This literal is then assigned as the value of a new mutable object of type HotelSizes.

CONVERSION OF AN OBJECT FROM ONE TYPE TO ANOTHER

OQL includes a number of operators for converting an object from one type into another. These include:

1) LISTTOSET—As the name suggests, this operator convert a list-object into a set-object which contains the same object, after any duplicates have been removed, e.g. LISTTOSET(LIST(1,2,3,3,4))= SET(1,2,3,4)
2) DISTINCT—This operator also removes duplicate objects from a collection-object. However, if the collection is a list (or array), the object returned is also a list (or array), with the same relative ordering of the remaining elements. If distinct is applied to a bag it returns a set. For example, e.g. DISTINCT (LIST (1,2,2,3,2,5)) = LIST(1,2,3,5); DISTINCT (BAG (1,2,3,3)) = SET(1,2,3)
3) ELEMENT—When applied to a collection-object containing one object, element will return the contained object, e.g. ELEMENT(SET(5)) = 5.
4) FLATTEN—This operator implements the unnest operator of the object algebra, e.g. flatten (LIST (SET(1,2), SET(2,3), SET(4,5)) = LIST(1,2,2,3,4,5).

EXAMPLE 3.29

1) Assume the list–object, HotelBookings, which contains Booking objects, for hotel reservations for a particular month. The elements of HotelBookings are in chronological order. The following will return the corresponding set-object.

```
LISTTOSET (HotelBookings)
```

The respective types of HotelBookings, and the object returned by the OQL are list<Booking> and set<Booking>. The other difference is that duplicate *objects will have been removed in the returned object and its elements will have no ordering.*

2) *The following OQL returns a list-object which contains the same objects as HotelBookings, but with duplicate objects removed. The relative ordering of the remaining elements is preserved.*

```
DISTINCT (HotelBookings);
```

3) *The next OQL illustrates how distinct is used to convert a bag into a set, in a manner similar to the use of listtoset to convert lists to sets. CustomersToday is a bag-object which contains Customer objects for customer who have made hotel booking inquiries during the day. The following OQL returns a set-object containing the same Customer objects, but with duplicates removed.*

```
DISTINCT (Customers_TODAY);
```

4) *This next OQL example uses **ELEMENT** to retrieve a single object from a collection, rather than a collection-object containing that object.*

```
ELEMENT(SELECT DISTINCT h
    FROM Hotel h
    WHERE h.Address = "The Grand, Honley");
```

The object returned by the embedded select query is of type set<Hotel> and the element operator returns the one Hotel object contained in it.

5) *This final example uses flatten to return a bag-object of Customer objects.*

```
FLATTEN (SELECT s.PlacedBy FROM Booking s)
```

The embedded select query returns an object of type bag<set<Customer>>. The set-objects it contains are the sets of Customer objects related to each Booking object in BookingS. The flatten operator then flattens out the sets, and returns an object of type bag<Customer> containing Customer objects in the sets.

OPERATOR COMPOSITION

OQL's language orthogonality makes it possible to compose expressions from other simpler expressions, as long as the types are consistent. In practice this makes it possible to construct and test a complex query in stages. OQL includes a query naming facility to support this mode of working.

A query is named using a define statement, e.g.

```
DEFINE ActiveCustomers AS
        SELECT DISTINCT (Customer)c
        FROM Customers c
        WHERE EXISTS(c.Booking);
```

The above OQL includes a select statement which returns a set-object containing Customer objects for customers who have made hotel bookings. The OQL does not execute this query, but assigns it a name, ACTIVE_Customers, that can be used in subsequent OQL statements instead of the text of the query.

By naming a query, we simplify other queries within which the named query is embedded. For instance, the above definition simplifies the following query which groups customers with orders, by city.

```
DEFINE CustomerAreas AS
        SELECT ca
        FROM Customers ca
        GROUP BY AREA:c.Address.City;
```

Once again the above does not execute, but simply defines and names a query for future use. Having defined the above two queries, we can now use them, for example to retrieve a list of customers with outstanding bookings, grouped and sorted alphabetically by city name, as follows,

```
SELECT sca
FROM  CustomerAreas sca
ORDERED BY sca.Area;
```

The above could have been expressed as a single but much more complex OQL query, as follows.

```
SELECT sca
FROM   (SELECT ca
        FROM (SELECT DISTINCT (Customer)c
              FROM Customers c
              WHERE EXISTS(c.Booking)) ca
        GROUP BY area:c.Address.City) sca
ordered by sca.Area;
```

There are obvious advantages in keeping things simple when using a computer, and the above series of subquery definitions have enabled us to do this, and avoid the complexity evident in the single query version.

A set of query definitions and a query can be put together to form a **query program.**

3.3 OBJECT-RELATIONAL DATABASES

Also included in the third generation of databases is the object–relational data model. This represents an evolutionary approach in which the relational data model is enhanced to include features normally associated with object-oriented systems. SQL is currently being revised to operate upon object-relational databases.

A new revision of SQL has been under development throughout the 1990s which will support object-relational database. This will then provide an International Standard for object-relational databases. This new version of SQL has been referred to as SQL3 in the working papers. The core features of this revision of SQL were eventually published in 1999 [Sigmod Record], and SQL3 was accordingly re-named SQL:1999. Other projects relating to SQL:1999 are still in progress. These concern the Object Language Bindings, Management of External Data, and OLAP facilities.

The new features of SQL:1999 include:
- Support for storing and manipulating very large data objects (LOBs)
- Object-Oriented Features
- Facilities to represent complex data relationships:
- Improved facilities for maintaining the integrity of databases

The general approach evident in SQL:1999 is to provide these and other additional features as optional extras for the database designer. For instance, SQL:1999 supports object identifiers, but it is up to the designer to decide if they are to be used or not—in the Object Data Model all objects have object identifiers. A consequence is that SQL:1999 is a very large language, compared to the original SQL standard, or the ODMG standards (ODL and OQL). On the basis of a page count, the syntax definition of SQL:1999 is approximately five times longer that the combined specifications of ODL and OQL in the ODMG standard! In this respect, SQL:1999 has lost one of the main qualities of the original relational data model, i.e. its simplicity. It has also lost its theoretical rigour—only a very small part of SQL:1999 is concerned with implementing the original Relational Data Model. The additional features are not formally defined.

In the following sections some of the more important new features of SQL:1999 are overviewed.

LARGE DATA OBJECTS

Inclusion of support for large objects is a response to the growing importance of textual and multimedia data. Documents and media objects cannot be easily accessed using previous versions of SQL, except as files external to the database, via the file names stored in the database. The problem has been that of handling such large objects. A page of a document typically required up to 40K of memory, a colour image 40M, and video 1G per hour.

SQL:1999 includes two new types to support large objects:
- Character Large Objects or CLOBs can be used to better support databases of documents.
- Binary Large Objects or BLOBs can be used to store media objects, such as audio, images and video.

This facility is illustrated in the following SQL:1999 table declaration.

```
CREATE TABLE museum_artifact
   (id_number            INTEGER,
    name                 VARCHAR(200)
    historic_notes       CLOB(32K)
    image_of_artifact    BLOB(40K))
```

In general large objects are accessed in the same way as the others, though there is only a restricted set of operations that can be performed on them. For example, it is not possible to perform "GROUP BY" or "ORDER BY" on large objects. In practice it may not be possible to retrieve a complete large object (a video for example) into the store of a workstation. SQL:1999 therefore allows large objects to be accessed in manageable chunks. This is done using "Locators". These are similar to the cursors used when word processing.

TRIGGERS
SQL:1999 includes a standarised syntax for triggers. Triggers are a way of implementing what are sometimes known as event–condition–action (ECA) operations in databases [Paton 99]. Some form of trigger has been introduced into a number of RDBMS but without a standardised format. The syntax is

```
CREATE TRIGGER <trigger_name>
[BEFORE|AFTER]   <trigger_event>
ON <table_name>
[REFERENCING <old_or_new_correlation_list>
[FOR EACH ROW|STATEMENT]
[WHEN <trigger_condition>]
<trigger_body>
```

The <trigger_event> is one of "insert" "delete" or "update" on a list of columns. The <old_or_new_correlation_list> allows the trigger to refer to before and after states of rows or whole tables. The FOR EACH ROW or FOR EACH STATEMENT feature allows triggers to be executed for each row affected or once (the default). The <trigger_body> itself is a sequence of SQL statements, not including transaction statements (such as COMMIT) or connection statements (such as DISCONNECT).

OBJECT-ORIENTED FEATURES
SQL:1999 includes features usually associated with object-oriented systems. These allow users to capture more of the meaning of the information represented as data, by creating User Defined Types (UDTs). These are types that users can define to extend the database for specific applications. (UDTs are similar to object types (see 3.1), but the operations are not restricted to operating on a single instance). Earlier

SQL standards provide a single abstraction for modelling entities, the table, and include built–in types (Integer, Character, etc.) which can be used as column types. This new extension is to allow relational database designers to define new data types for non-standard and application specific data. However, the instances of these UDTs can only exist within relational tables.

SQL:1999 also supports generalisation and specialisation hierarchies. These hierarchies are similar to subtype/supertype hierarchies in the Object Data Model (see 3.1). In SQL:1999 there are separate hierarchies for tables, and UDTs. This facility allows a table or a UDT to be redefined into a specialised form, reusing the original definition.

With the addition of UDTs, SQL:1999 provides two ways to model entities—as rows in tables and as values of UDTs. There is also considerable overlap between the features of these two abstractions—for example, they both support inheritance hierarchies and object/row identifiers.

UDT
A UDT definition includes:
* A type name
* the way in which instances are represented, i.e. the structures used
* the relationship to other types.

In addition, the operations (methods and functions) on a UDT must be defined. The definition of a UDT operation includes:
* an operation name
* its signature, i.e. the types of parameters it receives
* the type of result returned by the operation
* the way in which the operation is implemented.

The additions of UDTs to SQL has a number of advantages:
* It enables the database designer to more closely model the information that must be represented. The object-relational database designer can define UDTs (and tables) for each type of value and entity that they wish to represent and which cannot be represented using the built-in data types. As in the object databases, new types (UDTs) can be freely constructed from others.

- It then becomes possible for the DBMS to detect data manipulations that are inconsistent with the meaning of the data. SQL:1999 enforces constraints such that a value of one type cannot be assigned a value of a different type. Since UDTs allow users to define application-specific types, this constraint can effectively avoid nonsensical data assignments, such as setting the price of a product to its height! The latter is possible, if both are simply real numbers.
- As in object databases, by accessing instances of UDTs via the operators, the complexities of how the instances are represented are hidden from the user.

UDTs may be simple or complex. These are called respectively:
- Distinct types
- Structured types

DISTINCT UDT
A distinct UDT simply provides an application-specific name for a built-in type, as illustrated in Example 3.30. Columns of a table can be defined on distinct UDTs so as to give them a more specific meaning and to restrict their use to operations that are consistent with their meaning.

EXAMPLE 3.30
The following defines the Hotel table, but using distinct UDTs for the hotel number and hotel chain number.

```
CREATE TYPE hotel.numbertype
AS INTEGER FINAL

CREATE TYPE hotel_chain.number
AS INTEGER FINAL

CREATE TABLE hotel (
hotel_number            hotel.numbertype,
chain_number            hotel_chain.number,
address                 CHAR(30),
rooms            INTEGER);
```

Note that we have defined two new types, for values of hotel number and hotel chain number. These take the same values, as the built-in type INTEGER.

However, the fact that they are distinct means that, for example, the value of a hotel chain number cannot be assigned to a hotel number, using the following SQL

```
UPDATE hotel
SET hotel_number = chain_no;
```

Note also that the definitions include the term, "FINAL". This indicates that subtypes will not be defined on the UDT.

In addition, operations on distinct types can be defined to model the behaviour of the entities represented. Definition of operations on UDTs are described later.

STRUCTURED UDT
The values of structured UDTs are complex, i.e. they are composed of other values. Columns of a table can be defined on structured UDTs. Also, tables themselves can be defined on them. In the latter case, the instances of the stuctured UDT form the rows of the table.

A structured UDT is similar to an ODMG structure object type. Each instance is formed from a row of values, possibly of different types.

EXAMPLE 3.31
The following SQL:1999 code first defines a Structured UDT for addresses and a Distinct UDT for biographical details. These are then used in a Structured UDT that defines a person type. Finally, we define a table on the person type, instances of which will form the rows of the table.

```
CREATE TYPE addrtype AS
(street              CHAR (40),
town                CHAR (20),
county              CHAR (20),
post_code           CHAR(8)) NOT FINAL

CREATE TYPE biogtype AS CLOB FINAL

CREATE TYPE person AS
(name               CHAR(30),
```

address   addrtype,
biography   biogtype) NOT FINAL

CREATE TABLE people OF person

OPERATIONS ON UDT

These may be defined for UDTs in a similar way to which operations are defined for object types in an object database.

EXAMPLE 3.32

Many of the features of the SQL:1999 UDT facility are illustrated in the following example UDT declaration.

```
1    CREATE TYPE person_type
2    (       name VARCHAR NOT NULL,
3            SEX CONSTANT CHAR (1),
4            age UPDATABLE VIRTUAL GET WITH age
5                 SET WITH set_age,
6    PRIVATE
7            birthdate DATE
8            CHECK (birthdate < DATE '1992-01-01'),
9    PUBLIC
10           EQUAL DEFAULT,
11           LESS THAN NONE,
12           ACTOR FUNCTION age (:P person_type)
13                 RETURN REAL
14                 RETURN <CODE TO CALCULATE THE AGE>
15           END FUNCTION
16           ACTOR FUNCTION set_age
17                 (:P person_type, ...)
18                  RETURNS person_type
19                 < CODE TO UPDATE THE BIRTHDATE>
20                 RETURN :P
21           END FUNCTION,
22           DESTRUCTOR FUNCTION remove_person
23                 (:P person_type)
24                 RETURNS person_type
25                 <VARIOUS CLEAN_UP ACTIONS>
```

```
26                DESTROY :P;
27                RETURN :P;
28         END FUNCTION;
29    );
```

The Example 3.32 declaration is for a UDT, instances of which represent persons. As in the object databases, the type declaration specifies type properties (lines 2–4) and operations (lines 10–28). The implementations of the operations are also included in the specification (lines 14, 19 and 25). In this respect the UDT is more like a class than an object type.

UDT instances can exist only within a table—SQL:1999 currently retains the basic idea of the Relational Model, that all data is presented as values within tables. The SQL:1999 equivalent of the extent of a class in an object database is therefore a table envelope for an UDT—the rows contain the UDT instances. This is created by,

```
CREATE TABLE People OF Person;
```

Attributes of the UDT become columns of the table and instances are the rows, as shown below.

People

Name	Sex	Age
Barry Eaglestone	male	38
Mick Ridley	male	37
Carole Stainton	female	39

UDT instances can then be managed using the usual SQL select, update and delete statements (see Chapter 2).

OBJECT IDENTIFIERS

Object identifiers (OIDs) are an optional extra for an UDT. SQL:1999 supports three options:

1) with oid visible
2) with oid not visible
3) without oid

As in the Object Data Model, OIDs are unique and immutable identifiers used for referencing instances. A UDT declared "without oid" is called a value UDT, and must be referenced by its value. Value UDTs are like literals in the object databases. A UDT declared "with oid" is called an object UDT and is like a mutable object. Alternatively, a UDT may be explicitly declared as a value or object UDT, as in the Example 3.32 OBJECT UDT declaration (line 1). If the OID is visible, then it may by passed as a parameter.

If a column is defined on an object UDT, then it can either contain the UDT instances (this is specified using the "instance" keyword in the UDT definition), or the OIDs to reference the instances. The SQL:1999 "insert" statement illustrates the approach taken by which OIDs can be retrieved. Insert is extended to return the OID of the new row (instance) as an "alias",

```
INSERT INTO People <insert spec>
ALIAS NewPerson
```

SUBTYPE/SUPERTYPE RELATIONSHIPS
SQL:1999 supports subtype/supertype relationships between UDTs. Supertypes are declared using the "under" keyword in an UDT definition. For example, we can declare an ADT called Employee as a specialisation of Person as follows:

```
CREATE OBJECT TYPE Employee
UNDER Person
( ... );
```

This mechanism is the same as the subtype/supertype relationship in the object data model. Multiple supertypes are allowed. A subtype inherits the definitions of its supertypes, and also provides its own definitions. In this way a subtype can define a more specialised data definition without losing the properties and operations of its supertype. As in object databases, this mechanism also supports the re-use of type definitions— new types are built under older less specialised ones, rather than having to rewrite properties from scratch. An instance of a subtype is also an instance of all of its supertypes, but is associated with the "most specific type" (the lowest type in the type hierarchy of which it is an instance).

All operations on a type can be invoked on its subtypes, but there may be different implementations of the operation for each type. There is therefore potential for name conflicts. These ambiguities are avoided by the following rules:

1) When creating a subtype from two supertypes, if the two supertypes inherit an attribute from a common supertype, then only the one from the common supertype is inherited by the subtype. For instance, consider the situation where Employee_Customer is an SQL:1999 UDT, which is a subtype of Employee and Customer, which in turn are both subtypes of Person. Employee and Customer will both inherit Name and Address attributes from Person, thus causing a name conflict for Employee_Person. To resolve this, Employee_Customer inherits the Name and Address attributes from Person, rather than either Employee or Customer.

2) otherwise it is invalid to have the same attribute in two supertypes— one of them must be renamed.

UDT ENCAPSULATION

Encapsulation is the hiding of implementation details behind an interface, and is a major feature of the Object Data Model—instance characteristics (attributes, relationships and operations) provide an interface to objects of a particular type, but encapsulation means that the way in which those characteristics are implemented is invisible to the user. In SQL:1999, encapsulation is an optional extra which can be applied on a "sliding scale". Attributes and operations declared in a UDT definition can be either encapsulated (i.e. invisible to the user) or not. The three options are:

1) PUBLIC—this means that attributes and operations are visible to all authorised users.
2) PRIVATE—the attributes and operations are visible only within the UDT for implementation purposes.
3) PROTECTED—the attributes and operations are visible within the UDT and within all of its subtype.

The Example 3.32 UDT declaration includes both private (line 6) and public parts (line 9). The one private attribute is called birthdate, and is private because it is used only to compute the public (visible) age attribute. Private components of a UDT definition are there as parts of the implementation rather than the interface.

UDT OPERATIONS

As in the Object Data Model, SQL:1999 ADT operations can be defined to provide an interface by which its value can be accessed and manipulated. These operations can be for the following purposes:

1) To compare instance of the type (EQUALS, LESS THAN, etc.)— These determine the ordering and equality of instances, and can be used in standard SQL statement predicates.
2) To retrieve useful information from the instance—This type of operation is called a FUNCTION. An SQL:1999 FUNCTION operates on one or more UDT instances and returns a single value. Note that this contrasts with an operation on an object in object data models, which must operate upon a single instance.
3) CONSTRUCTORS/DESTRUCTORS—These create and delete instances and are automatically invoked by the SQL:1999 INSERT and DELETE instructions. It is only this type of operation that can create or destroy UDT instances.
4) To convert (CAST) instances into other types.
5) To change the value of an instance.

The Example 3.32 declaration illustrates a number of operator definitions. The definition of instance equality is the default one, i.e. instances are equal if the attribute values are equal.

```
10          EQUAL DEFAULT,
```

The less than operator is undefined.

```
11          LESS THAN NONE,
```

Operations which return useful values or update the UDT attribute values are called actor functions. The Example 3.32 definition declares two of these. The first retrieves useful information, i.e. the person's age.

```
12              ACTOR FUNCTION age (:P person_type)
13                  RETURN REAL
14                  RETURN <code to calculate the age>
15              END FUNCTION
```

The second example actor function alters the state of an instance, by setting the age attribute to a new value.

```
16              ACTOR FUNCTION set_age
17                  (:P person_type, ...)
18                   RETURNS person_type
19                  < code to update the birthdate>
20                  RETURN :P
21              END FUNCTION,
```

Finally, the Example 3.32 ADT definition includes a destructor function, which deletes an ADT instance of type person.

```
22              DESTRUCTOR FUNCTION remove_person
23                  (:P person_type)
24                  RETURNS person_type
25                  <various clean_up actions>
26                  DESTROY :P;
27                  RETURN :P;
28              END FUNCTION;
```

Operations can be implemented, either by a single SQL:1999 instruction, or as (external) functions coded in some other programming language.

A single SQL statement that implements an operation may be a compound statement, i.e. a block of statements together with local variables and exception handling. A compound statement can be thought of as a SQL:1999 program or procedure. Its syntax is:

```
<compound statement> ::=
    [ <beginning label>: ]
    [ <variable declarations ]
    BEGIN
        [SQL statements> ]
```

```
            [ <exception handler> ]
     END [   <ending label> ]
```

where the exception handlers have the form,

```
     EXCEPTION [ {WHEN <condition>
       THEN <SQL statements>)} ...]
```

The syntax for an external function definition is:

```
<external function declaration> ::=
        DECLARE EXTERNAL <external function name>
        <formal parameters>
        RETURNS <result data type>
             [ CAST AS <cast data type> ]
        LANGUAGE <language name>
```

SQL:1999 also includes new statements which can be used to program operations on UDTs. These include:

1) NEW/DESTROY—used in a CONSTRUCTOR/DESTRUCTOR to create/destroy a UDT instance;
2) ASSIGNMENT—assigns the result of an SQL expression to a variable, column or attribute of a UDT;
3) CALL—to invoke an SQL procedure;
4) RETURN—to return the value of an operation on a UDT.

There are also control structures to support sequences of SQL statements, looping (LOOP, LEAVE), branching (CASE, IF), and exception handling. The net effect of including these additional features it to move SQL:1999 nearer to a programming language, rather than simply a query language.

UDT POLYMORPHISM

SQL:1999 gives support to polymorphism, as does the Object Data Model. Polymorphism is the ability to invoke an operation on any of a number of different objects and to have that object determine what to do at run time. A polymorphic function is one that can be applied in the same way to a variety of objects. The techniques used are:

1) Overloading—multiple definitions of the same operation. Name resolution is determined by a set of rules which allow a processor to distinguish between them by examining the type of the input data.
2) Coercion—the ability to omit certain type conversions
3) Inclusion—the ability to manipulate objects of a subtype as if they were of a supertype.
4) Generalisation—the ability to specify that a parameter should take on the type of some supertype during processing a specific function call.

Resolution rules must determine which implementation of a named function should be executed. These rules choose the "best match" from candidates within the scope, as follows:

1) Begin with all functions in scope.
2) For each argument, determine the functions that are a best match, and take the intersection (one function).
3) "Best match"—exact match is better than matches based on type coercion (CASTING); an implicit conversion to the closest supertype is better than SQL or user-defined type coercion; implicit SQL-defined CAST is better than implicit user-defined CAST.

UDT SUMMARY

The general syntax for an SQL:1999 definition of an ADT is,

```
<UDT_definition>::=
        CREATE [OBJECT | VALUE] TYPE
        <UDT name>
        [ <Object identifier options> ]
        [ <supertypes> ]
        [ <attributes and operations> ]
```

Note that the definition specifies if the UDT instances are objects or values (which correspond to mutable objects and literals in the Object Data Model). Object UDT instances have OIDs which may or may not be visible. A UDT may have supertypes from which it inherits characteristics. The UDT instance characteristics are attributes and operations, which may be encapsulated (PRIVATE) or not (PUBLIC).

Alternatively, they may be accessible only to the type and its subtypes (PROTECTED).

PARAMETERISED TYPES
A parameterised type defines a family of UDTs, e.g. SET(N). These correspond to type generators in the Object Data Model, and can be defined using templates (Templates will be familiar to C++ programmers),

```
CREATE TYPE TEMPLATE <name>
      ( { <template parameters> } ... )
      <ADT body>
```

There are a number of built–in parameterised types, called generators, for generating standard structured types, e.g. LIST, SET, and ARRAY.

```
ARRAY {[ <lower> .. <upper>] } ...
      OF <base type>
LIST OF <base type>
SET OF <Base type>
CHOICE ({<identifier>:base type>} ...)
RECORD ({<identifier:<bae type>}...)
```

SQL:1999 TABLES
SQL:1999 also extends the table abstraction to make rows more like objects. For example, row identifiers (which are analogous to object identifiers) can be maintained as unique and immutable identifiers for the rows in a table. These can be used as a column value or foreign key. Any table can have a row identifier defined by specifying WITH IDENTITY in the table definition. The row identifiers are in an implicit column called IDENTITY which is ignored unless explicitly referenced.

There is also a subtable facility (analogous to subtyping). A table declaration can specify supertables, using

        UNDER <table name>

In this case all columns are inherited from the supertable.

```
CREATE TABLE person
(name CHAR(20),
 sex      CHAR(1),
 spouse      person IDENTITY);

CREATE TABLE employee UNDER person
(salary FLOAT)

CREATE TABLE customer UNDER person
(account INTEGER);
```

Operations on table rows can be associated with tables to implement object-like operations. These can be specialised for subtables to support polymorphism for those operations.

```
CREATE TABLE polygon
        (xvalue LIST(FLOAT), yvalue LIST(FLOAT));

CREATE TABLE rectangle UNDER polygon;

CREATE FUNCTION area (P polygon IDENTITY,
        xs LIST(FLOAT), ys LIST(FLOAT))
                RETURNS FLOAT
BEGIN ... END;

CREATE FUNCTION area (R rectangle IDENTITY,
        xs LIST(FLOAT), ys LIST(FLOAT))
                RETURNS FLOAT
BEGIN ... END;
```

There is also a row type facility by which a row is a new kind of data type. The components of row types are called fields. The aim is to provide a single data type that represents an entire row in a table, so that complete rows can be treated as values, stored in variables, passed as parameters, etc. These row types can also be used as types for columns, thus supporting a degree of relation nesting.

```
CREATE DOMAIN uk_address ROW
(       street CHAR(30),
```

```
            city CHAR(20),
            postcode ROW
                  (original CHAR(5) plus4 CHAR(4))
      );

      CREATE TABLE employee
      (       last_name CHAR(20),
              first_name CHAR(20),
              age  INTEGER,
              address uk_address
      );
```

SQL:1999 explicitly breaks with the original definition of a table as a relation, by allowing tables to be SETs, BAGs or LISTs.

The sections above detail only the object-oriented features of SQL:1999. SQL:1999 is an extensive and large language and includes many other data representation and data management features.

3.4 PERSISTENT PROGRAMMING LANGUAGES

The approach on which ODL is based contrasts with that of persistent programming languages, where a programming language is extended to provide "database"-like capabilities by making the data items or objects defined and manipulated by the programs persistent [Atkinson 96]. A persistent object continues to exist, even after the program that created it has terminated, until it has been explicitly deleted. The aim of a persistent object-oriented programming language is therefore to create a single programming environment for both applications and database programming.

Persistent object-oriented programming language systems and object database systems can be viewed as being complementary. The former are appropriate for systems where the application and the object database are tightly integrated (such as an object implementation of the ship's navigation system of Example 1.4), whereas object database systems are more appropriate for systems where the data is viewed as a separately administered resource, sharable by many applications.

3.5 SUMMARY

Developments in computing, particularly those associated with object-oriented programming, have led to developments in database technologies. There are two main directions: **object databases** which are built on similar data models to those used in object-oriented programming and **object-relational databases** which attempt to extend the relational data model with object features. Both attempt to add more meaning or semantics to the database. They also both allow for more complex media types, such as audio and video, within the database.

The object data model has **structural** and **manipulative** parts. These are implemented in object databases with an **object definition language** and an **object query language**. Object databases also have bindings that allow these to be embedded in programming languages. Just as the relational model has a relational algebra, implemented as SQL, object databases have an object algebra implemented by the pick and mix operations of **OQL**. There is no formal model underlying the object extensions of SQL to **SQL:1999**, the query language for object-relational databases.

Both object and object-relational systems have means of expressing features such as inheritance via subtype/supertype relationships, and encapsulation. They can both include complex structures and user defined types and incorporate behaviour via methods or triggers.

EXERCISES

(3.1)   What are the characteristics of the three generations of database technology?

(3.2)   What is meant by the expression, "the semantic gap", within the context of database technology.

(3.3)   Explain what is meant by the term, "structural semantics".

(3.4)   Explain what is meant by the term "behavioural semantics".

(3.5)   When using relational database technology, how are the behavioural semantics of the data represented?

(3.6)   What features of the relational model allow the representation of structural semantics?

(3.7)   What does ODMG stand for, and why is it important?

(3.8)   If a DBMS is said to be "ODMG compliant", what does that mean?

(3.9)   What do the ODMG standards define?

(3.10)   How is OQL different from SQL?

(3.11)   When using an ODMG compliant object database, it is necessary to use ODL and also an object-oriented programming language, such as Java. Explain the respective roles of ODL and the object-oriented programming language.

(3.12)   The ODMG standards define ODL/OQL binding. What does binding mean in this context.

(3.13)   For which programming languages are bindings defined within the ODMG standards?

(3.14)   Explain the roles of the Object Database Schema preprocessor and Programming Language compiler/linker when creating an object database application.

(3.15)   What is the OMG, and how is it different from the ODMG?

(3.16)   Explain the role of an object request broker.

(3.17)   What is the relationship between IDL and ODL?

(3.18)   What does UML stand for, and why is UML important?

(3.19)   Why was UML created and by whom?

(3.20)   The relational model has just the one type of structure for representing information as data, the table (or relation). How many types of structure does the object data model have, and what are they called?

(3.21)   What is meant by "object identity" and why is it important?

(3.22)   What is meant by "object state", and why is it important?

(3.23)   What is meant by "object behaviour" and why is it important?

(3.24)   Why is it important that an object's state should include attribute values?

(3.25)   How do attribute values in an object differ from column values in a relational table?

(3.26)   What is the purpose of an object key?

(3.27)   How does an object key differ from a key of a relational table.

(3.28)   Why are keys compulsory for a relational table, but optional for an object?

(3.29)   Explain what a relationship is within the context of object state?

(3.30)   Why do objects contain relationships, but not relational tables?

(3.31)   Is the object identifier part of the object state?

(3.32)   What is the difference between an object identifier and an object key?

(3.33)   Explain the terms object equivalence and object equality.

(3.34) Explain the difference between shallow and deep object equality.

(3.35) Give an example of where objects are equivalent but not equal.

(3.36) Give an example of where objects are shallow equivalent, but not deep equivalent.

(3.37) Give an example of deep equivalent objects.

(3.38) What is an object name, and what is it used for?

(3.39) Give an example situation in which object names should be used.

(3.40) What is meant by an object's interface?

(3.41) Explain the concept of encapsulation. Why is it important?

(3.42) Give examples of object operations that would be appropriate for object which represent salespersons. Include operations which have parameters and return a value.

(3.43) Distinguish between retrieval operations and update operations. Give examples of each that would be appropriate for an object that represents a customer's account.

(3.44) Operation side effect can be dangerous when using an object database. Explain what is meant by a side effect, and give an example of how they can have undesirable consequences.

(3.45) What is the difference between an object in an ODMG object database that represents a value and one that represents an entity.

(3.46) Distinguish between an object type, and object instance and an extent?

(3.47) Distinguish between an object type and an implementation class.

(3.48) An object type to represent books in a library has attributes which represent the ISBN, title, authors. It also has operations to represent the loan and return of the book. Specify this class using UML.

(3.49) Expand the UML specification in your answer to the previous question to also represent an object type for representing borrowers and the relationship between books and the borrowers who have loaned them.

(3.50) In the ODMG object model, how are relationships between objects identified? Refer to your answer to the previous question to illustrate your explanation.

(3.51) What is a complex object? Given an example of where one would be used.

(3.52) How is it possible for an object to be an instance of more than one type? Give an example.

(3.53)   What is the ISA relationship, and why is it so called? Give an example.

(3.54)   Distinguish between a subtype and a supertype. Give examples of each.

(3.55)   Within an object database we must represent information about vehicles. All have a maximum speed and capacity in terms of the load they can carry and the number of passengers. Some are wind powered and others are powered by fuel. Some are land vehicles, others are water craft, and others still can travel over land or water. Show, with the aid of a UML class diagram, how the inheritance mechanism of the object data model can be used to represent this information efficiently and in a natural way.

(3.56)   Explain the purpose of the ODMG DDL.

(3.57)   What is the function of a DDL "module". What information can it contain?

(3.58)   Distinguish between DDL class and interface declarations. Why would a schema include both? Give examples where this is necessary.

(3.59)   An ODL schema can include the following definitions. In each case, explain their purpose and give an example of where they might be used: deftype, const, exception.

(3.60)   ODL has a block structure. Explain what this means and why it is important. Why is the block structure particularly important when two independently developed schemas are combined.

(3.61)   Within the context of a DDL schema, what is meant by the term scope?

(3.62)   Two different modules, Module1 and Module2, both include definitions of Customer classes with an Address attribute. Show how these could be both referred to from another module, Module 3.

(3.63)   What are the components of a class definition? What is the purpose of each?

(3.64)   What are the components of an interface definition? What are the purposes of each?

(3.65)   Types are given names. Is it possible for two types to have the same name. If so, how are they distinguished?

(3.66)   What is the "extent" of a type?

(3.67)   Using ODL, define a class called Vehicle. Within your declaration, define a suitable extent, attributes to represent the maximum speed, maximum load and maximum number of passengers. There should also be a vehicle reference number that is used as the key.

(3.68) Using ODL, define a class to represent cars. This should be a subclass of the vehicle class defined in your answer to question (2.67). However, in addition to the attributes of vehicle, the car class should also include attributes for engine capacity and brake horsepower.

(3.69) Distinguish between a supertype and an extender class. Give an example where both would be used.

(3.70) A hovercraft is both a land and water vehicle, and therefore inherits the properties of both the LandVehicle and WaterVehicle types, which, in turn, both inherit properties of a Vehicle type. Illustrate how these types can be defined in ODL. (HINT: You will need to use a mixture of interfaces and classes and both forms of inheritance.)

(3.71) Define a class to represent products. Include definitions of product number, name and description attributes, and also define relationships with suppliers of the products.

(3.72) What is an "Exception" in an ODL schema. Give an example of where one could be used.

(3.73) Add to your ODL definition of a product class, in your answer to (2.71) the following behaviour: operations to change the name and description of a product, and an operation to return the suppliers of a product. Each definition should include appropriate parameters and exceptions.

(3.74) Distinguish between an operation on a type and a method. How are these defined in an ODMG schema?

(3.75) What is a "structure type"? Give an example.

(3.76) What is a "collection" type? Give an example.

(3.77) Using ODL, define a structure type to represent an entry in a telephone directory. Each entry will include a name, an address and a telephone number.

(3.78) Define a Set type to represent a telephone directory, using the structure type defined in your answer to (2.77).

(3.79) Distinguish between a Set and a Bag type. Give examples of where each would be used.

(3.80) Distinguish between a List and an Array type. Give examples of where each could be used.

(3.81)   Show how a Dictionary type could be used to represent a product catalogue, which names each product and also gives its price.

(3.82)   Illustrate the use of an enumerated type to classify customers as trade, private or special.

(3.83)   What is meant by "computationally complete"? In what way is OQL not computationally complete? Does this matter?

(3.84)   What is the relationship between SQL and OQL?

(3.85)   Express the following queries in OQL, on the object database shown in Figure 3.10:

(3.86)   Retrieve details of four and five star hotels. What type of object will your query return?

(3.87)   Retrieve details of hotels with more than 1000 rooms, as a list object, within which hotel objects are in ascending order of number of rooms.

(3.88)   Retrieve details of hotels, grouped into star ratings, i.e. all of the one star hotels, all two star hotels, etc. [HINT: use GROUP BY]. Describe the type of object returned by your query.

(3.89)   Retrieve the numbers of the customers who have a reservation in hotels in the "Happy Days" chain.

(3.90)   Explain what is meant by dereferencing. Given two Hotel objects respectively named HotelOfTheWeek and BestBuy, write two queries which respectively test to see if the hotels represented by the named objects have the same name, and if they are the same hotel.

(3.91)   In what way is OQL orthogonal? Give three examples of the simplest forms of OQL query, i.e. literals and object and property names. Show how the orthogonality of OQL allows these simple queries to be combined freely within a complex query.

(3.92)   Retrieve details of hotels which have more rooms that hotels in the "Happy Days" chain.

(3.93)   Retrieve details of customers who have not made any reservations.

(3.94)   Retrieve details of customers who have made only one reservation.

(3.95)   Write a query to test if "The Grand" is part of the "Happy Days" chain.

(3.96)   Hotel objects for five star hotels are stored in an array object called LuxuryHotels. These are in descending order of number of rooms. Retrieve the largest, smallest and third largest hotel from this array.

(3.97)   In addition to the LuxuryHotels array object, there is a list object called BestBuy hotels. Retrieve details of luxury hotels that are also best buys.

(3.98)   How can you use OQL, to change the name of the "Happy Days" chain to "Short Breaks Ltd" ?

(3.99)   Given two subclasses of Customer, i.e. PrivateCustomer and CorporateCustomer, show how you can invoice all customers with a simple query on the Customer class to execute an operation, InvoiceCustomer. Explain how late binding is applied when your query is executed. Modify this query, using a class indicator so that it only generates invoices for private customers.

(3.100) Create a bag object of hotels for which reservations have been made.

Part II

THE WEB

This Part examines the second of the technologies that are used within Web databases, namely Web technology. Specifically, this Part sets out to answer the following questions:

- How does a user place information on the Web?
- How does a user gain access to information on the Web?
- How does the Web transfer information between providers and suppliers?
- How are Web users and resources protected?

4

WEB
TECHNOLOGY

This chapter explains the basics of Web technology. Specifically, it sets
out to answer the following questions:
*   What is the Web and how does it operate?
*   How did the Web originate?
*   What are the main techniques and languages for utilising the Web?

One consideration that we have taken into account when writing this
chapter is the immaturity, rapid change and lack of standardisation of
Web technologies. Many different technologies are currently being used
to support Web-based systems. This is at least in part a reflection of the
youth of the Web. No single technology provides everything that is
needed and so in many situations there are choices that must be made
between different approaches. For example, with respect to technologies
that are explained later in this and later chapters, the implementer must
choose whether to execute the processing for an application at the server
or the client, whether to use JavaScript or Java, CGI or Servlets, or
whether to use Perl for CGI programming. In some cases these choices
reflect fundamentally different approaches where one technology offers
features or functionality not available with a different approach. But in
many cases the same functionality may be obtained using different
technologies. For example, the choice between Perl and Tcl as a scripting
language for CGI programming is likely to be driven by factors such as
familiarity with one or other of these languages, or the existence of
programs that must be modified to operate via the Web. We therefore
aim to provide an overview of the features of the main technologies and
highlight their relative capabilities, rather than provide a comprehensive
description of specific proprietary systems.

Section 4.1 introduces some of the basics of Web technology, such as the parts of the Web, what they do and how they fit together, i.e. the Web architecture, protocols and operations. This section also charts the origins and history of the Web. Section 4.2 introduces how information is made accessible via the Web. Section 4.3 then gives a tutorial on the standard language for storing information on the Web, i.e. HTML. Issues concerning the appearance and processing of Web documents are discussed in Section 4.4. In particular this section discusses Cascading Style Sheets, the Document Object Model and Web cacheing. Other technologies and techniques which can be used to dynamically create Web documents, such as CGI, Java and JavaScript, are introduced in Section 4.5. Finally, in Section 4.6 we review new developments (such as XML) and their implications. The chapter concludes with a summary and exercises.

4.1 THE WEB—BASIC CONCEPTS

In this section we overview the fundamentals of the Web. First we establish what the Web is and what distinguishes it from other types of computer network. The description includes a brief overview of the Internet, since the Web is built as an Internet application. The architecture, i.e. the parts of the Web and how they fit together, is then described. Accordingly, this section includes explanations of Web Servers, Web Clients, Web sites and browsers, and the HTTP protocol used on the Web. Finally, the origins of the Web are reviewed to provide a historical context.

WHAT IS THE WEB?

The Web uses the Internet to provide facilities for:

- storing information,
- finding and retrieving information,
- storing and executing computer programs,
- inputting and manipulating information.

These are features of computer systems in general. However, what makes Web facilities enormously powerful and revolutionary is the ability to use them from almost any part of the world, by almost anyone, and using low cost computer systems and communications resources. This is because the Web can be used by anyone with access to the Internet. The Web is now therefore literally everywhere, and can be used by almost anyone for almost any purpose. Use of the Web requires only minimal training and expenditure, and is largely unregulated.

The types of information that can be represented are largely restricted only by the imagination and skills of the Web applications designers and implementers. It is standard for information stored on the Web to be represented as text, numbers, images, graphics, sound or video. It is also possible for users to devise new ways of representing and accessing information. Further, information need not be stored as a static resource on the Web, since it can be accessed or generated by programs also stored on the Web, which can interact with users to vary the information and its presentation dynamically. Consequently, users of the Web cannot just retrieve information, but can also input and manipulate information. This enables users to use the Web to execute transactions, for example to buy and sell products from or to other Web users.

As well as being multimedia, information on the Web is inter-linked. Information is stored on the Web as 'Web documents' and these can include links. A link is used to address another part of the document or a different document, in the same way that this book includes references from one chapter to another, or to other publications. Information on the Web is largely unrestricted and unregulated. Consequently, anyone with access to a Web site can add any document they choose to the Web, and link it to any other existing document. Thus, the Web forms a global, inter-linked information source, to which anyone can contribute.

EXAMPLE 4.1

Bruddersfield Museum and Art Gallery uses the Web for publicity and to sell merchandise, such as replica jewellery and prints of paintings. The information that they store describes the contents of the museum and gallery, and also acts as a 'shop window'. This particular use of the Web illustrates the features described above:

- *The museum uses the Web to store multimedia data. In addition to textual descriptions of the artifacts and paintings, there are also pictures of them, and in some cases, such as antique musical instruments, there are sounds and video sequences.*
- *The museum's information on the Web can be accessed from anywhere in the world using a low cost computer, via an Internet connection.*

- *Users can interact with the information stored on the Web, via programs also stored on the Web, to make a "virtual" tour of the museum and gallery. These programs modify the image retrieved to give the user the illusion that they are walking from room to room and from exhibit to exhibit.*
- *Links are used within the Museum's Web documents, so that the reader can follow references between parts of the document (e.g. "...for more information see..."), and also to other Web documents maintained by other museum, (e.g. "...other examples of this type can be found at the Honley Folk Museum...").*
- *Users can also input and manipulate the information stored on the Web, in this case, to make a transaction to buy items from the museum's shop. To make a transaction, the user will input data indicating which items they wish to purchase, their credit card number, and the address to which the items must be sent.*

THE WEB AND THE INTERNET

The Web provides the facilities outlined in the previous subsection by supporting a particular way of using the world wide computer network called the Internet. In this subsection we describe the Internet and how it works, so as to understand better the capabilities of the Web. This explanation is simplified and avoids technical details on communications networks, which is a wide and complex area in its own right. ([Comer 00] provides detailed description of this field for those interested in the technical details.)

The power of the Internet stems from its use of a standard communications protocol. A communications protocol specifies the formats and rules by which data can be communicated. The Internet uses two tightly linked communications protocols call TCP (Transmission Control Protocol) and IP (Internet Protocol). These are often referred to as a single protocol called TCP/IP.

TCP/IP is used by the Internet to interconnect computer networks the world over. The Internet is therefore analogous to the international telephone network that connects national telephone systems such that international calls can be made between telephones in different countries. Consequently, the Internet has a hierarchical structure—at the lowest level computers may be connected to local area networks, which are in turn connected to wide area networks, which connect to national networks, which are connected by the Internet.

The Internet provides an infrastructure by which the computers it connects (these are called hosts) can communicate. However, it cannot store information or provide services. For information and services to be accessible via the Internet they must be stored or implemented on, or accessed via, the hosts. A program executing on a host to provide services for users is called a server. For example, a host that provided access to a digital library of documents would be implemented as a server. A program that accesses the services provided by a server is called a client. The idea that some computers request resources and others provide them, i.e. a client/server architecture, is key to the organisation and operation of the Internet.

The Internet supports various types of server. Examples are:
- FTP (file transfer protocol) servers—These support the transfer of files between file directories on the users' and the server computers.
- Gopher servers—These allow users to remotely search data stores.
- Mail servers—These allow electronic mail (email) to be sent between users of the Internet.
- News servers—These can be accessed to allow reading of and posting to news discussion groups.
- Web servers—These are used to implement the Web itself.

Different types of server use different communications protocols (based upon the TCP/IP protocols) that are specific to the tasks or applications of the server. For example, an FTP server uses a protocol that is specific to transferring computer files between hosts. Collectively, these protocols, together with TCP and IP, form the TCP/IP family of protocols.

TCP/IP
The TCP/IP protocol defines the rules and mechanisms by which co-operating computers can share resources across a network. TCP/IP is concerned with:
- how hosts find each other,
- how hosts establish a connection,

- how hosts use a connection to transfer data in the correct sequence and without error.

Other protocols in the TCP/IP family use this facility for specific applications, such as file transfer or email. However, the TCP/IP protocol itself has no knowledge of the meaning or application of the data it transmits.

The different protocols used in the Internet operate at different levels forming what is called a Protocol Stack (see Figure 4.1). The following is a simplified TCP/IP Protocol Stack, in which the TCP and IP protocols are sandwiched between application specific protocols and network specific protocols.

- Application Layer—At the highest levels, protocols are concerned with performing specific applications or tasks, such as transferring files or sending email between computers (examples are Telnet, FTP, and Gopher)

- Transport Layer—At the level below the Application Layer, protocols are concerned with communication between hosts. This is the concern of TCP and of UDP. UDP is the more primitive of the two protocols, since it is "connectionless". By this we mean that it does not need to establish a connection with the host to which a message is being sent. For this reason, when UDP is used to send a message to a host, it does not know if the message has been received. TCP, on the other hand, is used to establish a connection between two hosts so that they can transmit data, and is designed to guarantee that the data as a whole arrives at its destination, complete and in the correct order.

- Internet Layer—At this level, the IP protocol is concerned with the transmission of individual messages between hosts. The data to be sent is split into small parts by higher level protocols. Each part is transmitted in a message called an IP packet. The IP protocol is used to ensure that individual IP packets are correctly transmitted. IP can be viewed as being like a postal system. Each packet includes data and an address, in the same way that an envelope contains a letter and is addressed. IP then ensures that the packet eventually arrives at the host identified by the address. The route by which the packet arrives may involve transmission between many computers connected by the Internet. This form of protocol is described as packet switching.

- Network Interface Layer—In this layer the protocols are specific to different types of network, e.g. Ethernet, X.25, ATM. These may differ from network to network, and so some form of intermediary computer that translates between the different network protocols is sometimes required. This is called a gateway. A gateway provides Internet access from one network to another.

At each level of the Protocol Stack, modules supporting the same protocol communicate with each other, forming virtual communication links. However, the way in which they actually communicate is through the lower level protocols.

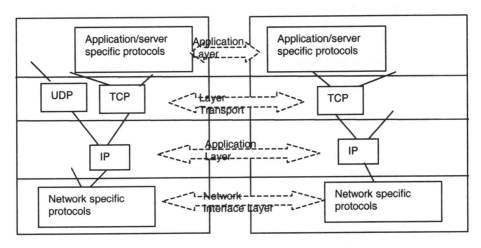

Figure 4.1 The TCP/IP Family Protocol Stack

IP ADDRESSES

The TCP/IP protocols identify each host by a unique address, called its IP Address. If we follow the analogy of the Internet being like the international telephone system, these correspond to the telephone numbers by which individual telephone connections can be uniquely addressed. An IP address is written as four numbers separated by dots. Each number is in the range 0 to 255. (123.234.5.67 is an example IP address.)

- IP Addresses are allocated by the Network Information Center (NIC). NIC allocates blocks of contiguous IP Addresses to organisations and regional networks. An IP Address comprises numbers that identify the network that the host is connected to, and the host itself. The exact way in which these are encoded within the IP address varies from network to network.

In addition, hosts are allocated symbolic addresses which can be used instead of the IP Addresses. These provide more meaningful logical names for hosts, and are implemented using a distributed system called the Domain Name System (DNS) which maps symbolic names to the numeric IP Addresses.

The symbolic names are constructed hierarchically, in a way similar to that by which the pathname of a file within a filestore is specified. However, whereas a file pathname is created by stringing together the names of the directories (or folders) within which the file resides, a symbolic IP address strings together the names of the sections or domains of the Internet within which the host is contained.

A symbolic IP address is made up of a list of names. These are separated by dots.
- The first name is that of the host.
- This is followed by a list of domain names.
- Domain names are sequenced from left to right, from the specific to the general.

In most of the world, the top-level domain name identifies a country, e.g. uk (United Kingdom), de (Germany), gr (Greece). In the USA it identifies an organisational sector, e.g. com (commercial organisation), edu (educational organisation). A second name then defines a subset of that domain, and so on, until the host has been identified. This is illustrated by the following example.

EXAMPLE 4.2

The following symbolic IP address is that of the host within the Department of Computer Science in Sheffield University:

dcs.sheffield.ac.uk

Note the hierarchical construction of the address:

- *The top-level domain name (uk) indicates that the host is within the UK domain.*
- *The second from top (ac) indicates that the host is within the academic community domain.*
- *The third from top domain is the domain for the university itself (sheffield for Sheffield University).*
- *Finally, on the leftmost side of the symbolic name is the name of the host itself (dcs for Department of Computer Science).*

The symbolic names are stored in name servers within and maintained by the organisations responsible for the networks linked by the Internet. The name servers are used to translate the symbolic names used by Internet users into the numeric IP Addresses used by the Internet protocols. The translation of a symbolic name into a numerical IP Address may require access to a number of name servers, moving progressively closer to the destination. For example, if a program is given the symbolic name in Example 4.2, it will request the name server for the uk domain for the IP Address, which in turn may request the ac name server, and so on.

Name servers can also store alternative names for hosts. These are called aliases, and provide names that are meaningful in different contexts for the same host. For example, aliases could be created so that the host at the University of Sheffield is known by alternative names, such as shef.ac.uk, sheffield.ac.uk, and www.shef.ac.uk. The aliases are often chosen so that the name conforms to some convention and may therefore be guessed. For example, www.shef.ac.uk conforms to conventions for addressing academic Web sites.

THE WEB AS AN INTERNET APPLICATION
The Web is one of a number of distributed applications, i.e. applications involving many computers, that use the Internet to provide the mechanism by which they communicate. Others include, FTP (file transfer protocol) and email.

SERVERS AND CLIENTS
The Web is implemented by programs that execute on computers connected to the Internet. The purpose of those programs is to make some of the computers behave as 'Web servers', i.e. computers that

provide information and services that can be accessed on the Web (Web resources). Other programs make computers act as "Web clients", i.e. computers that enable users to access the programs and information stored on the Web. Web-servers and Web-clients communicate via the Internet.

Web-servers are used to store the information and services that can be accessed by Web-clients. The space on a Web-server for storing these is called a Web site. A Web site is like a conventional file store in which the files contain the Web documents and other resources. Many documents are likely to be in the form of html files (see below), but they may also include plain text files, pdf files or other formats in which documents can be stored. The resources can include executable code, often called a script, to access programs and other types of server.

The Web client programs include browsers, search engines and proxy caches. The former two provide the end-user with a standard way of seeking and accessing information and other resources supported by Web servers, and are respectively described in the following two subsections. Proxy caches are a device for improving transmission speeds on the Web and are described later when Web caching is discussed (4.2 Web Caching).

BROWSERS

A browser is typically used to display Web documents and to follow the links they contain to access other Web documents or to move between different parts of a Web document. This corresponds to reading this book, and following links to related parts, e.g. see Chapter 1, or references to related documents e.g. (see [Eaglestone 98]). The documents displayed may be stored at a Web site as a Web document file, or alternatively the document may have been dynamically created by executing a script stored at the server.

Browsers are now included as standard software, sometimes bundled with the operating system (as if part of it). Other browsers are available free from Internet Service Providers (ISPs) or downloadable from the Net. Still others can be purchased at modest cost. Figure 4.2 shows the screen of a one of a number of widely used browsers, Internet Explorer [Internet Explorer]. The features and facilities are fairly standard, including the ability to access specific information or servers on the Web, to search the Web for information that satisfies users' queries.

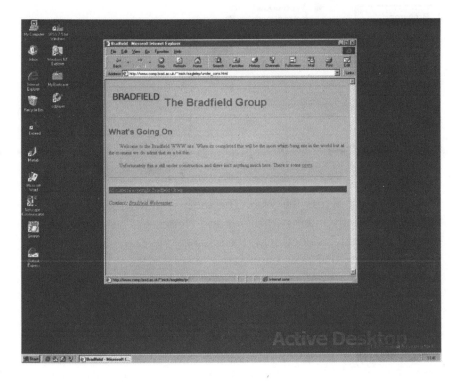

Figure 4.2 An example Web Browser screen

A Web server can be accessed simultaneously by many browsers. However, a connection between any one browser and a server will last for only one interchange of messages between them (see Figure 4.3). For example, once a browser has retrieved a Web document the connection is broken and must be created again if the browser then wishes to retrieve other documents. This has two consequences:

1) Servers are made simpler, since there is no need to maintain multiple communications channels.
2) There is no memory when a connection between a browser and a server is established of any previous connections, i.e. the protocol is "stateless". This means that other steps must be taken by browsers and servers to support transactions involving many interactions between the browser and server.

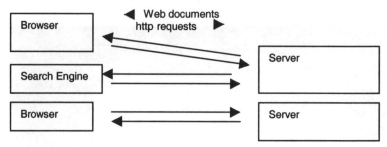

Figure 4.3 Clients and Servers

The range of browsers in use is wide and this has a strong impact on how users "see" and access the Web. The most widely used browsers are probably currently Internet Explorer and Netscape. These browsers are not as monolithic as they may seem, since there are many different versions of these that may, for example, display pages quite differently. Also the way in which browsers are used, e.g. full screen or not, images on or off, Java and JavaScript enabled or not, may affect how Web pages look. As more varied media are sent over the Web, users may receive this data in a number of ways. For example, video clips or Java applets (see below) may play within a browser or in separate dedicated windows. Also "minority" browsers, such as Lynx or Opera may only appear as being used by a very small percentage of users in some surveys, but from a worldwide audience that small percentage may still be many thousands of users. This variety is a strength of the Web, since it means that the Web is not dependent on any one piece of hardware or software. None of this need be a problem for Web authors if they remember these factors when developing Web applications. Not all users will "click here" to access information, they may "follow this link" with a variety of devices having seen (or heard) the information presented in a number of ways.

SEARCH ENGINES
Another significant type of client that accesses information on the Web is the search engine. Search engines have two roles:

1) Search engines assemble indexes to the content of documents stored on the Web.

2) They also provide search facilities for other clients. A client can access a search engine, and then submit search queries to it. The search engine will then use its index to locate relevant Web sites.

Since the Web is a decentralised structure, finding information can be hard and the development of search engines as an aid to finding information has been an important factor in making the Web usable. Most search engines are built around spiders. These are automated programs that follow links on Web pages. These enable the search engines to travel around the Web, building up their databases. The database of a search engine acts as an index to the content of the Web. The spiders access Web pages via the Web's communications protocol, HTTP (described in the following subsection), just as browsers do, but rather than display them they read the contents to build up their indexes and to find new links. The precise ways in which search engines work is not usually published for commercial reasons but more information on them, including guides for Web authors can be found at [Search Engine Watch].

THE UNIVERSAL RESOURCE LOCATOR (URL)

Each accessible Web resource has a unique address by which it is accessed, called a Universal Resource Locator (URL). These are also used within Web documents to form links and between Web documents and between Web sites. These features are illustrated in the example Web page described in Example 4.3 and shown in Figure 4.4.

EXAMPLE 4.3

Eagleley Hotels maintains Web pages for an online hotel booking service. The page for selecting a particular hotel or hotel chain is shown in Figure 4.4. Note that a link to the policy statement is shown as underlined text. The "Choose Chain" and "Choose Hotel" buttons also form links to other Web documents giving details of the hotel or hotel chain that the user selects. The "Eagleley Webmaster" text also appears underlined since that is also a link.

URLs may address many different types of resource that are available on the Internet. We shall discuss some of these later but our main concern will be with http URLs. This is the URL for a resource that will be delivered from a Web server using the http protocol, see below. The basic form of an http URL is

```
http://server/path
```

The parts of the URL, shown above are as follows:

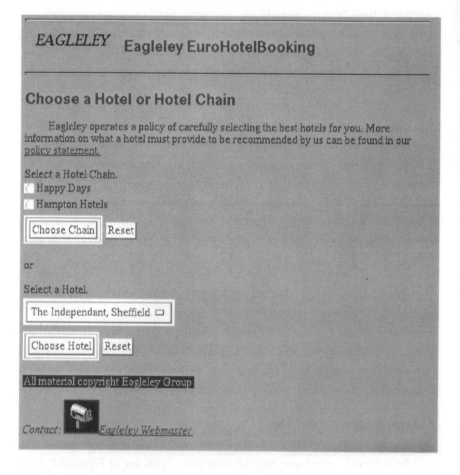

Figure 4.4 An Example Web Page for Eagleley Hotels

1) The first part, "http", specifies the protocol by which the Web resource addressed by the URL is accessed .

2) The second part, "server", is the name of the Web server on which the resource is located. This might be the IP address of the server but is more usually the DNS name for the server. The server name has the hierarchical structure shown in Example 4.2 above. For example, the Web server at that site might be "www.dcs.shef.ac.uk". The leading "www" in this example server name indicates a Web server

within the dcs.shef.ac.uk domain. It is a common convention, but only a convention, to name Web servers in this way. However, note that a server name in this form is also only a symbolic name, which will ultimately be translated into an IP address form. In fact a Web server may have many symbolic server names. Also, the server part may optionally include a port number. The convention is that Web servers operate on port 80. If a server runs on a different port this must be included in the server part of the URL, e.g.

```
http://www.eagleley.com:88
```

3) The third part of a URL, the "path" component, indicates the location of the resource on the server. This will have a form like

```
public/index.html
```

which indicates a path from the document root, via the directory structure of the Web server, to a particular file or other resource. The structure of Web sites is discussed in more detail below.

There are two important variants on the basic form of the path component of an http URL. These are:

```
path#fragment
path?search
```

1) The first variant is used to indicate a particular point, called a "fragment ", within a hypertext document. For example, the following URL addresses the part, 'appendix_1' of a Web document "annual_reports".

```
http://www.eagleley.com/annual_reports/
99.html#appendix_1
```

The detail of this form of URL is discussed in the HTML Tutorial below.

2) The second variant is used when the path indicates a resource such as an executable script. The "search" component can then hold parameters that can be passed to the script. For example, the

following URL holds the parameters, "city=berlin" and "month=july", for the Web resource, "available".

```
http://www.eagleley.com/available.pl
?city=berlin&month=july
```

This variant will be discussed further in the section on CGI and in the next part of the book.

HTTP

HTTP is the communications protocol used by the Web. Transfers from a server to a client by http are initiated by the client. The client will mostly be a browser (although servers may be contacted by other clients such as proxy caches and search engine spiders. HTTP operates as follows:

1) The client contacts the server with a document request. This will consist of a method (i.e. the name of an executable procedure associated with Web documents), a document address (the path part of a URL) and a specification of the HTTP version that is to be used. The following is an example document request:

```
GET /index.html/ HTTP1.0
```

A number of methods may be available, however not all servers will support all the HTTP methods. The most common methods are GET and POST.

2) The client can then send header information which will tell the server about itself, the User-Agent header and types of document it can accept. A blank line ends this header. The server may make use of this information to tailor what it sends to the client, e.g.

```
User-Agent: Mozilla/4.61 [en] (X11; I; SunOS
5.7 sun4u)Accept: image/gif, image/x-xbitmap,
image/jpeg, image/png, */*
```

3) The client can then send additional information, such as parameters to be sent to a script on the server via a POST method. A GET method would have sent this information in the search part of the URL, e.g.

```
GET available.pl?city=berlin&month=jul HTTP1.0
```

At this point the client has finished the first phase of the protocol. Responsibility for processing the transfer now moves to the server, which must respond to the request sent by the client.
4) First the server responds by returning a status line including an HTTP version and status code, e.g.

```
HTTP/1.0 200 OK
```

This indicates that the server uses HTTP 1.0 and that the request was successful. There is a range of server codes that can be sent to a client, however, most of these can be acted on by the client without the user being aware of them. Some codes that users may recognise, include error codes. An example is "404 Not Found". This code is sent when the requested document does not exist, and is often incorporated into an error message shown to the user.
5) Just as the client followed the request with header information, the server follows the status line with its header information. This can include information such as the type of the server, the format of the document to be returned (in Content-type), its size (in Content-length), modification time, etc. This information can include features such as a new location for a requested document sent in combination with a status code such as 301 or 302. A simple example header would look like

```
Server: Apache/1.3.6 (Unix)
Content-type: text/html
Content-length: 1001
```

A blank line terminates the header.
6) When the request has been successful, as in the example shown, the server would then send the requested data. This may be a copy of a file containing the requested document, such as the index.html

shown above, or the output from a script called by the GET or POST method using any parameters sent as part of the request, such as the output of available.pl with the parameters "city = berlin" and "month = jul" in the other example.

The above example http transaction is shown in Figure 4.5. On completion of the sequence shown the transaction is over and the connection between server and client is normally broken. If a "Connection: Keep Alive header" had been sent, the connection would have been maintained. This is useful for situations where a Web page is made up of a number of components, such as images, applets, etc., in addition to the basic html source file, and all these must be transferred to complete the Web page. Since HTTP is a stateless protocol, the client and server have no "memory" of the completed connection. Consequently any new requests must start completely afresh.

The description above outlines the 1.0 version of HTTP. More advanced features are available with HTTP 1.1, in the range of information passed in headers for example. However, HTTP 1.1 is still stateless.

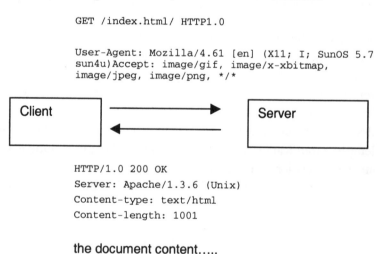

```
GET /index.html/ HTTP1.0

User-Agent: Mozilla/4.61 [en] (X11; I; SunOS 5.7
sun4u)Accept: image/gif, image/x-xbitmap,
image/jpeg, image/png, */*
```

Client → Server

```
HTTP/1.0 200 OK
Server: Apache/1.3.6 (Unix)
Content-type: text/html
Content-length: 1001
```

the document content.....

Figure 4.5 http request and response

THE HISTORY OF THE WORLD WIDE WEB

The history of the Web itself begins at the start of the 1990s with Tim Berners-Lee at CERN, the European Particle Physics Laboratory in

Switzerland. The Web was intended to allow easy collaboration between researchers, possibly at remote sites and working on different projects, by providing them with a common means of sharing information. The Web was intended, from the start, to be scalable and decentralised.

Though the history of the Web begins in the 1990s, it also has a prehistory composed of two strands, one more theoretical strand stretching back to the 1940s and the other more practical strand stretching back to the 1960s.

The theoretical strand is that of hypertext theory, and later practice. A hypertext document set is one in which there are links between related parts of the documents, and where those links can be followed by the document reader. Hypertext is the basis of the way in which information sources are represented and inter-linked when stored on the Web. The origins of hypertext may be found in Vannevar Bush's notion of the memex as elaborated in "As We May Think" [Bush 45]. Although not using modern technologies or terminologies, Bush envisaged the establishment of "trails" through a "mechanised file and library". This theoretical prehistory continues through the pioneering work of Ted Nelson, which established the terms "hypertext" and "hypermedia" and the long running Xanadu project [Nelson 95, Xanadu], and on to an increasing body of work through the 1980s (and on through the 1990s) that led to the development of a number of isolated systems. Isolated is not meant as a derogatory term. We want to contrast the aim of many hypertext systems, which was to provide links between and within a fixed set of documents on one system, with the aim of the Web which was a more all embracing attempt to link between many documents on many systems. For example, even in the mid 90s documentation for the Ingres DBMS was delivered on a proprietary hypertext system which provided extensive linking and cross-referencing through a 1000+ page documentation set. This system supplied on a single CD ROM replaced a printed technical documentation set that took over a foot of shelf space. Many of those documents, or later versions, can now be found in pdf format on the Computer Associates Web site.

The practical strand of Web history is that of communication between computers. It began with the military funded and focused ARPANET [1] which started in the late 1960s. This strand then progressed through the transformation of ARPANET into education and research funded networks, and the developments such as TCP/IP, ftp, email etc., and the building of an infrastructure of physical links and accepted protocols that now make the WWW possible.

Only when these two strands come together do we have the potential to create the Web

The Web is now about 10 years old. Its birth is usually given as 1990. It may seem in some ways older because of its fast rate of growth—Web years are often equated to real months. And it has become so much a part of life that it is hard to imagine life before the Web in some ways. This also makes it seem that the Web leapt fully formed into the world. In one sense this is true. Many of the essential elements of the Web, i.e. the basic idea of HTML, servers, clients and the protocol, were there at the start of the 1990s. The newness and phenomenal growth and penetration of the Web is apparent when we consider its treatment in very recent publications. For instance, a 1994 issue of the Communications of the ACM, which is aimed at a very computer literate and aware audience has a surprisingly introductory feature entitled "The World Wide Web" by Tim Berners-Lee and others at CERN [Berners-Lee 94]. This article is only a small part of the special issue focus on "Internet Technology" and in the article the WWW is compared to WAIS and Gopher. The WWW is shown to have overtaken WAIS in terms of the number of servers from 93 to 94 but was still smaller than Gopher.

4.2 HOW DOES A USER PUT INFORMATION ON THE WEB

Having established the concepts and historical roots of the Web, we now overview, in this section and the next, how it can be used. This section specifically answers the question, "How do users place information on the Web?" It therefore describes one of the two main components, i.e.

---

[1] ARPANET took its name from the US Department of Defense Advanced Research Projects Agency.

Web sites, in more detail. The second component, Web browsers, is described in the following section, when we answer the second question, "How do users access information on the Web?".

The structure of this section is as follows. First we describe the Web servers and Web sites. We then overview how information can be represented on Web sites. In particular, we describe the current *de facto* standard languages that are used for this purpose, i.e. HTML, Java and JavaScript.

WEB SERVERS

The Web provides facilities to store and access information and services. These are accessed from a Web client using a browser. The information and services that can be accessed in this way are stored either at Web sites implemented on Web servers, or alternatively Web servers may provide a route (a gateway) by which information stored on some other system can be accessed.

The Web server is a process running on a host computer waiting for HTTP requests to come in. On a UNIX system the server usually goes by the name of httpd (http daemon). This is similar to the way a DBMS server is usually a process running on a host waiting for requests to connect to a database to come in.

A server must be configured in a number of ways. Each server may have its own way of doing this, but a common method is that used by NCSA and Apache servers, which account for a large proportion of all Web servers. These simply use four files: *httpd.conf, srm.conf, access.conf, mime.types*. These are set up to suit local circumstances by the person running the Web server, the webmaster, just as a database administrator will configure a database management system. Many of the configuration details may be unknown to users putting information on the Web site, just as database users may only know a little of how a DBMS is configured and run. However, sometimes users will need to know some of this information in order to get their Web pages working in the manner they wish.

The server configuration files are used as follows:

- They establish how the server runs, e.g. on what port it listens, its name and any aliases, and what logging information is kept.
- They also configure how resources on the server are processed and delivered, such as setting up virtual directories (see below).
- Limits on access to particular resources by certain users or from clients in particular domains can also be set.
- By defining MIME (Multipurpose Internet Mail Extension) types, this sets the type of files, as designated by file extension, and consequently determines how they should be treated. HTTP has inherited this system which as its name implies originated with Mail systems.

THE STRUCTURE OF WEB SITES

Web sites are used to store information and provide services that are made available to Web users via browsers (described in the following section). These are installed on Web servers.

A Web site has a structure that is normally associated with the file store of a computer. In fact, once a Web site is installed, it appears simply as a part of the file system of the users' computer system. The Web site exists for the users of that site as a set of directories, each of which can store files and other directories. Information accessible on the Web is stored in the files.

The directories and files on a Web server may be located on the server, or on other servers. However, this physical distribution is not apparent to users, who see a hierarchy of directories, similar in appearance to the directories of a file store on a PC. The root directory, i.e. the directory at the top of the hierarchy is created when a Web site is first created. This is typically called WWWRoot and will be contained within a directory also with a default name, such as InetPup or WebShare. WWWRoot is the root directory for the Web site and is the home directory for the site created. This home directory is accessed using either the URL or IP address of the Web site.

Directories can store information as files, as well as other directories. Information stored within the files is represented as documents, called Web Pages, which can be coded in various languages and accessed using a browser (described in the next section), providing the browser includes the appropriate parser for the language(s) used to encode the document. The standard language for presenting information on the Web is called HTML (Hypertext Markup Language). However, there are other languages that can be used for this purpose. HTML and other Web languages are described in following subsections.

The home page for a Web site is stored as a file in the Home directory, and this contains the information that is accessed by the URL or IP Address. A blank home page will be automatically created when a Web site is created, and given a default name, typically default.htm or index.html, depending on the server used.

The Home directory of a Web site is located within the file system of the computer on which the server is installed (though not necessarily as the root of the file system). All subdirectories and their files of the Root directory can be accessed using the appropriate URL and path name, as illustrated in the following example.

EXAMPLE 4.4

The Eagleley group organises the material on its Web site into a number of directories below the root directory. One example is that information based on the company's annual reports is stored in an "annual_reports" directory. The URL below would access the 1999 document.

```
http://www.eagleley.com/annual_reports/99.html
```

In addition, it is possible to add to the Web site directories that are not physically stored as subdirectories of the Root directory. These are called virtual directories. The technique is also sometimes called aliasing. For example, a Web page can be created in a user's (conventional) directory, and then made accessible at the Web site by including it as a virtual directory. The alternative strategy is to physically create a new subdirectory of the Root directory and then to copy the Web page file into it.

A Web server will include tools for creating a Web site, and for adding, deleting or editing virtual directories. Note that when a virtual directory is deleted from a Web site, it still remains in its physical situation. Virtual directories can be thought of as links to physical directories stored elsewhere in the file system.

REPRESENTING INFORMATION ON THE WEB

Information is represented on a Web site as Web documents stored as files within the Web site directory or its subdirectories. Web documents can be created using various languages. The most commonly used is called HTML.

Web documents are typically text documents, but can also contain other media, such as images, sounds and video. They are therefore called media documents. A Web document can also contain programs that execute on the client system which accesses it, or on the server system. This facility provides enormous potential for novel applications.

HYPERLINKS

Web documents can contain links between different parts of the document and to parts of other documents, possibly stored on other Web servers. For this reason, they are also called hypermedia documents—the term "hyper" refers to this ability to create links that can be navigated using Web browsers to move directly from one part of a document to other related parts, or from one document to another. For example, hyperlinks can be used to connect a document to documents that it references. Example 4.3 and Figure 4.4 illustrated these properties.

Web documents are usually encoded using HTML (hypertext markup language). HTML is a markup language. A markup language allows the contents and presentation of a document to be described by including code within the document itself to identify and delimit its different parts, and to specify how they should be interpreted by browsers. This contrasts with other meta-languages (i.e. descriptive languages), where the descriptive code is separate from that which it describes. For example, in a relational database system (see Chapter 2), the description of the database structures is stored separately from the data itself. Users of the Unix operating system will be familiar with examples of markup languages, such as Latex and troff. However, both are untidy examples, since both Latex and troff have dual roles, specification of the format of data, and also how data should be presented or displayed.

The origins of HTML lie in a more general markup language, called SGML (Standard Generalised Markup Language) [Goldfarb 91]. SGML is in fact a meta-language for defining markup languages, and has a sound theoretical basis. HTML started as an SGML-like application and moved to a formal definition as an SGML application as it progressed through its different versions. SGML itself has, since the growth of the Web, given birth to a new meta-language XML (Extensible Markup Language) [XML Cover Pages]. XML and its implications are discussed at the end of this chapter.

4.3 AN HTML TUTORIAL

Skills in the use of HTML are essential for building effective Web applications, in the same way that SQL skills are important for those who wish to develop relational databases. Often HTML code is automatically generated by Web Document authoring tools. These are supported by Web browsers and by many word-processors. For example, the Microsoft Word word-processor provides the option to edit and save text as an HTML document. However, to fully exploit the capabilities of the Web it is still often necessary to access and directly modify HTML code.

We therefore present an HTML tutorial in a similar style to the SQL tutorial in Chapter 2. This progressively takes readers through HTML features. The major parts of HTML are illustrated by building up a simple Web page. The aim here is not to give an exhaustive guide to all the HTML tags and their uses but rather to indicate the fundamental features of HTML. Readers are encouraged to work through the tutorial and also the exercises at the end of this chapter using a computer to implement the example Web pages.

HOW TO CREATE HTML DOCUMENTS

HTML documents can be written directly in HTML code, using an appropriate text editor, such as Notepad in a Windows environment, SimpleText on a Macintosh, and vi, pico or emacs in a UNIX environment. The file created should have an extension name ".html" (or ".htm" in environments where the extension is limited to three letters, as in Windows 3.x). This meets the MIME type convention outlined earlier. Other tools can be used for creating HTML documents. Word processing systems such as Word allow documents to be saved as HTML. Some browsers also have a document creation mode as well as the document viewing one. While such tools have some advantages, such as productivity, and may be useful for converting existing documents to HTML, they can also produce HTML of uncertain quality.

The HTML documents that you create in the course of this tutorial can be opened and viewed using a browser. Normally, you will open Web documents stored at Web sites, using their URLs. However, when developing and testing a Web document it is also possible to open it from local filestore. This can be done using the "File menu" of the browser and selecting the operation for opening a file, e.g. '"Open", "Open Page", "Open File with Browser", "Browse..." or "Choose File...", etc., depending on the browser that you are using.

It may also be useful to readers to view HTML code for documents accessed on the Web, for example, to analyse how their features are achieved. This is also possible with a browser, using the "View" menu and by selecting "source", "Document Source", etc., depending on the browser.

A VERY SIMPLE HTML EXAMPLE

The first HTML example (Example 4.5) defines a minimal Web page. In fact, it has no content at all (the Web document is a blank screen!) and serves only to illustrate the form of HTML tags.

EXAMPLE 4.5

The following HTML defines a blank Hypermedia document.

```
<HTML>
<HEAD>
</HEAD>      }
<BODY>
</BODY>      }
</HTML>
```

Example 4.5s HTML illustrates a number of HTML features.
- We can see the basic form of an HTML tag. This is, the name of the tag enclosed in angle brackets e.g. <BODY>.
- We can also see the use of paired start and end tags e.g. <HEAD> and </HEAD> which effectively define a container for the part of

the document content specified by the tag pair. Note, the end tag must have the same name as the start tag but with a leading "/". (These pairs are indicated by the braces, "}", which are not part of the HTML.)

- We can also see that some tags occur within the scope of others e.g. <HEAD> ... </HEAD> is within <HTML> ... </HTML>

Some further points can be made with this simple HTML example:

- The tags are shown in upper case. This has been common practice so as to make the tags stand out from normal text which is mostly in lower case. This may be a less significant issue if an HTML aware editor is used for Web page creation, since this may well highlight tags by some other means such as colour.
- HTML tags are in fact case insensitive, so <BODY> and <body> are equivalent and we could match the opening <BODY> with a closing </body>.

COMMON ERRORS—OVERLAPPING TAG PAIRS

Example 4.5 is a valid (if trivial) piece of HTML. We will consider what *valid* means in more depth further on. However, even with such a simple piece of code, there is still scope for error. Common errors are illustrated in the following examples.

EXAMPLE 4.6

The following HTML is invalid because of overlapping tag pairs, as indicated by the braces.

```
<HTML>
<HEAD>
whatever
<BODY>
</HEAD>
</BODY>
</HTML>
```

We can see that the HEAD and BODY tags overlap, that is one is not closed before the other opens (as shown by the braces). We have the sequence

```
<HEAD><BODY>whatever</HEAD></BODY>
```
which is not valid HTML. It can be seen that the "whatever" content is both in the head and the body.

In general a tag pair must be wholly contained within any outer tag pairs.

We should also note that the layout of the HTML is not significant. The two HTML examples in Example 4.6 will have the same effect. However, it may be considered good practice to lay HTML out clearly where possible, putting tags on separate lines from the content. However, the layout of HTTP headers sent by a Web Server before the HTML itself, is significant.

COMMON ERRORS—REPEATED SINGULAR TAGS

Some tags may occur only once in an HTML document, as illustrated in Example 4.7.

EXAMPLE 4.7
The following HTML is not valid since it contains two bodies.

```
<HTML>
<HEAD>
</HEAD>
<BODY></BODY>
<BODY></BODY>
</HTML>
```

VALIDITY AND INVALIDITY

Although we are still considering an HTML page that has no content it is worth considering what we mean by valid and perhaps, in contrast, what works. Valid HTML satisfies the HTML language specification. In the previous examples we have not mentioned what specification that is. However, we can add to our HTML document a DTD (Document Type Definition) that specifies what version of HTML we are claiming our document meets. An example is

```
<!DOCTYPE HTML PUBLIC "-//W3C//DTD HTML 4.0
Transitional//EN">
```

This can be added as the first line of our HTML document, before the opening HTML tag in order to declare that this HTML meets the 4.0 specification in its "loose" or "transitional" form. By adding this line we are saying that the way we use subsequent tags is with the meaning given to them in that standard.

However, what works and what is valid are two different things. Browsers, in general, are very accepting of errors in HTML. For example, an early version of Netscape accepted pages with multiple bodies and some Web authors have exploited this "feature" [Musciano 97 p 12]. In fact, many browsers pay no attention at all to the DTD and simply interpret the HTML tags according to their own built-in set of rules. Also, unknown tags are ignored. Consequently, the Example 4.8 HTML will have exactly the same effect at that in Example 4.5.

EXAMPLE 4.8

The following HTML is not valid, since "RUBBISH" is an unknown tag. The RUBBISH tags will therefore be ignored.

```
<!DOCTYPE HTML PUBLIC "-//W3C//DTD HTML 4.0
Transitional//EN">
<HTML>
<HEAD>
</HEAD>
<BODY>
<RUBBISH> </RUBBISH>
</BODY>
</HTML>
```

ADDING CONTENT TO HTML

We are now in a position to start to add some real content to our example HTML. HTML is a markup language and the tags already introduced are applied to the content of Web documents to specify how that content is to be structured and presented.

HEADINGS AND PARAGRAPHS

Example 4.9 illustrates how HTML can be used to markup text. The purpose is to specify how the text is to be structured and hence displayed. Specifically, the example illustrates how headings and paragraphs of a Web document are specified.

EXAMPLE 4.9

The following HTML defines the Web document shown in Figure 4.6. Note the use of the tags, TITLE, H1, H2 and P. These specify respectively that the text contained in the tag pair should be displayed as the document title, headings, and a paragraph.

```
<HTML>
<HEAD>
<TITLE>Statement of Ownership</TITLE>
</HEAD>
<BODY>
<H1> Eagleley EuroHotel Booking</H1>
<H2>Statement of Ownership</H2>
<P>
Eagleley EuroHotelBooking is a wholly owned
subsidiary of the
Eagleley Group.
</P>
</BODY>
</HTML>
```

Eagleley EuroHotel Booking

Statement of Ownership

Eagleley EuroHotelBooking is a wholly owned subsidiary of the Eagleley Group.

Figure 4.6 The Web document specified by the Example 4.9 HTML

Note the structure of the Example 4.9 HTML. In it we have:
- a title which occurs in the HEAD section of the HTML
- headings H1 and H2 which occur within the BODY
- a paragraph which occurs within the BODY.

All of these tags act as containers, that is, the content appears between start and end tags. Formally, the combination of a start tag, the content and the end tag, is called an **element**.

It is possible to omit some end tags, since the closing of some tags can be inferred by the opening of a subsequent tag. For example part of our body could have been:

```
<P>
Eagleley EuroHotelBooking is a wholly owned
subsidiary of the
Eagleley Group.
<P>
```

```
The Eagleley Group was established in 1998 and
is a private limited company owned by B.
Eaglestone and M. Ridley.
</BODY>
```

In this case, the closure of the first paragraph can be inferred by the opening of the second, since it is not possible to nest paragraphs inside one another. The second paragraph is implicitly closed by the end of the body.

This approach of omitting implicit closing tags can be found in many Web pages. In fact, early versions of HTML defined <P> as a separator rather than the start of a container and it is still often used as if it were only a separator between paragraphs. However, in general we believe that it is good practice to explicitly close HTML tags, even when it would still be valid HTML to omit the end tags. One good reason for this is that style sheet support in browsers generally works better with all end tags present. Another reason is that your pages are not then at the mercy of the, possibly faulty, interpretation of the HTML by all the many different browsers that will view your pages.

LINKS

The Web page we have presented so far is a dead end on the 'information superhighway', that is it has no links to anything else. However, one of the powers of the Web is the ability to create a network of links between related information and services. In HTML this is done by adding links from within one HTML document to others. For example, we can add links with the anchor tag, <A ...>...</A>, as illustrated in Example 4.10.

EXAMPLE 4.10

The following HTML specified the text "Eagleley Group" as a link to another Web page, addressed by the URL "http://www.eagleley.com/index.html".

```
Eagleley EuroHotelBooking is a wholly
owned subsidiary of the
<A HREF =
"http://www.eagleley.com/index.html">Eagleley
Group</A>
```

The link in Example 4.10 is to another Web page, in this case the Eagleley Group Home page. When the Web document is displayed on a browser, the user has the option of selecting the link text, " Eagleley Group", within the displayed document. This will cause the addressed Web document to be displayed.

The structure of the anchor tag is more complex than the previous tags we have looked at. Following the starting "<" and tag identifier, "A" (for anchor), we have

```
HREF = "http://www.eagleley.com/index.html"
```

This occurs before the start tag is closed i.e. ">". This is then followed by the link's content; i.e. the text which a browser will display as the link. The link content is then followed by the closing tag </A>.

"HREF" is an attribute and "http://www.eagleley.com/index.html" is the attribute value. In this case the attribute is a hypertext reference and its value is therefore the address of what we are linking to. The value is given by the URL.

ABSOLUTE, PARTIAL AND RELATIVE LINKS

In Example 4.10 the link is an **absolute link,** i.e. the full URL is given. The full URL specifies the protocol to be used, the domain name, and the pathname, as in Figure 4.7.

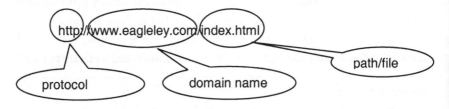

Figure 4.7 The components of a URL

The full URL may be abbreviated in some circumstances. It is possible to omit the protocol, the domain name and some path information. Relative links can be specified as the value of an HREF attribute. These give the location of a page relative to the location of the current Web page. For example, consider the following situation:

- the Example 4.10 HTML is stored at URL,
  http://www.eagleley.com/exampledoc.html.

- the link in the Example 4.10 HTML is rewritten as

```
HREF = "index.html"
```

In this case the link is a relative link, since it does not provide the full URL. Therefore the browser can create the full URL by using the path component and the domain name of the current Web page with the information specified in the link. Thus, the relative link becomes:

```
HREF = "http://www.eagleley.com/index.html"
```

In the example above the link is given relative to the current Web page. It is also possible to indicate links by their relative position from a different URL. This is done by setting the base URL. A base tag, <BASE>, can be included in the HEAD of an HTML document and then all relative URLs in the document are resolved from that base URL. Thus if we had

```
<BASE HREF= "http://www.eagleley.com/public/">
```

in the HEAD of a document, a subsequent link of

```
HREF = "/index.html"
```

would not resolve to the index.html of the current directory or to index.html in the root directory, but to

```
HREF = "http://www.eagleley.com/public/index.html"
```

It is also possible to give URLs to a point within a document. URLs discussed previously refer to an entire document. However, references to a fragment are particularly useful within large Web documents. Creating an anchor at a point in a document in the following way does this.

```
<A NAME="top_of_the_page">
```

This can then be referenced as

```
go back to the <A HREF="#top_of_the_page">top</A>
```

LINKS TO DIFFERENT TYPES OF SERVER OR RESOURCE

On many Web pages, the links will usually be of the most common type, i.e. an http URL. However, various links are available such as mailto URLs. For example we could add a contact email address with

```
<A HREF="mailto:info@eagleley.com">
Eagleley Webmaster</A>
```

Following this link, i.e. the text " Eagleley Webmaster" in the example, should activate an email tool which will automatically create a new email message addressed to info@eagleley.com.

Other types of link can be to ftp servers, Gopher servers, WAIS files and to newsgroup servers, etc. The type of link is specified by the protocol part of the URL. For example, the links to the above types of server are respectively specified by the following protocols: ftp, gopher, WAIS and news.

Links may also be made with an http URL to other document formats. These might be plain text or pdf (Portable Document Format). The latter can be used where precise layout of a document is important. A link to a plain text file might look like

```
Instructions on installing the software can be
found
<A HREF="plaintexts/install.txt">here.</A>
```

This uses a relative URL but indicates the file can be found in a directory "plaintexts" off the current location, unlike the example above where the relative URL referenced a resource in the same directory. The file extension "txt" also indicates that this is a plain text document as opposed to an html document. The server delivering the documents needs to be configured correctly to do this. The MIME type information uses file extensions to denote the type of document and hence what http header information should be sent.

A pdf document might be referenced as

```
If you agree please sign and return one of our
<A HREF="contracts/faust.pdf"> standard
contacts</A>
```

In these cases the text and pdf files will be delivered by the server in response to the user's request. What the user sees will depend on their browser set up and is discussed in a later section.

The links above have all been created with the anchor tag <A>. However, there is also a separate <LINK> tag within HTML which, although little used, provides a framework for defining the relationships between documents rather than actual links in documents.

LISTS

HTML includes the facility to construct lists. There are two basic types, ordered lists, denoted by <OL> and unordered lists, <UL>. Ordered lists have attributes for setting the starting number and the style of numbering. For example <OL START = 3 TYPE = a> would create a list that was numbered with lower case letters starting at "c", the third letter in the alphabet. This tag has attributes and attribute values expressed in a similar way to those used above. This type of list would usually be presented in the Web document in a form something like the following:

>   c. First item in the list.
>   d. Second item in the list
>   ...

Example 4.11 illustrates the use of lists.

EXAMPLE 4.11

The HTML code below represents a list of Eagleley Offices in a number of ways.

1) *In this first example within the <UL> </UL> tags we have four list items enclosed within the list item tags <LI> </LI>.*

```
<UL>
<LI>Eagleley UK: Huddersfield</LI>
<LI>Eagleley USA: New York</LI>
<LI>Eagleley USA: San Francisco</LI>
<LI>Eagleley Switzerland :Geneva</LI>
</UL>
```

2) *Lists may be nested. This is illustrated below by including another list as part of the list item for Eagleley USA. This is shown indented but the source code layout has no meaning.*

```
<UL>
<LI>Eagleley UK: Huddersfield</LI>
<LI>Eagleley USA:
    <UL>
       <LI>New York</LI>
       <LI>San Francisco</LI>
    </UL>
</LI>
<LI>Eagleley Switzerland: Geneva</LI>
</UL>
```

Most popular browsers will present lists in similar ways, often indenting the text slightly and starting each item with bullets. Nested lists will often have a different bullet style. However, lists do not have a fixed presentation. One example rendering of the Example 4.11 (2) code is shown in Figure 4.8. Given the differences between browsers, it is strongly recommended that you try the appearance of lists in various browsers and do not make undue assumptions about how the list will appear. It is acceptable to refer to "the third item" in a list in the text but you should avoid referring to item (i) since that might be represented by something similar, such as i.) or simply i.

- **Eagleley UK: Huddersfield**
- **Eagleley USA:**
    - New York
    - San Francisco
- **Eagleley Switzerland: Geneva**

Figure 4.8 Sample list display

TABLES

HTML also includes the ability to construct tables within a Web page. These should be used for tabular information and not simply used as a layout tool for lining up text on a Web page. This is because the effects are very unreliable in many viewing situations. We could use tables to present the Eagleley office information since this can be viewed as a grid containing countries and corresponding cities. A simple presentation would be

```
<TABLE border = 1>
<TR><TD>Eagleley
UK</TD><TD>Huddersfield</TD></TR>
<TR><TD>Eagleley USA</TD><TD>New York</TD></TR>
<TR><TD>"</TD><TD>San Francisco</TD></TR>
<TR><TD>Eagleley
Switzerland</TD><TD>Geneva</TD></TR>
</TABLE>
```

In the above examples we use an attribute "border" with a value 1 to indicate that the table should have a visible border. Within the table tags we have a number of table rows <TR> </TR> each of which may contain a number of items of table data within <TD> </TD>. In this case each row has two columns. For our convenience we have laid out the source code so that each row of the table is on one line of source code. Tables may also include column headers indicated with <TH> </TH>. For example, we could have inserted the following after the opening table tag and before the first row of table data

```
<TH><TD>Organisation</TD><TD>Office</TD></TH>
```

This is often presented in a bolder text form than normal data. Tables have a large number of other features, such as the ability to position the data within the cells in different ways, set background colours, add captions, etc. Not all of these features may be standardised or supported by all browsers. Therefore, you should check current HTML standards and how well these are implemented by browsers before using the more advanced features. Within tables the use of closing tags, even where these can be inferred, is strongly recommended since this is a known problem with browsers.

Tables may be nested. For example, we could have structured our information so that the offices of Eagleley USA are represented in a separate table within the larger table, thus;

```
<TABLE border = 1>
<TR><TD>Eagleley
UK</TD><TD>Huddersfield</TD></TR>
<TR><TD>Eagleley USA</TD>
    <TD>
    <TABLE>
        <TR><TD>New York</TD></TR>
        <TR><TD>San Francisco</TD></TR>
```

```
      </TABLE>
      </TD>
   </TR>
   <TR><TD>Eagleley
   Switzerland</TD><TD>Geneva</TD></TR>
   </TABLE>
```

The above HTML will define the display in Figure 4.9, or something like it, depending on the browser used.

Eagleley UK	Huddersfield
Eagleley USA	New York San Francisco
Eagleley Switzerland	Geneva

Figure 4.9 Sample table display

IMAGES

Images can be inserted into a Web page by including the <IMG> tag in HTML. Unlike the tags above, IMG has no end tag. An example would be

```
   <IMG SRC="eagleley_trans.gif" ALT="EAGLELEY." >
```

This code is used in the Figure 4.4 example. The tag, as used here, has two attributes: SRC whose value gives the filename that contains the image, so that it can be fetched via HTTP, and ALT whose value gives alternative text that can be used as a substitute, for example when images are not loaded. The IMG tag can have a number of other attributes largely for presentational purposes, indicating its size and alignment on the page, etc.

HTML FORMS

The FORM tag opens the way for user interaction with a Web page, by giving a user a way of inputting information and sending this to a server. The FORM is contained within <FORM>...</FORM>. The opening tag is usually of the following format

```
<FORM METHOD=GET ACTION="available.pl">
```

The attributes should be familiar from the discussion of HTTP above, since the first is an HTTP method and the second the URL that will be requested via the method given. The action shown uses a relative link but other forms of URL could be used here. A number of other elements may occur within the form tag, but the most significant is the <INPUT> tag. This allows the user to submit information to the resource named in the action. Information may be submitted in a number of ways, for example, by directly entering data or choosing from a list in the form.

An example form is shown below. This shows a number of features, such as attributes given to the <INPUT> tag. These set the parameter name, type of input and size of the data entry item. Other INPUT tags include the SUBMIT one which sends the form data as defined in the ACTION and a RESET one to clear the form. The value attribute of these sets the text displayed, for example, on a button. Within the form, text and formatting tags can be seen.

```
<FORM ACTION= "available.pl" METHOD=GET>

<P>
 Find out more about Eagleley's
'Summer in the City' offer. Enter the city of
'your choice.
</P>

<INPUT TYPE =text NAME =city size=28>
<P>
Select the month.
</P>

<input type=radio name=month value="jun"> June
<BR>
<input type=radio name=month value="jul"> July
<BR>
<input type=radio name=month value="aug">
August
<BR>

<INPUT TYPE=SUBMIT VALUE="More information">
<INPUT TYPE=RESET VALUE ="Clear Form">
</FORM>
```

Forms will be discussed in more detail later in the book in the context of building Web database applications.

STRUCTURE AND PRESENTATION

Thus far in this tutorial we have said only a little about the appearance of the page. HTML tags have been introduced to declare parts of the content to be a title or a heading, etc. However, we have emphasised the structural markup of the Web page and what each part represents, rather than how it will appear.

The structural markup is a very important aspect of HTML and one which is often neglected.

- By defining the structure we have a means of producing truly cross platform content that can be understood and used effectively with, not only the commonly used graphical browsers such as Netscape and Internet Explorer, but also by significant Web page visitors such as search engines' spiders.
- Well-defined Web pages in terms of structure will also work well in environments, such as speaking browsers for the blind and partially sighted and mobile browsers that may have limited screen space and graphic capabilities.
- Correct use of structure will in general future proof your Web pages for the applications you do not know about at present but which may be very significant for your Web pages in the future.

HTML also contains a number of essentially presentational features. These were mostly introduced at an early stage in the history of HTML. Although still supported by browsers, presentation features are now deprecated in newer versions of HTML, usually in favour of style sheet methods of providing presentational information. A simple example, that does not even need style sheets, is in how we emphasise text. HTML contains a BOLD tag. We could therefore use this to highlight Eagleley's name.

```
The<B>Eagleley Group</B> was …
```

However, it is better to use a structural alternative

```
The <STRONG>Eagleley Group</STRONG> was ..
```

On many browsers the effect will be the same, i.e. the same font size and type will be used and "Eagleley Group" rendered in the bold version of that font. The structural version is, however, more likely to give a better result in a number of situations. For example, if a user has set their browser to already use bold versions of fonts then <BOLD> text will not stand out. <STRONG> text, which can be highlighted in another way, e.g. with a larger font or different colour, will stand out.

The advantages of structural markup can also be seen with headings. If text is marked as a heading, a search engine can use that information in the short displays of what is on a Web page. On the other hand, if the heading was indicated using representation markup, by specifying normal text in a large bold font, the user might see the same appearance but the search engine would not see the distinction between that "heading" and normal text.

Headings also show what may be considered to be a weakness in the structural side of HTML. We have used a top level heading <H1>, followed by the next level <H2>. In fact, HTML has levels from <H1> to <H6>. This would seem to be a sensible hierarchical way to use headings. However, this hierarchy is not in general enforced by HTML editors or validators and it is common to see headings start at <H2> and for presentational reasons the next level to be used might be <H4>.

Other tags such as <CITE>, <CODE> and <ADDRESS> give structure to the text in a Web page and as a *side effect* a certain sort of presentation.

SOME MORE ADVANCED FEATURES

It is possible to consider the visual appearance of a Web page and still produce HTML that works in a wide variety of situations. For example, we could substitute or complement some of the links used in earlier examples with the following piece of HTML.

```
<!-- standard footer -->

<DIV>
<HR>

<A HREF="http://www.eagleley.com/">
<IMG SRC="home.jpg" ALIGN="LEFT" ALT="Home
"></A>
```

```
<A HREF="mailto:info@eagleley.com">
<IMG SRC="envelope.jpg" ALIGN="RIGHT"
ALT="Email "></A>

</DIV>
```

Here we have set up a standard piece of HTML that might be used at the bottom of a number of pages on the same site. There are a number of features that we can consider.

- There is a comment, i.e. the text "standard footer" between <!-- and --> . In general HTML comments are enclosed within <!-- and -->. Note, however that comments within HTML can be problematic, particularly when character sequences such as -- or > are found within the commented text, as can be the case with JavaScript.

- The fragment of HTML is enclosed within a DIV. This groups this part of the HTML into one section. This can then be used to apply features to the section as a whole, directly by setting an attribute for the DIV e.g. <DIV ALIGN = "center"> or via style sheets where the type of section would usually be given by setting the class attribute e.g. <DIV CLASS = "footer">.

- In the DIV we also have the use of a presentational feature, the horizontal rule <HR>. Like the image tag discussed above and the line break <BR> this tag is complete and has no corresponding end tag.

- Here we also have hyperlinks but these contain images rather than text within the anchor tags. As in the earlier use of an image, an ALT text is provided so that the page will still appear sensible and usable with or without images. Representations of this code are shown in Figures 4.10 and 4.11.

Figure 4.10 "Standard footer" as displayed in Netscape

```
Home Email
```

Figure 4.11 "Standard footer" as displayed in Lynx

WRITING GOOD HTML

In the tutorial sections above we have outlined some of the main features of HTML. This did not cover all the tags in HTML or some important related issues such as style sheets, which are discussed separately below. The Web itself contains many other tutorials and the specifications of HTML (at the W3C Web site, www.w3.org) and the HTML underlying any Web page you visit can be seen, usually via a "View Source" option in a browser. These sources and the use of a validator as discussed in the next section should enable you to produce good HTML. By good we mean HTML that is syntactically valid and works well in a number of viewing situations. The differences in the ways different browsers present Web pages will be discussed in 4.3.

HTML VALIDATION

Familiarity with the basics of HTML are essential for any Web author but fortunately authors do not have to check all their HTML by hand since there are computer programs to do this. These are HTML validators. Since HTML is an SGML application, validators are generally SGML parsers. They read through HTML source code, applying the rules specified by the DTD and report any errors. They come in two basic forms, online and offline.

1) Online validators appear as Web pages. An example is the validator at W3C (http://validator.w3.org/). These allow authors to submit Web pages or fragments of code for testing.
2) Offline validators are computer programs that take HTML as input and report errors (or success). Those coming from a programming background may like to compare this with the way a compiler parses program source code and reports any errors.

Checking that a Web page works in a browser may be a start to the validation process, but it is no substitute for real validation. Browsers are built to be forgiving in what they display. That is, they will ignore, or try to make sense of, errors and show something. However, not all browsers will make the same allowances. They will not all interpret errors or omissions in the same way.

A related issue is checking Web pages for accessibility. Some HTML constructions may make Web pages harder to use for those with disabilities. The HTML may be syntactically correct, so it will pass validation, but it may be unusable to many of your potential audience. Particular uses of structural features such as tables for presentational purposes may not make sense in some browsing situations. Services like [Bobby] offer advice and testing of Web pages on these issues.

4.4 PRESENTATION AND PROCESSING OF WEB PAGES

The preceding section overviewed features of the *de facto* standard language used to markup information stored on the Web. This section discusses two related issues, the presentation and processing of information on the Web. The first subsection describes cascaded style sheets, since these are used to suggest how sets of pages should be represented. The second subsection discusses the Document Object Model (DOM). The DOM is of great potential importance, since it attempts to establish a standard way of defining the structure of Web documents, so that programs, such a search engine spiders, can process them. Finally, in the third subsection we discuss Web caching, a technique for reducing the speed of Web page retrieval.

CASCADING STYLE SHEETS

In the preceding sections we have stressed the desirability of specifying structure over presentation in HTML. This is not to say that the appearance of HTML is unimportant. What must be remembered is that it is almost impossible to *fix* how a Web page will appear. There are too many variables in the viewing situation which are out of the Web author's control. These include

- the type of browser
- the screen size
- the proportion of the screen given to the browser
- the proportions of the browser
- the facilities enabled on the browser (e.g. Java and JavaScript)
- the fonts available to the browser
- the user's preferences (e.g font sizes, types and colours).

In order to attempt to ensure some consistency of presentation, Web authors can *suggest* how a Web page should appear by specifying a style sheet to be used with the page. This is done in the head of an HTML document with

```
<LINK REL=Stylesheet HREF="whatever.css"
TYPE="text/css">
```

EXAMPLE 4.12

The Eagleley group wants to maintain a consistent look to its Web site and also allow for the periodic update of this look. Rather than tailor the look of each page, it makes its pages appear in a house style by referring to a style sheet. The style sheet is shown below.

```
BODY     {color: navy; background-color:
         lightblue;}
H1       {color: blue;font-family:
         sans-serif;}
H2       {color: blue;font-family:
         sans-serif;}
H3       {color: blue;font-family:
         sans-serif;}
H4       {color: blue;font-family:
         sans-serif;}
H5       {color: blue;font-family:
         sans-serif;}
H6       {color: blue;font-family:
         sans-serif;}
P.ANN    {margin-left: 10em;margin-right:
         10em; font-family:monospace;}
P.LIT    {text-indent: 2em; font-family:
         serif;}
P.REV    {color: lightblue;
         background-color: navy;
         font-family:serif;}
```

This is done by including

```
<LINK REL=Stylesheet HREF="house.css"
TYPE="text/css" MEDIA =screen>
```

in the head of documents. The effects of this style sheet can be seen in the earlier examples in Figures 1.6 and 1.8. This style sheet is also used for the pages shown in Figures 4.2 and 4.4. This sheet sets the colours to be used for background and headings and the types of font. Note that a particular font is not specified, since that may not be present on all browsers. Three styles of paragraph are also specified:

- *ANN for announcements using a fixed width font*
- *LIT for normal text with a leading indent*
- *and REV which appears in reverse.*

Changes to the style sheet will affect all the pages on the site that reference it.

Web authors can use style sheets to give a guide to browsers over many features of the appearance of Web pages. Style sheets are said to be cascading since there is a hierarchy of preferences that can be used in displaying a page and style sheets should not for example overrule a user's own settings. This might be important, for example, for a colour-blind user who can only see certain colour combinations, or for a partially sighted user who might need all text to be shown in larger than normal font sizes. The implementation of all aspects of style sheets by browsers is still uneven. A good guide to the theory and pitfalls of practice can be found at [CSS Pointers Group].

DOM: THE DOCUMENT OBJECT MODEL

The W3C is in the process of standardising the Document Object Model (DOM), which defines a structure for Web documents. This may seem strange, given that we have previously stressed the unstructured nature of Web documents. However, although Web documents are relatively unstructured in that there are few compulsory parts, particularly in the body, every document has some sort of structure.

The DOM allows the structure of Web documents to be addressed in a formalised way. For example , DOM specifies that if a Web page contains a number of forms, these become the members of a forms array. Similarly, images on the Web page can be referred to as members of the images array and links are in a links array. Thus parts of the Web page can be referred to, e.g. the third image (arrays start at 0) is

```
image[2]
```

Within these objects further structure can be addressed, e.g. the source URL for the third image is

```
images[2].src
```

This is important to us is because it offers a programmatic interface to HTML (or XML, see below) documents, by defining a standard internal representation to them. The interface is platform and language neutral. This is achieved by using the OMG IDL for its specification (see the previous chapter for other uses of IDL). This can then be used as the basis for particular language bindings such as Java and JavaScript. Java and JavaScript programs can then address and dynamically update parts of a Web page, for instance in response to a user's input or as time passes.

WEB CACHING

Web pages may not be served directly from their original source but may arrive at the browser from a cache, or temporary store. The material in the caches may be HTML, images, pdf files or any other material transmitted to a Web browser from a Web server. This is important for any Web application but may be particularly so for Web database systems. The reasons for using caches are primarily pragmatic ones, i.e. to make the Web seem quicker and reduce costs by not re-transmitting data that has previously been supplied. There are two sorts of these caches to consider: the browser cache and the proxy cache.

BROWSER CACHES

Browser caches may come in two parts: a memory cache and a disc cache. For our purposes they can be treated as the same since their effect is the same. With a browser cache, rather than fetching a new copy of a page from a server, a copy from the cache may be presented. This improves performance, for example, when using a browser's Back button to display the previously accessed Web document. In this case the page will only be as old as the current session, but in other cases the page retrieved from the cache may come from an earlier session.

It is of course common to have a means of overriding browser caching, such as Netscape's feature of forcing a reload of a page if the Shift key is held down when clicking on Reload.

The browser cache is a very localised one, available only to the particular browser application. (In practice, there may be a number of separate caches if a user has more than one browser. Further, it would be possible for one disc cache to be used by more than one browser, although such a non-competitive attitude does not always seem prevalent in the world of Web browsers.)

The usefulness of browser caches is particularly evident when you get a number of pages from a site, may of which use the same menus, images and other graphics. One copy of these can be used on many pages, thus avoiding the need to download what may be large parts of a page.

The effect of this form of caching is often very apparent: users can observe the first page that is viewed at a site arriving slowly but subsequent pages being presented more quickly.

PROXY CACHES
Proxy caches are stores of previously retrieved Web material held, not on the user's own computer, but on some intermediary machine, such as an ISP through which Web traffic is normally routed.

When proxy caching is used, if one user, in for example the UK, requests a page held on a server in the US, the proxy cache will be checked. If the page is not held, the page will be fetched from its server and delivered to the user, and a copy will also be saved in the proxy cache. A subsequent user requesting the same page would then receive the copy from the proxy cache. The delivery from the cache would not normally be distinguishable from delivery from the real source to the user.

The proxy cache administrator will decide what pages to cache, and how long to keep them before they are regarded as stale and not used. It might, for example, be decided in the UK not to cache UK pages but to cache pages coming across the Atlantic, so as to reduce transmission costs and time delays. Use of the domain name to determine where a Web page comes from may be a simple minded approach, since, for example, not all ".coms" are in the US, but it may be a good guestimate.

The proxy cache is as we can see from this description a shared cache in contrast to the browser cache.

The benefits of caching can be lost if for example the same image is referenced in a number of different ways. The cache may not be able to reconcile these as being the same image and consequently download multiple copies. Web caching may also distort the picture users have of how many hits their site gets, since an unknown number of hits might be satisfied by pages from a cache. This can lead to Web page authors believing that caches are by definition a bad thing and trying to defeat them. This is often a bad response and it is better to accept that pages will be cached and to work with this.

There are two main ways in which Web authors can affect caching: via HTML Meta tags and HTTP headers.

1) HTML Meta Tags are put into the <HEAD> section of a Web page. These can be used to mark the page as non-cachable. This strategy will only affect browser caches, which read the HTML, not proxy caches which do not in general look into the HTML. This can be effective in situations where you want a user returning to a page, via a Back button for example, to get a fresh copy. This might be the case when returning to an HTML form which you wanted to be blank rather than containing previously entered values.

2) HTTP headers, i.e. the information sent by the server prior to the HTML itself, can be used to pass on caching information. This is the preferred way to control cachability of Web documents. Full details of this can be found in the HTTP Specification at the W3C Web site. These headers may be set by the Web server itself or generated by cgi scripts. The header can include an Expires entry which can be used by a proxy cache to determine whether a document is still fresh or if a new copy needs fetching. The newer HTTP 1.1 specification has greater facilities in the form of the Cache-Control header.

4.5 DYNAMIC WEB PAGES

Up to now we have concentrated on how documents are created and how they can be delivered via HTTP. We have mentioned that the resources requested may not be simply files. Instead, the resource may be the output of programs, or scripts, run on the server. In this section we will outline some of the main technologies for providing dynamic content which will then be used in the next part of the book for building Web database applications.

Technologies for dynamic content cover server side and client side processing.

- Server side programs are those that run on the server as is the case with CGI (Common Gateway Interface) but are called from a browser, possibly with values provided by a user on a Web page.
- Client side programs are those that run on the browser as is the situation with JavaScript.

We also introduce Java which can be used for both types of programming, running on a client as an applet or on a server as a servlet.

CGI

The Common Gateway Interface is a standard that allows HTTP requests to be made for resources rather than pre-existing documents. It provides a way of calling up a program, often referred to as a script, on a server. That script can be passed additional information, such as parameters from an HTML form. The output of the script is then sent back to the user. This is often an HTML page built dynamically by the script, but can be any sort of resource, e.g. audio or video clip.

The CGI specification [CGI spec] does not specify any particular programming languages to be used. In fact many different languages are in use for CGI programming. What it specifies is the ways in which information is passed. It is then up to CGI programmers to access this information in the language of their choice.

Most CGI programming uses two HTTP methods, GET or POST. These methods have different ways of passing information to the server.

1) The GET method passes information as the search component of the URL (see above).
2) The POST method passes the information as a data stream on the standard input to the script.

In the example used above in HTML forms, if the user chooses June, the following URL is sent as a GET method

```
available.pl?month=jun
```

The query fragment of the URL, "month=jun" is known as the "QUERY_STRING" and is available to the CGI program as an environment variable of that name. This is a relatively simple query string consisting of a single name and value. More complex strings may consist of a number of name/value pairs, usually separated with an "&". Special characters such as spaces and newlines will be encoded in the query string and it is the job of any CGI program to decode the information passed to it.

If the form had used a POST method the URL would not have included the query string. The "available" script would have been called on its own and the query string would have been passed, via HTTP, to the script's standard input. The length of data coming in this way is made available by another environment variable "CONTENT_LENGTH".

Some CGI programs accept input by both GET and PUT methods. This can be done with the use of another environment variable "REQUEST_METHOD" which can be tested to see which method was used and then appropriate action taken to read the query string in whatever form it was sent. Full details of all the variables available to CGI programs are given in the CGI specification.

Both the GET and POST methods have advantages and disadvantages.
- The main advantage of GET is that, since the information to be passed is present in the URL it can be 'bookmarked' or included directly in a hyperlink and so be used, without a form.
- The POST method has the advantage that there is no limit to the amount of data that can be passed, whereas the size of data in a GET method may be limited and either the browser or server may truncate data.
- Another issue is whether sending a query via CGI more than once can cause a problem. Most browsers prompt users before sending POST requests but do not for GET. Therefore multiple requests via a GET are possible, if for instance a user reloads or double clicks. Web authors need to ensure that their applications can deal correctly with this.

There will be many factors affecting the choice of CGI programming language, one of these may be the ease of decoding information passed to the program. A number of languages, such as Perl, have sets of routines already available to make this easier. Examples of using CGI to access databases will be found later in the book and a comprehensive guide to CGI programming can be found in [Gundavaram 96].

JAVA

In this section we provide a brief introduction to Java and outline why it is significant. More details and examples of using Java, with databases for Web systems occur in Chapter 6. This section is not intended to provide an introduction to programming in Java, many other books and online resources can do that. Users wanting more information are well advised to start at Sun's Java site [Java].

Providing dynamic content was seen by many people as a very desirable feature once the Web started to become popular. One solution is that outlined above, using CGI to provide that content from the server. Another possible solution is to provide a way of running programs in the browser, i.e. on the client. This requires a programming language, not just a markup language like HTML.

Although this client-side approach is an enticing possibility, it is also a dangerous one. A program running on a client might do a lot of good things such as provide animated demonstrations, but it might also do bad things such as delete files. This highlights one difference of the Web's client-server model to that of traditional computing client-server architectures: on the Web the model is an un-trusted one. Clients and servers have little knowledge of one another. Also, a necessity for a programming language for Web pages is that it should run on many platforms. Since the Web is a decentralised system clients may run on many different hardware and software combinations. Web authors should not make assumptions about clients that they known little about.

Java offered a solution to these problems. Its roots were in a project within Sun known as "Oak" which was intended to provide a small, reliable and machine independent language for use in a variety of devices. Java can offer this independence by executing in a virtual machine. Java programs, instead of being compiled to machine code (specific to one machine), are compiled to byte code which can then be run on any machine that has a Java Virtual Machine (JavaVM). This does mean that someone must have written a Virtual Machine for your type of computer and you must have it installed, but this is still a much simpler situation than having to provide a program in many different forms and send the correct one to each client. The virtual machine approach also means that it is possible to run programs securely. This is because the security limits can be put into the virtual machine which can be trusted, and these will limit the resources any "un-trusted" program can access. These are the features that make possible Java programs running on a client, i.e. applets.

The speed with which applets were deployed and the breadth of support given to Java within browsers is testimony to the fact that Java filled a need. The ongoing debates and legal battles over Java standardisation and certification still cast a shadow over Java. However, the Web clearly needs an open cross platform programming platform, and Java has the potential to be it.

Java has also quickly established itself as the programming language of choice in many situations beyond applet programming. It includes many features that are needed or useful in software development generally, such as:

- Java is an object-oriented language. This has many advantages, including ease of implementing modern design methodologies.
- It is a strongly typed language. This has advantages in allowing compile time checking and can aid the development of robust code.
- It is easier to use than some other object-oriented languages. In particular Java's developers learnt a number of lessons from C++. Features such as the absence of pointers, garbage collection and no multiple inheritance are significant here.
- It has features needed for large scale programming projects. Many applications will be much larger than applets.
- It has networking features built in.
- It has windowing features built in. Java came with an Abstract Window Toolkit which fitted in with the platform independence mentioned above. This made programming for a number of GUIs possible.

The general-purpose nature of Java also has a spin off for Web use. We will see later that it is possible to re-use or simply modify Java code so that it is possible to use it within applets, servlets or more traditional CGI programming. Since Java is compiled to byte code, which is then interpreted by the JavaVM, there have been concerns about whether it can ever be as efficient as straightforwardly compiled code. Progress has been made in these areas both in terms of producing more efficient byte code and virtual machines and also in terms of compiling to native code where needed. For most Web applications this is not a significant issue, since delays are generally due to slow transmissions across networks rather than slow processing.

JAVASCRIPT

We start this section by looking at what JavaScript is, what it can and cannot do and why it matters. We use the name JavaScript in a generic sense. Here JavaScript refers to the scripting language originated with Netscape and its implementation as JScript by Microsoft, which is now being standardised as ECMAScript. (The standard is ECMA-262 and it is planned that this will become an ISO standard too.) JScript is commonly called JavaScript or sometimes javascript.

JavaScript is a cross platform scripting language with object-oriented features that can provide us with a programming interface to the DOM. JavaScript offers the possibility of making Web pages dynamic. It does this by enabling us to have sections of code within the HTML of a Web page, marked by <SCRIPT></SCRIPT>tags (or in a number of other ways). This code can allow us to test the value of variables, for example, set by a user on a form or in the user's environment. JavaScript can perform actions based on the values of such variables or based on events such as mouse clicks or movements. The actions performed can be conditional on these values or events. Thus, JavaScript is a *programming* language in contrast to HTML itself, which is only a *markup* language. It therefore offers possibilities that are not available within HTML itself. Although we should remember that JavaScript offers all this within the client, the combination of HTML and processing at the server may be equivalent or more powerful.

Some of the things that make JavaScript important within the Web context are worth emphasising:

1) The cross platform nature is important. This means that we can use it without regard for the hardware or software used by the user. (However, there are limits to this that we discuss below.) This contrasts with other alternative scripting languages which might be used in Web pages, such as VBScript, which we would only expect to find on a Microsoft Browser running on a Microsoft operating system.

2) JavaScript is a scripting language that is widely supported by browsers. It would be possible to use Perl as a scripting language in Web pages. However, for security reasons, since these are programs running on a client, it would have to be a restricted subset of Perl. Like JavaScript, Perl does satisfy the requirement for being cross platform, since, although Perl originated on Unix systems, implementations can be found for many operating systems and hardware platforms. However Perl is not supported as a scripting language by browsers.

JavaScript was originally known as LiveScript. Its name was changed to JavaScript when the initial hype over Java was at something of a peak, possibly as a marketing move. Consequently, the name, JavaScript, has caused confusion for na•ve users between it and Java. However, the two languages are distinct. JavaScript is not simply a cutdown and interpreted version of Java.

There are a number of features that are common to JavaScript and Java:
- They both have a common syntactic parent in C. Consequently, many constructions, such as a *for* loop, are very similar.
- Both languages are object-oriented languages or at least have features that support object-orientation. Neither might be regarded as totally object-oriented by purists, unlike languages such as Smalltalk where everything is an object.

The differences include:
- Java is a strongly typed language whereas JavaScript, like most scripting languages is untyped.

Both have a strong cross-platform basis. This suggests that the pair of languages may find their places in Web programming, each doing tasks for which they are appropriate and the similarities between them may be beneficial for programmers who are working with both languages. Problems resulting from differences between them in areas such as scoping rules (which are beyond the scope of this book), may outweigh the benefits of their similarity.

WHEN TO USE JAVASCRIPT

JavaScript can offer useful extras to Web pages. It can provide additional ways to navigate within Web sites and to achieve good-looking presentational features. However, although JavaScript is a programming language, there are a number of things that it cannot do. It cannot access file systems. Since it runs on client computers this is a good thing. There is also one exception to this, since it can access a browser's cookie file. Cookies are discussed later in the book in the context of building Web database applications. What is perhaps most important to remember is that JavaScript cannot be relied on as the basis of a system. There are a number of reasons for this.

- Not all browsers support it.
- Some users turn it off.
- There are still bugs in implementations.
- There are still differences between implementations .

A good survey of the problems, as well as positive features of JavaScript, can be found in [Flanagan98]. Search engines represent a small number of very important users who will not be using JavaScript. Consequently, sites that depend on JavaScript, particularly for navigational purposes, may find that their contents never get indexed, as the search engines cannot progress beyond the home page. Given the current situation, the conclusion must be to use JavaScript as an extra but never to depend on it.

4.6 NEW DEVELOPMENTS

At the start of this chapter we noted that Web technology is still undergoing rapid change. There are a number of features, such as the DOM and Cascading Style Sheets, which are discussed above but are still undergoing development.

- Standardisation of the DOM will allow more sophisticated programmatic control of Web pages, allowing for more sophisticated client processing.
- Developments in Style Sheets, especially for the presentation of Web pages in other media, such as spoken and printed, may have an influence on wireless devices and mean that more material can be presented as HTML, rather than in more specialised formats.

The DOM and style sheets are likely to be important technologies in the future, but their exact form is still uncertain. New generations of browsers (such as that of the Mozilla project [Mozilla]) and the features they do (and do not) support will also have an impact on what is available on the Web and how it looks.

It is possible to identify a number of areas where HTML can be considered weak. Examples are areas such as poetry and playscripts, since HTML does not have suitable tags for the structures needed. This is perhaps not surprising given its origins in a scientific community. But there are still other areas, such as Mathematics where there are also no appropriate structures for formulae. One solution to this is the development of specialised markup languages (MathsML and perhaps PoetryML). One way in which this may be possible is via XML (see below). HTML itself has now become relatively stable and it seems unlikely that many extra tags will be added. HTML 4.0 did not add a lot of new tags to HTML 3.2, and in fact deprecated the use of a number. However, HTML 4.0 did allow the addition of a CLASS attribute within any tag. This combined with the DOM and CSS may allow much more fine control of structure and presentation of the existing structures in HTML.

A guide to what the future might hold can be found in [Berners-Lee 99] and the World Wide Web Consortium site [W3C] also contains many documents showing areas under discussion and development.

XML

The single most important development is XML (Extensible Markup Language). XML is a new meta-language . It is like SGML, but somewhat simplified to make application development easier (XML was referred to as SGML Lite when it was first developed). Consequently, it is easier to build XML parsers, which makes XML more suitable for the Web environment than SGML.

What is significant about XML is the extensible part, i.e. the facilities for defining new tags. Consequently, we now have HTML with a relatively stable and small set of tags, but if we require other tags, these can be defined in XML. One important XML development is RDF (Resource Description Framework) which is a format that allows the specification of metadata (i.e. information about information). This feature can be used in an XML namespace to include structural information. This allows us, for example, both to declare a part of a document as the author's name, and also to specify in metadata what we mean by the term author. This information might then be used both to present the document in a browser and also to index it by a search engine.

XML will enable specialised applications and groups of users to talk in richer languages than are available in plain HTML. Examples of this are MathML and CML (Chemical Markup Language). These are still in development and the browsers that support this are also in early stages. XML code that is not understood by a browser, like HTML markup that a browser does not know about, should just be ignored. Consequently, in theory it should be possible to use this framework to create Web pages that are usable by anyone but that have richer content for those with access to the XML content. For example, a Web page could refer to a chemical compound for HTML browsers, and for CML-enabled browsers also show a diagrammatic view.

The examples above are about the presentation of XML delivered as Web pages; the other important aspect is the development of the use of XML XSL (Extensible Stylesheet Language) a proposal for a language that would transform XML documents into, for example, HTML for Web delivery. This facility would allow a company to keep all of its data in XML format and use this to drive typesetting for printed catalogues and also produce HTML for Web delivery of the catalogue information.

Earlier we noted that HTML is an SGML application. With the development of XML we also now have XHTML " This is a reformulation of HTML 4.0 in XML 1.0." according to the W3C. A simple piece of XHTML code is shown in the following example which updates the

Example 4.9 code. XML tags are case sensitive and the ones we use here are defined in lower case. Note that XHTML documents should be, what is known as, well-formed. That is, they should have closing tags and correctly terminated empty tags. This is shown in the form of the horizontal rule tag below.

EXAMPLE 4.13

The Eagleley Group is in the process of converting to XML. This is the statement of ownership Web page converted to XHTML.

```
<?xml version="1.0" encoding="UTF-8"?>
<!DOCTYPE html
    PUBLIC "-//W3C//DTD XHTML 1.0 Strict//EN"
    "DTD/xhtml1-strict.dtd">
<html xmlns="http://www.w3.org/1999/xhtml"
xml:lang="en" lang="en">

<head>
<title>
Statement of Ownership
</title>
</head>

<body>
<h1> Eagleley EuroHotel Booking</h1>
<h2>Statement of Ownership</h2>
<hr />
<p>
Eagleley EuroHotelBooking is a wholly owned
subsidiary of the
Eagleley Group.
</p>
<hr />
</body>
</html>
```

4.7 SUMMARY

This chapter has overviewed features of the Web. Specifically, it has explained how it works, how data is stored on the Web, how data is accessed on the Web and new developments.

The **Web** is an **Internet** application for inputting, storing, accessing and manipulating data, and for storing and executing programs. The Internet is a network which connects computers and computer networks the world over. It achieves this using the **TCP/IP** protocols.

The computers connected by the Internet are called **hosts**. The programs executing on a host to provide services is called a **server**. The Internet supports various types of server, such as FTP, Gopher, and Web servers, each of which uses a different protocol at the **Application Layer** of the **Protocol Stack**. At the **Transport Layer** the **TCP** protocol allows communication between hosts. Below this, at the **Internet Layer**, the **IP (packet switching)** protocol supports transmission of individual messages between hosts. Lower still, at the **Network Interface Layer**, the protocols are specific to the computer networks the Internet connects.

Hosts in the Internet are identified by **IP addresses**, allocated by the **NIC**. In addition, hosts are allocated symbolic names, stored on **name servers**. These are mapped to IP addressed by the **DNS**. Symbolic names are constructed hierarchically from **domain** names.

The Web is based on a **Client-Server architecture**, whereby Web services stored on **Web servers** are accessed by **Web clients**, via the Internet. The space on a Web server for storing **Web documents** and other Web resources is called a **Web site**, which appear like a conventional file store. The executable code contained in Web documents to access programs and other types of server are called **scripts**. Web documents can store **multimedia** information and can also contain **hyperlinks** to other Web documents. Thus the Web creates a worldwide **hypermedia**. Web client programs for accessing Web resources stored on servers are called **browsers**. Web resources are uniquely addressed by **URLs**. These may address Web documents, fragments of Web documents, and other resources such as scripts. In the latter case, parameters can be specified in the URL. The Web protocol is called **HTTP**. This is a stateless protocol for transmitting a request from a client to a server, and the response from the server to the client.

The Web originated at the start of the 1990s at **CERN** as a network for collaboration between researchers. The theoretical and practical origins of the Web are respectively the work on **hypertext** and **ARPNET**.

A Web server is configured and maintained by a person called its **webmaster**, to establish how the server runs, how resources are processed and delivered, the access restrictions, and **MIME** types. A Web site has a hierarchical structure, like a file space. The root directory, typically called WWWRoot, contains the **home page**, other files and other directories. The latter may be **virtual directories**, located elsewhere using **aliasing**. Directories store information as files. The information is represented as documents called **Web pages.** The standard language for presenting information on the Web is **HTML**. HTML started as an **SGML**-like application.

Web documents are typically text, but can also contain programs that execute on the client or server systems, respectively called applets and servlets. A Web document can also contain hyperlinks between its parts, or with other Web documents. Links can also be to other types of server. These links are specified using URLs.

HTML is a markup language. The structure and presentation of parts of a document are specified using **HTML tags**. Though HTML can specify the presentation of the marked up information, individual browsers may differ in the ways in which they represent a document. In practice, it is therefore often better to specify the structure of a document so that a browser will present the document in a way consistent with this strcture.

HTML code can be validated, either using an online or offline **validator**.

Cascading style sheets are used to suggest how documents should be presented. Individual Web documents can specify a particular style sheet. However, the suggestion may be overruled by individual browsers.

The **DOM** is an attempt to standardise the structure of Web documents. This is important, since it makes it possible for programs to process Web documents in general.

Web caching improves retrieval times by caching accessed Web documents, either in the browsers (**browser caching**), or on an intermediary machine (**proxy cashing**).

Web documents can be **dynamically** created by programs or scripts that are run on servers (**server side**) or clients (**client side**). **CGI** provides a standard way by which HTTP requests can be made to resources other than pre-existing documents. CGI usually uses two HTTP methods, **GET** to pass information as the search component of the URL, and **POST** which passes information as a data stream on the standard input to the script. **JAVA** provides another way of dynamically creating Web documents. Using JAVA we can embed programs (called **applets)** within a Web document). The applets will be executed in clients. This is possible because JAVA runs in a trusted environment (the **JAVA Virtual Machine**) and is therefore also platform independent. Scripts can be written using various programming languages, including **JavaScript** and **Perl**.

Browsers for access information and services on the Web are now standard software, sometimes bundled with the operating system, available free from ISPs, downloadable from the Net, or purchased.

New developments include the ongoing work on DOM and Cascading Style Sheets and also **XML**, which allows new user-defined tags to be specified.

EXERCISES:

(4.1)   List four general facilities provided by the Web.

(4.2)   In what way does the Internet differ from previous wide area networks?

(4.3)   What is the Internet?

(4.4)   What is the relationship between the Internet and the Web?

(4.5)   What does the acronym TCP/IP refer to?

(4.6)   Sketch the TCP/IP protocol stack and explain the role of the four layers.

(4.7)   Distinguish between an Internet host, a server and a client.

(4.8)   Give four examples of types of server accessible via the Internet.

(4.9)   What is an IP address?

(4.10)   What does NIC stand for, and what is its role with respect to IP addresses?

(4.11)   A symbolic version of an IP address is constructed from domains. Explain what a domain is, and how the symbolic name is constructed.

(4.12)   What is the DNS?

(4.13)   What is the role of an Internet name server and how is it used?

(4.14)   Distinguish between Web server, Web site and Web document.

(4.15)   Name three types of Web client program, and explain their purposes.

(4.16)   What is an ISP and what does it do?

(4.17)   Name two widely used Web browsers. Outline their functions.

(4.18)   How does a Web search engine work? What is the role of a search engine "spider"?

(4.19)   Connections between a browser and server last only for the retrieval of a single document. Give one advantage and one disadvantage to this strategy.

(4.20)   The Web is used through a wide range of browsers. Discuss the advantages and disadvantages that are a consequence of this diversity.

(4.21)   What does URL stand for, and what are the uses of URLs?

(4.22)   Consider the URL, http::/www.eagleley.co.uk:88/index.html. Discuss the meaning of each of the components of this URL and how they relate to each other.

(4.23)   There are two widely used variants on the path component of a URL. Give examples of these, and explain their uses.

(4.24)   What does HTTP stand for and what is its significance within the Web?

(4.25)   Outline how the HTTP protocol works, i.e. the interchange of messages between a client and a server.

(4.26)   Describe an HTTP document request.

(4.27)   The most common methods invoked by a document request are GET and POST. What do these methods do?

(4.28)   HTTP requires a client to send header information after a document request. What information will this contain?

(4.29)   What additional information does HTTP allow a client to send following the header information?

(4.30)   Within HTTP, what is the purpose of the status line returned by a server on receipt of a document request, and what information will it contain?

(4.31)   HTTP allows a server to follow a status line with header information. What is the purpose of this, and what information can be sent?

(4.32) After sending status line and header information, a server sends the requested data. What happens next?

(4.33) Within HTTP, what is the significance of a "Connection: Keep Alive header" message?

(4.34) Who invented the Web and how does the original version differ from the Web as it is today?

(4.35) Information representation in the Web is based upon hypertext theory. Where did this originate and how did it evolve into its current form on the Web?

(4.36) What role does ARPANET have in the history of the Web?

(4.37) The managing director of a small manufacturing company has asked you to explain what is meant by a Web server, in simple but tangible terms. Write a short explanation.

(4.38) What is an http daemon?

(4.39) Within NCSA and Apache servers, the server is configured using four files: httpd.conf, srm.conf, access.conf and mime.types. Explain the role of each of these.

(4.40) What does the title, webmaster signify?

(4.41) What does MIME stand for, and why is it important within the context of the Web.

(4.42) A Web site is often likened to a file store. Explain the similarities and differences.

(4.43) What is the relationship between a Web site and a Web page?

(4.44) What does HTML stand for, and why is it important within the context of the Web?

(4.45) Explain what is meant by aliasing, or virtual directories, within the context of a Web site. Give an example of how this concept is used.

(4.46) What is a hyperlink? Give an example of one in an HTML document.

(4.47) What is the relationship between SGML, HTML and XML?

(4.48) HTML is a markup language. What is a markup language, and how does it differ from a schema language, such as ODL?

(4.49) What is the purpose of an HTML tag pair? Give a simple example.

(4.50) Define a simple HTML document with a header "SIMPLE EXAMPLE" and a body "This is my body".

(4.51) What do we mean by "Valid HTML"?

(4.52) What happens if a browser receives HTML with the following irregularities: an invalid tag, overlapping tags, multiple singular tags, missing closing tags?

(4.53) What is the purpose of the <A ...> ... </A> tag pair in HTML?

(4.54) Specify two Web documents, one with the name of a department, and the other with the name of the head of that department. Create hyper links between the two pages so that users can navigate between them.

(4.55) Consider the URL, http://www.eagleley.com.uk/index.html. Explain two ways in which this URL could be shortened within an HTML hyperlink, by using the facility for relative links.

(4.56) Define in outline, an HTML document with three parts, "Part 1", "Part 2" and "Part 3". Within the document create hyperlinks between the parts, by positioning named anchors.

(4.57) Modify your answer to (4.56) to include also a link to an email tool, for sending messages to MD@eagleley.com.

(4.58) Further modify your answer to (4.57) to include a link to a document stored in text form, located at "manuals/newinfo.txt".

(4.59) Define an HTML document with a header, "Lists page", and within its body, two lists. The first should contain the letters of the alphabet. The second should contain the ten numerical digit.

(4.60) Define an HTML document that displays as a table, with columns for names of countries and their three largest cities. Experiment with displays, colours, fonts, etc.

(4.61) Define an HTML document that displays the Eagleley logo, stored in a file, images/logo.gif.

(4.62) Define an HTML form by which name, address and telephone number can be entered.

(4.63) Explain why it is often better to specify in HTML the structure of a document, rather than the exact presentation.

(4.64) Define an HTML document that represents, as closely as you can, the front cover of this book. You should include links to the McGraw-Hill Web page and also to the Web page for the book.

(4.65) How can HTML be validated?

(4.66) Give examples of online and offline HTML validators. Describe the different ways in which they are used.

(4.67) Why are cascading style sheets so called? When should they be used?

(4.68)   Give examples of the information that can be specified in a style sheet.

(4.69)   Modify the example style sheet in Example 4.12, to define a style for the book cover Web page in your answer to (4.64).

(4.70)   What does DOM stand for and why is it important?

(4.71)   Why is Web caching sometimes necessary?

(4.72)   Differentiate between browser caches and proxy caches.

(4.73)   Under what circumstances would it be desirable to override caching.

(4.74)   Explain the two main ways in which Web caching can be influenced, using HTML.

(4.75)   In what way are dynamic Web pages dynamic? Give three examples of when a dynamic Web page should be used.

(4.76)   What is meant by the terms "client side" and "server side" processing?

(4.77)   What does CGI stand for, and why is it important?

(4.78)   What does the "CGI specification" specify?

(4.79)   Most CGI programming uses two HTTP methods, GET or POST. Explain the functions of these, and give examples of when they would be used.

(4.80)   How would a CGI program use the REQUEST_METHOD and CONTENT_LENGTH variables?

(4.81)   How is a CGI program invoked by an application? Give an example of one such application.

(4.82)   What is Java and from where did it originate?

(4.83)   What is the JavaVM. Why is this important within the context of the Web.

(4.84)   What is an Java applet? Explain how Java applets can be used to provide client side processing. Give examples of what Java applets can be used for. What restrictions are there within which an applet must operate and why are these important?

(4.85)   Explain in greater detail what we mean when we say "the Web clearly needs an open cross platform programming platform, and Java has the potential to be it."

(4.86)   List and identify and explain six characteristics of Java that make it suitable for Web applications.

(4.87)   An alternative to using CGI to provide Web pages with dynamic contents is to use Java programs.

(4.88)   What is a Java servlet, and what is it used for?

(4.89)   What is JavaScript and why is it important within the context of Web applications?

(4.90)   Distinguish between Java and JavaScript? What features do they have in common?

(4.91)   How do we include JavaScript within HTML documents?

(4.92)   JavaScript is cross platform by nature. Whey is this important within the context of the Web?

(4.93)   What are the pros and cons of using JavaScript or Perl as a scripting language in Web pages?

(4.94)   What is the relationship between JavaScript and LiveScript?

(4.95)   What are the advantages of using JavaScript as a scripting language within HTML pages?

(4.96)   Give four reasons why JavaScript cannot be relied on as the basis of a system.

(4.97)   Why is the use of JavaScript significant when considering visibility of a Web site to search engines?

(4.98)   What is the relationship between XML and HTML? What additional features does XML provide and why are they important?

(4.99)   Why is the DOM of potentially greater importance in the future?

(4.100) Explain why XML is of potentially greater importance in the future.

(4.101) What does XSL stand for, and why is it important?

(4.102) The managing director of a small manufacturing organisation wishes to be briefed on the basis of the Web and why it may be important to her company. Write a short report.

Part III

WEB DATABASES

This Part examines the systems that can be created by combining Database technology and Web technology. Specifically, this Part sets out to answer the following questions:

- How are Web Database systems designed?
- What technologies are available for building Web database systems?
- How are issues of security, identity and transactions handled?

5

WEB DATABASE DESIGN

This Chapter describes a design method for Web database systems. Using it we create a design of the Web pages and the database that they connect to. The technologies that can be used to implement the Web database system design are described in Chapter 6, which also covers design issues and techniques for transaction control, and for privacy, security, and integrity maintenance.

Our method for designing Web database systems is based upon that in [Atzeni 99]. This method uses conventional relational database design techniques based upon Entity-Relationship (ER) modelling. However, the techniques have been adapted and extended also to model Web pages.

Section 5.1 overviews the Web database design process. It introduces the tasks involved, their inputs, outputs, and aims. The subsequent sections describe each of these tasks in greater detail. Data analysis is described in section 5.2. In particular, the section overviews ER modelling techniques by which a conceptual model of the information to be represented in a database is created. Section 5.3 then describes the way in which a conceptual model of the information to be represented in Web pages is created, using an adaptation of the ER model. Sections 5.4 and 5.5 respectively overview the logical design of the database and of Web pages. Section 5.6 concludes the chapter with a summary, followed by exercises.

5.1 THE WEB DATABASE DESIGN PROCESS

In this section we overview a method for designing Web database systems. First we describe the stages of conventional database design.

We then examine additional complexities and stages necessary for designing a Web database system. The design method described is based on the method introduced in [Atzeni 99]. The subsequent sections then will take you through each of the stages of the Web database system design method in greater detail.

CONVENTIONAL DATABASE DESIGN METHODS

Methods for designing database systems are well established. Two main approaches are entity relationship (ER) modelling, which is used mainly for designing relational databases, and object data modelling, typically using UML, with which object databases are designed. Here we concentrate on the former, since relational databases remain the mainstream technology, particularly for data intensive Web applications.

The process of designing a database follows the steps in Figure 5.1. The starting point is a description of the organisation the database is to serve and the requirements for the new system. This is because the database approach is to represent data such that it has the same structure as the information that it models (see Section 1.1 Database Technology: The Database Approach to Information Systems). The advantage is that the database is then sharable by all relevant applications including future ones. It is therefore necessary to focus the design of the database on the relevant part of the world, rather than specific applications.

The database design process proceeds by moving progressively from an abstract analysis of the information to be stored in the database, to a physical description of how the database will be implemented.

The description of the organisation and system requirements are derived through a preliminary requirements analysis phase. In this, information is typically gathered in the following ways:
- by observing the organisation's working;
- by talking to the individuals, and particularly those who are experts within different areas of operation within the organisation;
- by inspecting documents within the organisation and in particular, those used to record data;
- by surveying experts within the areas of operation using questionnaires;

- by using other information already known by the individuals carrying out the design exercise.

This information gathering exercise will result in a documented description of the organisation, possibly made up of a set of descriptions, each from the viewpoint of a different area of operation. These descriptions are gathered as a preliminary to logical database design.

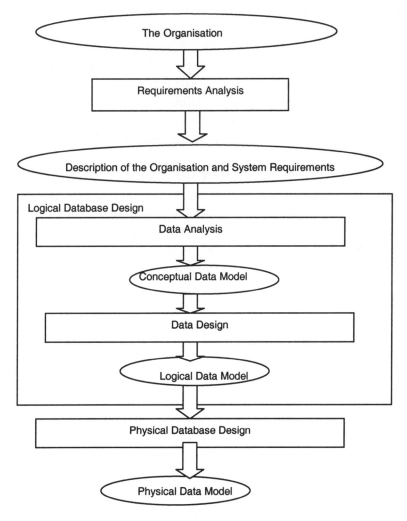

Figure 5.1: Database Design

The aim of logical database design is to design a database using the structures of the data model that the DBMS supports (see Section 2.1 What is a Data Model?). The result is a logical data model that describes the logical structure of the database. In the case of a relational database system this would define a set of tables (see Section 2.2 Relational Databases). For an object database, the logical data model would define a set of classes (see Section 3.1 Object Databases).

Logical database design takes place in two stages:

1) Data analysis is the process of describing the organisation in terms of the phenomena that must be represented within the database. This description is called a conceptual data model.
2) Data design is the process of defining a logical data model that implements the conceptual model as a database. The logical data model used the structures supported by the DBMS being used.

Following on from the logical database design, the physical database design process (described in Chapter 6) determines how the logical structures of the database, specified in the logical data model, should be implements such that the performance and use of computer resources of the database system are acceptable. Physical design is concerned with implementation issues, such as file structures and access methods.

WEB DATABASE DESIGN

The design of a Web database system, rather than a conventional database system, adds two complications:

1) Web page design—This concerns:
   a) Web data representation—i.e. presentation of data, as Web pages, retrieved from the database or input by the user.
   b) Web data association—i.e. design of the links for navigation within and between Web pages.
   c) Web interface design—i.e. design of the Web page features, including the use of graphics, animation, etc.
2) Design of the connectivity between Web pages and the database—This concerns:

a) Web database logical mapping—i.e. definition of the mapping between the data displayed in the Web pages and the data stored in the database.

b) Web database physical mapping—i.e. implementation of the mechanisms by which data is passed between the Web pages and the database.

Before discussing a Web database design method that addresses the above issues, it is first necessary to establish the limitations of this method. In this chapter we are concerned specifically with Web database design, rather than the broader and more complex area of Web application design. Therefore, the limitations of the method we describe are as follows:

1) We consider only those design issues that relate directly to the data in the database and that are displayed in the Web pages (i.e. Web data representation and association, and Web database logical and physical mapping). Other issues, such as the layout and features in the Web pages, e.g. graphics, animations, etc., are beyond the scope of our design method.

2) We consider only those Web pages that are explicitly designed for the application under consideration. Links to other pages outside of the system are not modelled. To include these would create an explosion in the complexity of the design, since the Web supports a single vast worldwide collection of inter-linked pages.

The Web database design method derives a series of models that represent the data stored in the Web pages, in addition to the data in the database. As with databases, the structure of a Web database can be represented at different levels of abstraction, corresponding to the conceptual, logical and physical models of a conventional database system:

- The conceptual Web data model should show the structure of the information represented by the Web pages.
- The logical Web data model should show how the conceptual structures are actually represented within the Web pages.
- The physical Web data model should show how the logical model of the Web pages is implemented.

The Web database design method therefore introduces design task for defining each of the above models. Consequently, the conventional database design process is expanded, as shown in Figure 5.2.

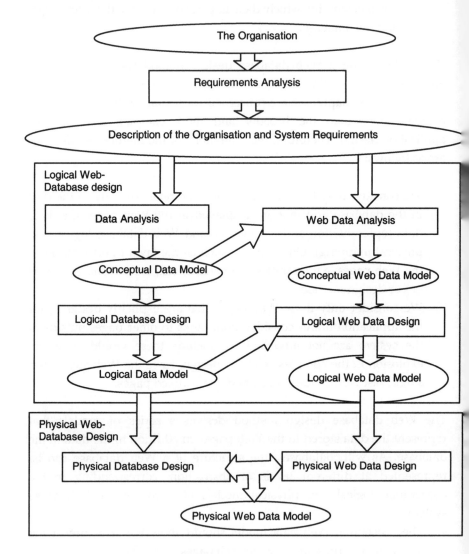

Figure 5.2: Web Database Design

Note the following additions to the conventional database design process in Figure 5.1.

1) Web Data Analysis defines a conceptual model of the information that the Web pages are to represent, as well as the information that the database must represent.
2) Logical Web Data Design defines the data structure of the actual Web pages, including the links between their parts and to other Web pages.
3) Physical Web Data Design designs how the Web pages are to be implemented and connected to the database system.

Note also that there are corresponding design tasks and models for each level of abstraction, respectively for designing the database and Web pages.

However, an important difference between the logical design of the Web pages and of a database is that the former are designed to support specific applications, whereas a database is design for all relevant applications, including future ones not yet thought of. Therefore, an important input into the Web data analysis is the set of specific requirements for the Web database application.

The relationship between data analysis, in which the conceptual model for the database is derived, and Web data analysis, in which the conceptual model of the information content of the Web pages is defined, can vary. This is because Web database systems can be designed within two scenarios:

1) A database may be designed specifically to support a data intensive Web application.
2) Alternatively, the Web application may be designed as an application of an existing database system.

In the former case the "Description of the Organisation and System Requirements" upon which the data analysis and Web data analysis are based, is a description only of the Web application. Therefore, all of the database is relevant and tailored to the requirements of the Web application. In the latter case, the Web database is one of a number of applications of a predefined database. Therefore the description upon which the data analysis is based describes the organisation the database is to serve, but the Web data analysis must then identify the part of the resulting conceptual model that is relevant to the Web application. This latter task is therefore similar to that of defining a view or external model for a conventional database application (see 2.2 Relational Databases, Views) when designing an application for a conventional database system.

In the following sections we explain and illustrate the stages of Web database design shown in Figure 5.2. Data analysis, Web data analysis, data design, and Web data design are respectively explained in sections 5.2, 5.3, 5.4 and 5.5. Physical database design and Web page design are discussed in Chapter 6.

5.2 DATA ANALYSIS

In this section we describe the data analysis stage of logical Web database design. This section also establishes basic concepts and techniques for Web data analysis, which is described in Section 5.3.

Data analysis is the first stage of the logical Web database design process. Its objective is to determine the natural structure of the data that the database will store. Data analysis, or data modelling as it is sometimes called, takes as input a description of the organisation and the system requirements, and produces a conceptual model of the part of the world about which the database is to represent information. In the case where the database is designed specifically to support a Web application, the analysis is based upon a description of that application only.

A conceptual model defined in data analysis describes the world in terms of the phenomena about which the data is to represent information, their properties and the relationships that can exist between them. The conceptual model is therefore defined using a semantic data model, i.e. one designed to represent the meaning of the data. Most commonly, the Entity Relationship (ER) data model [Chen 76] is used. However, with the emergence of object-oriented technologies, both for database and Web systems, the Unified Modeling Language (UML) [Rational] is also used in greater frequency. In this section we shall consider only ER modelling, and assume that the database will be implemented using a relational DBMS. (The use of UML to specify object databases is illustrated in Chapter 3.)

TYPES AND OCCURRENCES

When discussing data analysis it is necessary to distinguish between types and occurrences. A conceptual model for a database will describe the types of thing that are of interest, rather than the actual occurrences of those things. The occurrences will be described by the data that is stored in the database.

EXAMPLE 5.1

Eagleley wishes to represent information about customers, i.e. phenomena of type customer. B.Eaglestone is an actual customer, and is an occurrence of a phenomenon of type customer.

ENTITIES, ATTRIBUTES AND RELATIONSHIPS

During data analysis, the structure of the information that is to be represented in a database is usually thought of in terms of three types of component:

1) Entities—An entity is a phenomenon that has independent existence in the real world and about which there are facts in which we are interested. Each occurrence of an entity must be uniquely identifiable. That is to say, it must have properties that provide a unique name for it.
2) Attributes—Facts about an entity are to do with some quality, feature or characteristic of the entity. We call a particular type of fact an attribute.
3) Relationships—Facts about an entity may identify other entities, e.g. a fact about a customer may be that he deals through a particular sales office. These cross-references between entities form relationships or associations between entities. Sometimes we will wish to represent facts about a relationship, in which case the relationship is another entity, called an association entity.

When performing data analysis the database designer takes a very selective view of the world and classifies the things that he or she observes within the context of the intended database. However, classification of the phenomena relating to an organisation as entities, attributes and relationships can be subjective. For example, is marriage a relationship, an entity or an attribute? In fact marriage may be viewed as any or all of these. Analysis of the world is subjective and different individuals may produce different, but equally valid analyses. An entity is very much in the eye of the beholder. The important thing is that what the designer identifies as an entity does correspond to something in the real world about which he or she is interested and which exists independent of whether or not facts are known about it. For example, a customer may be thought of as an entity, because the customer does not cease to exist if we do not know the customer's name and address.

ENTITY RELATIONSHIP MODELLING

The ER Model [Chen 76] is widely used in data analysis to express the conceptual model, especially in relational database design methods. Using this model, the "building blocks" from which a conceptual data model is constructed include symbols for representing types of entities, their attributes and relationships between them. Entities and relationships are represented in a diagrammatical form. In an ER diagram:

- Boxes represent entity types,
- Diamonds and connecting lines represent the type of relationship that can exist between them.
- Numbers in square brackets at the ends of relationship lines are used to denote the minimum and maximum numbers of entities that can participate in an instance of the relationship. This is called the cardinality of the relationship.

EXAMPLE 5.2

Customer, booking and hotel type entities and the relationships between them may be depicted using the ER model shown in Figure 5.3. The diagram depicts the following:

- *Three entities types—Customer, Booking and Hotel. These entities are represented by boxes.*
- *Two relationship types—These are represented by the diamonds and connecting lines. The numbers in square brackets at each end of a relationship line, e.g. [0,n], specify the cardinality of the relationships, i.e. they indicate how many occurrences of the entities may participate in a relationship. The two numbers in brackets respectively give the minimum and maximum number of entities that can participate. The relationship cardinalities in Figure 5.3 specify the following:*

- *an occurrence of Customer may be related to zero, one, two or more occurrences of Booking, but each occurrence of Booking is related to only one Customer;*
- *an occurrence of Hotel may be related to zero, one, two or more occurrences of Booking and each occurrence of Booking may be related to many occurrences of Hotel.*

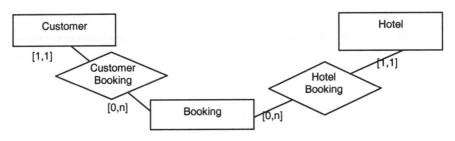

Figure 5.3 ER Model of Customers, Hotels and Booking

In order to determine the cardinality of a relationship it is necessary to consider it in both directions. If entities of types X and Y are related we must consider how X is related to Y, and also how Y is related to X. The following types of relationship may be identified:

1) A relationship between X and Y is one-to-one if each occurrence of X is related to one and only one occurrence of Y, denoted [1,1], and each occurrence of Y is related to one and only one occurrence of X. This is shown diagrammatically as follows:

2) A relationship between X and Y is one-to-many, if each occurrence of X may be related to one, two, or more occurrences of Y, denoted [1,n], but each occurrence of Y is related to only one occurrence of X, denoted [1,1]. This is shown diagrammatically as follows:

3) A relationship between attributes X and Y is many-to-many, if each occurrence of X may be related to one, two or more occurrences of Y, and each occurrence of Y many be related to one, two or more occurrences of X.

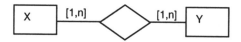

4) A relationship between attributes X and Y is zero-or-one-to-many, if each occurrence of X may be related to one, two or more occurrences of Y, but occurrences of Y are related either to one occurrence of X, or none.

The above types of relationship are illustrated in Example 5.3.

EXAMPLE 5.3

Examples of relationships with different cardinalities are illustrated below:

1) *The following is an example one-to-one relationship.*

   A department has only one manager and a manager manages only one department.

2) *The following is a zero-or-one-to-many relationship.*

   A hotel is either independent or part of only one hotel chain, but a hotel chain may include many hotels.

3) *The following is a many-to-many relationship.*

Zero, one, two or more customers have stayed at each hotel, and each customer has stayed at zero, one, two or more hotels.

The ER model also includes notation to represent attributes, and to specify those that are used as the keys, as illustrated in Figure 5.4. Note that in Figure 5.4, attributes are shown as "circles on sticks". Black circles are used to denote the keys.

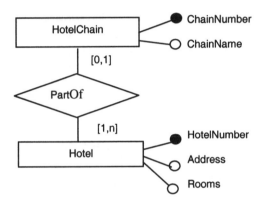

Figure 5.4 ER Diagram with entities, relationships and attributes

Figure 5.5 illustrates other ER model notations for composite keys and generalisation/specialisation relationships. Note the following features:
- A bar across a set of attribute (e.g. Name and Address of Person) shows that a key is composed of the attributes linked by the bar.
- The line that connects attributes of an entity to the relationship line that associates it with a second entity (e.g. InvoiceItem) denotes that the key is composed of the identified attributes and also the key of the related entity (i.e. InvoiceNumber and ItemNumber combined).
- The broad arrow connecting entities (e.g. from Customer to Person) indicates that the entity at the start of the arrow is a specialisation of the entity at the point of the arrow, and therefore inherits its properties (i.e. Customer is_a Person).

DATA ANALYSIS METHODS
Data analysis methods generally fall into one of two categories—top-down and bottom-up, though some methods include a bit of each.

Top-down is working from a general analysis of phenomena to the detail, and bottom-up is the opposite.

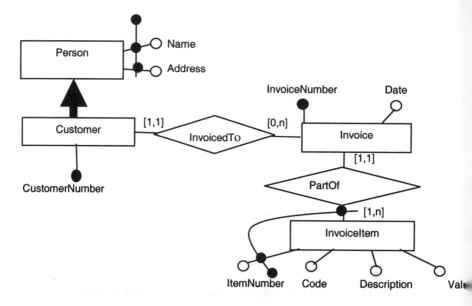

Figure 5.5 ER Model to illustrate composite keys, and generalisation/specialisation.

BOTTOM-UP DATA ANALYSIS

The bottom-up approach to data analysis is to work from the attributes upward towards the entities and relationships that are to be represented in the database. This method is sometimes called data aggregation or synthesis. This approach can be likened to viewing the world as comprising free-floating facts, and then analysing how they interrelate in order to make some sense of them.

Bottom-up data analysis is based on the notion that entities are implicit in the data values. By analysing all attributes referred to in descriptions of the organisation, it is possible to identify the relationships between them and hence the existence of entities. The entities are implied by those data items that determine other data items. Data items that determine others are the natural keys (i.e. the identifiers of the entities represented in the database, rather than identifiers of the database structures).

EXAMPLE 5.4

A customer number is related to just the one customer name, and so the customer number attribute is said to determine the customer name attribute. We therefore deduce the existence of an entity, occurrences of which are identified by the values of the customer number attribute. Customer number is the natural key of this entity.

The bottom-up data analysis process is as follows:

1) IDENTIFY DATA ITEMS

Data items are identified in descriptions of the organisation to be served by the database and the system requirements. They may be identified from for example, the fields on some data recording form, or the contents of the organisation's files and records.

EXAMPLE 5.5

An example organisation maintains a file containing details of customers. By inspection, we may identify a number of data items, including the following:

> *CustomerNumber*
> *CustomerName*
> *Customer's Organisation*
> *ContactTelephoneNumber*
> *ContactAddress*
> *PaymentDetails*

2) IDENTIFY RELATIONSHIPS BETWEEN DATA ITEMS

The designer must now identify:

- those attributes that are related to other attributes;
- the types of those relationship, i.e. one-to-many, one-to-one, many-to-many, or zero-or-one-to-many (see above).

The relationships identified then provide a basis for deducing the entities.

EXAMPLE 5.6

Continuing with the analysis of attributes identified in step (1) (Example 5.5), there are many ways in which values of the attributes identified may be related, but the designer must identify just those relationships that he or she thinks are relevant to the structure and activities of the organisation. Different designers may come to different, but equally valid conclusions as to what the relevant relationships are. In this example, the designer reasons the existence of the following relationships.

- *Customer's Organisation is related to the CustomerNumber attribute for each customer in the organisation.*
- *CustomerNumber is related to the attribute, ContactTelephoneNumber, by which he or she may be contacted, and also to CustomerName, ContactAddress and PaymentDetails.*

These relationships are sketched in the diagram in Figure 5.6.

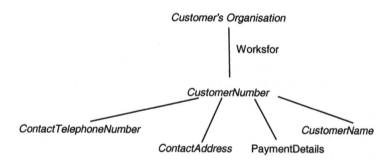

Figure 5.6 A sketch of the attributes and relationships identified in Examples 5.5 and 5.6

Initially all of the relationships between attributes are represented as one-to-one, but the diagram will be modified later to indicate the actual relationship cardinalities, as they become apparent.

We next have to determine the cardinality of each relationship. This requires the analyst to reason about the maximum and minimum number of attribute values that can participate in a relationship. Each relationship must be considered in both directions.

EXAMPLE 5.7

Continuing with the example data analysis (Examples 5.5 and 5.6), the cardinalities of the relationships are as follows:

- *Each customer will be a private customer, or will represent a particular organisation, but an organisation may have many representatives, and so the "WorksFor" relationship between Customer's Organisation and CustomerNumber is zero-or-one-to-many.*
- *Each customer has a unique name and contact address. However, many customers may have the same name and contact address. The relationships between CustomerNumber and CustomerName, and between CustomerNumber and ContactAddress, are therefore one-to-many.*
- *Each customer may have many contact telephone numbers (e.g. home, office, mobile) and the same number may be used to contact different customers. The relationship between CustomerNumber and ContactTelephoneNumber is therefore many-to-many.*

These cardinalities are added to the sketch in Figure 5.7.

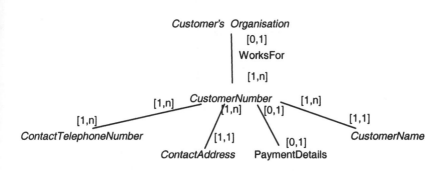

Figure 5.7 A sketch of the attributes and relationships identified in Examples 5.5, 5.6 and 5.7

3) IDENTIFY ENTITIES
Entities are deduced from the attributes and relationships identified in steps (1) and (2) above. An entity is deemed to exist where there appear to be attributes that name it and others that represent facts about it. The following types of relationship therefore imply the existence of an entity.

- Many-to-one relationships—In an occurrence of this type of relationship the value of the "many" attributes determines a value of the "one" attribute, and so we assume the values of the "many" attributes are the names of entities and the "one" values represent facts about those entities.

EXAMPLE 5.8

There is a many-to-one relationship between CustomerNumber and CustomerName and ContactAddress. This is because for any one occurrence of CustomerNumber there is only one value of CustomerName and one value of ContactAddress. The converse is not true, since, for example, there may be more than one John Smith, or there may be two employees living at 25 High Street, Leeds. We therefore have a situation where the value of CustomerNumber determines the value of CustomerName and the value of CustomerAddress.

Consequently, we deduce that there exists an entity type, occurrences of which are named by a value of CustomerNumber, and facts about which are represented by the values of CustomerName and ContactAddress. We therefore add a Customer entity to the conceptual model for the database, or the Web data, depending upon the design activity (see Figure 5.8).

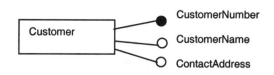

Figure 5.8 The customer entity identified in Example 5.9

In general, where there is a many-to-one relationship the 'many' attribute is assumed to provide the name of an entity, and the 'one' attribute is assumed to represent a fact about the entity.

- Zero-or-one-to-many relationships—In an occurrence of this type of relationship, a value of the "many" attribute determines a value of the "zero-or-one" attribute; though some values of the "many" attribute may be unrelated to any of the "zero-or-one" attribute values. We therefore assume that the values of the "many" attribute are the names of entities, and the values of the "zero-or-one" attributes are the names of other entities which are sometimes related to them.

EXAMPLE 5.9

In our analysis in Examples 5.5–7, we identified that there was a zero-or-one-to-many relationship between Customer's Organisation and CustomerNumber. We can therefore deduce the existence of two entities, one identified by values of Customer'sOrganisation, and the other identified by values of CustomerNumber (already deduced in Example 5.8), and so the data structure diagram becomes as shown in Figure 5.9.

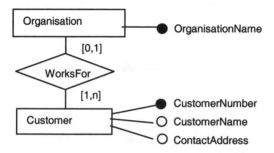

Figure 5.9 Entities and relationships deduced in Example 5.9

In general, where two attributes are related in a zero-or-one-to-many relationship, two entities named respectively by the "zero-or-one" and the "many" attribute values are implied.

- Many-to-many relationships—This type of relationship identifies three entities. The values of the two sets of "many" attributes in the relationship each identify an entity, and the relationship itself is considered to be an association entity.

EXAMPLE 5.10

There is a many-to-many relationship between CustomerNumber and ContactTelephoneNumber because customers may share a telephone number with other customer. Also, there may be many telephones by which a particular customer can be contacted. We therefore deduce the set of entities. These are:

- *the Customer entity, which is identified by CustomerNumber.*
- *the Telephone entity, which is identified by ContactsTelephoneNumber.*
- *the entity, occurrences of which represent the fact that a particular customer can be contacted on a particular telephone. This third entity may be thought of as an entry in a telephone directory.*

The data structure diagram therefore becomes as in Figure 5.10.

Note that a many-to-many relationship is replaced by two one-to-many relationships. All many-to-many relationships may be broken down in this way.

- One-to-one relationships—These may imply one or two entities. The two attributes in the relationship may simply be alternative identifiers for a single entity, or they may identify two distinct entities.

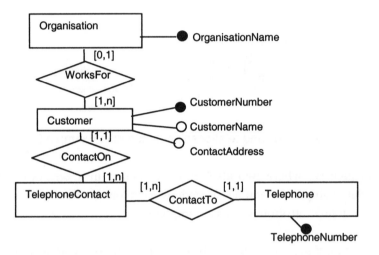

Figure 5.10 The ER model derived in Examples 5.5–5.10

EXAMPLE 5.11

There are no one-to-one relationships in our running example. Instead consider the following two examples of a one-to-one relationship:

1) *There is a one-to-one relationship between an employee's payroll number and their National Insurance number. In this case these are alternative identifiers (keys) for the one entity, employee.*

2) *There is a one-to-one relationship between department name and the employee number of its manager. The manager and department both have an independent existence, are uniquely identifiable, and there are facts about them which are of interest. We therefore deduce two entities, employee and department, related by a one-to-one ManageOf relationship.*

At the end of this bottom-up data analysis we have identified entities and their attributes, and have also identified the relationships between these entities.

4) COMBINE THE DATA MODELS

The above analysis may be performed for a number of descriptions of the organisation, each from the perspective of different activities. The set of data models so produced must then be combined to form a single data model, which will be the basis from which the database itself is designed. Models may be merged where they include the same entity types, in which case the lists of entity attributes for common entities must be merged. This combining may be iterative and may involve some re-analysis and re-definition or renaming of entities, attributes and relationships.

TOP-DOWN LOGICAL DATA ANALYSIS

Top-down or entity-attribute-relationship data analysis works from the real world, to the entities that are of interest within the real world, to the relationships between those objects, to the properties of those entities. The following processes are applied and the result is a conceptual data model of the organisation.

1) IDENTIFY ENTITIES

An entity is a thing that has independent existence and about which we wish to represent information. We can deduce the existence of entities by reasoning about the organisation, and in particular about the activities that take place and the data that is recorded within it. The grammar of a written description of the operation of the organisation provides clues that help identify the entities. An entity is usually referenced in text by a noun or a noun-phrase.

It is not always easy to distinguish between entities and attributes. An attribute may also be referenced by a noun or a noun phrase. We distinguish between an entity and a property or attribute through the following reasoning—an entity has existence of its own, whereas an attribute only exists as a property of an entity. For example, customer is an entity type because a customer exists whether or not we know details of his or her customer number and name. The latter two are attributes of a customer because they exist only as facts about the customer.

This distinction may be somewhat blurred and there may be cases where the designer could legitimately choose to treat a referenced phenomenon as either an entity or an attribute. For example, a customer's address exists whether or not we know of its attributes, but it may be of interest only as an attribute of a customer. An important property of an entity is that each occurrence is uniquely identifiable. That is to say, it must have attributes or groups of attributes, which uniquely identify it; these form its keys in relational terminology

We will work through an example similar to that used in the discussion on bottom-up data analysis, to illustrate top-down design.

EXAMPLE 5.12
Consider the following partial description of the workings of the organisation, provided by the sales officer.

"... A new customer is allocated a customer number. In addition the following details are recorded: the name of the organisation that the customer represents (if any), the customer's name, contact address, and also one or more telephone numbers by which they can be contacted...."

Through analysis of the nouns and noun phrases of the above text, we identify the following which may be entities.

> *customer*
> *organisation*
> *contact*
> *telephone*
> *(telephone) number*
> *(department's) name*
> *(customer's) name*
> *(contact) address*

Of the above, the first two are clearly entities. "Contact" refers to customer. Telephone satisfied the properties of an entity, i.e. it exists independently, it is uniquely identifiable, and there are facts about it tha we wish to know, i.e. its number. However, it is a matter of judgement as to whether we wish to model telephone as an entity or as a property of a customer. In this case we can argue that telephones are interesting only in the context of contacting specific customers, and therefore it makes sense to model them as attributes of customers. The last four are attributes rather than entities, since they are all properties of one of the above entities. Thus we deduce the existence of the entities, customer and organisation. Thus, our evolving conceptual model is as in Figure 5.11.

```
┌──────────────────┐          ┌──────────────────┐
│ Customer         │          │ Organisation     │
│                  │          │                  │
└──────────────────┘          └──────────────────┘
```

Figure 5.11 The ER Model derived in Example 5.11

2) IDENTIFICATION OF RELATIONSHIPS BETWEEN ENTITIES

Having identified a set of entities, the next step is to determine if and how pairs of entities are related. These relationships represent the types of connections that can exist between the real world phenomena represented by the entities. There are many ways in which objects may be connected. Some examples are given below.

Once again, the grammar of the organisation description provides clues which assist the identification of relationships. A relationship is implied by phrases of the type: "has......." or "requires a number of......" or "is a part of.....". This type of phrase references one entity in describing another.

An objective of this analysis is to identify only those relationships which are direct links between entities. For example, an organisation may be related to a customer who is related to a spouse who works for a different organisation, but we are not interested in directly modelling this indirect relationship between departments.

In some cases a relationship may already have been identified as an entity. This will be the case when that relationship is given a name, e.g. "...marriage is the union between this man and this woman...." Here, marriage will have been identified as an entity, which is in fact a relationship between two other entities, man and woman.

EXAMPLE 5.13

Continuing the analysis of Example 5.12, by inspection we identify the relationship, customer represents organisation. Thus, the data structure diagram becomes as shown in Figure 5.12

The type of the relationships must now be determined. This is done through a similar reasoning to that used in bottom-up data analysis (see above). However, whereas in bottom-up design we reasoned about values, here we must reason in terms of the real world entities themselves.

Figure 5.12 The ER Model derived in Examples 5.12 and 5.13

EXAMPLE 5.14

Consider the "represents" relationship in Figure 5.12, To determine the relationship cardinality, we must ask, how many customers may there be who represent a particular organisation, and how many organisations may a particular customer represent? The answer depends on the real world constraints. In our case study, we assume that each customer may represent only one organisation, but some are private customers who do not represent any organisation. Further, an organisation may be represented by many customers. This is therefore a zero-or-one-to-many relationship from organisation to customer, as shown in Figure 5.13.

Figure 5.13 The ER model derived in Examples 5.12–14

3) IDENTIFY ENTITY ATTRIBUTES

The third stage is to identify the types of fact about the entities that must be represented in the database. Again, the grammar of the organisation description gives clues which aid this task. Attributes are implied by nouns and noun-clauses, as are the entities themselves. The attributes are implied where the noun or noun-clause identifies something that is a property, quality or characteristic of some entity.

EXAMPLE 5.15
Returning to the example descriptive text in Example 5.12, the following attributes may be deduced

Entity	*Attribute*
Customer	*customer number*
	name
	contact address
	contact telephone numbers
Organisation	*organisation name*

Further, we can reason that since the customer number and organisation name attributes will be unique for each instance of Customer and Organisation, respectively, they can therefore be used as keys. Thus, the ER Model becomes as in Figure 5.14.

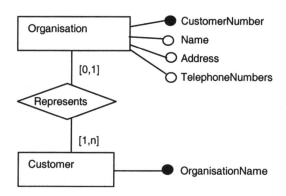

Figure 5.14 The ER model derived in Examples 5.12–15

4) COMBINE ANY SEPARATE MODELS

This is the same process as for bottom-up design. A number of descriptions may have been analysed and the different conceptual models must be merged.

The small case study provides a trivial example, but does serve to illustrate the essential features of ER modelling and the bottom-up and top-down approaches. Note that the former method is the more formal. Consequently, top-down analysis relies more on the analyst's judgement. This will often result in a simpler conceptual model (as in the examples), since the analyst will filter out entities, relationships and attributes that do not make sense or are not useful within the context of the problem. (A fuller explanation of ER modelling can be found in various books, such as [Batini 91].)

In the next section we discuss how the above techniques are also adapted for Web Data analysis.

5.3 CONCEPTUAL MODELLING OF WEB PAGES

Web data analysis derives a conceptual model of the data to be represented within the Web pages. The inputs to this process are the description of the organisation and the system requirements, together with the conceptual model for the database of which the Web database system is an application. In this section we describe how the ER model and analysis techniques are adapted for this purpose.

To illustrate this process we shall use the case study in Example 5.16.

EXAMPLE 5.16

EagleleyHotels plans to support online accommodation reservations via the Web. The (simplified) ER Model for the database of which this is an application is shown in Figure 5.16. The Web pages to support this application will be organised as follows

- *A home page contains links to pages containing details of each hotel, and also links to pages with details of each hotel chain.*
- *Hotel chain pages present details of the chains and are linked to the relevant hotel pages. The page for a particular hotel chain will display the name of the chain and a contact address, telephone and fax number. The page also lists the addresses of the hotels in that chain as anchors to links to the pages on which details of each hotel are displayed.*
- *Hotel pages present details of the hotels, i.e. the hotel address, its star rating, contact telephone and fax numbers, the number of rooms and the minimum and maximum room price per night. There is also a link from each hotel*

page to the relevant hotel chain page and also a link to the online booking page.

- *The online reservation pages for each hotel displays a form for entry of details of the client, dates of the proposed stay, and the type of room(s) required. When a form is filled in and submitted, a "provisional" reservation is recorded in the database. Also, the system will automatically email the reservation request to the relevant hotel, who will send reservation and room tariff details to the customer for confirmation, depending on room availability.*

EXTENDING ER MODELLING FOR WEB DATA MODELLING

A Web database system supports database applications through interaction via Web pages. The Web pages therefore play a similar role to that of a view (see Section 2.2 Relational Databases: Views) or an external model (see 1.1 Database Technology: The Database Management System). That is, they separate out the part of the database that is relevant to the application and hide the rest. Like a view or an external model, Web pages for an application represent entities, attributes and relationships as data.

When designing the data content of the Web pages it is important to address the ways in which a Web page is different from a relational table. Consequently, new features must be included in a conceptual model of the Web pages. Specifically, there are two aspects of Web Pages that require extensions to the ER model.

1) Hypermedia links—The hypermedia created by the Web pages (see Section 4.2 How Does A User Put Information On The Web?: Representing Information on the Web) explicitly provides navigation paths between related entities. These are provided by the links within and between the Web pages. These can be represented in the conventional way within an ER diagram, as relationships. However, the relationship lines must become arrows, to show the direction of each link.

2) Web application-specific concepts—The Web pages themselves represent concepts that are important to the user, for example, since these may provide access points into the hypermedia. These concepts will often correspond to entities, relationships or attributes within

the conceptual model of the database. However, at other times they do not. In such cases, the concepts that do not correspond to abstractions in the database conceptual model must still be represented in the conceptual model for the Web pages. We represent these as ovals, called concept boxes.

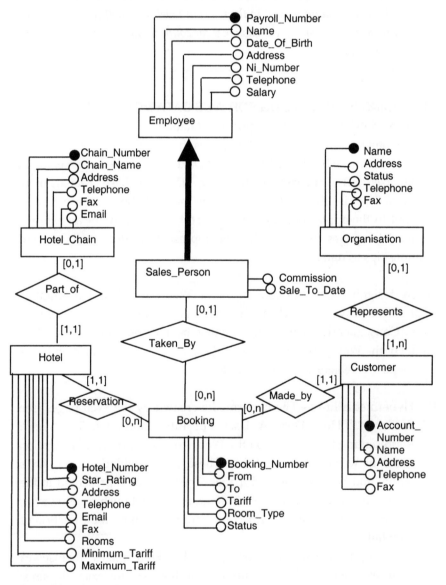

Figure 5.15 The ER model for the database for which the case study in Example 5.16 is an application

The above adaptations of the ER model are illustrated in Figure 5.16, which is the conceptual model for the case study Eagleley Hotel Online Booking system. (A description of how this model is derived is given in the following subsection.)

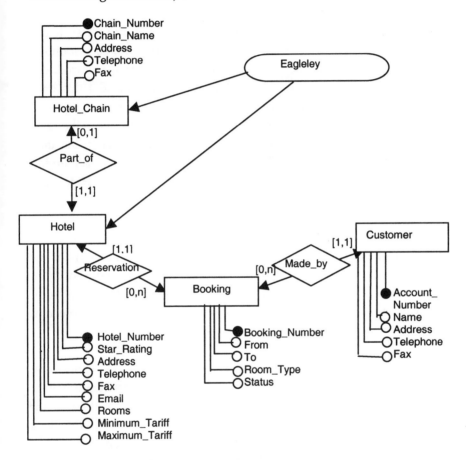

Figure 5.16 Conceptual (ER) model of the Eagleley Hotel Online Booking Hypermedia

Note the inclusion of the two new features discussed above, to model the additional information represented by Web pages:

1) Directional relationships—Unlike relationships in an ER model (see previous section), the ones in Figure 5.16 have arrow-heads. This is

because the links within and between Web pages are directional. A page can include the URL of another page to allow a relationship to be navigated, but the inverse link is optional and has to be explicitly specified as a link in the destination page. For example, since hotel pages contain links to the relevant hotel chain page and hotel chain pages contain links to relevant hotel pages, the Part_of relationship has arrow heads at both ends.

2) Web application-specific concepts—The entry point to the system as a whole is provided by the home page. There is no corresponding concept in the ER model for the database. We therefore introduce a new concept in the Web conceptual model to represent this entry point, called "Eagleley". We use a new symbol, the oval, to represent Eagleley. This type of symbol is called a concept box. From the home page it is possible to access Web pages which detail specific instances of the hotel and hotel chain entities. The Eagleley concept is therefore connected by arrows that associate it with the Hotel and Hotel_Chain entities.

WEB DATA ANALYSIS

Web data analysis, like data analysis (see 5.2 Data Analysis) for the database, is the process by which a conceptual model is produced. In the previous subsection we showed how the ER model is adapted to model the way in which information is represented in Web pages. We now explain the process of deriving that model.

Web data analysis follows data analysis so that the process can take as input both the description of the organisation and system requirements, and the conceptual model of the database. The aim is to use the description to select from the conceptual model the part that is relevant to the Web application, and to identify and specify the additional Web application-specific concepts and directional relationships.

The aims of modelling the information that Web pages will represent, prior to the detailed design of the Web pages themselves and the connectivity with the database, are: as follows:

1) We establish the mapping between the information presented on the Web pages and that stored in the database upon which the detailed design of the Web pages will be based. Also, by presenting it in a

straightforward digrammatical form, it is possible to communicate and explain this conceptual design to the future users of the system and thus check the validity of the design.

2) We check the validity of the database with respect to its intended use in the Web database application. This analysis should help us to identify required information missing from the database.

3) The conceptual model of the Web pages gives us a basis for verifying that the detailed design and implementation of the Web pages is correct.

4) By approaching the design problem in stages, working from the conceptual level to the physical implementation, we avoid the technical complexities, such as the design and implementation of page features and Web database connectivity mechanisms, from occurring at too early a stage. Basically, we defer the complexities of implementing the Web system until we have a clear understanding of what we must implement.

The process then proceeds in two stages, as in Figure 5.17.

WEB DATA EXTRACTION

The aim of the first of the two phases of Web data analysis is to define the part of the conceptual model of the database that is relevant to the Web database application. Therefore the process takes as its inputs the database conceptual model and the requirements for the Web database system. The latter are analysed for references to the former. Where these exist, the references' abstractions are included in an ER model of the Web data.

As in Data Analysis (see 5.2), the grammar of the description provides clues as to which entities, attributes and relationships should be included.

- Entities are implied by nouns and noun phrases.
- Relationships are implied by phrases of the type: "has......." or "requires a number of......" or "is a part of.....". This type of phrase references one entity in describing another.
- Attributes by are implied where the noun or noun clause identifies something that is a property, quality or characteristic of some entity.

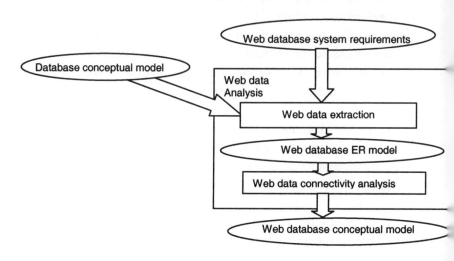

Figure 5.17 Web Data Analysis

You will remember from the previous discussion of data analysis that the classification of concepts can be subjective, since the same concept can often be classified as either an entity, relationship or attribute, depending on the perspective and perception of the analyser. However, this is less of a problem for the Web data analyst, since that classification has already been made within the conceptual model for the database. Web data extraction is therefore a more straightforward task of identifying concepts referred to in the Web application description and determining if any of those concepts are modelled in the conceptual model of the database.

For each candidate entity, attribute or relationship, the designer seeks corresponding abstractions in the conceptual model of the database. The matched concept, if it exists, is then added to the conceptual model for the Web database application.

The matching of concepts in the conceptual model with those named in the requirements description may be complicated by differences in the ways in which phenomena are described in the Web application description and within the database conceptual model. For example, the entity Customer in the conceptual model is referred to as client in the description, and so on. The analyst must therefore reason in terms of the meanings of the terms and phrases, rather than simply matching character strings.

In cases where the database is specifically defined to support the Web applications, all of the conceptual model will be relevant, and so this stage becomes trivial.

Having extracted those concepts referred to in the Web application description, it may then be necessary to add additional concepts of the conceptual model for completeness. These are added so as to avoid any "loose ends". The completeness rules that must be applied are as follows:

1) Entity attribute completeness—If an attribute is added to the ER model for the Web pages, the entity of which it is an attribute must also be added.
2) Entity identify completeness—For each entity added to the ER model for the Web pages, the attributes that form its primary key must also be added.
3) Referential completeness—If a relationship is added to the ER model for the Web pages, then all of the entities that participate in that relationship must also be added.

The above process is illustrated in Example 5.17.

EXAMPLE 5.17
The Web data extraction phase of Web data analysis for the application in Example 5.16 proceeds as follows. The analyst seeks to identify concepts referred to in the descriptive text and that are also represented in the database conceptual model (Figure 5.16). The analysis therefore follows a similar process to that used for data analysis, i.e. the text is scanned for grammatical clues that imply entities, attributes and relationship. Initially, we seek the nouns and noun clauses in order to identify the entities and their attributes. We then seek references to the relationships that associate them. The concepts identified and the corresponding concepts in the conceptual model are as follows:

(hotel) reservation	*Booking entity*
hotel	*Hotel entity*
accommodation }	
hotel chain	*HotelChain entity*
chains }	
client	*Customer entity*
(hotel chain) name	*Name attribute of HotelChain*
(hotel chain) contact address	*Address attribute of HotelChain*
(hotel chain) contact fax	*Fax attribute of HotelChain*
((hotel chain) contact	*Telephone attribute*
telephone numbers	*of HotelChain*
(hotel) address	*Address attribute of Hotel*
(hotel) star rating	*Stars attribute of Hotel*
(hotel) contact	*Telephone attribute*
telephone numbers	*of Hotel*
(hotel) contact fax number	*Fax attribute of Hotel*
(hotel) minimum room	*MinimumTariff attribute*
nightly tariff	*of Hotel*
(hotel) maximum room	*MaximumTariff attribute*
nightly tariff	*of Hotel*
(reservation) dates	*From and To attributes of Booking*
(reservation) room type	*RoomType attribute of Booking*
(reservation) provisional/	*Status attribute of Booking*
confirmed	

Note the differences in terminology used in the application description and in the database conceptual model, i.e. client and Customer, accommodation and Hotel, chain and HotelChain, reservation and Booking. This analysis task is therefore one of determining the meaning of the terms used, rather than simply matching character strings.

Certain entities, attributes and relationships are not referred to in the requirements statement and are therefore omitted. For example, there is no reference to the Organisation, Employee or Salesperson entities and associated relationships. Also, though the Tariff entity of Booking is referred to, this is in the context of activities that take place outside of the system, i.e. during direct hotel to customer communications.

Once the entities and attributes have been identified, the analyst must seek references to relationships between entities, so as to determine which relationships should be included in the Web data conceptual model. The relationships referred to in the text are between hotels and the hotel chains, and between reservations and the relevant customer and hotel.

The analyst now checks the above concepts for completeness.

- *Applying the* Entity attribute completeness rule no entities are found to be missing, since in all cases where an attribute is referred to, so is the entity of which it is an attribute.
- *Applying the Entity attribute completeness rule, we add the following attributes since they are primary keys of the entities: ChainNumber, AccountNumber, HotelNumber, BookingNumber.*
- *Applying the Referential completeness rule, there are no additional entities, since for each relationship referred to, all participating entities have also been referred to.*

Thus the ER model for the Web pages is as in Figure 5.19. Note that Organisation, Salesperson and Employee have been omitted, since these are not referred to in the application description.

WEB DATABASE CONNECTIVITY ANALYSIS

This task is to analyse the Web database application description in order to identify the access points into the system, and the navigation paths between and within the Web pages. On the basis of these the following modifications are made to the Web page conceptual model:

- Where an access point does not correspond to a concept represented in the ER model for the Web pages, it is added as a concept box.
- Where a navigation path is identified, the ER model is analysed to see if this corresponds to a relationship. Accordingly, arrow-heads are added to the relationship connecting line in the ER model, to show the direction of the navigation.

This process is illustrated in Example 5.18.

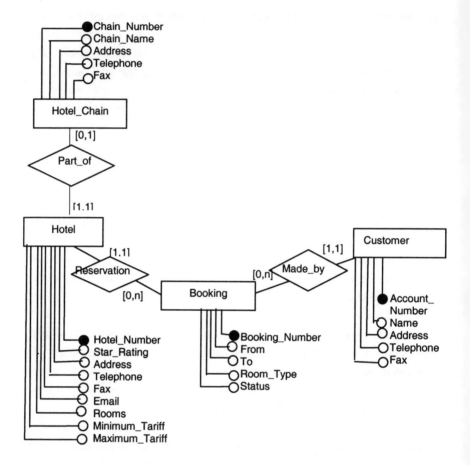

Figure 5.18 ER Model for the Example 5.17 Web database application

---

EXAMPLE 5.18
The connectivity analysis of Example 5.17 proceeds as follows:

- *Example 5.17 refers to the "home page" for the Eagleley Hotels online booking service. This provides the access point, but does not correspond to any of the concepts in the database conceptual model. A concept box is therefore added to the Web pages conceptual model, labelled "Eagleley", since this represents the concept of the whole system.*

- *There are access paths from the home page to the hotel and hotel chain pages, and so arrows are included from the "Eagleley" concept box to the Hotel and HotelChain entities.*

- *There are naviagation paths from each hotel page to the relevant hotel chain page, and also from the hotel chain page to the pages for hotels in that chain.*

The relationship between Hotel and HotelChain entities is therefore bi-directional, and this is shown by a double-headed arrow.

- *There is also a link from the hotel page to the reservation page, and so the relationship line from Hotel to Booking becomes an arrow.*
- *Details of clients (or customers) and bookings are both entered and displayed on the reservation page. The relationship between Customer and Booking is therefore bi-directional, and is represented by a double-headed arrow.*

Thus, the conceptual model for the Web pages becomes, as previously shown in Figure 5.16.

5.4 DATA DESIGN.

This second phase of logical database design is to represent the natural structure specified in the conceptual data model as a database structure. The designer will seek to use the structures supported by the DBMS to represent the entities, attributes and relationships of the conceptual data model. In an RDBMS these must all be represented using tables. The designer must find a way of representing the entities, attributes and relationships as tables, without loss of information or unnecessary duplication of data values.

A conceptual data model is transformed into a relational database by applying the following rules:

RULE 1: RESOLUTION OF MANY-TO-MANY RELATIONSHIPS.

Any many-to-many relationship may be replaced by two one-to-many relationships. This is done by introducing an entity that represents the association between two of the participating entities. The new association entity will have any attributes of the relationship that it models.

EXAMPLE 5.19

We illustrate the application of Rule 1 by applying it to the Figure 5.19 ER model. Note that this ER model is a variation of part of the ER diagram in Figure 5.16. In particular, we now model a booking as a relationship between a hotel and a customer, rather than as an entity. Note also, that the relationship is now many-to-many, since a customer may make many bookings, and a hotel may be booked by many customers. Also, there are attributes of the relationship, rather than the participating entities.

If we apply Rule 1 to the ER model in Figure 5.19 we produce the model in Figure 5.20. Note that the many-to-many Reserves relationship is replaced by an association entity that we have called Reservation. Two one-to-many relationships relate each instance of the association with one Hotel and one Customer entity.

RULE 2: REPRESENTATION OF ENTITIES

Each entity in the ER diagram becomes a table. Each property becomes an attribute in the relation. A primary key is selected.

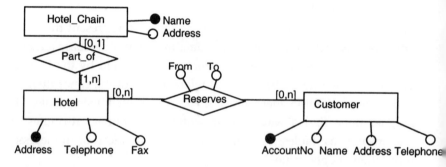

Figure 5.19 The ER Model in Example 5.19 prior to application of Data Design Rule 1

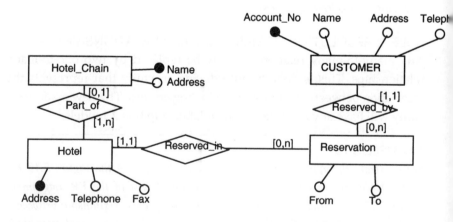

Figure 5.20 The ER Model in Figure 5.19 after application of the data design Rule 1

EXAMPLE 5.20
Applying the Data Design Rule 2, to the ER model in Figure 5.20, we derive the following table definitions:

```
TABLE   Hotel_Chain (
        ATTRIBUTE Name
        ATTRIBUTE Address
)


TABLE Hotel (
        ATTRIBUTE Address
        ATTRIBUTE Telephone
        ATTRIBUTE Fax
)


TABLE Customer (
        ATTRIBUTE Account_No
        ATTRIBUTE Name
        ATTRIBUTE Address
        ATTRIBUTE Telephone
)
TABLE Reservation (
        ATTRIBUTE From
        ATTRIBUTE To
)
```

RULE 3: ONE-TO-MANY RELATIONSHIPS.

The primary key of the "one" (parent or owner) table migrates to the "many" (child or member) table. Thus each row in the "many" table may cross-reference a row in the "one" table. These "migrated" primary keys become foreign keys (see 2.1 Relational databases).

EXAMPLE 5.21
If we apply the Data Design Rule 3 to the conceptual model in Figure 5.20, the relational database design becomes, as follows:

```
TABLE   Hotel_Chain (
        ATTRIBUTE Name
        ATTRIBUTE Address
)


TABLE Hotel (
        ATTRIBUTE Address
        ATTRIBUTE Telephone
        ATTRIBUTE Fax
)


TABLE Customer (
        ATTRIBUTE Account_No
        ATTRIBUTE Name
        ATTRIBUTE Address
        ATTRIBUTE Telephone
)

TABLE reservation (
        ATTRIBUTE Hotel_Address
        ATTRIBUTE Account_No
        ATTRIBUTE From
        ATTRIBUTE To
)
```

Note that the key attributes of Hotel and Customer have been added to the attributes of Reservation, respectively to implement the one-to-many relationships, Reserved_in and Reserved_by.

RULE 4: ZERO-OR-ONE-TO-MANY RELATIONSHIPS.

These are relationships that hold only for some of a particular type of entity. For instance, we may have marriage as a relationship between a man and a woman, but some men and some women are unmarried. These relationships may be represented by a separate table, in the same way that many-to-many relationships are (see Rule 1).

EXAMPLE 5.22
If we apply the Data Design Rule 4 to the conceptual model in Figure 5.20, the relational database design becomes, as follows:

```
TABLE  Hotel_Chain  (
       ATTRIBUTE Name
       ATTRIBUTE Address
)

TABLE Hotels_In_Chain  (
       ATTRIBUTE Chain_Name
       ATTRIBUTE Hotel_Address
)

TABLE Hotel  (
       ATTRIBUTE Address
       ATTRIBUTE Telephone
       ATTRIBUTE Fax
)

TABLE Customer  (
       ATTRIBUTE Account_No
       ATTRIBUTE Name
       ATTRIBUTE Address
       ATTRIBUTE Telephone
)

TABLE Reservation  (        '
       ATTRIBUTE Hotel_Address
       ATTRIBUTE Account_No
       ATTRIBUTE From
       ATTRIBUTE To
)
```

Note that the Hotels_In_Chain table has been added to implement the zero-or-one-to-many relationship Part_of, and the keys of the two entities that it relates are its attributes.

The above is an implementation of the example conceptual data model. However, further adjustments may still be made to this design, for example, to remove any unnecessary duplication of information that may still exist within the design, or to make the database design more suitable for the requirements of time critical or high priority applications.

NORMALISATION

The normalisation process is applied to further improve the design of a relational database. It does this by applying part of the theory of relational databases in which some wisdom about what is, and what is not, a good database design is formally defined. These notions are expressed in terms of sets of restrictions, each of which excludes certain undesirable properties from database designs. These sets of restrictions are called normal forms, and normalisation is the process of creating a database design that does not violate them.

Database design methods invariably include normalisation at some stage. Typically, a method will prescribe that bottom-up or top-down data analysis is followed by data design to produce a gross database design, and then normalisation is applied to improve it.

Normalisation achieves a good database design by reducing the amount of data duplication. Data redundancy is undesirable for three reasons:

1) Data redundancy is a consequence of an unnatural representation of information. Since a particular instance of an entity or relationship occurs only once within the real world, it should be represented just the once in the database.
2) It causes problems when the database is updated. Updating a data item will cause inconsistency unless all other copies of that data item are also updated.
3) It causes the database to take up more storage space than is necessary.

Many normal forms have been defined, but there are six that are well established in the theory of databases. These are:
- First Normal Form (1NF)—This is concerned with simplifying the structures in a database so as to ensure that each data value represents a single fact and is accessible given only the table name and key value.
- Second Normal Form (2NF), Third Normal Form (3NF), and Boyce Codd Normal Form (BCNF)—These are all concerned with

eliminating the duplication of data that represents single-valued facts.

- Fourth Normal Form (4NF) and Fifth Normal Form (5NF)—These are concerned with eliminating the duplication of data which represents multi-valued facts. 4NF deals only with cases where multi-valued facts are independent of each other. 5NF or Project/Join Normal Form deals with the cases where multi-valued facts are not independent of each other

The above normal forms define progressively tighter restrictions on the design of a relational database. Therefore, a database that satisfies 2NF will also satisfy 1NF, one that satisfies 3NF will satisfy 2NF, and so on.

Mainly, it is only the first four of the above normal forms that are used in practice. These are illustrated below using examples based upon the relational table in Figure 5.22. This table has been contrived to illustrate the faults that normalisation removes. (Formal definitions of the normal forms can be found in the following: 1NF, 2NF and 3NF in [Codd 70]; BCNF in [Codd 74], 4NF in [Fagin 77] and 5NF in [Fagin 79]. An intuitive guide to these normal forms is given in [Kent 83].)

Hotel_Booking

Hotel_No	Chain_No	Cust_No	From	To	C_Addr
H2	HC3	C1	1/9/00	3/9/00	Chez Frank
H2	HC3	C2	1/9/00	2/9/00	Mon Repose
H3	HC2	C1	2/8/00	7/8/00	Chez Frank

Figure 5.21 Example Badly Designed Relational Table

Hotel_Booking represents information about reservations made by customers (identified by a customer number (Cust_No)) to stay in specific hotels (identified by a hotel number (Hotel_No)). The hotels are parts of hotel chains (identified by a hotel chain number (Chain_No)). Also, the address of the customers is recorded (C_Addr). The hotel reservation is from a specific arrival date (From) until a specific check-out date (To).

FIRST NORMAL FORM (1NF)

1NF imposes the restrictions that rows of a table may contain only values that cannot be split into smaller component values. This ensures that each attribute value represents a single fact.

1NF is built into the definition of the original relational data model [Codd 70], which requires columns to be defined on atomic domains. The advantages are simplicity and uniform access to all facts represented in the database. No relationships or entities may be hidden within complex structures. However, this restriction has been lifted in the most recent version of SQL, i.e. SQL:1999 (see 3.2 Object-Relational Databases) which allows the values in columns to be made up from other values. For example, SQL:1999 allows arrays of values or rows of values to appear in columns of a table.

A consequence of 1NF is that a bad (unnatural) database design will make it necessary to represent the same information more than once. The subsequent normal forms, i.e. 2NF, 3NF, BCNF, 4NF and 5NF, have been defined to remove this problem.

The Figure 5.21 table does in fact satisfy 1NF, since the values in each column are simple values. However, it is deliberately badly designed to demonstrate the problems that subsequent normal forms are contrived to remove.

KEYS AND FUNCTIONAL DEPENDENCIES

2NF, 3NF and BCNF exclude unnecessary duplication of data values that represent single-valued facts.

EXAMPLE 5.23

ChainNo in HotelBooking is an example of data that represents a single-valued fact. Its values represents facts concerning the identification numbers of hotel chains, and these are single-valued facts because there is only one number for each hotel chain.

Unnecessary duplication of single-valued facts occurs when a table represents information about more than one type of entity. For example, each row of HotelBooking represents facts about both a customer and also a booking. Therefore it is necessary to duplicate customer information for each booking made by the customer. In general, such situations can be defined in terms of the keys and the relationships between the columns of a table.

KEYS

Keys are important in normalisation since they provide the names of the phenomena represented by the rows of a table. For example, the key of a table that describes hotels is likely to be the hotel's name or identification number.

EXAMPLE 5.24

The key of HotelBooking is a combination of the columns HotelNo, CustNo, From, since that will uniquely identify any booking.

Certain data values are the natural keys of the entities that must be represented in a database. For example, Cust_No is the natural key of the Customer entity. In general, a good database design should ensure that the natural keys coincide with the table keys. Normalisation achieves this.

FUNCTIONAL DEPENDENCIES

The relationships between columns are important because they show situations when entities other than those named by the keys are also described by the table. The relationship between columns whose values identify objects, and columns whose values represent single-value facts about those objects is modelled by a functional dependency (FD). The concept of an FD is explained below with the aid of an example.

The entity identifying columns and those that represent single-valued facts about the entities in Figure 5.21 are as follows:
- A booking is uniquely identified by the columns HotelNo, CustNo and From.
- Columns that represent other single-valued facts about a booking are the values of To, CAddr, and ChainNo.

The above relationships between columns are modelled by FDs as follows:
- Since the column, To, is a single-valued fact about the entity identified by columns, HotelNo, CustomerNo, and From, we say that

To is functionally dependent on (HotelNo, CustomerNo, From), or alternatively (HotelNo, CustomerNo, From) functionally determines To. This FD is written,

HotelNo, CustNo From → To

- Similarly, the following FDs also hold:

HotelNo, CustNo, From → CAddr
HotelNo, CustNo, From → ChainNo

The above FDs mean that for any specific booking there can be only one value of the "To" time, and only one customer address and hotel chain number. (As our analysis progresses we will identify other FDs characterised by HotelBooking.)

The left-hand side of an FD is called the determinant, and the right-hand side, the determined column. In general, the columns on the left-hand side of an FD include the natural keys of the entities represented in the database.

SECOND NORMAL FORM (2NF)

2NF prohibits the situation where each row of a table represents single-valued facts about more than one entity, and where the identifiers of those entities are contained in key values. This situation is outlawed by requiring that tables are in 1NF and that there are no partial FDs on a table's key. A partial FD on a key is an FD where the determinant is part of a key.

EXAMPLE 5.25

The key of HotelBooking is (HotelNo, CustNo, From). However, CustNo on its own determines the value of CAddr, and the value of HotelNo on its own determines the value of ChainNo. The FDs that hold for HotelBooking therefore include:

HotelNo, CustNo, From → To, CAddr, ChainNo
CustNo → CAddr
HotelNo → ChainNo

The second two of the above FDs are partial FDs on the key. HotelBooking therefore violates 2NF.

A partial FD on a key occurs when the key includes the identifier of more than one entity, and the table also includes single-values facts about more than one of those entities. In the example, a key value identifies a booking, but also includes the identification of a customer and a hotel. A value of CAddr represents a fact about a customer, a value of ChainNo represents a fact about a hotel chain, and a value of To represents a fact about the bookings.

Partial FDs on a key are a bad thing because they result in data redundancy. In the example it can be seen that for each booking made by customer C1, the address 'Chez Frank' must be replicated. Similarly, for each reservation in hotel H2, it is necessary to duplicate the fact that that it is part of the hotel chain, HC3. Data redundancy of the above type has three undesirable consequences.

1) It is not possible to represent certain types of information. For example, if there are no current bookings by customer C1 then there will be no record of their address.
2) Update anomalies may occur when individual rows are inserted or amended. For example, if the customer address is changed in one row of HotelBooking, this may cause inconsistency with other rows which record bookings made by the same customer.
3) Redundancy obviously causes more store to be used than is necessary.

A table is normalised to 2NF by splitting it up so that its columns are distributed over a number of new tables. This splitting up of the original table is done strategically so as to remove the partial FDs on the keys, but without any loss of information. The process is as follows:

Step 1: Where there is a FD on part of a key, $X \rightarrow Y$ say, form a new table within which X is a key, and in which the columns determined by X are also included.

Step 2: Form a new table which is defined on the columns of the keys of the original table, and in which are also every column which is **not** functionally determined by just part of the key.

EXAMPLE 5.26

HotelBooking is put into 2NF using the above process as follows.

Step 1: There are two FDs on part of the key (HotelNo, CustNo, From),

$$CustNo \rightarrow CAddr$$
$$HotelNo \rightarrow ChainNo$$

We therefore create two new tables (CustNo, CAddr) and (HotelNo, ChainNo) in which CustNo and HotelNo are the respective keys.

Step 2: The key of the original table and the remaining columns form a new table (HotelNo, CustNo, From, To)..

In this way the table HotelBooking becomes the tables given in Figure 5.22.

Customer

CustNo	CAddr
C1	Chez Frank
C2	Mon Repose

Hotel

HotelNo	ChainNo
H2	HC3
H3	HC2

Booking

HotelNo	CustNo	From	Too
H2	C1	1/9/00	3/9/00
H2	C2	1/9/00	2/9/00
H3	C1	2/8/00	7/8/00

Figure 5.22 Example Relational Tables in 2NF

Note, that all of the FDs still hold for the new database and there has been no loss of information, but the database is now in 2NF because there are no longer any partial FDs on the keys in any of the three new relations. Note also that the data duplication has now been removed, the address of a particular customer, and the hotel chain of a particular hotel, are now recorded only once.

THIRD NORMAL FORM (3NF)

3NF prohibits the situation where each row of a table represents single-valued facts about more than one entity, and where the identifiers of those entities are contained in key values and also in non-key columns values. 3NF does this by imposing the same restrictions as does 2NF, but also prohibits transitive FDs of non-key columns on keys.

A transitive FD of a non-key column on a key occurs where a non-key column is functionally determined by another non-key column which is also functionally determined by a key. For example, if column X is a key, and columns Y and Z are not parts of a key, then there is a transitive FD of Z on X if $X \rightarrow Y$ and $Y \rightarrow Z$.

3NF is explained in the following example, through further examination of the Hotel table in Figure 5.22.

EXAMPLE 5.27

To illustrate 3NF, we slightly extend the Hotel table in Figure 5.22 to include two additional columns, ChainName and HotelName. The extended table, HotelPlus is shown in Figure 5.23. This introduces some new problems. HotelPlus is still in 2NF, since the key is still HotelNo. However, there is now clearly some unnecessary duplication of data. The name of a hotel chain is duplicated for every hotel in that chain. This is because ChainName is determined by ChainNo, which is not the key. HotelPlus therefore violates 3NF. The offending transitive FD is as follows:

$$HotelNo \rightarrow ChainNo \rightarrow ChainName$$

HotelPlus

HotelNo	ChainNo	ChainName	HotelName
H1	HC3	Hotels-R-Us	Imperial
H2	HC3	Hotels-R-Us	Majestic
H3	HC2	Hotel-U-Like	Bayview

Figure 5.23 Example Badly Designed Relational Table

Transitive FDs on a key occur when each row in a table describes more than one entity, one of the entities being named by the keys, but other objects being named by non-key attributes. In the example a row contains facts about both a hotel (identified by the key value, HotelNo) and also about an hotel chain (identified by ChainNo).

Data redundancy may occur where there are transitive FDs on the key. For example, details of hotel chain HC2 are repeated because they have two hotels. This redundancy may cause inability to represent certain types of information, and may result in update anomalies, as was a consequence of partial dependencies on the key and which were removed by 2NF normalisation.

1) Information about an entity of the type identified by a non-key attribute cannot be represented if there are no associated entities identified by the keys. For example, HotelPlus cannot represent information about a hotel chain which has yet to acquire hotels.
2) Update anomalies may occur when a row is altered, or a new row is inserted. For example, if the chain name of HC2 is changed in one row, it will also be necessary to alter it in the rows for the other hotels in that chain.

The following procedure transforms a 2NF table that violates 3NF into a set of tables that satisfy 3NF table.

Step 1: Where there is a transitive FD on a key, $X \rightarrow Y \rightarrow Z$ say, form a new table (Y, Z) within which Y is a key and which contains columns determined by Y.

Step 2: Form a new table which is defined on the columns of the keys of the original table and every column which is **not** transitively functionally determined by a key.

EXAMPLE 5.28

The above process is applied to HotelPlus as follows.

Step 1: The transitive FD on the key is

$$HotelNo \rightarrow ChainNo \rightarrow ChainName$$

and so a table is formed on (ChainNo, ChainName).

Step 2: The original key is HotelNo, and the column that is not transitively dependent on the key is HotelName, and so a second table is formed on (HotelNo, HotelName).

The 3NF tables so derived are shown in Figure 5.24.

HotelChain

ChainNo	ChainName
HC2	Hotel-U-Like
HC3	Hotels-R-Us

Hotel

HotelNo	ChainNo	HotelName
H1	HC3	Imperial
H2	HC3	Majestic
H3	HC2	Bayview

Figure 5.24 Example Relational Tables in 3NF

Note that after normalisation to 3NF, all unnecessary duplication of single-valued facts in the example tables has been removed. For example, the information that the hotel chain HC3 is called Hotels-R-Us is now stated only once.

SUMMARY DEFINITION OF 1NF, 2NF and 3NF
An easily remembered summary definition of 1NF, 2NF and 3NF is as follows.

> Each non-key column is dependent on the key (1NF),
> the whole key (2NF)
> and nothing but the key (3NF).

A FINAL NOTE ON NORMAL FORMS
Other normal forms have been defined as a basis for further improvement to the design of relational databases. Above are mentioned BCNF, 4NF and 5NF, and many others are defined in the literature on relational database theory. However, most practical database design methods restrict themselves to the application of the normal forms described above, i.e. 1NF, 2NF and 3NF.

It should also be noted that normal forms provide only a crude basis for database design. Normalisation will not always produce the best design, since many of the subtleties of the meaning of data are not apparent in an analysis of data based on FDs and keys alone. For example, normalisation may fail to identify where natural keys are for different entities, e.g. where there is a one-to-one relationship, and normalisation may split up data that is always accessed together. Further, there may be alternative designs which satisfy 3NF, some of which provide a more natural representation of the information than others. Normalisation should therefore be applied to suggest improvements to the design of a relational database, and to check the correctness of the initial data analysis, but the database designer must use judgement to decide on the most natural and appropriate design. Database design is still an art, rather than a science.

5.5 WEB DATA DESIGN

In this section we describe the process by which the data structures of the Web pages are determined. The process takes as input the Web conceptual model and defines a schema for each Web page. The notations used to represent Web page schemas are described in the next subsection. This is followed by a subsection in which the Web data design method is described.

LOGICAL WEB PAGE SCHEMAS

A Web page provides access to Web resources by displaying information, and by allowing users to interact with the page. For example, a user may interact by filling in displayed forms, and by clicking on icons or text to initiating the execution of processes. Users may also access other Web resources by clicking on the anchor text of the links. In addition, users can interact with Web pages through the standard interface features of a browser (see Chapter 4).

Web pages can be complex, both in terms of the features they display and the associated processes. However, when designing the data component of Web pages we are concerned only with data that is retrieved from the database and displayed, with data entered by users, and with the links or access paths to data accessible via other pages. At this stage of the Web database design process, we therefore design the data content of each page but ignore other complexities, such as the other Web page features and the way in which the database connectivity is implemented. These complexities can be considered at a later stage during physical Web database design (see Chapter 6), once the information content of the pages has been specified.

We have already studied how a logical view of data is achieved during data design (see 5.4 Data Design). This view is specified by the logical data model, which is implemented as a logical database schema. For Web data design we use a similar technique. We specify the data content of Web pages as logical Web page schemas. These specify the structure of the data that is displayed and/or input via each Web page. A Web page schema can be thought of as the record structure definition of the Web page, in the same way that a logical schema for a table in a relational database defines the structure of the rows in the tables.

The characteristics of Web pages require that some additional features be added to conventional logical schema languages. Specifically we must be able to define the following:

1) The structures of unique pages—Some of the pages in a Web database application will have a fixed structure and content when displayed, for example, the home page in the Example 5.17.
2) Structures common to many pages—More often, the Web pages of a Web database system are dynamically created from data retrieved from the database to describe different instances of entities. Thus, there are sets of pages within a Web database system that will have a fixed structure but different data values. For example, all of the Hotel pages will include the same data fields, but with different values.
3) Links—The logical Web page model must be able to represent the inter-page links, since these represent associations and navigation paths between the data represented in each Web page.
4) Complex data structures—The structure of a Web page, in terms of the data represented, can be more complex that the structures allowed in a relational database. A relational table can have only simple values in its columns (this restriction is called first normal form (see 2.2)), however, a Web page can contain fields with nested structures and also lists of values. For example, the "Hotel Chain" Web pages include a list of links to the relevant hotel pages, where each link field in the list comprises two component fields, the anchor and the link itself.

In our Web database design method we therefore describe the structure of Web pages using a schema (similar to a table definition in a relational database, or a class definition in an object database). There will be one schema for each unique page, and one to describe each set of pages with a common structure. The notation used is similar to that of the ODMG ODL (Object Definition Language) used to define classes in an object database (see 3.1). An example is given in Figure 5.25.

```
PAGE-SCHEMA HotelChain
{
        STRING          ChainNumber
        STRING          ChainName
        STRING          ChainAddress
        STRING          Telephone
        STRING          Email
        LIST_OF         (Hotel: LINK(STRING HotelAddress;
                        *Hotel)) Hotels
}
```

Figure 5.25 Web Page Schema for the Hotel Chain Pages

Note that the Web page schema (Figure 5.25) defines the data fields (or attributes) displayed in the Web page.
- The general structure of a Web page schema is as follows: It starts with the keyword "PAGE-SCHEMA", the name of the schema (HotelChain), followed by a list of field definitions within braces.
- Complexly structured data fields (e.g. Hotel) are defined by including the definition of the nested structures within brackets.
- Repeating data items are indicated by the keyword, "LIST_OF".
- In addition to the usual field types, e.g. STRING, INTEGER, etc., there are also link fields. These represent links within the Web page and therefore comprise the anchor and the address (denoted by preceding a page schema name with an asterisk).

A graphical representation of Web pages schemas, again using notation introduced in [Atzeni 99], is shown in Figure 5.26. In the diagram, boxes represent schemas and arrows represent the links.

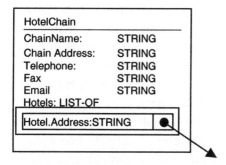

Figure 5.26 Graphical representation of the logical Web page schemas for the Eagleley Hotels Online booking system.

Note that the Hotels field in Figure 5.27 has a complex value, which is graphically shown by nested boxes. The outside box represents the "LIST_OF" values, and the inner box represents the individual values in that list, each of which comprises the anchor value (HotelAddress) and the link to the Hotel page. The latter is represented by an arrow, which in the completed diagram will point to the box that represents the Hotel Web page.

The advantage of the graphical notation, as with ER diagrams, is that it better facilitates both validation and verification. Verification is the process by which we establish that the design is a correct implementation of the requirements. Validation is that process by which we establish that the design is for a valid solution.

- Verification—The graphical notation provides a representation of the complete system in terms of the data in the Web pages and the links between them. This can be used to check that the information in the Web conceptual model has been represented. Also, it can be used to verify that the navigation paths between the entities are implemented either by including the associated data in the same page, or by providing a link between pages that display the related data.
- Validation—This notation can also be used to explain the design to future users, and to trace the ways in which the system will be used for characteristic use cases. This should help to identify omissions, inaccuracies or cases where the implementer has misunderstood the user's requirements.

Web page schemas are derived from the Web conceptual model. This can be done by first sketching the Web pages that support the Web database application, so as to identify the data fields in each of the Web pages (ignoring other Web page features). The field names used in the schemas should be those used in the database schema, so as to establish the exact mapping between the database and each Web page.

- Concept boxes—Typically, these will be implemented as pages. For example, the concept "Eagleley" will be presented by the home page.
- Entities—Attributes of each entity must be represented, typically on the same page, or on directly linked pages.
- Relationships—Relationships between entities must be represented by including the data for associated entities on the same page, or by linking the respective pages.

The validity of the design is tested by tracing how the pages will be used, in given use scenarios.

Figure 5.27.gives Web page sketches for the case study application. Note that these provide a simplified and stylised depiction of what the final system will look like. The sketches concern the data that will be presented in the Web pages, but not the detailed design of how they will be presented.

Schemas are defined for each of the sketched Web pages. The field names used should be those used in the database schema, so as to establish the mapping between the Web pages and the database. A full set of schemas for the Eagleley case study Web database system is given in Figure 5.28.

Finally, the Web page schemas are brought together to form a single integrated graphical representation of the Web database system, using the notation discussed above. The graphical representation of the case study system is shown in Figure 5.29.

The Web page schemas together with the database schema form the logical Web database system design. The ways in which this can be implemented are discussed in Chapter 6.

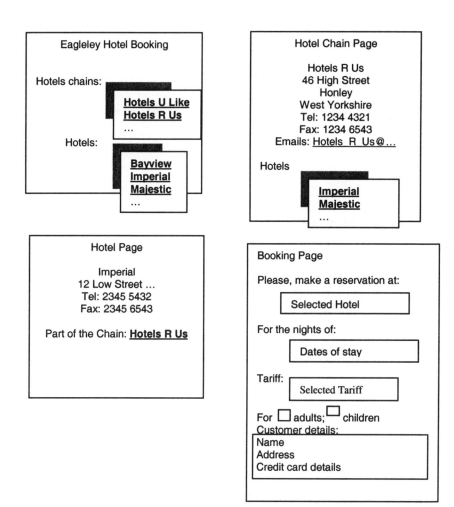

Figure 5.27 Sketches of the Web pages from the Eagleley Hotels Online Booking System

```
PAGE-SCHEMA Eagleley UNIQUE
{
        LIST_OF
            (STRING HotelChain.Name, *Chain) HotelChains;
        LIST OF
            (STRING HotelAddress, *Hotel) Hotels;
)
```

```
PAGE-SCHEMA HotelChain
{
        STRING   ChainNumber
        STRING   ChainName
        (...)Hotel.Address
        STRING   Telephone
        LIST_OF (STRING HotelAddress; *Hotel) Hotels;
}
```

```
PAGE-SCHEMA Hotel
{
        STRING   ChainNumber
        STRING   ChainName
        (...)ChainAddress
        STRING Telephone
        LIST_OF (STRING  HotelChain.Address; *Hotel)Hotels;
}
```

```
PAGE-SCHEMA Reservation
{
        STRING   CustomerName
        STRING   CustomerAddress
        STRING   CustomerTelephone
        (STRING HotelAddress; *hotel);
        DATE   From
        DATE   To
        STRING   CreditCard
}
```

Figure 5.28 Web Page Schemas

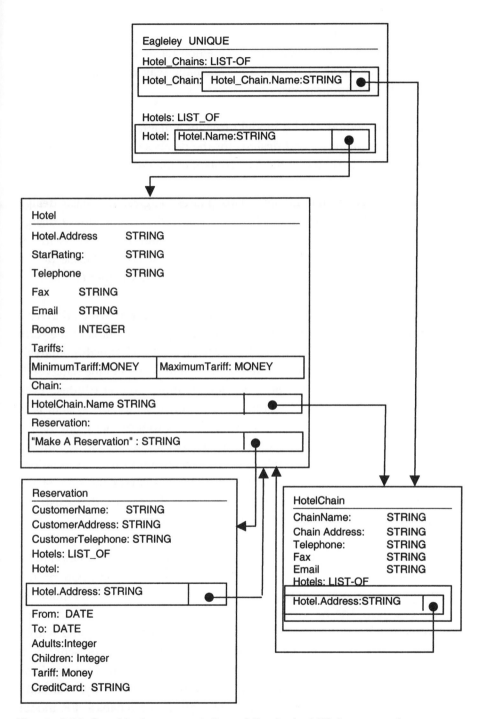

Figure 5.29 Graphical representation of the logical Web page schemas for the Eagleley Hotels Online booking system

5.6 SUMMARY
In this chapter, we have described a method for designing Web database systems. This method provides a systematic way of designing a data-intensive Web applications.

Within the method, the **ER model** provides a diagrammatic language for representing analyses and designs for the database system and has also been adapted to represent the data content of the Web pages.

Web database design involves two phases. **Logical database design** defines the logical structure of the database. **Physical database design** then determines the way in which the logical design will be implemented. The method described is a logical Web database design method. Physical Web database design is covered in Chapter 6.

The first phase of Web database design is **data analysis** which derives a **conceptual model** of the database. The conceptual model is in the form of an ER model. This is derived by applying **entity relationship analysis techniques**, in which the information to be represented in the database is interpreted in terms of **entities, relationships** and **attributes**. Data analysis takes as input, descriptions of the organisation the system is to serve and the system requirements, and can produce many alternative designs. Two approaches to data analysis are **bottom up** and **top down**. The former infers entities, relationships and attributes from associations that can exist between data values. The latter analyses the part of the world that the system is to serve in terms of the entities that exist, the associations that can exist between them, and their properties.

Web data analysis produces a conceptual model of the information to be represented in the Web pages. The input is the description of the organisation and system requirements, and also the conceptual model of the database. The ER model is adapted for this purpose. Relationships are given direction to model the navigational **links** between and within Web pages, and **concept boxes** are introduced to represent **Web application-specific concepts** that do not occur in the database conceptual model. Web data analysis is in two phases. Firstly, **Web data extraction** defines an ER model of the part of the database ER model relevant to the Web database system. Secondly, in **Web database connectivity analysis** the links between the entities and other Web application specific concepts are identified and represented in the ER model for the Web database application.

The next two phases, **data analysis** and **Web data analysis** concern the ways in which the conceptual models of the database and the Web database application are logically implemented.

Data analysis takes as input, the conceptual model of the database, and derives a representation of it using the logical structures supported by the DBMS. An RDBMS is used, and so the purpose is to define tables to implement the ER model of the database. After replacing any many-to-many relationships with two many-to-one relationshsip, entities are represented as tables. Other tables are defined to represent associations between entities, where appropriate. **Normalisation** is also applied to improve the database design. Normalisation is the modification of the database design so as to conform to various constraints, called **normal forms**. These are defined in terms of the table keys and dependencies between columns, to exclude unnecessary duplication of data. Three normal forms are applied, to ensure that each column is determined by the key (**1NF**), the whole key (**2NF**) and nothing but the key (**3NF**).

Finally, **Web data design** determines the data structures of the Web pages. These are defined as Logical Web page schemas, which specify the data items in each page, including any with complex structures and those that provide links.

EXERCISES

(5.1)   Describe the stages of a conventional database design method. What are the inputs, outputs and purpose of each?

(5.2)   Why do database design methods concentrate on entities types, rather than instances? In your answer give an example of an entity type and an instance of it.

(5.3)   Describe the stages of a Web database system design method. Identify those stages that have been added to the stages identified in your answer to (5.1), explaining why they are needed, and what are their inputs, outputs and purpose.

(5.4)   The stages of Web database design can be grouped into those that are part of logical Web database design, and those that are part of physical Web database design. Explain the meanings of the terms logical and physical in this context. Why are both needed?

(5.4) What is meant by a semantic data model?

(5.5) What is the purpose of a conceptual model and of a logical model within the context of a Web database design method? Why are both needed?

(5.6) Distinguish between data analysis and data design. Why are both required?

(5.7) Upon which abstractions is entity relationship analysis based, and why is it relevant to Web database system design?

(5.8) Distinguish between top-down and bottom-up data analysis methods.

(5.9) Explain why the ER model has to be extended to represent conceptual models of Web applications.

(5.10) Web database design complicates the conventional database design process. Identify five additional complexities that must be addressed.

(5.11) Identify two scenarios within which a Web database is designed. How do these affect the Web database design process?

(5.12) What are the stages of Web data analysis?

(5.13) What properties does a phenomenon have to have in order to be considered as an entity?

(5.14) Distinguish between an attribute and an entity. Explain why the address of an employee could be considered as either.

(5.15) Distinguish between a relationship and an attribute of an entity. Explain how a line manager of an employee could be considered as either.

(5.16) Why is a semantic data model, such as the entity relationship model, used in data analysis, and not the relational data model?

(5.17) An association entity is both an entity and a relationship. Explain how this can be so. Give an example of an association entity that can be identified when modelling the relationship between a student and a course that they have taken.

(5.18) What is meant by the cardinality of a relationship. Consider the problem of modelling the entities and relationships that exist within a family. Give examples of relationships with cardinalities of one-to-one, one-to-many, many-to-many, and zero-or-one-to-many. Represent each using the entity relationship model.

[Hint: the relationship between mother and father has a one-to-one cardinality].

(5.19) Depict the following using the entity relationship model, book and borrower entities, where the book key is its ISBN and the borrower key is a borrower number. The diagram should also depict the relationship between book and the borrower it is on loan to, the title and authors of the book, and the name, address and telephone number of the borrower.

(5.20) Depict using the entity relationship model, bed (in a hospital) entity, patient entity and the relationship between a patient and their bed. The bed key is the combination of ward number and bed (within ward) number.

(5.21) Depict, using the entity relationship model, department and division entities, showing the relationship between departments and the divisions that they are part of. The key for a department is a combination of the division number and department (within division) number. The model should also represent the division and department names.

(5.22) Add an employee entity to the model in your answer to the previous question, and depict the relationships between a department and its head, between a division and its head, and between employees and the departments of which they are members. The combination of division number and employee number within division is used as the key for employees.

(5.23) Data analysis can be performed in a bottom-up or top-down manner. Briefly describe these two approaches, highlighting the differences.

(5.24) In bottom-up data analysis, the fact that a book ISBN determines the title and authors of the book implies the existence of a book entity type. Explain the reasoning behind this inference.

(5.25) In a bottom-up data analysis of a library system, a many-to-many relationship is identified between the book ISBN and borrower number attributes, since there can be multiple copies of any one book, and a borrower number can be related to the many books that they have on loan. What entities can you infer from this relationship?

(5.26) In a bottom-up data analysis two attributes identified are CompanyCarNumber and EmployeeNumber. These are related, in that some employees have a company car assigned to them. What entities can you deduce?

(5.27) What clues does the grammar provide for the data analyst who is seeking to identify entities, attributes and relationships from a description of an organisation. Give examples.

(5.28) Both entities and attributes may be described by nouns and noun clauses. How does the analyst distinguish between them? Give examples.

(5.29) Consider the following statement and use bottom-up data analysis techniques to identify entities, attributes and relationships:

"The library stocks books, identified by an ISBN. Each book has a title one or more authors, and a publisher. There can be multiple copies of a book. A borrower can borrow up to six books at any one time, for up to three weeks. When a loan is made, the ISBN, borrower number, date of loan and return data are recorded. When a borrower registers with the library, their name, address, telephone number, sex, date of birth and the date are recorded."

(5.30) Identify entities, relationships and attributes by analysing the following statement (using both top-down and bottom-up data analysis techniques):

"Students attending Honley University enrol on courses. There are prerequisites for enrolment—i.e. the student must have certain qualifications, or be accepted by Dr. Brown the admissions tutor. The institute currently has 3,000 students enrolled. Once enrolled, the student will accumulate credits by taking various course modules, such as Programming and Object Databases. A grade is awarded for each completed module. The grade will be A, B, C, D or E. A represents distinction, and E a fail. Students may be full time or part time."

(5.31) A Web database application is required by Honley University (see 5.30), for storing and retrieving student records, so as to retrieve details of their courses, modules taken and their grades. Perform a Web data extraction and Web database connectivity analysis for this application.

(5.32) Draw an ER diagram for a Person entity showing the relationships *MarriedTo*, *ParentOf* and *ChildOf*.

(5.33) Draw an ER diagram for part of the ship's navigational system showing how various classes for oil rigs, ships of different types and buoys share attributes via inheritance.

(5.34) The statement in 5.30 includes examples of entities at too high and too low a level of abstraction, and also redundant, irrelevant and vague terms. Identify and classify these.

(5.35) Identify the is_a relationships implied by the statement in 5.30. Analyse each in terms of its usefulness within the admissions database.

(5.36) Explain how Honley University could be viewed as either an abstract or a physical entity.

(5.37) Represent the following structure as an ER model:
"The University of Honley is a technical university, with five faculties, each with departments."

(5.38) Show how the management structure within Honley University, can be represented by a single employee entity and appropriate relationships.

(5.39) Define the type and cardinality of each relationship defined in the previous questions.

(5.40) Identify the attributes implied by the text in 5.30.

(5.41) Define first normal form (1NF). What are the advantages of enforcing 1NF, and what are the disadvantages?

(5.42) What is meant by the terms functional dependency, table key and natural key? Why are these important in normalisation?

(5.43) Define second normal form (2NF). Why does a database that does not satisfy 2NF cause potential problems?

(5.44) A relational table has been designed to represent information about the projects upon which employees of a company work. The table therefore comprises the following columns: employee number, employee name, employee's address, project number and project name. An employee number and project number are both unique. Employees may work on many projects and many employees may work on a project. Identify the keys of this table, and the functional dependencies. Explain why the table does not satisfy 2NF, and what the consequences might be. Describe how the table can be decomposed into tables which do satisfy 2NF.

(5.45) Define third normal form (3NF). Why does a database that does not satisfy 3NF pose potential problems?

(5.46) A relational table is designed to represent details of projects. Its columns are, project number, employee number of project leader, project name, host department and head of host department. Each project has a unique number, a leader and a host department. Each department has only one head, but can host many projects. Identify the table keys and functional dependencies. Explain why the table does not satisfy 3NF and what the potential consequences are. How can the table be converted into tables which do satisfy 3NF?

(5.47) Explain the difference between validation and verification. How is a Web page schema respectively verified and validated?

(5.48) How must the entity relationship model be extended to model the data associated with Web pages?

(5.49) Explain the purpose of a concept box in an entity relationship model of a Web database system. Give an example of where one would be used.

(5.50) Explain why relationships in an entity relationship model of a Web database system are depicted as arrows. Give examples of where the arrows would be single and double headed.

(5.51) Sketch Web pages that could be used for a Web database system to purchase cinema tickets. The system should have a number of pages, starting with a home that displays the films showing at each of the six screens. This is linked to a booking page for each of the screens. The booking page should allow the customer to enter the time and date at which they wish to view the film and their credit card number.

(5.52) The database for the Web-based cinema ticket system in the previous question stores details of customers, screens, films, and bookings. Draw an entity relationship diagram that represents these entities, the relationships between them and attributes that are relevant to this application.

(5.53) Design a set of relational tables to represent the entity relationship model in your answer to the previous question. Draw examples of the tables with sufficient data to convince yourself that your design is valid.

(5.54) The cinema ticket system is required to display details of films and the screen on which they are showing. It is also required to allow users to make bookings for each screen at dates and times of their choosing. When a user makes a booking they must enter their credit card number. Derive an extended entity relationship model to represent the structure of the information to be represented by the Web pages.

(5.55)   In the Web database system design method, two notations are used to represent Web pages. Why is this advantageous? What are the respective roles of the notations?

(5.56)   Web data analysis involves Web data extraction and Web data connectivity analysis. Explain the inputs, ouputs and purpose of these two tasks.

(5.57)   Define the three completeness rules that the entity relationship model for a Web application must satisfy.

(5.58)   A Web application is required to allow borrowers to search for books on the basis of author or title. Sketch the Web pages involved, and perform a Web data extraction on the data model in your answer to 5.29. Explain what modifications you have to make to ensure that each of the three completeness rules is satisfied.

(5.59)   Perform a Web Database Connectivity analysis for the system in 5.29. Explain what modifications you must make to the Web data model in order to represent the navigation paths identified.

(5.60)   How is a many-to-many relationship between entities resolved during data design. Illustrate your answer by considering the many-to-many relationship between Parent and Child.

(5.61)   How are entities represented as relational tables during data analysis? Illustrate your answer by considering an implementation of the entities in your answer to 5.29.

(5.62)   How is a one-to-many relationship represented as relational tables during data design? Illustrate your answer by considering how you would represent publisher and book entities and the publishes relationship between them.

(5.63)   How is a zero-or-one-to-many relationship represented as relational tables during data analysis? Illustrate your answer by considering how you would represent borrower and book entities and the OnLoanTo relationship between them.

(5.64)   Design relational tables to represent the entity relationship model in your answer to question 5.52.

(5.65)   Represent the Web page schemas in your answer to (5.58) using the graphical notation (as in Figure 5.30).

(5.66)   Explain how the Web database system in your answer to (5.58) will be verified and validated.

(5.67)   Write a short report on the difficulties of Web database systems design for the manager of a company that is just switching from a conventional relational database system to one in which database applications will be accessible via the Web.

6

IMPLEMENTATION OF WEB DATABASES

This chapter describes technical options for implementing a Web database system. Specifically, it sets out to answer the questions:

- How is a database implemented?
- How is a database system connected to the Web?
- What technologies are available?
- What technologies are appropriate?

The starting point is a logical design of a Web database system. Methods that can be used to produce such a logical design have already been described in the preceding chapter. We now overview technologies that can be used to implement the logical design of a database, and to connect the database to the Web pages. This chapter is therefore primarily concerned with physical file structures and access methods for implementing databases, and with Web database connectivity. The latter term refers to those software tools and techniques that can be used to make a database system accessible via the Web. As is the case with all Web technology, this is a rapidly evolving area, and there is a constantly changing range of approaches and tools that can be used. Here we focus on the general approaches, and illustrate these with the most widely used tools currently available. Examples of the general techniques are described and illustrated with case studies. However, it should be noted that this is a rapidly evolving area. For example, the major database vendors, such as Oracle Corp, Informix, Sybase and IBM have all been working with the Web industry to improve their proprietary Web database system products.

The following approaches to Web database connectivity are covered:
- Client side approaches using browser extensions and external applications
- Server side approaches, using:
  - HTML preprocessors
  - Generic and proprietary CGI scripts
  - Server API applications
- Java based solutions

Techniques for transaction control, privacy and security, integrity maintenance, etc. are also overviewed, since these are critical to the successful operation of the Web database system.

The structure of the chapter is as follows. Section 6.1 overviews physical database design. That is, design of the storage structures and access methods to be used to implement the logical structures of the database. The architectural options for connecting the database system to the Web are then overviewed in Section 6.2. Subsequent sections detail the technologies available. Technologies for client and server processing are respectively covered in sections 6.3 and 6.4. Java has a particularly important role in Web database systems, and so is covered separately in section 6.5. We conclude this part of the chapter with a discussion of the implementation choices in section 6.6. The final part of this chapter covers related issues, i.e. transactions (section 6.7), security related issues (section 6.8) and the use of a database to store the Web site itself (section 6.9). The chapter concludes with a summary and exercises.

6.1 PHYSICAL DATABASE DESIGN

Physical database design is the phase in the design process wherein the designer decides how the database is to be stored. A DBMS will usually support a number of alternative physical representations of the logical data structure (see Chapter 5 Web Database Design) and the designer must select the most appropriate. It is therefore essential that designers understand advantages and penalties associated with each alternative.

The designer's objectives are to select physical representations for each logical structure such that the database has the following properties:
- data may be accessed with acceptable speed;
- the database does not use up too much of the computer's store;

- the database is reasonably resilient to catastrophes. It should always be possible to recover a damaged database system, and if only part of the system fails it should still be possible for the remainder to "limp" along.

The above objectives are such that the designer will often achieve one at the expense of the others. For example, making the database efficient for one application may slow down other applications and make the database larger. The designer must therefore come to some compromise design.

Physical design decisions should be based on knowledge of the following.
- Logical database design—The designer must know which structures are to be included in the database. In fact it may be decided that the logical design should be changed so as to favour certain applications.
- Quantities and volatility of data—The designer should know the numbers of data instances that are likely to occur in each table or of each class, the frequency with which each will be altered, and the rate at which each table or class will grow. This is necessary to establish the resources, e.g. the amount of disc space, required to store the database. This knowledge is also necessary to select the most appropriate file structures and access methods.
- The ways in which the data is to be used—Ideally, the designer should know for each database application:
  - the frequency with which the application will be run;
  - its ranking compared with other applications to indicate relative importance;
  - the longest acceptable time for the application to execute.
- Transaction properties—Also, for each transaction which can occur during an application, the designer should know:
  - the number of times the transaction is generated each time the application is run;
  - the tables and columns, or classes, accessed by the transaction, and the type of access, i.e. retrieval, update, delete or insert;
  - the longest acceptable time for the transaction to execute.
- Costs associated with storing and accessing data, given each of the available representations of relations or classes—For any given file organisation the designer must be aware of how it affects the speed

with which records may be accessed, inserted and deleted; and also store overheads, i.e. the amount of store in addition to the data, necessary to implement the representation.

Though, in theory it is possible to use the above information to calculate costs and advantages of different designs, it is more usual to base a design on general properties of different representations. The designer will select representations that appear to make the database efficient for anticipated data manipulations, and then improve the design on the basis of its actual measured performance. This "implement-test-improve" method of physical database design is used because DBMS make it relatively easy to detect and correct inappropriate design decisions. DBMS support facilities which allow the database administrator (DBA) to monitor the operation of a database system during its life-time, and to tune it, i.e. alter the physical design, without disrupting the running of the system. The designer may therefore experiment with different representation of the database and iterate towards a physical database design that gives acceptable access speed, use of computer resources, and reliability.

Physical database design typically proceeds as follows.

Step 1: An initial physical database design is arrived at through analysis of the database applications. The table or class representations that appear most appropriate for the anticipated data manipulation are selected.

Step 2: The initial design is tested. A "test" database is created with realistic amounts of data. If real data is unavailable then "fake" data must be contrived. The anticipated data manipulations are then timed, or "bench-marked". These tests should be as realistic as possible. For example, if the database system is to be a multi-user system, then the database should be tested with simultaneous data manipulations.

Step 3: The initial design will be modified to remove the shortcomings revealed in Step 2. "Bottle-necks" should be identified and if possible the physical design modified to remove them.

Step 4: During its operational life-time, the database system's performance should be monitored and modifications should be made so as to correct inappropriate design decisions, adjust to changing requirement, and maintain the storage structures being used.

STORAGE STRUCTURES

DBMS typically support a number of alternative representations of tables or the instances of a class. These are usually represented as computer files in which each record represents a row or a class instance. Various direct access techniques are then used for rapidly locating the records that represent the rows or instances that satisfy specified search conditions.

A file comprises fixed-size pages, each possibly containing many records. A page is the "unit of transfer" to and from main store. When a file is read from, or written to, complete pages are transferred, not just the relevant records.

The files are handled by the operating system, and accordingly DBMS usually sit on top of the operating system's file manager. As follows:
- A user or application program will make requests to the DBMS using a database language such as SQL or OQL. These requests are expressed in terms of the logical database, i.e. tables or classes.
- The DBMS will then issue the corresponding requests to the file manager in terms of the files and pages that are used to represent the tables and rows, or class instances.
- The file manager in turn accesses the corresponding blocks of data on the computer's storage devices.

The mapping between the objects in the logical database and objects in the physical database is defined in the storage schema. The physical database designer must specify details of the database to both the DBMS and the operating system. The designer must specify:
- to the DBMS, the file structures that are to be used to represent each to the logical structures;
- to the operating system, details of the operating system environment within which the database is to operate. In particular the designer

must specify where each file is to be physically located—i.e. on which storage device and in which directory.

The positioning of files is important for a large database because it effects both performance and resilience to system failure. The designer should position the files so as to achieve the following:

- Balanced use of the computer resources—This is necessary to reduce the risk of bottle-necks at the channels between storage devices and the main store, such as may occur if all of the database is stored on a single storage unit. Better performance may be achieved by spreading the data over a number of storage devices. This makes available more channels and takes advantage of the fact that many storage devices can operate simultaneously.

- Physical partitioning of the database—This is desirable because if all of the database is stored on one storage device, a breakdown of that device will cause all of the database system to crash with it. By strategic distribution of the database across a number of devices the designer can ensure that when one device fails, there will still be sufficient of the database available for some applications to run. This partitioning is just one of a number of ways by which database resilience can be ensured.

Representations of logical structures vary from DBMS to DBMS. However, there are a number of basic techniques. These are outlined in the following subsections.

HEAP FILES AND SERIAL SEARCH

The simplest file structure that may be used to represent a table or instances of a class is a heap file. A heap file is constructed as a list of pages, and when a new record is inserted it is simply stored in the last page of the file. If there is insufficient space left, an extra page is added.

Two advantages to using a heap file are as follows:

1) Fast record insertion—Insertion is faster for a heap file than for any of the alternative file structures. With other structures it is necessary to search for the correct place in which to store the new record, to allocate space in which to store the record, and possibly to insert other information to enable that record to be rapidly located at some

later time. In a heap file new records are simply added to the end of the file.

2) Economic use of store—It is necessary only to store the data records. There are no store overheads.

The disadvantage is that the only possible method of accessing records in a heap file is by serial searching, i.e. searching a file, record by record, from beginning to end. Each record must be tested to see if it represents information that satisfies the search condition. The search must continue until the last record because there may be more than one record that satisfies the search condition. This is therefore the slowest of all methods of record retrieval.

When records are deleted from a heap file it is not possible to immediately reclaim the space. This means that the performance of a heap file will progressively deteriorate as it gets clogged up with deleted records. A heap file which is frequently updated must therefore be periodically recreated by the DBA so as to release the space occupied by deleted records.

Heap files are appropriate in the following situations:
- when a batch of records is to be inserted, for example when a table is first created and populated with rows. However, once populated it will often be appropriate to alter the representation to a structure that supports faster retrieval.
- when a file is only a few pages long. In that case search times will be short, even using a serial search.
- when every record of a file is accessed (in no particular sequence) whenever the file is used.
- a heap file may sometimes be appropriate as part of some other structure. For example, it may be appropriate to store a large file as a heap file, but also to have indexes (see below) for fast access on specific attribute values.

Heap files should not be used in the following situation:
- when only selected rows of a table, or instances of a class are to be accessed. The only way of locating selected rows is by serial searching and that is the slowest of all methods.

ACCESS KEYS

When accessing data, a search condition is used to restrict the rows that are retrieved. For example, consider the following SQL that queries the Hotel table.

```
SELECT *
FROM Hotel
WHERE ChainNumber = 'HC1' AND Rooms > 100;
```

The time taken to execute this query can be decreased if the file used to store the Hotel table is organised such that the DBMS can go directly to the records that store rows that have specified values of ChainNumber or Rooms. When a file is organised to provide direct access to records on the basis of values of specific properties, then those properties are called access keys. (A heap file of course does not support any access keys.) The primary key of a table is usually implemented as an access key by default. However, all of the properties named in a search are candidate access keys, and the designer must decide which of those candidates should actually be used.

The most appropriate access keys can be selected on the basis of how "tight" they are. A tight access key is one where there are relatively few records containing specific values of it. If there are many such records, the access key is said to be "loose". For example ChainNumber would be a tighter access key than Rooms for the Hotel table; since there are few rows with any specific value of ChainNumber, but many for each of the values of Rooms that we may wish to test for, e.g. Rooms > 100.

To illustrate extreme examples, consider the problem of accessing an ElectoralRegister table that contains details of voters in a district. The column Sex would be an extremely loose access key because searching on a value of Sex will restrict a search to only 50% or so of the rows. On the other hand the combination of the columns, Name and Address, would provide an extremely tight access key because testing for specific values will restrict the search to just one row.

Tight access keys are desirable because they can be used to rapidly restrict a search to just a few rows or objects, and there is then relatively little work still necessary to test the rest of the search condition. In general, the tightest candidate access key is used for each table or class.

In the above examples, ChainNumber would be used in preference to Rooms as access key for Hotel; the combination of Name and Address would be used in preference to Sex as access key for ElectoralRegister.

Where there is no obvious choice, the designer must then take into account other factors, such as the relative importance and frequency of the different applications.

Having selected access keys, these can be implemented using various data structures, as described below.

SORTED FILES

The speed of certain types of access may be improved by making sure that the records of a file are stored in some specific order. Specifically, this will speed up the processing of records if the sequence of the file corresponds to the sequence in which they must be processed. Also, sorting a file will speed up the location of records with specific values of the field on which the file is sorted (the access keys). This is even the case for certain logical structures that have no sequence, e.g. a table in a relational database, or a set or bag collection object in an object database.

The latter improvement in the speed of retrieval is achieved because by maintaining sorted files it is then possible to use an alternative and faster way of accessing records, i.e. the binary search. Binary search is the technique of repeatedly halving a file and searching the half in which the required record resides. The process can be likened to that of searching for a clock hidden in a tree trunk, using a chainsaw and stethoscope. The tree is cut in half, and then the half in which ticking can still be heard is halved, and so on, until the ticking stops. The following example demonstrates the significant improvement binary search gives over serial searching.

Consider a Customer table for which CustomerNo is the primary key. Customer represents details of customers C1, C2, C3, C5, C7, C9, C12, C15 and C19, and the records of the file which represents this table are sorted into CustomerNo sequence.

The binary search can be used to execute the following SQL,

```
SELECT *
FROM Customer
WHERE CustomerNo = 'C9';
```

in the manner depicted below.

Records: C1   C2   C3   C5   C7   C9   C12   C15   C19

The binary search proceeds as follows:

1) The middle record, (C7) is accessed. C9 is greater than the CustomerNo in this record, so the required record must be in the top half of the file.
2) The middle record of the top half of the file, (C12) is accessed. C9 is less than C12 and so we conclude that the required record is in the lower half of the top half of the file.
3) The middle record of the lower half of the top half of the file, (C9) is accessed, and the required record is located.

Note that the above binary search requires 3 record accesses, where a serial search would have required 5.

A problem of sorted files is that of maintaining the sequence when new records are inserted. The position in the file of the new record must be found and then space must be allocated in which to store it. In fact, sorted files are usually used within the context of indexed file structures, described later. Some RDBMS do allow heap files which represent tables to be sorted, but make no attempt to maintain the sequence when new records are inserted; they are simply added to the end. The sorted file therefore reverts to a heap file structure.

HASH FILES

In many cases, the fastest access to records in a file is achieved using a technique known as hashing. Hashing is the process of calculating the location of a record (the page address) from the value of an access key.

The computed address is called the record's home address, the access key is also called the hash key, and the calculation necessary address to compute the home address is called the hashing function. Records in a hash file will appear to be randomly distributed across the available file space and for that reason hash files are sometimes called random files. Hashing potentially provides the fastest access to a record via an access key. This is because when it works at its best a record may be retrieved by reading just one page.

A record is inserted into a hashed file as follows:
- A hashing function will compute from the access key value the home address at which the record should be stored for optimum retrieval.
- A collision is said to occur when a hashing function returns the same home address for different access key values. Consequently, both records should be stored in the same page. However, when a collision occurs one possibility is that the page addressed by the home address is full. In that case, the record must be stored somewhere else as an overflow record.

A record with a particular access key value is accessed as follows:
- The home address is computed from the access key value using the hashing function
- The page addressed by the home address is searched.
- If the record is not contained in its home page, other pages must be searched to see if the record is stored as an overflow record.

When overflow does occur, the overflow record must be stored such that it can be located efficiently, and it does not increase the likelihood of future overflow, by occupying the home page of other records. To illustrate some approaches to this, here are four techniques for managing overflow records:

In progressive overflow, an overflow record is placed in the next available location after the home address. When the last page is reached, it is necessary to loop back to the first. When searching for a record, the record is deemed not to exist if an unused record store is located before the record is found.

A variation on progressive overflow is chained progressive overflow where overflow records are chained to the home address. This is done by storing the address of the first overflow page in the home address page, the address of the second in the first, and so on. This reduces the number of page reads necessary to locate an overflow record.

A problem with progressive overflow is that the overflow records occupy the home addresses of other records and increase the likelihood of other overflow records. A technique for avoiding this is to store overflow records in a special overflow storage area, reserved for them only.

Another variation is rehashing. This is the technique of applying a different hashing function to overflow records to find an alternative home address. This second home address may be in a special overflow area.

Clearly, the performance of a hashed file deteriorates as the number of overflow records increases. The objective of the hashing function is therefore to evenly distribute records over the available pages so as to minimise the number of collisions, and hence minimise the number of overflow records and the consequential increase in record access time.

Static hashing techniques assume a fixed allocation of space when the file is created. When that space becomes over-full it is said to be saturated and the DBA must then allocate extra space and recreate the file. Dynamic hashing is a technique whereby saturation is avoided because additional space is automatically added to the file when pages become full, and records are then automatically redistributed.

Where hashing is used it is necessary for the DBA to monitor its effectiveness. The DBMS must therefore provide the following information.
- How much of the address space allocated for the storage of a hash file is occupied. When this space becomes more than 70% full the DBA should allocate more pages and recreate the file.
- Statistics about the average number of pages that must be read in order to retrieve a record. This depends on the number of overflow records, and how they are handled. When the average number of

page accesses becomes excessive, the DBA should recreate the file. When recreating the file, the number of overflow records can be reduced to a minimum. This is done by recreating the file in two phases—firstly all records that will fit into their home address pages are stored, and only then are the overflow records inserted.

Hash files should be used in the following situation:
- when retrieval is always on the basis of the value of a single access key.

Hash files are inappropriate in the following situations:
- when retrieval is on the basis of pattern matching. For example hashing could not be used to retrieve rows from a Customer table for customers whose names begin with "Mac", or from a Hotel table for hotels with hotel numbers which begin with "99".
- when retrieval is on the basis of a range of values. For example, hashing could not be used to retrieve details from a Hotel table of hotels with between 1000 and 2000 rooms.
- when access is on the basis of values of only part of the access key. For example, if a Customer table is stored as a hash file with hash key (Name, Address), then hashing could not be used to retrieve details of employees at a particular address, or with a particular name.

INDEXES

Indexes are an alternative to hashing as a mechanism for direct access to records with given access key values. An index is a collection, the elements of which are access key values, along with the addresses of the records within which each value is stored. By searching the list of values, the address of required records may be located. Searching for a record using an index is usually much faster than serially searching through the data records, because an index is relatively short; each index record comprising only a single access key value and an address. On the other hand, access via indexes is not as fast as access using hashing. Hashing (at its best) requires a single page access, but using an index it is necessary to read pages in which the index is stored as well as those in which the data record is located.

There are a number of advantages of indexes over hashing.

- Indexes provide access to sequences of records. For example, a Hotel table with an index on the Rooms column will provide direct access to rows for hotels with a specific number of rooms, e.g. 200, or if required for hotels with the number of rooms in some band, e.g. 300 to 700.

- Indexes may be used to implement many access keys for one table or class, whereas there can be only one hash key. It is possible, for example, to hash on an access key, and then support secondary access keys using indexes. The cost of each additional index is the storage space it occupies, and slower updates because the DBMS must update all of the indexes of a table or class whenever the table or class is updated.

In some RDBMS indexes are visible as tables. An index table has one row for each row of the table to which it is an index. Each index table row includes two values, an access key value, and the address of a row in the indexed table that contains that value. The user may not directly alter an index; its values are changed only by the DBMS to reflect changes to the indexed table.

Many RDBMS make it easy for users or the DBA to experiment in order to find the most effective combination of indexes. SQL for example includes the "create index" instruction to add a new index on some specified access key and the "drop index" instruction to remove an index.

An index table is an example of a full index, i.e. one that addresses every single record. A B-tree is another example. A partial index is one where the data records are stored in access key sequence and the index addresses the pages, rather than individual records. ISAM files, also described below, are based on partial indexing. There can be only one partial index for a file because the data records can have only one sequence, but there may be many full indexes.

An index is not always visible, e.g. as an index table, and strictly speaking it should not be. An index is just an implementation device for speeding up data accesses. Whether or not an index is visible, there are a number of ways in which it may be stored. It may be stored as a heap file, but the time it takes to search an index may be decreased using the previously mentioned techniques, i.e. the index may be sorted, or it may be stored as a hash file. However, there are a number of file organisations specific to indexes, and the more widely used ones are described in the following sections.

MULTI-LEVEL INDEXES
The shorter the index, the faster the search. When an index is large the search time can become significant because it then becomes necessary to store the index across many pages. A solution to this problem is to split the index up into a number of shorter indexes and to provide an index to the indexes. This creates a two-level index.

INDEXED SEQUENTIAL ACCESS METHOD
Indexed Sequential Access Method (ISAM) is based on partial indexing. The data records are stored in access key sequence and the index addresses the pages, each of which will contain a sequence of records rather than an individual record.

The access time will be approximately the same for all records in an ISAM file immediately after the file has been constructed, but may lengthen for some records as a result of file updates. This is because the index is fixed for the life of the file, and therefore rigidly determines the page in which each record should be stored. However, pages will eventually fill up, and then records must be stored as overflow records in other pages, usually chained to the relevant home address overflow records page. Overflow records are stored in a separate overflow area. This deterioration in access time becomes rapid when many new records in the same key range are inserted, or when the key range is repeatedly extended. In the latter case the inserted records will all overflow from the last page of the file.

The above problem of "fixed for life" indexes are not shared by all "ISAM" implementations. Many implementations described as ISAM do overcome the above restriction by dynamically adjusting and extending the indexes, sometimes in a way similar to that used by B-Trees, described later.

The DBA must monitor the performance of an ISAM file, and recreate it when overflow records cause access times to deteriorate excessively.

B-TREES

A B-tree is a type of multi-level full index. B-trees are widely used because they are largely self-maintaining. They expand and contract automatically according to the number of data records in the file. In this way the uneven deterioration in access speeds that occurs when an ISAM file is updated is avoided. A B-tree keeps itself balanced such that it always takes approximately the same time to access any data record. It does this by ensuring that each component index has no less than some fixed minimum and no more than some fixed maximum number of entries. Also, being a full index, every single record is addressed from the index and there is therefore no need to store the data records in sequence; they may be stored as a heap file. There may therefore be many B-trees for a single file of data records.

The balance of a B-tree is maintained by the following mechanism:

- When an index becomes too full, a new index is created and the entries are distributed between the two. The parent index is adjusted to take account of the new index and the redistribution of index entries. If the parent again becomes too large, it is similarly split, and so on. A similar contraction of the B-tree occurs when deleting a record causes an index to have too few entries.

The are many varieties of B-tree, but a description of one of the more common ones, the B+-tree, will illustrate the basic technique. We shall construct a B+-tree to provide access to the records which store the rows of the Customer table in Figure 5.23.

The B+-tree that we shall construct will be of order 1. This means that each index will have a minimum of one test value and a maximum of two. In general a B-tree of order n has a minimum of n and a maximum of $2*n$. A component index, or node, in an order 1 B+-tree comprises store for three addresses or pointers, and two test values. We depict a component index diagrammatically as shown below, where the asterisks (*) represent pointers to records or to other nodes, and the other boxes contain test values. A test value is an access key value used for searching the index.

Test value1	*	Test value 2	*

There are many variations in the detail of how B-trees are constructed and used. However, in general a B-tree is constructed from nodes, in a similar way to that as illustrated in Figure 6.1. Note that:

- Each node includes one or two test values, and there is a pointer to another node or to a data record on each side of each test value.
- A test value indicates the lowest access key value in a particular node. The pointer to the left is the address of the node that indexes the preceding records, and the pointer to the right addresses the node that includes the test value.
- The leaf nodes of the B+-tree, i.e. the nodes that point to the data records, are linked so that records can be accessed in access key sequence.

Thus, nodes form a multilevel index. The single node at the first level contains text values that indicate the range of access key values indexed by each of the nodes at the next lower level... and so on.

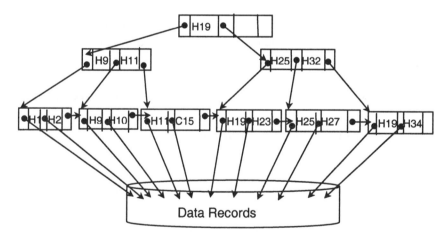

Figure 6.1 Example B+-tree

An advantage of a B-tree is its uniform performance. A B-tree is self organising such that the search path remains the same length for each record. For example, every record in the example B-tree is accessed by searching two node indexes, to locate the leaf node which addresses the required data record.

When a new data record is inserted, the index nodes are also updated. Appropriate entries are added and where a node would become larger than is allowed, an extra node is created.

Deletion of a record from a B-tree is the insertion process in reverse. Instead of expanding to accommodate the new test values and pointers, the B-tree contracts. When a test value and associated address are removed from a node and that node becomes too small, the node is deleted from the tree, and any test values and addresses that were in the node are redistributed to other nodes. The parent nodes are adjusted in a similar way.

Indexes are slower but more versatile than hashing. They should be used in the following situations:
- when pattern matching is used to retrieve rows. B-tree and ISAM files are based on access key sequence, and so it is possible to retrieve on the basis of the left most part of the access key. For example it is possible to retrieve Employee records with names that start, "Mac", using a Name index
- when rows are retrieved on the basis of a range of access key values. For example, it is possible to retrieve details of hotels with between 1000 and 2000 rooms from a Hotel table using an index on the Rooms column
- when using the leftmost column of a multi-column access key. It is possible for example to access details of customers at a specific address using an index on (Address, Name).

B-trees are preferable to ISAM:
- when the table is frequently updated. An ISAM file will deteriorate in this situation because its index is fixed and cannot accommodate a changing spread of access key values without resorting to record overflow
- when the table is so large that it is costly to recreate. A B-tree re-organises itself whenever it is updated
- when sorting on the access key is required. Updates to an ISAM file will cause the records to lose their access key sequence but the sequence will always be maintained in a B-tree.

ISAM is most appropriate in the following situations:
- when the file is infrequently updated. An ISAM file which has not been updated will give faster access than a B-tree, because the B-tree has an extra level of indexes, i.e. the leaf nodes which contain the record pointers
- when the table is to be simultaneously manipulated by a number of users. This is because since the ISAM index does not change, it is not necessary to take any precautions to avoid problems of multiple concurrent updates of the index
- when all of the data records are to be accessed serially. With a B-tree the sequence is determined via the leaf nodes, but in an ISAM file, the data records may be processed without reference to the index.

CLUSTERING

Clustering is the technique of storing related records physically close together. The advantage of doing this is that it reduces the number of page accesses necessary to process a group of related records.

For example, consider the situation where details of invoice and invoice items are respectively represented in the Invoice and InvoiceLine tables. An application which produces the invoice for a stay in a hotel, one with six invoice lines say, will have to access the corresponding row in the Invoice table, and also the corresponding six rows in InvoiceLine. If these rows are all stored in separate pages then the application must access seven different pages. However, if we arrange for records in the file that stores InvoiceLine to be clustered on InvoiceNo, then the six InvoiceLine rows will probably be stored in the same page, and so only two page accesses are necessary. By clustering on InvoiceNo we mean storing records with the same InvoiceNo value physically close together.

Some RDBMS support cluster indexes whereby records with the same access key value are stored physically close together.

Clustering should be used in the following situation:
- when an application accesses groups of rows which have some common attribute value.

A table may have only the one clustering index, and so where there is more than one such application, the designer must decide which is the most important. Where applications have equal importance, then clustering on the tightest attribute is likely to be more effective. This is because a large cluster is likely to spread across a number of pages, thus slowing down the application, and also using up space which should be occupied by other clusters.

CHANGES TO THE LOGICAL DATABASE DESIGN

The logical database design methods attempt to produce a design that reflects the natural structure of the data, rather than the ways in which it is used. However, a consequence may be that data required by any particular application may be dispersed across a number of different tables, or stored with other data that the application does not require.

The designer may sometimes conclude that an application is sufficiently important to justify denormalising the logical design. Of course, a consequence is that some data redundancy is then re-introduced, and applications must be programmed to cope with it.

Sometimes the logical database design will include tables with many attributes, but certain applications will need to access just a few. For example, a pay-roll application will only wish to access attributes in an Employee table which relate to rates of pay. It takes less time to access shorter records, and so the designer may choose to split up a relation so as to place groups of attributes required by different applications in different relations. This is called vertical fragmentation.

PHYSICAL DATABASE DESIGN—SUMMARY

Physical database design is the process of deciding how to implement the logical data structures. The designer must select the most appropriate of the storage structures supported by the DBMS for each structure. The choice will be based on the logical database design, the volume and volatility of the data, the ways in which applications will manipulate the data, and the costs associated with each representation.

A physical database design is usually tested by bench-marking data manipulation of a test database, and will be tuned throughout the life of the database by monitoring its performance and making adjustments.

Four methods of representing tables are using heap files, sorted files, hash files, and indexes (e.g. ISAM or B-tree).

A heap file is a chain of pages where new records are simply added to the end, and is appropriate when a batch of records is being inserted, or when a file is only a few pages long. The disadvantage is that record access is slow because serial searching must be used. Serial searching involves accessing each record, from the first to the last.

Other file organisations make it possible to speedily access records given the value of some access key, i.e. specific attribute or attributes. Attributes used in the search conditions are candidate access keys, and the tightest candidate access keys should be implemented.

Record access speed can be improved if the file is sorted. Binary searching may then be used to access records with a specific value of the access key, i.e. the attributes on which the file is sorted. Binary searching is the process of repeatedly halving the part of the file that contains the required record. Sorted files are appropriate when data objects are normally accessed in some specific sequence.

Hashing is the process of locating a record by calculating its address from the access key value. Hash files provide the fastest access to records for exact search key matchihg, but are not appropriate when retrieval is on the basis of pattern or range matching. Also, they do not support sequential access to records.

An index is a table of access key values and associated record addresses. Indexes are slower but more versatile than hashing. They should be used when retrieval is based on pattern or range matching.

Two types of index structures are ISAM and B-trees. ISAM is an example of a partial index, because the data records are in access key sequence and the index addresses pages, rather than records. A B-tree is an example of a full index because every record is addressed by the index. ISAM files have a static index and therefore deteriorate when records are inserted, but provide faster access and give less problems when simultaneously used by many users, than B-trees. B-trees on the other hand maintain themselves by expanding or contracting according to the number of data records, and so are more appropriate when re-creating the file structure is expensive, or when the file is frequently updated.

Clustering is the technique of storing related records physically close together, and should be used where applications process groups of rows or objects with some common attribute value.

Sometimes the designer may choose to alter the logical database design to favour certain applications. This may be done by combining tables, i.e. denormalising, so as to remove the necessity for an application to perform a join; and by vertical fragmentation, i.e. splitting a table so as to place the groups of attributes used by different applications in different tables. Vertical fragmentation has the advantage of producing files with shorter records, and these may therefore be accessed faster.

Physical database design is a complex and technically demanding task, and the information in this section merely gives a brief overview of issues, methods and techniques. In practice the designer should have a good technical knowledge of the operating system and the DBMS.

6.2 WEB DATABASE CONNECTIVITY

Having implemented the database component of a Web database system, there are still technical choices to be made concerning how it is connected to the Web pages by which it is used (and how those Web pages will be created). The term Web database connectivity refers to those software tools and techniques that can be used to make a database system accessible via the Web. In this section, we recap on the architecture of Web applications, i.e. their components and how they fit together and identify the different architectural options for Web database systems. This is preliminary to a detailed overview, in subsequent sections, of the main approaches and technologies that can be used within this framework.

THE WEB ARCHITECTURE REVISITED

Web-based applications must be constructed within the client server architecture described in Chapter 4. To recap, a Web database system will involve the following parts:

1) Client systems—These display the Web pages that provide the user interface to the Web database system. These are displayed using a browser.
2) Web Server systems—These store the Web documents, scripts and programs. The Web documents are the marked up versions of the Web pages that are displayed by the browsers, and may also include scripts relating to the dynamic aspects, such as retrieval, manipulation and updating of data in the database. The programs also implement the dynamic aspects of the system. They may implement the database system or provide an interface to it, for example, as a CGI script.

The database system component may be implemented as extensions to the servers or browsers, or may be external to the Web. The application software may therefore be constructed either to execute within the relevant clients (client side) or the relevant servers (server side). In either case, the software that executes can act as a "gateway" to some other system that provides database services.

- There are two general client side approaches. These are, to extend the browser itself, for example, using scripts, add-ons, or applets, or alternatively, the browser can be linked to other (external) applications.
- The server side approaches are either to embed executable code (scripts) within the Web page source, which currently is typically coded in HTML (e.g. as in Active Server Pages (ASP)), or to create other programs that are executed when accessed by the client (e.g. as in CGI or programs written using the server API).
- Systems may use both client side and server side approaches, by distributing their processing between the client and server.

Systems may be built from specially constructed software. In addition, systems may use generic software tools for executing general aspects of Web database systems. These are called middleware. Middleware can be defined as a generic system that provides platform independence, and supports standard interfaces and protocols in addition to distribution. Within the context of Web database connectivity, middleware is an approach where the clients, the Web database connectivity mechanism, and the underlying database systems are implemented as independent components of a system. Examples of middleware include X/Open

Distributed Transaction Processing (DTP) Model [Atzeni 99], JPernLite: Extensible Transaction Services for WWW [Yang 98], and.Object Transaction Service (OTS) [OMG 97].

Unlike the previous approaches, middleware factors out the standard functions of Web database connectivity into a third component. This has two advantages. Firstly, it has flexibility, since it provides a way to link existing legacy systems and the information they contain to newer applications based on Internet, intranet, and object-oriented technology, without having to totally rewrite these applications. It also significantly improves the performance by reducing the load on underlying Web or database systems.

A further consideration for the implementer is continuity between Web transactions. Given the statelessness of HTTP, the Web protocol, Web database systems have one important characteristic that distinguishes them from traditional client-server applications, i.e. a connection supports only one Web transaction. Connections to the database must therefore be recreated if the database transaction involves a sequence of user interactions, via the client. Consequently, when discussing how these approaches can be used, it is also necessary to examine how to support sequences of transactions (see 6.10 State and Transactions).

Given these options, the designer of a Web database system must make decisions whether to access the database from the client or server and at which of these to process the application. A related decision is the choice of technology to be used to implement the system. In the following subsections we outline the architectural options. The choices of implementation technology are discussed in subsequent sections.

CLIENT SIDE APPROACH
In this approach the application is executed by the Web client system, rather than the server.

Two client side approaches are:

1) Browser extension—The browser is extended to give additional functionality. This is done using plug-ins (on Netscape and Internet

Explorer), ActiveX controls (Internet Explorer), or using Java applets and JavaScript.

2) External applications—These are typically existing database clients on the client system, and are launched by the Web browser to provide additional services. This latter approach is similar to that of using a server side gateway to execute other systems.

The latter approach is useful, for example, to connect legacy systems to the Web. Legacy systems are those that pre-exist, and for reasons of complexity, resources, support, etc. are still used but can no longer be developed. Through the use of legacy systems we can preserve the investment in them and potentially provide a quick solution. However, there are drawbacks. These include:

• Systems which utilise legacy systems are not portable, since they are both platform and language dependent.

• They are also difficult to change, since the legacy systems themselves cannot be altered.

SERVER SIDE APPROACH

The server side approach is to execute the application processing on the server computer system. For example, access to the database system may be from the server. The operation of this approach involves the following procedures:

1) Data must be sent from a client to a server.
2) The data must be processed on the server.
3) Results must be sent from the server to the client.

Step 1) will often involve an HTML form to enter parameters to be passed to the server. This data is then processed in Step 2). Techniques for undertaking that processing include:

• HTML Preprocessors.
• CGI scripts.
• Server API applications.

Within these approaches, there are choices of programming language open to the developer. Pre-processors such as Active Server Pages (ASP) or Java Server Pages (JSP) may allow different languages to be used, such as VBScript or Java. CGI Scripts, for example, may be written in many languages.

Scripting languages, Perl in particular, are playing an important role in Web applications. Two reasons for this are their simplicity and portability. However, server side programs can also be written in Java as CGI programs or Servlets.

For Web database systems, whatever language is used there must be a method of making a database connection from that language. This is done, typically, using JDBC to connect Java to databases, DBI for Perl, or ODBC for more general use.

IMPLEMENTATION CHOICE— CLIENT OR SERVER?
Having overviewed architectural choices open to the implementer, this subsection now discusses some of their pros and cons, and the complexities of each.

Client-server applications are distributed between two computer systems, respectively providing an interface (the client) and a service (the server). Traditionally one of the attractions of client-server applications in computing has been the ability to reduce the workload placed on a server by performing as many functions as possible on a client machine. The rationale is that whereas a client can be dedicated to the execution of the application for the current user, the server must provide services for many other users from other clients.

Client and server systems may execute on different computers, possibly with different operating systems, architectures, etc. However, they may often execute on the same machine. For example, the client may be literally a system on the individual user's desktop in the form of a PC or workstation. Alternatively it may execute on a larger computer, implemented as a local server system but operating as the client to a mainframe, for example, in an organisation's remote headquarters. Often one reason for the latter situation is to minimise the amount of network traffic between client and server. Similar considerations apply to the client-server aspects of Web Database systems.

EXAMPLE 6.1

Consider a case where the staff at the Eagleley HQ office must access the Eagleley database via a Web system. The staff run their browsers on the computer they use for office-related processing in general (office.eagleley) and connect to the Eagleley Web server (www.eagleley) to access resources, such as the database. Both the office system and Web server system are implemented on the same physical computer, known by more than one name in the DNS. Eagleley's American office staff have configured their local computer system in exactly the same way, but connect to the database and other resources via the Web from several thousand miles away. Subsequent upgrades to the HQ computer system result in office.eagleley and www.eagleley becoming separate machines. However, note that across these different situations the same client-sever model is used.

It can normally be assumed that there may be a more fundamental server element in Web Database systems since that is where the database will be situated. Distributing to the clients many of the application-specific tasks can therefore reduce the workload on the server. In particular it may be beneficial to implement on the clients those processes that are associated with providing the interface to the database. Also, as in Example 6.1, in some cases the client and server architectural model may be kept, even though client and server functions are carried out on the same computer.

In general, client side scripting is more appropriate for implementing small-scale functionality, such as animation of Web pages, data validation and calculations, whereas server side should be used for large-scale complex processing. One obvious practical advantage to distributing processes on this basis, between the client and server, is that if some functions take place at the client, a number of possibly slow connections can be avoided. However, the consequences of the allocation of processing to client or server requires careful analysis, both from performance and human computer interaction perspectives. To illustrate possible complexities, we explore below an apparently simple example, i.e. client side validation of data entered by a user (Example 6.2).

EXAMPLE 6.2

Imagine a situation where we require the user to fill in a form on which certain fields are mandatory. Enforcing that constraint on a single Web page (or applet screen) may be more effective than letting the user submit a form with a missing field, since the latter requires the system to send an error page back.

The latter strategy in Example 6.2, i.e. returning an error page to indicate a missing field, may also create other problems that should be avoided.

1) Should the page simply tell the user that there was an error, hopefully indicating what was missing and perhaps what input would be acceptable? If so, the user is then forced to navigate back in their browser to the previous data entry page, so that the missing data can be entered and resubmitted.

2) An alternative strategy to that of returning an error page that simply identified a data entry error, is to also include on the error page a new version of the form. On this page the user can add the missing information and re-submit the form. However, this can lead to a confusing sequence later if the user "backs" out of the site, using the browser facility for returning to the previous page.

3) Another option is to open the error page in another browser window, but this is a feature known to be unpopular with some users.

If enough information can be provided it may be possible to perform processing, such as data validation, at the client. However, the issue of whether the client has sufficient resources to process the information must be considered. If one's aim is to minimise delays to the operation of an application, a solution that replaces connection delays with slow client processing may be no solution at all.

We now explore the complexities that may occur when determining if sufficient information can be held on a client for specific processing, by considering another apparently simple data validation example (Example 6.3).

EXAMPLE 6.3

Consider a case where a name and address entered into a form by a user must be validated. This could be done at the client using any of the following:
- *the facilities of HTML forms*
- *Java*
- *JavaScript*

Other scripting language, such as VBScript, also offer similar power to the above, but are available in more limited browsing situations. We will therefore consider only JavaScript, since this exemplifies the typical client based scripting language.

In this apparently simple case (Example 6.3) complexities are revealed by considering how one small part of the name, that is, title (Mr, Ms, Dr, Prof., etc.) can be validated. Though client side processing provides a preferred way of validating data prior to submission of an HTML form to the server, the unexpected complexities of this simple example make this choice less than straight-forward.

Some design options and associated problems are as follows:

1) Checkboxes and radio buttons—These can be used as one option for validating a field in an HTML form. Using a checkbox we can offer a fixed number of valid choices to the user. The problems here are that the user may "check" no box or more than one. This does not satisfy our requirement that the inclusion of a title is mandatory and that only one response is allowed. It would be possible simply to take the first response and ignore further choices, but that hardly constitutes validation. Also, starting a checkbox with a filled-in default cannot satisfy our requirements, since the default can be cancelled by the user. Assuming that one title, e.g. Mr, is an acceptable default is probably not wise either.

2) Radio buttons—This option might at first seem an attractive alternative. By its nature one (and only one) choice can be made. However it is normal to have one choice checked by default. If there is no default and the user makes no choice the result may not be relied on. By making one choice the default you risk annoying or insulting a large part of your user population. The system could offer

"None" as the default but that will not be satisfactory if a value is required.

3) HTML Form Select option—Similar problems exist with the select option within an HTML form. The first select choice in the form appears as a default and can only be avoided by permitting a blank input.

The issue of what is an acceptable input may be more complex than suggested above. Should we accept "Dr" or "Prof."? Since this is the **World** Wide Web perhaps we should also accept "Herr" and "Snr" Adding these options may make the form large and cumbersome to use and therefore a database solution may be more appropriate.

A database approach to the problem could be to have a table "ValidTitle" containing what were felt to be acceptable titles and to check user input against this table. Alternatively, this list could be held in some other form in the system. Database 4GLs often offer validation lists held in screens, but these are more limited in use being tied to one input screen and are closer to the HTML form options discussed above.

If we adopt the strategy of using a database of valid titles, how might such a table be used to validate user input? There are both client and server based processing alternatives. The user could be allowed to enter their title into a blank space and that input compared to the table. Differences in case and punctuation might be ignored so that a user who entered "MR" or "Mr." might be accepted, and registered by the system as "Mr" What remains flexible is still where this validation takes place.

In a server based version the user's data from the form would be transmitted to the server. Then, within a program that connected to the database, that input would be tested against the values in the ValidTitle table. Depending on the result, processing could continue or an error report page could be produced and sent back to the user. There might be a number of data items from one HTML form, some or all of which need validation in this way.

In a client based version the contents of the ValidTitle table would have been sent to the client as part of a Java or JavaScript data structure. The values in that data structure could then be tested against the user's input.

This testing could be done as soon as the user leaves the data entry field. Valid input would allow the user to progress to other data entry fields and errors could bring up a dialogue box, possibly including the valid title list so that the user could now select one.

It would also be possible to create a simple HTML form dynamically reading the values from ValidTitle if an HTML form solution was appropriate. This might be the case if we wanted to use standard forms of title such as "Mr" but were not concerned if no title was given.

This may seem like overkill for such a small matter as the title. We may however actually be undertaking more than one task. The data entry may be for one use, for example, sending out a printed brochure. However, this application may be effectively building a database of contacts to whom we may write in the future and when we do so we would like to be able to create well-personalised letters.

From the above discussion of how a fragment of a simple problem can be implemented, it should be apparent that implementing a Web database system is made complicated by the problem of optimum process distribution, and by the wide range of alternative technologies and approaches available to the implementer. However, there are some general advantages and disadvantages that can be identified for client and server side approaches.

Advantages of Client Side
- Advantage of distribution of processing—By performing some of processing associated with a Web database application on the server, the communications between client and server can be reduced.
- Speed of feedback—Client side processes can provide instant feedback to users, without having the overhead of transmission across the Internet from the server.
- Added Web-page functionality—Server side processing can be used to create interactive Web pages and forms. In general this approach allows greater user interface flexibility.

Disadvantages of Client Side
- Environment dependencies—Server side processing may be dependent on the features of the platform and browser of the client where it is executed.
- Security—The source code, delivered from the server, is not secured.
- Download time - Because the pages must also include the code to be executed by the client they will be larger and take longer to download.
- Programming limitations—The restrictions on processes executing in the client mean that client side processes cannot access certain systems and there is only limited error handling and debugging support. Also, variables can be accessed only within a single page.

Advantages of Server Side
- Dependencies—Server side processing is independent of the browsers being used. Also, Web pages can be customised for the different browsers used, before they are sent to the client.
- Security—Source code is secured.
- Download time—Only HTML pages, not code, to download.
- Programming limitations—These are fewer than for client side. Server side scripts can interface directly with the database and have direct access to HTTP server variables, and can use global variables.

Disadvantages of Server Side
- Difficulty—There is generally a lack of debugging tools for server side scripting. Also, this tends to be used for more complex problems, and the programming environment and languages are consequently more complex.
- There is no direct control over the user interface.

6.3 CLIENT PROCESSING

In this section we look at different options available if processing is to be done on the client, rather than at the server. This section is deliberately very brief since the main language for implementing client side processing, i.e. Java, has a general use in Web database systems, and is therefore covered in a separate section (see 6.8 Java). Also, as noted above, there is a fundamental bias toward server side processing in Web database systems, since typically that is where access to the database is supported. This section describes the ways of implementing the two basic approaches to client side processing, i.e. browser extension and external applications.

BROWSER EXTENSIONS

Browser extensions give additional functionality. This is done using plug-ins (on Netscape and Internet Explorer), ActiveX controls (Internet Explorer), or using Java applets and JavaScript.

Browser extensions can be created with:

1) Scripting language interpreters, e.g. JavaScript—These execute the JavaScript code within HTML when the document is received.
2) Bytecode interpreters, to implement the Java Virtual Machine (JVM) to interpret Java—These execute the Java classes downloaded in <APPLET> tags in HTML documents.
3) Access to Operating System resources—These are platform specific additions such as Dynamic Link Libraries (DLL). The processes in the libraries will interpret files based on their MIME type as indicated by the file extension. ActiveX is another browser specific technology. It provides a way to extend the functionality of Internet Explorer, for example, to access files and databases.

EXTERNAL APPLICATIONS

External applications are typically existing database clients on the client system, and are launched by the Web browser to provide additional services. An advantage of using an external application for accessing the database is that it can interact directly with the DBMS, using its transaction management system. The alternative approach of accessing the database via the server means that interactions between the client and server are not controlled by the DBMS transaction management.

6.4 SERVER PROCESSING

In this section we look at the different options available if processing is to be done on the server rather than at the client. This is a lengthy section by comparison with the preceding one, since this is the approach that most of current technology addresses.

A major division can be made between two different approaches to server side processing, i.e. between server side scripting and the use of

CGI. Similar facilities are available with both approaches and the same languages may even be used. However, we can characterise them as:

- With Server Side Scripting the program is embedded in the HTML.
- With CGI the HTML is embedded in the program.

In both cases the result is the same. In response to an HTTP request from a client (for a URL possibly including path information or parameters sent via standard input) an HTML Web page is delivered. The difference between the approaches is that, using server side scripting the Web page contains instructions that are executed, whereas with CGI a program is execution to create a Web page.

In this section we concentrate on dynamic processing, that is generating Web pages "on the fly" from a database in response to a request, but we will also consider other approaches to building Web pages from a database (see 6.9 A Web Site in a Database). Although we look at the use of Java in scripting and CGI we will also consider the range of ways Java can be used separately (see 6.8 Java).

The section is structured as follows. First, general techniques of server side scripting are discussed. Subsequent subsections then describe and illustrate some specific systems for implementing server side scripting. These are ASP, JSP, PHP, server side JavaScript, server side includes, and ColdFusion. Other less widely used systems are also overviewed. The second part of this section discusses scripting languages. The criteria for choosing a pre-processor for server side processing, and the relative pros and cons of the systems and languages are reviewed. The third part of this section overviews the CGI mechanism, and within that context consider PERL, INGRES-ICE, and O2-O2WEB. The section concludes with a discussion of the problems with using CGI and how these can be overcome using the Server API.

SERVER SIDE SCRIPTING

There are a number of different and competing technologies that can be grouped together for comparison purposes. They are all effectively pre-processing systems for HTML. That is, directives can be embedded into Web pages, and are then processed by the server when the pages are delivered to a user. The Web server processes these pages and dynamically produces an HTML document that is sent to the browser.

The Web server is made aware of the need to pre-process a Web page through various mechanisms. The commonly used mechanism is to identify the files with a particular extension: for example ".shtml" for HTML with server side includes, or ".asp" for active server pages.

A problem with using scripting languages in this way is the extent to which the extensions used are tied to one server (or a limited number of servers). There is not (at least not yet) a truly cross platform scripting language. This is not to say that there are not efforts to get there, either through market domination or more formal standardisation processes. In the meantime we can outline a number of the significant choices in this area.

Pre-processor instructions usually have a fairly standard form, appearing in angle brackets or comment delimiters within the HTML, as can be seen from the Figure 6.2 example fragments of HTML in which are embedded PHP (see PHP below) and ASP (see ASP below).

```
<HTML>
...
<?PHP echo "Hello World";?>
...
</HTML>

<HTML>
...
<% Response.Write("Hello World") %>
...
</HTML>
```

Figure 6.2 Example HTML with embedded PHP and ASP directives

Note the use of the bracket pairs, "<?" ... "?>" and "<%" and "%>", respectively, as containers for directives in PHP and VBScript.

The following subsections now discuss specific systems for server side scripting.

ASP (ACTIVE SERVER PAGES)

ASP originated with Microsoft and was initially only available for the Microsoft Internet Information Server or Personal Web Server. VBScript is its default language and is used in the Figure 6.2 example. JScript, Microsoft's implementation of JavaScript, is also supported. For systems committed to Microsoft products, especially if the implementers have existing code or knowledge of Visual Basic, ASP represents a straightforward way to create dynamic Web pages.

ASP has a number of built-in objects. These include:
- Response object—This is used for sending information to a user. Note that the Response object's "Write" method is used in the code fragment in Figure 6.2.
- ActiveX Data Objects (ADOs)—ADOs are used to access databases via ODBC. Databases are registered separately with the "Data Source Administrator" and can then be recognised via ODBC drivers when referenced from within ASP code.

The fragment of ASP code in Figure 6.3 shows how we could open the case study bookings database, select some data, process it and close up

```
<%
Conn.Open "bookings"
Set RS = Conn.Execute (SELECT * FROM hotels")
       .

       .
code to loop through processing result set
       .
RS.Close
Conn.Close
%>
```

Figure 6.3 Example ASP code

The Figure 6.3 code uses an object, Conn, to provide a connection to a database called "bookings". Conn methods are used, for example, to open the connection (Conn.open) and to execute SQL queries (Conn.Execute). Results are returned (as the RS object). After processing the results of the

SQL, both the results object and database connection are terminated (RS.close and Conn.close).

Access to COM (Component Object Model) and DCOM (Distributed Component Object Model) objects can also provide a means of accessing code in other languages.

Though originally only available for Microsoft's Web server products, ASP versions are now available for Unix based systems, for example from [Chilisoft]. Third party support also means that PerlScript can now be used as a scripting language. PerlScript offers Perl syntax and many of the facilities of Perl within ASP and may make an ASP route more popular to those less familiar with VBScript. However, the PerlScript option is currently only available for Microsoft based systems. Although the range of platforms and ways of using ASP are increasing it remains fundamentally limited to a Microsoft way of doing things.

JSP (JAVA SERVER PAGES)
JSP is an attempt to offer a similar style to that of ASP (see above). JSP therefore provides the same sort of facilities as in ASP. However, whereas ASP typically used VBScript, JSP supports Java as the scripting language within HTML, as is illustrated in the following fragment of code.

```
<% out.println("Hello World"); %>
```

JSP is one of a number of ways in which Java can be used. The wider role of Java is considered in more detail later (see 6.8 Java). Although there is wide cross platform support for Java in general there is still only limited support for Java via JSP. Within the Java code, access to a database is made via JDBC (see 6.8, Java, JDBC).

PHP
PHP is now recursively named (*ala* GNU), PHP Hypertext Preprocessor, but originally stood for Personal Home Page. It is an open source scripting language available for a number of platforms. PHP is often linked with MySQL or PostgreSQL, since the combination of the freely available databases (for Unix) and scripting language provide a complete package for developing Web database applications. PHP is available for a

larger number of DBMS, including proprietary systems such as Informix, Oracle and Sybase. It also has facilities for connecting to an ODBC driver, which can be used as a way of connecting to the many other database systems that support ODBC. PHP can even access data stored in the .dbf format used by dBase and other similar systems.

The syntax of PHP borrows strongly from C (and Perl and Java). It also has a wide range of functions that will seem familiar to C programmers, such as "printf" and "strcmp". Like most scripting languages PHP is not strongly typed and supports a Perl like way of creating variables. For example, the following fragment would create a string variable called "name" and initialise it to contain the string "Barry".

```
$name = "Barry";
```

PHP accesses a database via calls to PHP functions. There is a set of functions for each supported DBMS. Although these sets are similar it is necessary to tailor applications to a particular database system. Consequently an application using a PostgreSQL database would connect with "pg_connect", execute a query with "pg_Exec", obtain the result with "pg_Result" and close the connection with "pg_Close". Similarly, an Oracle based application might need "ora_Logon", "ora_Parse", "ora_Exec", "ora_Fetch" and "ora_Logoff". Such functions are available for most DBMS, normally prefixed by a database identifier e.g. pg_ for PostgreSQL. The differences in functions do reflect some differences in the operation of the different database systems but still result in a less independent way of connecting to a database than other choices such as Perl DBI or JDBC. An indication of the range can be seen from the following different functions for disconnecting from a database.

```
pg_Close      PostgreSQL
ora_Logoff    Oracle
oclLogOff     Oracle 8
msql_close    mSQL
mysql_close   MySQL
ifx_close     Informix
obdc_close    ODBC
```

Within the range of functions there are also differences in arguments and return values, for example most of the functions above return true or false but the Informix function always returns true even if the named database connection is not closed. As one book on PHP admits "PHP needs more database independence" [Hilton 00 p 16]. This means that updating a PHP based system to connect to a different database may not be a simple task. One solution to this would be to connect via the ODBC functions but these are regarded as slow and somewhat unreliable and should perhaps only be used as a last resort.

SERVER SIDE JAVASCRIPT

This originates with Netscape and is available for their server. It has the advantages of a large common part with client side JavaScript which was originally developed by Netscape. It uses JavaScript as the scripting language. This may be an advantage for sites that already have JavaScript expertise from client side programming. The source files will look similar to pages with client side JavaScript but of course these will be processed on the server and "pure" HTML will be transmitted, unlike pages containing client side JavaScript where the JavaScript is transmitted. It should be noted that the standardisation of JavaScript, as ECMAScript, is limited to the client side. Although client side JavaScript has become widespread server side JavaScript has not.

SSI (SERVER SIDE INCLUDE)

SSIs can be considered the parent of all other HTML pre-processors. It is the original pre-processor that came with the Apache Web server, although its facilities are now supported on other Web servers. At one level, SSI may seem to have limited facilities compared to some of the pre-processors above. The number of SSI instructions is much smaller than the large number of PHP functions for example. However it is possible to "escape" to the system to execute a program in any other language, via the

```
<!--#exec ...-->
```

command[3], and to include any file, possibly the output of the previous exec command, using the

```
<!--#include … -->
```

command. Therefore it should be possible to achieve the same results as can be obtained with other pre-processors. However, this may be at the cost of code that is less comprehensible and less easily maintainable. In the area we are concerned with, i.e. linking to a database, although SSI itself contains no database related commands, "exec" and "include" can be used to achieve linkage with a database. For example the "exec" command could be used to run a report against a database and then the "include" command used to read the contents of that report into a Web page.

EXAMPLE 6.4

Eagleley EuroHotel Bookings has a largely static page but wishes to add a small dynamic feature, i.e. a listing of cities with late booking offers. To achieve this it uses SSI to call a report that produces a list of cities with the lowest rate. A fragment of the page (which will have an ".shtml" extension so that it is always parsed by the server) is shown below.

```
<P>
Special rates for last minute bookings in:
<!--#exec cmd="RunLastMinReport"-->
<HR>

<!--#include file="LastMin.out"-->
<HR>
```

The first line instructs the Web server to run the RunLastMinReport program. This is a script that sets some environment variables, so the Web server can access the database correctly and then runs a report stored in the database. At the heart of the report is a piece of SQL of the form

---

[3] In the use of exec we assume a Unix system. Similar commands and facilities should be available to Web servers running on other operating systems.

```
SELECT DISTINCT City
    FROM LastMinuteBookings
    WHERE Rate = ( SELECT MIN(rate)
                       FROM LastMinuteBookings
                       WHERE Date ='today');
```

This SQL selects the cities with the lowest rates today. We do not know how many will be selected. Let us assume it is London and Berlin. As a result of this query, the cities and some suitable formatting is written by the report to the file LastMin.out which is then read into the HTML by the "include" instruction. This produces the following fragment of HTML.

```
<P>
Special rates for last minute bookings in:
<HR>
London<BR>
Berlin<BR>
<HR>
```

The report produces each city followed by <BR> as a piece of formatting. If instead of just the names we wanted to make the cities into links, then we could modify the report to create something like

```
<A HREF="CityInfo/CityName">CityName</A><BR>
```

for each city where CityName was filled in for London, Berlin, etc.

In the example above we have not considered what might happen if something goes wrong. If the database is not reachable or the report does not run what HTML will be produced? The example as shown will either produce no report at all and hence will not produce a list of cities, or it will produce no report but will read in an old list of cities produced by an earlier execution of the report. Clearly neither is desirable. No output available will produce a bad looking page and an old output may produce an incorrect Web page, since the cities listed may be from an earlier date. This could be tackled in a number of ways.

A further SSI instruction could be added, after the "include" command, to remove an old report so it is not reused e.g.

```
<!--#exec cmd="rm LastMin.out"-->
```

This does not solve the problem of what happens if we have no output. One solution to this is to have a default message. This could be stored in a file and the "exec" command modified to copy that default. We could then have a file LastMinDefault.out that contained the text "For last minute information phone Beechwood 4-5789
". Then the second "exec" could be changed to

```
<!--#exec
cmd="cp LastMinDefault.out LastMin.out"
-->
```

The report will then be overwritten after it has been used. This will result in the default message being inserted into the Web page if the report cannot be run. If the report runs and produces an error message or a blank output the default message will still be overwritten.

Another strategy is to only remove the report occasionally (in this case daily would be appropriate) and allow a slightly old report to be reused. This could be done independently of the database and Web server with something like Unix's "cron" facility.

If we do not require the report to be very up to date it is possible that the overhead of parsing the HTML and executing the instructions for every request for the page could be avoided. This could be done by producing a completed static HTML page as a report from a database, on a regular basis rather than dynamically every time it is requested.

The use of the "exec" command may also have security implications, since it can call any program on the Web server and that program will execute with the same permissions as the Web server itself.

In addition to JSP, there is another way to use Java in a pre-processing style. In many applications, Java Servlets are used to create whole Web pages and will be considered in detail later in this chapter. Servlets can be called from within HTML with a <SERVLET> tag. As with other SSIs, files with a ".shtml" extension are parsed and then the servlet code is executed to produce HTML. This is very similar to JSP, except that there is a reference to Java code embedded in the Web page rather than Java code itself. For example instead of the "Hello World" code used above, a HelloWorld servlet, which has the same effect could be called, as shown

```
<SERVLET CODE=HelloWorld>
</SERVLET>
```

COLDFUSION

ColdFusion is a proprietary product from the Allaire Corporation which has a similar approach to the server side scripting technologies discussed above. It can be used on a number of different Web servers and can connect to a range of databases. ColdFusion is different from the other technologies in that it does not use code within comment delimiters, but instead uses its own mark-up language CFML (ColdFusion Markup Language). CFML has a similar syntax to HTML but an extended set of tags (around 70 in all) which can be used to create dynamic content, including connections to databases. These CFML files are processed on the server and standard HTML delivered to the browser in the same way that ".asp" files are processed and normal HTML delivered up to a browser.

The following fragment of CFML can be compared with the ASP example above.

```
<CFQUERY NAME ="HotelList"
DATASOURCE ="Bookings">
select * from Hotels
</CFQUERY>

<CFOUTPUT QUERY = HotelList">
#HotelName# #City#<BR>
</CFOUTPUT>
```

The above code includes a new tag "<CFQUERY>", which includes information on the database. This can have other parameters such as username and password. This creates a named query, which is then used in the "<CFOUTPUT>" tag. The code shown will produce a list of hotel names and cities. Unlike the ASP example there is no need to use a loop construct to iterate through the result set. Other tags such as "<CFINSERT>" and "<CFUPDATE>" allow other forms of access to a database.

ColdFusion can connect to databases via ODBC drivers, native drivers or OLE-DB, depending on the database and platform used. Plans for ColdFusion include the ability to include JSP as well as CFML. ColdFusion's facilities make dynamic Web page construction easy, especially for developers coming from a HTML, rather than programming, background, but the results are tied to a proprietary product and the set of databases it supports.

OTHER

There are pre-processors other than those mentioned above, but these tend to be much more limited because they are tied to specific products. One example of this is Lite, the scripting language that comes with mSQL. Also in the area of proprietary products we should consider offerings like ICE from Computer Associates as a part of Ingres. ICE (Internet Commerce Enabled) is a single product (i.e. one executable program) but can be used in a number of different ways. We will consider some of these later when looking at CGI routes to database connection. It also includes an ICE Macro facility that allows the user to embed directives in an HTML page in the form

```
<!--#ICE[keyword='value']-->
```

This is clearly the same approach as that of other pre-processors.

SERVER SIDE SCRIPTING—SUMMARY

In the above subsection we have overviewed some of the major pre-processors used for server side scripting. These have a lot in common. Specifically, they allow fragments of code to be inserted into HTML or its variants, which are processed on the server side. Thus the approach provides the ability to deliver dynamic content within Web pages.

In the above overview we have described examples of individual pre-processors, highlighting their specific features, strengths and weaknesses. However, for developers of Web systems, the specific server may determine the choice of pre-processor. This is not a good state of affairs. If there is a choice between servers then familiarity with one product (or what it is similar to) may be a factor. For example, if the developer uses Microsoft products, such as Visual Basic, then ASP may be an obvious choice since it can use VBScript as its scripting language. Existing code in Java may lead to JSP which uses Java. A knowledge of Client Side JavaScript may prompt the developer to use Server Side JavaScript. For Web database systems, the connections that a pre-processor offers to specific databases may be the key factor.

COMMON GATEWAY INTERFACE (CGI)

This subsection consider how server side processing can be umplemented using CGI (see also Chapter 4 CGI). CGI is an interface by which executable programs can be created to execute on a server, and which are separate from the HTML Web pages. This contrasts with the approach described in the preceding subsection, in which pre-processors are used to allow executable code to be included in HTML.

CGI programming can be written in many programming languages. This is because CGI is merely an interface, i.e. a way of passing information to and from a program. Therefore CGI simply provides a general facility that enables us to execute some instructions on the server. However, for Web database systems, what is significant is whether, and with what restrictions, the language can access a database.

Since many different languages are in use for CGI programming, in some cases if an existing application is being transferred to the Web it will make sense to keep it in the original language with modifications to accept parameters from an HTML form for example. If a new system is being developed a choice of programming language will have to be made. Three choices are as follows:

1) Many CGI applications use scripting languages such as Perl and TCl rather than compiled languages like C or Pascal.
2) It may even be possible to use within a CGI program the facilities for shell programming provided by the operating system, rather than using a programming language.
3) Some DBMS include programs, such as report generators, that may be used directly as the program for CGI programming. In later

subsections this facility will be illustrated by describing the CGI tools provided by one relational DBMS, Ingres, and one object DBMS, O2.

Of the above, scripting languages and in particular Perl have become the dominant ways of doing CGI Programming. There are a number of factors which account for this trend:

- Firstly, most CGI programs are relatively small. Typically they take a few parameters, process them in some way, possibly reading from and writing to files and produce some textual output. This sort of programming can be prototyped quickly in scripting languages.
- In some cases the sort of processing required is similar to that already being done using scripting languages. The fact that much early CGI programming was by people who were also system administrators and already used scripting languages on a regular basis should not be ignored.
- Modern computing languages support a number of features such as strong typing and modularity which may be considered crucial for large scale software development, but these features may not be essential factors in CGI developments. Whether in the future, as Web systems become more complex, the advantages of scripting languages continue to outweigh their disadvantages remains to be seen. However, scripting languages can of course evolve to include features which may be needed for "programming in the large".

One weakness of using scripting language is that, in general, they have a disadvantage in terms of efficiency, as interpreted languages, compared to compiled languages. This too may be overcome if a scripting language can be interpreted for prototyping but compiled for real use.

PERL

Perl has the typical advantages of a scripting language, but also has excellent features for the sort of text manipulation commonly needed in CGI programming. As it has become popular as a CGI programming language it has also built up a body of useful code that can be re-used. Its open source status is an advantage here. In particular, the CGI, DBD and DBI modules of Perl (explained below) mean that many facilities are available "off the shelf" and a large part of an application may be built by joining existing building blocks together. In principle this is no different from the range of standard libraries that C programmers use, but in practice the specific functionality available in Perl makes it an obvious choice for many applications.

Perl programmers can write their code from scratch, but in general it makes sense to use existing code available in the wide range of Perl modules. Particularly, when programming for Web database systems, there are three modules that are likely to be utilised. These are:

- CGI.pm module—This module provides an easy way to perform various tasks common to many CGI programs. It includes simple ways to get parameters into the program and easy output of HTTP headers and HTML. None of these operations are particularly hard, but using the CGI.pm module makes for simpler coding and gives easier to read and maintain code. Example code for decoding form information without CGI.pm can be found in [Gundavaram 96].

- DBD and DBI modules—Originally, a number of DBMS-specific Perl modules were available for connecting to databases. Examples are ora-perl for Oracle, and ing-perl for Ingres. More recently, these DBMS-specific modules have been superseded by the DBD and DBI modules. These are a range of database driver (DBD) modules and a single database interface (DBI) module. The advantage of DBI is that it provides a common interface to a range of different databases, since the database specific features are factored out into the DBD module. A consequence is that transferring an application from one DBMS to another should only be a matter of replacing one driver module with another, since the interface provided by the DBI module is common. In practice there may be some more complications if non-standard SQL has been used or if one DBMS does not support a full SQL implementation.

The code in Figure 6.4 illustrates a number of features of using Perl. When executed, the example Perl code will display a list of hotels in a given city. However, not that this example has been simplified for clarity, by minimising the amount of error checking. Consequently, this code is usable, for example, if the city name has been selected from a list on a form, but is not be suitable for a form into which a user types the city name. This is because there is no way of coping with differences in capitalization or spelling or with any abbreviations of a city name. Also, the Perl code assumes that only one matching city will be found, and the program does not deal adequately with the situation in which no rows are retrieved. Note also, that the line numbers are included for ease of reference in the following explanation and are not part of Perl.

Figure 6.4 Example Perl code

```
1.  #!/usr/local/bin/perl

2.  $ENV{'LD_LIBRARY_PATH'}="/home1/ingres/lib";
3.  $ENV{'II_SYSTEM'} = "/home1/ingres";
4.  $ENV{'PATH'} = "/home1/ingres/bin";

5.  use DBI;
6.  use CGI;

7.  $q = new CGI;
8.  print $q->header,
9.  $q->start_html('Hotel listing'),
10. $q->h1('Hotel listing');

11. $City = $q->param('City');

12. my $dbh = DBI->connect("dbi:Ingres:bookingdb","www","" )
13. || die "Connection failure to $data_source:
14. $DBI::errstr";

15. my $sth = $dbh->prepare(
16. qq{
17. SELECT  Hotel
18. FROM Bookings
19. WHERE City = '$City'
20. ORDER BY Hotel
21. })
22. || die "Statement prepare failure: $DBI::errstr";

23. my $rc = $sth->execute
24. || die "Statement execute failure: $DBI::errstr";

25. print $q->p,
26. 'City: ',$City;
```

Figure 6.4 Example Perl code—continued

```
27. while (($Hotel) = $sth->fetchrow_array)
28. {
29.      print $q->br,
30.      'Hotel: ',$Hotel;
31. }

32. print $q->hr,
33. $q->end_html;

34. die $sth->errstr if $sth->err;

35. $dbh->disconnect;
```

Figure 6.4 Example Perl code—concluded

The program in Figure 6.4 is a Perl script which will be executed by the Perl interpreter (line 1). To enable the program to access a database a number of environment variables must be set (lines 2–4). These variables require setting for any access to the database and would be defined in a user's environment if they were accessing the database directly. On a Unix system the variables might be in a ".cshrc" file, for example. Since the script will use the CGI and DBI modules these must be invoked (lines 5–6). The CGI module is then used to produce a simple way of outputting the HTTP header (line 8) and HTML itself (lines 9–10). Without CGI.pm the tags as well as the content would have been needed. The value of the City variable taken from the form is put into the Perl variable $City (line 11). The DBI module is then used to make a connection to the Ingres "bookingdb" database, as the user "www" with no password required (lines 12–14). On success this returns the database handle object "dbh", which is used in subsequent interaction with the database. The SQL query is then prepared (lines 15–22). Different quoting styles (q{...}) may be needed in some circumstances. For example, qq{..} allows us to use the single quotes necessary for constructing the SQL statement and also allows the inclusion of the variable name $City, which will be substituted with the form value. The statement is then executed (lines 23–24). Using the CGI.pm module, a new paragraph is started and then the city information is printed (lines

25–26). The results from the select statement are then looped through, again using the CGI.pm module to control the output (lines 27–31). Finally, a horizontal rule and ending tags (</BODY></HTML>) are output (lines 32–33) and the database connection is closed (line 35).

INGRES-ICE

Recent versions of the Open Ingres DBMS have included a CGI program, ICE (Internet Commerce Enabled), that can be used for simple access to Ingres from Web pages. We consider it briefly here as an example of the sort of proprietary Web gateway available with relational systems.

ICE can be used in a number of ways, such as executing SQL statements, running database reports and executing database procedures. In all of these cases an HTML form whose action is a "call" to the ice program is run. Different hidden variables in the form are set to establish which database and as what user a connection will be made. If the form includes "ii_query_statement", the SQL in that variable is run. The SQL statement may include variables whose values are other fields on the form. The ice program provides default headers and footers, and converts the results of any select query into an HTML table. It provides a standard success message for other operations, such as inserts.

More complex operations on the database can be performed by naming a database procedure in the form with the "ii_procedure" variable.

The uses of ICE above would be suitable for prototyping but do not allow for the development of complex systems or customized Web pages. It is possible to use ICE in more sophisticated ways. Specialized success messages can be output by setting an "ii_success_message" variable in the form. More significantly, the normal output screen can be ignored and a different Web page used by setting an "ii_success_url" variable. This will allow a completely customised result to be prepared. The URL used can be generated dynamically and the page it references may also be dynamically created.

Customized output from queries is also availabl: by using the "ii_report" variable. This causes ice to run a database report rather than a plain SQL query. The report itself contains an SQL statement, but its output can be controlled to allow whatever formatting of the query results in a Web page the user wants. The ice program also includes the macro facility mentioned earlier.

One limitation of ICE is that it is restricted to a single query statement on a form, but multiple statements can be used by including them in ICE macros.

The following example shows a simple use of ICE calling the SQL statement used in the Perl example above.

```
<FORM ACTION="/cgi-bin/ice" METHOD="POST">

<INPUT TYPE=hidden NAME="ii_userid" VALUE="www">
<INPUT TYPE=hidden NAME="ii_database"
VALUE="bookingdb">

<INPUT TYPE=HIDDEN NAME="ii_system"
VALUE="/home1/ingres">
<P>
City?: <INPUT TYPE=text NAME ="City" SIZE=20>

<INPUT TYPE = hidden NAME="ii_query_statement"
VALUE ="SELECT Hotel FROM Bookings WHERE City =
':City' ORDER BY Hotel">

<INPUT TYPE="SUBMIT" VALUE="Do the search">
<INPUT TYPE=RESET VALUE="Clear this form and start
over">

</FORM>
```

We can modify the above code to use a report (HotelsInCity) which will produce a customized output Web page rather than the default. ICE uses the GET rather than POST method here. Both can be used with ICE, developers will need to use the appropriate method. We also introduce an error message and logging information.

```
<FORM ACTION=" /cgi-bin/ice" METHOD="GET">

<INPUT TYPE=hidden NAME="ii_userid" VALUE="www">
<INPUT TYPE=hidden NAME="ii_database"
VALUE="bookingdb">

<INPUT TYPE=HIDDEN NAME="ii_system"
VALUE="/home1/ingres">
<INPUT TYPE=HIDDEN NAME="ii_report"
VALUE="HotelsInCity">

<INPUT TYPE=HIDDEN NAME="ii_html_logfile"
VALUE="/tmp/ice">
<INPUT TYPE=HIDDEN NAME="ii_output_dir" VALUE="/tmp">
<INPUT TYPE=HIDDEN NAME="ii_log_type" VALUE="BOTH">

City? :
<INPUT TYPE=text NAME="City" SIZE=20>


<INPUT TYPE="SUBMIT" VALUE="Do the search">
<INPUT TYPE=RESET VALUE="Clear this form and start
over">

<INPUT TYPE=HIDDEN NAME="ii_error_message"
VALUE=" Nothing that matches your request. Please
recheck your input.">
</FORM>
```

The advantages of ICE, and systems like it, is that they allow rapid prototyping. Also, they will provide a route for legacy applications to be moved to the Web, since established database procedures can be used. Existing reports may also form the basis of reports that produce Web pages.

It can be seen that much of the detail of connecting to the database is in the form. Details of the output layout may be in a report specification. This contrasts with the Perl, and other scripting language CGI approaches. A plain form with no database information is used in the

Perl example and all the database connection and output layout is performed in one program.

O2-O2WEB

The Object Database, O2, includes a number of means of connecting a database to the Web. These are a Java binding and JDBC, an ODBC interface, O2ODBC, and O2WEB its CGI toolkit.

O2WEB includes a CGI script "o2web_gateway" which can be passed the system name (effectively a container for a number of databases), a database name and a query. The query will be an OQL, rather than SQL, query. Since the pure query part of SQL is a subset of OQL many queries will look familiar to SQL users. Of course other more complex queries may also be possible. O2 automatically produces a Web page in response to the query. It provides default HTML headers and footers and an appropriate way of displaying the query results. This provides a way of rapidly prototyping systems.

The default headers and footers can be customized for all pages by writing new header and footer methods for the database and on a per class basis by writing new "html_header" and "html_footer" methods for any class. These methods are stored in the database itself.

The default methods for displaying data itself mean that, for example, a query (like the one used in the Perl example) that resulted in a list of hotel names would be presented as an HTML unordered list presenting the hotels' names. Since OQL offers the ability to query the database in ways that are not possible with SQL there is a wide variety of default ways of displaying results. These will use the default display methods in the database for the type of object retrieved. Since this is an object database the query result is an object, as opposed to the query result from a relational system which is always a table. For example, in OQL we can ask whether there is a Grand Hotel in Vienna.

```
"Grand Hotel" IN
        (SELECT Hotel.Name
         FROM Hotel IN Hotels
         WHERE Hotel.City = "Vienna")
```

The result of such an existential query is true or false and the result would be a Web page with "yes" or "no" on it.

If the result had been a complex object, e.g. the hotel itself rather than just its name, the result would have been a list of links. The link text would be the hotel's name (its default display method). Following a link would take you to a new page displaying the single hotel object in more detail.

Just as the headers and footers can be customized so can the display of objects themselves. An "html_report" method can produce a modified way of displaying the data. For example we could customize any queries that returned hotels to always display their name and address and an image. Since O2 is an object database it is quite simple to store an image as part of the hotel object. Both the hotel's name and image could be made links to further information.

In the examples above we have considered the production of HTML pages from an O2 database. In addition to the standard headers and footers used above, O2 also has "prolog" and "epilog" methods. The "prolog" output would normally include the standard HTTP headers and mime type information. The "prolog" method can be overridden to provide a different type of header. This could be used so that instead of an HTML page a pdf document or jpeg image could be returned. This would be suitable if a class in the database contained documents or images. For example, in the Eagleley example we could have a Contracts class in the database. A suitable instance from this class could then be returned directly as a pdf document in response to following a link. The link would send an OQL query via the CGI gateway and return the document.

Updates to an O2 database can also be made via the Web gateway program. In this case rather than a query being passed, the URL will reference a method that updates the database.

O2WEB provides a means of accessing a database with default styles that can then be customized. This is achieved via methods stored in the database. This is an elegant solution since the default methods allow quick prototyping and the customization of methods can be made as wide or narrow as desired, reflecting the relationships between objects in a database. All of the methods used are themselves part of the database. The database itself can also contain the source for the HTML forms that will query the database. The flexibility of an object database system means that all the components of a Web database system can be kept in the database itself.

The only problem is of commitment to a proprietary product. Although the OQL used to query objects and ODL used to define the objects might be transferable many methods might be database specific. This can be a problem with object solutions other than O2's. Increased used of Java as the programming language for writing the database methods may make solutions like this more generic and transferable between systems in the future.

PROBLEMS OF CGI
The main problem of CGI is that of efficiency, but there are also issues of security and identity. The security and identity issues, that is, what rights the CGI process has, are discussed later (see Section 8.8 Security, Privacy and Identity). The efficiency problem with CGI is that a new process must be started up each time the CGI program is invoked. This can be slow and wasteful. For example, excessive delays may occur if the Perl interpreter has to be started to do a small amount of processing and is then closed, only to be restarted for another process soon after. This is a problem for any CGI application, but the problem for Web database systems can be particularly acute. This is because a Web database system has an additional overhead of making the connection to the database. (Note that the same efficiency and overhead problems also affect some of the HTML pre-processor systems.)

There are a number of solutions available, such as "FastCGI" and "mod_perl". In general these take the approach of integrating the CGI process into the Web server. This can be achieved relatively simply when using open source software such as Apache, Perl or PHP. The Web server is rebuilt to include the additional features and these are left running and do not need invoking afresh each time they are used. There is an extension to mod_perl called mod_perl+, which allows persistent database connections to be maintained. [Labrinidis 00] surveys the effectiveness of these options. However, a general limitation is that the solutions are often specific to one Web server.

EXTENDING THE SERVER FUNCTIONALITY USING ITS API

The strategy, described in the previous subsection, of extending CGI by integrating it into the Web server (e.g. FastCGI and mod_perl), can be generalised as a Server API (Application Programming Interface) approach. Another example of this approach is a JAVA API route using Servlets. The latter is discussed separately below.

An example Server API is the ISAPI (Internet Server Application Program Interface) for the Microsoft Windows NT IIS Web server. The API is a published interface and the programs that are written using it become part of the Web server. These programs are computed as dynamic-link libraries (DLLs). When the Web server is executed, these are loaded into memory and then await requests from clients.

A Web server API application can provide services in a similar way to CGI scripts. For example, it is possible to write applications that execute on the server when an HTML form is posted.

API applications have also been created by software vendors to perform generic functions. An example is the Microsoft Internet Database Connector (IDC) that uses ISAPI. As well as using ISAPI to interface with the Web, IDC also uses a standard interface for connecting to relational databases.

IDC uses two types of files, stored at the Web site. These are:

1) Internet Database Connector (with extension ".idc")—This file specifies the database and database manipulations.
2) HTML Extension files (with extension ".htx") - These specify how the Web page in which the results of the database operation is constructed.

As with CGI, the IDC application can be executed by submitting an HTML form or following a link to the "idc" file. These are respectively coded in HTML as illustrated

```
<FORM  METHOD="POST"
ACTION="/scripts/example.idc">
<A
HREF="http://eagleley.com/scripts/bighotels.idc
">
```

Examples of an "idc" file, and a part of an "htx" file in which results are displayed, are as follows:

```
bighotels.idc
Datasource: Web SQL
Username:   be&mr
Template: example.htx
SQLstatement:
+ SELECT name, address
+ FROM   hotel
+ WHERE rooms > 1000

bighotels.htx
<TABLE BORDER>
   <%begindetail%>
      <%if CurrentRecord EQ 0 %>
         <caption>Hotels with more than 1000
          rooms:</caption>
         <TR>
            <TH>Name</TH> <TH>Address </TH>
         </TR>
      <%endif%>
      <TR>
         <TD><%name%> </TD>
         <TD> align="right">$<%address%></TD>
      <TR/>
   <%enddetails%>
</TABLE>
```

Note that the "idc" file identifies the data source and user, and cross references the "htx" file which specifies the format of retrieved data. The "idc" file also includes the SQL statement to be executed to access the database. In general, this approach separates out the database access (into the "idc" file) from the presentation (in the "htx" file). This is similar to the separation of data description (in database schemas) and processes (in database applications) in a conventional database system.

6.5 JAVA

In this section Java is considered as a language for implementing processing in Web database systems. This separate coverage of Java reflects its dominant role within Web technologies, which is partly a consequence of its power, versatility and extensive use within Web applications.

Java can be used within each of the architectural options (see 6.2), i.e.:
- for processing on the client, via Applets,
- for server side processing, using Servlets, possibly via Java Server Pages (JSP) (see 6.4), or as a CGI programming language.

In addition, Java has a number of advantages over other programming languages, i.e.:

1) The programming language itself—Java is a network aware object-oriented language with features, such as garbage collection; strong typing and absence of pointers. These features make code development easier than using many other object-oriented programming language, e.g. C++. As a network aware language it also has a security model that will allow it to be used safely on clients and servers.

2) The Java virtual machine (JVM)—Java code is compiled, not to an executable code that runs on a particular piece of hardware, but to bytecode, a portable format that can then be run on any type of machine on which the JVM is implemented.

3) The library of classes and interfaces—Like C and C++, Java is a small language, in that it has a limited number of reserved words and functions in the language itself. However, there are many common tasks that can be accomplished by the use of standard pieces of code provided in libraries.

In the following subsections we outline a number of ways Java can be used in Web database systems to exploit the above advantage. Topics covered are:

- how Java programs can access relational databases using JDBC and its alternative,
- the use of Java applets and servlets, respectively to implement client side and server side processing,
- the use of Java for CGI programming,
- the Java relational query language SQLJ,
- and the ODMG standard for accessing object databases from Java.

Much more information can be found about Java in a growing number of books, although [Hamilton 98] and [Hunter 99] are particularly useful for database and servlet issues. There is also a wealth of information online at [Java] and its specialised sections such as [Java Servlets] [JSP] and [JDBC].

JDBC (Java Database Connectivity)

In whatever fashion Java is used, a method of connecting to a database is needed. We therefore discuss within the following subsections the principal method used, i.e. JDBC. JDBC is an application programming interface (API) and is implemented as a set of classes and interfaces in Java. These support the following operations:

- making connections to a database,
- sending SQL statements to the database, and
- returning the results from the database.

Details of how JDBC is used are given below, in the context of the different ways of using Java for both client and server processing.

JDBC is one block of library code, i.e. a package. This means that any Java program, whether an applet, servlet or application, can use the same JDBC code to pass information to and from a database. A Java program accesses the JDBC classes and interfaces by inputting the package. This is specified by the following Java code

```
input java.sql.*;
```

The uses of the JDBC classes that are imported by the above code are described and illustrated, in the following subsections, within the contexts of the different uses of Java.

JAVA APPLETS

Java applets are small applications sent, as bytecode, from a server to execute on a client. The applet will then run on the client machine, doing computations, controlling the display, etc. Applets can be used in Web database systems also to communicate with a database, typically, using JDBC classes.

An applet can make a connection to a database and although the main processing of the applet will be done on the client, data can be retrieved from or written to the database on the server. A JDBC database connection that an Applet makes is separate from the normal HTTP connection made between a Web client and server. Unlike the HTTP connection, which is stateless, a JDBC connection can persist. This means that one connection can be maintained over a number of different "screens" of an applet.

The fragment Java code in Figure 6.5 implements an applet, and demonstrates a number of features of using Java to connect to a database. We will not consider in detail how the results generated will be displayed by the applet, or the error checking. Instead the example is used to illustrate the manner in which JDBC is used and its basic functions. Note that the lines of code are numbered so that they can be referenced, but the numbers are not part of Java.

Figure 6.5 Example Java Applet in which JDBC is used

```
1.  import java.applet.Applet;
2.  import java.sql.*;
3.  …
4.  …

5.  public void run()
6.  {
7.    String url =
8.       "jdbc:subprotocol//host:port/database";
9.    String query = " select hotel,city
10.     from booking order by hotel,city";
11.   try
12.   {
```

Figure 6.5 Example Java Applet in which JDBC is used—continued

```
13.    Class.forName("drivername.classname");
14.  }
15.  catch(java.lang.ClassNotFoundException ex1)
16.  {
17.    //Error handling code
18.  }

19.
20.  try
21.  {
22.    Vector results = new Vector();
23.    Connection con =
24.      DriverManager.getConnection
25.        (url,"user","passwd");
26.    Statement stmt = con.createStatement();
27.    ResultSet rs =stmt.executeQuery(query);
28.    while (rs.next())
29.    {
30.      String HotelName = rs.getString(1);
31.      String CityName = rs.getString(2);
32.      String text = (" " + HotelName + " , " +
33.        CityName);
34.      results.addElement(text);
35.    }
36.
37.    stmt.close();
38.    con.close();
39.    setResults(results);
40.  }
41.  catch(SQLException ex2)
42.  {
43.    //Error handling code
44.  }
45.}
```

Figure 6.5 Example Java Applet in which JDBC is used—concluded

The above Java example illustrates the following features of the applet facility:

- Note that the above Java example illustrates how the Java applet facility is provided within the language as a set of conventional Java classes, i.e. the classes needed are imported (lines 1–2).
- The necessary preparations to connect to a database and execute SQL are made as follows:
  - A URL to be used when connecting to the database is constructed (lines 7–8) as a string.
  - An SQL query is constructed as a string (lines 9–10).

In many applications both of these strings, i.e. the database URL and SQL, will be built up from information passed in as parameters. Here we show a simple case where the database connection and query are fixed. Once the database and SQL are defined, the example Java proceeds as follows:

- The database driver classes are loaded (line 13).
- A database connection is then made (lines 23–25) adding user and password information to the URL when a Connection object is created.
- A statement object is then created (line 26) ready to send SQL statements to the database.
- The executeQuery method of the statement object is then used to pass the query and the results are put into a ResultSet object (line 27).
- The program then iterates through the result set (lines 28–35).
  - The result set's getString method is used to extract the hotel and city names into string variables that are then used to build up a piece of text that can be displayed on a browser via a results object (lines 30–34).
  - The getString method's parameter is the column index, i.e. 1 for the first column hotel, etc (line 30). The column name could have been used instead, e.g.

```
String hotelName = rs.getString("hotel");
```

- The Statement and Connection objects are then closed (lines 37–38).

JAVA SERVLETS

Java Servlets are a way of using Java for server side processing, rather than on the client as occurs with applets. An advantage of servlets is that they can be used with Web clients that do not support Java, or do not have Java enabled.

Like JDBC, Java Servlets are a Java API. Consequently, Servlets offer a way of extending the server's functionality, in the same way as other server APIs, such as mod_perl or Fast CGI. However, Java servlets have the advantage over these alternatives of Java's portability to many different platforms.

The efficiency gains of integrating the CGI functionality into the server also apply to servlets. Also, since servlet code runs in a JVM on the server, it is not necessary to write specialised versions for each Web server or operating system.

Example Java code to implement a servlet is given in Figure 6.6. In this example, the Figure 6.5 applet code is modified to work as a servlet. Once again, numbering is included for ease of reference, but is not part of Java.

Figure 6.6 Example Java Servlet in which JDBC is used

```
1. import java.io.*;
2. import java.sql.*;
3. import javax.servlet.*;
4. import javax.servlet.http.*;

5. public class hotellist extends HttpServlet
6. {

7.    public void doGet(HttpServletRequest req,
8.                        HttpServletResponse res)
9.    throws ServletException, IOException
10.   {
11.     res.setContentType("test/html");
12.     PrintWriter out = res.getWriter();
```

Figure 6.6 Example Java Servlet in which JDBC is used—continued

```
13.     String url =
14.         "jdbc:subprotocol//host:port/database";
15.     String query = " select hotel,city
16.                     from booking
17.                     order by hotel,city";

18.     out.println("<HTML>");
19.     out.println("<BODY>");

20.     try
21.     {
22.        Class.forName("drivername.classname");
23.     }
24.     catch(java.lang.ClassNotFoundException e1)
25.     {
26.        // Error handling code
27.     }

28.     try{
29.        DriverManager.getConnection
30.           (url,"user","passwd");

31.        Connection con =
32.        DriverManager.getConnection(url,"jdbc","");
33.        Statement stmt = con.createStatement();
34.        ResultSet rs =stmt.executeQuery(query);
35.        System.out.println("<P> Hotel,      City");
36.        while (rs.next())
37.        {
33.           String hotelName = rs.getString(1);
34.           String cityName = rs.getString(2);
35.           out.println("<BR> " + hotelName + " , "
36.           + cityName);
37.        }

38.     out.println("</P>");
39.     stmt.close();
```

Figure 6.6 Example Java Servlet in which JDBC is used—continued

```
40.        con.close();
41.    }
42.    catch(SQLException ex2)
43.{
44.        // Error handling code
45.    }
46.    out.println("</HTML>");
47.    out.println("</BODY>");
48.  }
49.}
```

Figure 6.6 Example Java Servlet in which JDBC is used—concluded

The bulk of the code dealing with the database connection in Figure 6.6 is the same as in Figure 6.5, and has already been explained. The main change in the servlet in Figure 6.6 to the applet code in Figure 6.5 concerns how the output is performed.

- As with the JDBC classes, the servlet classes are imported (lines 1–4).
- The servlet, hotellist, can then be defined as a specialisation of the general class, HttpServlet (line 5).
- The doGet method (starting in line 7) is invoked whenever the server receives a GET request for this servlet, which might be, for example, from an HTML form with an action, e.g.

```
<FORM ACTION ="/servlet/hotellist" METHOD =GET>
```

- An HttpServletResponse object (line 8) then handles the output. The HttpServletRequest "req" (line 7) is not used since this servlet does not process any input parameters, such as form variables.

Servlet code can produce an entire HTML page, as in the example above, or it can operate in the server side scripting style, adding content into an existing Web page via server side includes or JSP.

JAVA CGI
Java can also be used as a CGI programming language. In fact, given the similarity in the ways in which these are respectively coded, Java for any

one of these may be re-used to implement the other with relatively little change.

In the Figure 6.7 example we show how the code in the Figure 6.5 applet above can also form the basis of a Java program run on a server as a normal CGI program. Since Java is compiled to bytecode and therefore is not directly executable, in order to execute the Java CGI, it is first necessary to run the JVM which then executes the Java bytecode. This is done by calling a script, e.g.

```
#!/bin/csh
java hotellist
```

The program in Figure 6.7 is simplified again by omitting error checking.

Figure 6.7 Example Java CGI in which JDBC is used

```
1. import java.sql.*;

2. public class hotellist
3. {
4.   public static void main (String args[])
5.   {
6.     String url =
7.        "jdbc:subprotocol//host:port/database";
8.     String query = " select hotel,city
9.                     from booking
10.                    order by hotel,city";
11.    System.out.println("Content-type: text/html");
12.    System.out.println("");

13.    System.out.println("<HTML>");
14.    System.out.println("<BODY>");

15.    try
16.    {
17.      Class.forName("drivername.classname");
18.}
```

Figure 6.7 Example Java CGI in which JDBC is used—continued

```
19.      catch(java.lang.ClassNotFoundException e1)
20.      {
18.        // Error handling code
19.}

20.      try{
21.         DriverManager.getConnection
22.           (url,"user","passwd");

23.         Connection con =
24.         DriverManager.getConnection(url,"jdbc","");
25.         Statement stmt = con.createStatement();
26.         ResultSet rs =stmt.executeQuery(query);
27.         System.out.println("<P> Hotel,      City");
28.         while (rs.next())
29.         {
30.            String hotelName = rs.getString(1);
31.            String cityName = rs.getString(2);
32.            System.out.println("<BR> " +
33.            hotelName + "," + cityName);
34.         }

35.         System.out.println("</P>");
36.         stmt.close();
37.         con.close();
38.      }
39.      catch(SQLException ex2)
40.      {
41.        // Error handling code
42.      }
43.      System.out.println("</HTML>");
44.      System.out.println("</BODY>");
45.   }
46.}
```

Figure 6.7 Example Java CGI in which JDBC is used—concluded

The only significant changes from the applet in Figure 6.5 to the CGI program in Figure 6.7 are the addition of the System.out.println statements. These are used as follows:

- to produce an HTTP header (lines 11–12). This contrasts with the modification from the applet code to a servlet (Figure 6.6), where producing the HTTP header was handled by the servlet's HttpServletResponse setContentType method.
- to produce HTML headers and footers (lines 13–14, 43–44)
- Other System.out.println statements output the data itself in a suitable form (lines 32–33).

Note that applets, servlets and Java CGI programs differ only in the way they handle output. For example, in the servlet and CGI examples the servlet code uses an HttpServletResponse object for its output, while the CGI program sends its output to stdout. These similarities make possible a strategy for writing generic Java code which will execute as either applet, server or CGI. This is done by coding the output statements as separate output methods.

ALTERNATIVES TO JDBC

JDBC has already become a widely used means of connecting to databases. It is mainly used to connect to relational databases, and in fact JDBC contains a number of features that assume that the database it connects to will be a relational one. The need to provide a means of accessing relational systems was clearly a driving force behind the development of JDBC. However, since JDBC largely provides a means of passing SQL commands as strings to a database, it can also be used to access other sorts of database provided they can accept SQL. This facility can be used, for example, to utilise SQL front ends to some older network and hierarchical systems, as well as to flat file systems. Also, some Object databases may be accessed with SQL.

One area where JDBC is weak is its inability to fully exploit the object features of Java. A simple mapping of complex structures between Java and a database allowing permanent storage of those structures would simplify many programming tasks. JDBC is still limited by the "impedance mismatch" between databases and third generation programming languages. This refers to the fact that relational databases operate on a table at a time, which does not interface well with programming languages that process only one (possibly complex) record at a time.

One feature of JDBC not considered above is that it can be used to address metadata (i.e. data about data), as well as data itself. In the previous examples (Figures 6.5–6.7), in which JDBC is used, the structure of the table being queried is known. For example, the booking table is known to contain hotel and city columns. JDBC also contains a set of metadata classes that allow the metadata, usually held in system tables in the database, to be queried. In this way applications can discover and then use the names of tables and the names and types of columns within those tables.

For many applications, the use of metadata is not necessary since the details of the database will be known. The use of metadata does however, allow the development of generic methods that can be re-used in many different applications. [Hunter 99] gives a very useful example of using metadata with a generalised HTMLResultSet class whose output is an HTML table. The code could be used to format the output of any SQL select statement as a table in a Web page. The metadata information provides the database column names which are used in the HTML table's header and the Java ResultSet produced from the SQL query provides the table's data.

JDBC is often described as a low level API, since SQL commands are called directly, e.g. a method like executeQuery() takes an SQL statement as its parameter. Since it is a low level API it can also be used as the basis for building other APIs, such as SQLJ described in the next subsection.

SQLJ

One example of a higher level API is SQLJ. SQLJ is an embedded SQL for Java, similar to the embedded language interfaces provided for other languages such as COBOL and C. An embedded language is a language that can be used within another language to provide added functionality.

In one sense the situation for embedded languages is now different to that of these earlier ones, e.g. for C or Cobol. This is because in the past there has been no common low level API for databases. For example, embedded SQL in C had to be translated into database specific function calls. This situation changed for databases with the emergence of ODBC as a standard API. SQLJ is now being standardised as part of SQL99 (see Section 3.2 Object Relational Databases) and is being promoted by many database vendors, such as Oracle.

SQLJ has a number of advantages and disadvantages compared to JDBC:

- Since SQLJ is a higher level API, code development is simpler. There may be a bonus to this if Integrated Development Environments (IDE) also support SQLJ.
- SQLJ allows a number of checks to be made; these include syntax checking and type checking. Online checking, where the existence of tables and columns to be accessed is tested, may also be possible.
- SQLJ allows only the construction of static SQL statements. JDBC is needed if applications use dynamic SQL.
- SQLJ Translators may include vendor specific features to allow users to exploit non-standard features of a database. There may be an advantage in using those features. However, a disadvantage is a lessening of portability.
- Because JDBC came first there is already a large body of JBDC code and expertise that can be re-used.
- JDBC only requires knowledge of the JDBC driver and that the database will accept the SQL commands.
- Use of an embedded form of SQL means that we must have access to a preprocessor to convert the embedded SQL into calls in the host language.

We therefore anticipate that SQLJ will gain in popularity and have an increasing role in Web database systems.

ODMG JAVA BINDING

The ODMG Java binding provides a similar facility to the JDBC facility described above. The main difference is that Java objects and methods are defined to access object databases, rather than relational. Accordingly, the language used is OQL (see Section 3.1. Object Databases), rather than SQL. The difficulty here is the lack of standardisation across object databases. Although the major ODBMS vendors are members of the ODMG there are still wide variations in the bindings and query languages used with their respective object databases. For this reason the ODMG Java binding is not yet likely to provide the same degree of database independence as JDBC.

6.6 WEB DATABASE IMPLEMENTATION CHOICES

Having outlined the approaches and some of the tools for connecting a database system to the Web, the following section provides guidance on which facilities to use in actual Web database systems. In covering this area we focus on the main approaches, rather than on specific database, Web server and Web browser products.

The design considerations covered in the following subsections are:

- Client Processing: Java or JavaScrip—We discuss the major options in language choice for client side processing.
- Graceful degradation—This is the desirable property whereby a system can still operate, possibly at a reduced capacity, in the absence of certain facilities.
- Browser Detection—This is a technique for tailoring content and appearance for different browsers.
- Feature Bloat—This is the tendency to add features unnecessarily.
- User Interface Issues—That is, how HCI factors apply to Web systems.

CLIENT SIDE PROCESSING: JAVA OR JAVASCRIPT

In this subsection we consider the dilemma, if processing is to be done at the client, should Java or JavaScript be used? Two considerations are examined.

1) Although some activities could be implemented in either language, some facilities are only available in Java.
2) This choice will substantially affect the look of the application, since client processing with Java means that interaction will be with an applet rather than Web pages.

APPEARANCE

One consideration is the appearance of the Web database applications. An application designer has more control over many aspects of the appearance of an applet than over a Web page. For example, the size, layout and colour of an applet can be specified within the applet and cannot be overridden by the browser. On the other hand, the appearance of a Web page can only be suggested by the designer and may be overridden by a browser's preferences. However, the appearance of an applet is not as fixed as, for example, a Windowed application for Microsoft Windows, a Macintosh application or a Unix application using X. The precise appearance of an applet varies on different platforms. This is because the features of Java's AWT (Abstract Windows Toolkit) may be implemented in different ways. Features, such as scroll bars, can be included in a design, but their appearance may depend on the system on which they are executed. Variations in fonts across platforms can also produce unexpected effects. In contrast JavaScript can be seen as adding features to HTML pages. It may be decided that the familiar appearance of Web pages is worth maintaining, as opposed to the different look and feel of an applet.

DATABASE CONNECTION

From a database point of view there is one very important difference between using Java and JavaScript, i.e. the ability to establish a connection to a database. JavaScript does not offer a way to connect to a database[1]. On the other hand, Java has JDBC which can be used to create and to maintain a connection to a database. The database processing will still take place at the server[2], but other parts of the application's processing can be carried out at the client. This will allow the development of an application that can pass information to and from a database in a seamless fashion within one applet.

If client processing is to be done with JavaScript, the application will have to be broken into a number of separate interactions with the database. An HTML page and its JavaScript code can be generated, possibly dynamically, from a database and results of a user's interaction with that page returned to the database. These interactions can be extended to become a sequence of pages, with state maintenance (see below) if needed. However, in the latter case we have moved a long way

---

[1] Here we are discussing client side JavaScript. Server side JavaScript does have access to a Database object.

[2] The database server may of course not be on the same machine as the Web server. Nonetheless the processing is taking place at a server rather than the Web client.

from a pure client processing model to what is essentially a hybrid. That is not to say that it is not a workable solution, just a different one.

DATA VALIDATION

Some client processing that can be done with JavaScript can be compared to some database 4GLs. These languages, for example the Oracle 4GL, provide an environment in which developers can specify localised processing and the transfer of information to and from the database. (Here we refer to information rather than data, since some facts which are metadata such as the names and or specification of columns and tables as well as the data in them may be being processed.) In such a 4GL a developer might wish to validate a data item entered by a user. For example, the application may check that an order quantity is a positive integer or that a date is in the future. Such a validation could be carried out by code associated with the input screen or the application. In general this has the advantage of checking user's input immediately, that is without communicating it to the database. Such a check does not invalidate the need for an integrity constraint within the database that makes the same check. The reasons for this approach to data validation include:

- The 4GL may offer the means to give the user a more informative error message than that coming from the failure of the database integrity check. "Order must be in the range 1-100." may be preferably to "Insert into table order failed.".
- The 4GL may be able to offer some messages immediately, i.e. when the user moves off a field. Database messages might only come later when a complete SQL statement (or number of statements) has been constructed and executed.
- The need for the check in the database itself will still exist since the application we are considering may not be the only route to insert (or change) the data item.

JavaScript validation is very like the 4GL validation described here. It can offer immediate feedback and helpful messages. The immediacy may be greater and more significant with a Web application. The need to see this as a supplement to, rather than a substitute for, a database integrity check is however stronger. The use of a 4GL cannot be avoided by traditional non-Web application, but some Web users may turn off JavaScript. In this case we are discussing a scenario which is not completely JavaScript dependent, that is, we use JavaScript as a bonus rather than relying on it.

Validation of data with Java covers similar ground. We can test values as soon as a user leaves a field, etc. What Java offers in addition is the ability to communicate with the database on the same screen of the applet using JDBC so no fresh Web page is downloaded. Using JavaScript such a database connection will involve downloading a new page. The page may be a dynamically created one that looks the same, or very similar. In either case we have moved beyond purely client processing.

GRACEFUL DEGRADATION

The notion of graceful degradation is always an important one when designing Web database systems. Graceful degradation is the feature whereby a system can continue to operate, perhaps with a reduced functionality, after some part of that system has failed or is missing. Humans have this capability. For example, if someone breaks a leg, they will still able largely to continue their role in society. Graceful degradation is an important feature for all computer systems (or even all systems—we like the idea that railway signals should failsafe) but this is especially the case for Web systems. Many features of Web systems, such as images, the use of cookies, stylesheets, JavaScript or Java, may be enabled or disabled by a user. Also, some or all of those features may not be available on a particular browser. However, it remains important that the Web system continues to provide its basic services. A graceful degradation strategy is therefore one that has a fallback position. An example is where the system offers navigational aids on a site using JavaScript but also the equivalent via normal HTML hyperlinks. The advantage is that the JavaScript enabled users may have a bonus but non-JavaScript users are still catered for.

To further illustrate the issue of graceful degradation when designing a Web system, consider the situation where nominally text only browsers, such as lynx, are used. These may in fact have features such as the ability to display images, but may not use those features in the way a Web page author expects. This does not mean that no system should use those features, but it does raise questions about whether it is appropriate to rely on any of those features. For example, should a designer produce a page where the links are implemented as visually attractive graphics, such as a picture of a cottage for a HOME link? In practice, this is sensible only if the designer also uses an ALT ="Home" in the HREF. Without the ALT text, the page is not usable by a browser that does not load images. In fact, when using recent version of HTML, e.g. the HTML 4.0 DTD, specification of images without a text alternative is invalid.

BROWSER DETECTION

Browser detection or browser "sniffing" is a technique by which incompatibility between the features required by a Web system and those supported by a particular browser can be detected. For example, this technique can be used to test if JavaScript is enabled. Having identified the browser, the author may then take "appropriate" action. However, this appropriate action is too often a basically insulting message telling the user to get what the author thinks is a better browser. As a strategy, browser detection fails on a number of points.

- No one knows all the different browsers in the world (let alone their versions) and their capabilities.
- Some browsers misrepresent themselves, partly to avoid problems of users attempting to identify them.
- If you do detect the browser, what do you do? Can you maintain an ever-increasing range of different pages with the same basic content but tailored to each browser variant?
- Even if you detect the browser, has the feature you want to use been turned off?

FEATURE BLOAT

The needs of a Web Database system should have been determined by a requirements analysis that will have specified the functionality that the system must fulfil. This should of course be true for any system development, including any Web system. Web systems in general, as any Web surfer will have seen, seem to be particularly prone to feature bloat where features are added because "we can do them" rather than because "we need them". Some features may be associated more with the appearance of the Web pages or the ease of user interaction. Examples of this are the use of style sheets (see Chapter 4 Cascading Style Sheets). Some technologies, such as JavaScript, may be used for issues of functionality as well as ease of user interaction. In the following subsections we will concentrate on the issues of functionality, although these cannot always be cleanly divorced from ease of user interaction issues.

USER INTERFACES AND THE WEB

One important factor to remember in building Web Database systems (in fact any Web system) is that the user interface is, by the nature of the Web, less controllable than is the norm for computer based information systems. This may be particularly notable if, for example, when transferring a system built using a database and its 4GL onto the Web. On the Web there is much less control of what an application looks like or how it behaves. The look of a Web application is much more under the control of the user than the application developer. The application developer may suggest what the system will look like and may test it on common browsers but each user may see the application in a different way (or not see it all but hear it via a speaking browser).

The "look" of a Web application can be determined in a number of ways.
- HTML.
- Fonts, tables, paragraphs, headings, breaks, and indents.
- Browser differences.
- Detecting the browser and assuming things from that.
- Style sheets.
- JavaScript.
- Differences between Java implementations on different platforms.
- User preferences for colour, fonts, for example to cope with sight problems.
- User screen resolution and the actual browser window's shape and size on the screen.

The influence of any of the above factors may result in an application with an appearance which is very different to that which the developer intended. This lack of control must be borne in mind by the developer, who must accordingly focus on the logical structure and features of an application, rather than the fine detail of how it will look.

USER INTERFACES AND THE INTRANET

Though Intranet applications might be regarded as different to those on the Web, they should still be built with the same considerations for variation between user situations, as when developing Web applications.

Many of the caveats applied to Web applications must also be applied to Intranet applications.

The browsing environment of an intranet is likely to be more strictly controlled, for example by a company policy of only using one browser, perhaps even possibly one version of that browser. Also, organisation wide configuration of systems might be in place. This could cover factors such as enabling JavaScript and Java. However, making too many assumptions or exploiting particular features of a browser does not allow for smooth future development. If you exploit the way your application looks because of what is essentially a quirk of a browser will it still be satisfactory after a workplace wide upgrade to a new release of the same browser, let alone a decision to use a different browser as standard? A system designed for use on Netscape in the sales office should still work when salespeople in the field access it on mobile phones with built in browsers. Even within what is believed to be a controlled workplace environment the developer should still ensure that the application will run on browsers with non "normal" settings, e.g. an application designed primarily for full screen use should also operate within an A4 shaped browser window.

USER INTERFACES AND CONTROL

The general conclusion for Web systems is that the designer should stop thinking in terms of "How do I force the user?" or "How do I make...?". In newsgroups discussing the Web such questions are frequent and are often answered wisely, but often not to the questioner's satisfaction, with "You don't force but you can suggest".

The underlying philosophy of Cascading Style Sheets is a good indication of this approach. Style Sheets are not intended to force a particular appearance on a page but rather to suggest an appearance. The cascading part is the hierarchy of authority given to different style sheets so that a user's specific needs have greater authority than the settings of an individual page. For example, if the implementer wishes to emphasise some text by increasing its size, it is better to do this by suggesting that it should be larger than normal text, rather than fixing it at a particular point size 16 pt is larger to someone with a normal size of 12 pt but smaller if you usually use 20pt.

The way HTML forms work can also provide a useful example. It is common practice to use a select tag with a number of options to obtain a user input that is from a known range. Browsers commonly implement this as a pull down menu. This works well in an example such as the following fragment where we wish to set the variable, location, to one of four cities.

```
<select name =location size =1>
<option>Berlin
<option>London
<option>Paris
<option>Warsaw
```

The above code works much less well when it is necessary to choose from a pull down that includes all the states of the USA followed by all the countries in the world. Such a pull down list might be created automatically from a database, so its total size might become larger than expected. How different browsers, now and in the future, can present these options is beyond the control of the system developer. The distinct features of Web systems are leading to the development of a separate branch of HCI concerned with "Web usability" [Nielsen 00].

6.7 STATE AND TRANSACTIONS
In this section we examine one important aspect of Web database processing that remains a problem. That is, transaction management. We first explain the concept of a transaction and review the standard techniques for ensuring that database transactions are correctly executed. The section then overviews the added complexities and current solutions relating to Web database systems.

TRANSACTIONS
The concept of a transaction is fundamental to the safety of database processing. This concept can be explained by examining the relationship between a database and the organisation that it serves. A database typically represents a "snapshot" of a part of the world. It represents information about relevant entities, facts about them and association between them that are valid at the time of the "snapshot". Therefore when the world changes, information about the world should also change to maintain the validity of the database. When a database is

updated to reflect those changes, it is important that processes that access the database should retrieve data from a single and consistent snapshot. In particular, they should be safeguarded from accessing data that is a consequence of updates to the database that are as yet uncompleted.

The purpose of transaction management is to provide those safeguards. A transaction is a sequence of instructions which alter the database so as to represent a single change in the world, and/or which retrieve information about a single "snapshot" of the world to support some task. Transaction management ensures that each transaction satisfies certain properties so as to provide the above safeguards. The four properties are known as the ACID properties, and are as follows:

- Atomicity—That is, the transaction should execute in its entirety, or not at all. If for some reason it is aborted, the database should be left as if the transaction had never started.
- Consistency—A transaction should transform a database from one consistent state to another.
- Independence—Transactions should be independent of each other. In general, conventional transaction management gives a user the illusion that they have a computer system to themselves without any other users, who might potentially interfere with their work.
- Durability—This property requires that once the transaction has completed, the changes that it has made persist until another valid transaction makes further changes.

When these properties are enforced, a transaction acts as a unit of recovery in a database system. The DBMS will make sure that either all of the instructions of a transaction are executed as a single task, or none of them are.

The potential problems associated with transactions are as follows.

INCOMPLETE OR ABANDONED TRANSACTIONS

A transaction may fail for some reason (e.g. because of a programming error), or it may be abandoned (e.g. a user who wishes to make a hotel reservation finds that there are no available rooms).

A database language, such as SQL, will include instructions for indicating the start of a transaction. Other instructions can be used to indicate that the transaction has successfully completed, i.e. a COMMIT instruction, and to indicate that the transaction should be abandoned, i.e. ABORT or ROLLBACK.

- After a COMMIT the changes made by the transaction are made permanent (until the next update) within the database. Until that time changes are unknown to other transactions, and therefore to other users.
- ROLLBACK causes the data values that have been changed by the transaction to be re-assigned the values that they had immediately before the transaction started.

A DBMS is able to undo the updates made by a failed or abandoned transaction because it keeps a record, typically on a file called a transaction log, of all changes made to the database.

INTERFERENCE BETWEEN TRANSACTIONS

Problems that transaction management must avoid occur when transactions execute concurrently, as illustrated in the following scenarios.

SCENARIO 1—A LOST OPERATION

Consider the two transactions in Figure 6.8, executing concurrently. These transactions respectively raise the minimum tariff for hotel "H3" by £2.10 and £2.20.

Transaction 1	Transaction 2
UPDATE Hotel	UPDATE Hotel
SET MinTariff = MinTariff	SET MinTariff = MinTariff
+ 2.10	+ 2.20
WHERE HotelNo = 'H3'	WHERE HotelNo = 'H3'

Figure 6.8 Example ambiguous concurrent transactions

Note that both transactions update the same row of the hotel table, but add different values to the MinTariff attribute. This situation is clearly ambiguous. For example, it may reflect consecutive price rises, or alternatively, it may reflect two inconsistent attempts to record a single price rise.

Now let us consider how the transactions in Figure 6.8 could execute and produce invalid results. One possible sequence is shown in Figure 6.9.

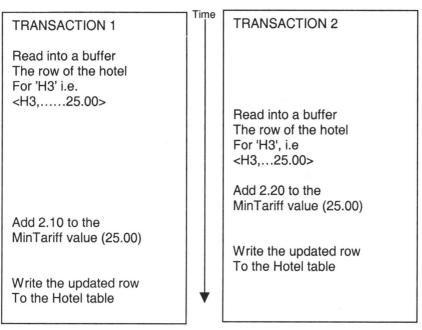

TRANSACTION 1	Time	TRANSACTION 2
Read into a buffer The row of the hotel For 'H3' i.e. <H3,......25.00>		
		Read into a buffer The row of the hotel For 'H3', i.e <H3,...25.00> Add 2.20 to the MinTariff value (25.00)
Add 2.10 to the MinTariff value (25.00)		
		Write the updated row To the Hotel table
Write the updated row To the Hotel table		

Figure 6.9 Example of transaction loss

Given this sequence in Figure 6.9, on completion of the above two transactions the MinTariff value will have been incremented by 2.10. The effect of transaction 2 will have been lost. This is because computations are performed on copies of the rows, rather than directly on the table data.

SCENARIO 2—RETRIEVAL OF INCONSISTENT DATA

Consider the two transactions executing concurrently as shown in Figure 6.10. These transactions respectively retrieve and update the minimum tariff for hotel "H3".

This second scenario is devised to illustrate situations when retrieval and update transaction interfere, causing invalid reports. Note that in the first transaction in Figure 6.10 the user retrieves the minimum tariff for hotel

H3 and then checks to see if it is above or below average. The second raises the minimum tariff for hotel H3.

Transaction 1	Transaction 2
SELECT HotelNo,MinTariff FROM Hotel WHERE HotelNo = 'H3' SELECT AVG(MinTariff) FROM Hotel	UPDATE Hotel SET MinTariff = MinTariff + 2.20 WHERE HotelNo = 'H3'

Figure 6.10 Example of an update transaction that affects concurrent retrieval transactions

Now let us consider how they could execute and produce invalid results (see Figure 6.11).

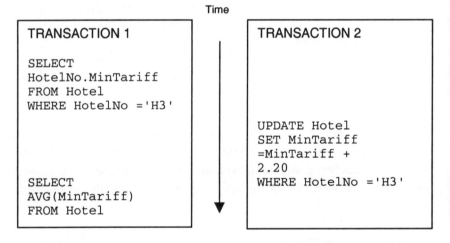

Figure 6.11 Example of interference between concurrent transactions

On completion of transaction 1, a user will have retrieved inconsistent data, since the minimum tariff will have changed between retrieving it and computing the average.

Though the above scenarios are not life threatening, it is possible to imagine other situations, such as a banking system concerned with the movement of funds, where the loss of an update or retrieval of inconsistent data could be catastrophic or expensive. Also, it is important to guarantee correct execution of all transactions so as to establish amongst the population of potential users confidence in Web-based database systems and services.

One way of preventing the types of interference between transactions illustrated above is to ensure that concurrent transactions are serialisable. By this, we mean that, though the transactions execute concurrently, the result is the same as if they executed one after the other in some sequence. Conventional transaction management ensures that concurrent transactions are serialisable. The techniques that are used to ensure this are outlined in the following subsection.

LOCKING AND DEADLOCK AVOIDANCE
Serialisability is usually assured by applying locks to the data being accessed or updated by transactions.

- If a transaction needs to access some data, then a lock is applied to that data so as to stop other transactions from changing it. This ensures that the transaction has access to a database which represents a single consistent "snap shot" of the world.
- If a transaction wishes to alter some data, a lock is applied to the data to ensure that other transactions do not access that data until the alterations are complete.

Locking is a means by which users can change parts of the database and not conflict with one another. The purpose of locks is to stop two (or more) users from trying to change the same data at the same time. It also stops one user from updating data while it is being read by another user or being read while it is being updated.

In general it is a good idea to lock as little of the database as possible so that users are less likely to be affected by one another's actions. In relational databases whole tables or large parts of tables have sometimes been the smallest unit that could be locked. Object databases should be able to lock at the level of individual objects.

There are a number of different locking strategies that may be used by DBMS. These may allow locking at different levels (tables, rows, individual object, type extents, etc.).

Most commercial DBMS support the following lock types:

1) A read lock must be taken before data can be read, and this will stop another user writing to (updating) that data, which would require a write lock. It may be possible for a number of read locks to be held on the same data.
2) A write lock must be held before data can be updated and will stop another user from reading or amending that data.
3) An upgrade lock is used when an application reads data which it may later decide to update (upgrade locks are used specifically to avoid a condition known as deadlock, which is explained later).

TWO-PHASE LOCKING
Most commercial DBMS use a locking protocol call two-phase locking (2PL). In order to ensure serialisability 2PL applies the restriction that:

- After releasing a lock, a transaction cannot acquire other locks.

The two phases of 2PL are therefore in phase one, locks are acquired, and in phase two, locks are released. This is illustrated below in Figure 6.12, which is a re-working of the scenario depicted in Figure 6.11, but with 2PL applied.

Note that the above sequence has resulted in the first transaction retrieving a total that does now correspond to the retrieved quantities in the hotel table at the time. This has been achieved by delaying the execution of transaction 2. The overall effect of applying the lock is to create the same result as when running transaction 1 and then transaction 2 in sequence. The transactions are therefore serialisable.

It is left as an exercise for the reader to re-work the other scenario above, but including locking so as to avoid the problems.

DEADLOCK
In some situations deadlock can occur when two or more users are attempting to lock parts of the database, and a cycle occurs. The database management system should be able to detect such situations and resolve

them by choosing between the users in some way to break the deadlock, or stopping them all and forcing a restart of a number of transactions.

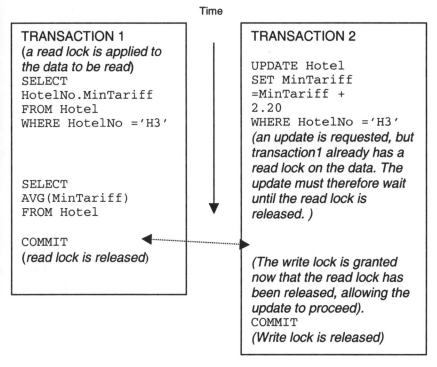

Figure 6.12 Example of the use of locking to avoid interference between concurrent transactions

Deadlocks can be prevented from occurring by requiring each transaction to lock all the data that it will need when it starts. This can be done by applying an upgrade lock, such that the locking can be changed from a read to a write lock later if necessary. However, the disadvantages of this strategy are that data is locked for the full duration of a transaction; and it is necessary to lock whole tables (or classes), since the pages and rows (or objects) to be accessed are not identified until the appropriate commands are executed. This is an example of a pessimistic locking strategy, because it always takes precautions to avoid the deadlock which may not actually occur.

An optimistic locking strategy allows deadlock to occur, and then breaks the deadlock. A deadlock is detected by periodically searching for a cycle in the "who is waiting for whom" relationships. When a deadlock is detected the DBMS selects a victim transaction (or victims) and aborts it (or them). Some systems then automatically restart the transaction(s), while others return an appropriate status message so that the application program may take some appropriate action. Users should be unaware of deadlocks. The disadvantage of optimistic strategies is that when there are many concurrent transactions, many deadlocks may occur. Some transactions may then be significantly slowed down because they repeatedly deadlock, abort, and restart.

Deadlocks can also be avoided by ensuring that where possible each user accesses a copy of the required data, but this is not always feasible or desirable, since shared access to data is one of the main attractions of database systems.

Some DBMS allow the DBA to choose between different locking strategies, both pessimistic and optimistic, and also to set the level at which locks are applied, e.g. to tables or pages or type extents or objects. By monitoring the performance under different strategies, the DBA may then determine the most effective concurrency controls.

TWO-PHASE COMMIT
The above transaction management techniques are applicable only for transactions on a single database system. In cases where multiple databases are involved there must also be a higher (global) level of transaction management to ensure that all of the component transactions are either committed or aborted. The technique most used for this purpose is called Two Phase Commit (2PC).

2PC operates by first checking that all subtransactions will be able to commit (the first or preparation phase) and then by allowing them to commit (the second or execution phase). This is managed by a co-ordinator process which sends messages to each participating system, for example, to determine if they are ready to commit. If any one participating system is unable to commit, all are aborted.

WEB DATABASE TRANSACTIONS
When a Web database system is constructed, the Web is interposed between the user and the database system. This creates a number of complexities, with respect to transaction management, in addition to

those discussed in the previous section. In particular, there is the problem of the Web protocol, HTTP, which does not maintain connections between clients and servers. This poses the question, Since HTTP is a stateless protocol is there a way of identifying a number of requests as parts of a single transaction from one user? The W3C has considered developing a "Session Identification URI" but at present there are four main techniques that can be used to provide session tracking:

- Hidden variables
- URL rewriting
- Cookies
- User Authentication

These techniques provide a way of tracking a session, i.e. a sequence of interactions with one user. They provide a way of passing information, such as a simple identifier, or more complex data, e.g. a name and address, through a number of operations. In this way, the appearance of a continuous connection between the user and the database is maintained, even though the link may be broken and remade repeatedly.

An alternative strategy is to perform the interaction with a database via an applet which makes a separate connection to the database in which state can be maintained.

To further explore the problems of Web transaction we consider a series of scenarios.

EXAMPLE 6.5

A transaction updates a hotel booking table by making a reservation and also initiating billing in another table. Clearly, both parts must happen. We don't want the reservation made without the billing and we don't want the billing without the reservation.

In the above example both database operations can be made to take place in one interaction with the database. All the information can be passed from a single form for example. One connection is then made to the database and then two SQL statements executed, the single transaction completed with an SQL commit and the connection broken. If either SQL statement fails the transaction as a whole is aborted, the database remains consistent and a message can be sent to the user. This is a true database transaction with no need for the maintenance of state beyond this interaction.

EXAMPLE 6.6

If we show a list of vacancies to a user and the user then selects one to make their booking we do not want another user to have seen the vacancy and be able to make the same booking.

In the second example with a non-Web based system, viewing the vacancies and then making the booking would normally be a single transaction. Reading the vacancies would take a read lock on the table. This stops other users updating the data. Making the booking would update the table and complete the transaction. A write lock would be place on the data prior to this update. While the transaction is in progress and the write lock is in effect, other users cannot see the data selected by the first user and therefore will not be able to try to book it too.

The above situation is not simply translated to a Web based system. On the Web, reading the vacancies and delivering them to a user will be a single database connection and operation. That transaction will then be over, and closing the database connection will always complete a transaction. Therefore we may deliver the same vacancy list to a number of users all of whom may try to make the same booking. The booking operation may be a transaction in its own right, as in the first example. All attempts after the first to make the booking will fail. This may look confusing to the users who have seen an apparent vacancy but are unable to book it.

Modifying the logic of an application may solve some transaction problems. For example, if all interactions with the database can be kept to one HTML form then one transaction (and one connection) may be possible. Other solutions to these problems are available by performing some form of session tracking. If we can associate some identifier with a user's operations it may be possible to simulate state and transactions. In the examples above, if the vacancy table has an attribute to show a pending interest from a user it may be possible to mark parts of the table and stop them being shown to others. The simple SQL to return part of a table to a user might be

```
SELECT * FROM vacancies WHERE city = "Barcelona"
```

In order to add a user id, the SQL might become

```
SELECT * FROM vacancies
WHERE city ="Barcelona" AND user _id NOT null;
UPDATE vacancies SET user_id = :user_id
WHERE city ="Barcelona" AND user_id  NOT null;
```

where :user_id is an identifier that can be read in by one of the session tracking mechanisms.

This modifies the interaction so that the user only gets unlocked rows and then locks what they see. The counterpart to this is that these rows must be unlocked subsequently. This can be done as an additional SQL statement when a booking is made with

```
UPDATE vacancies SET user_id = null
WHERE userid = :user_id
```

A problem remains with interactions that are not completed. We do not want parts of the database to remain locked if no booking is made, so some form of timeout will also be needed.

By adding identifiers to the database and using them (as illustrated above) we can provide transaction-like features. This is at a cost of increased complexity. A transaction is completed or abandoned with the SQL commands commit and rollback (or abort). Completing or undoing a sequence of database operations identified with an application based id may be more complex. Within a transaction, all changes are made pending completion, whereas with the simulated transaction, changes will have actually been made and need undoing. A transaction which is designed to undo the effects of another is called a compensating transaction. Also, the necessary sequence of operations may need working out individually for each application.

HIDDEN VARIABLES

A simple way to pass information through a sequence of Web pages is via hidden variables in HTML forms. In addition to the fields completed by a user, a form can have other hidden fields. The values of all the fields, hidden and visible, are passed to the server when the form is completed.

Hidden variables can be used in a number of ways.

An application could be built with an initial form that requested a name and address, or other id such as credit card number. This information is passed to the Web server which then includes the information as hidden variables in a new form. The user enters new information on the second form and this is passed along with the original information back to the server.

The following example shows what a later form in a sequence might look like. The form would have been created dynamically to include the hidden session variable with the value seen.

```
<FORM ACTION= "city.cgi" METHOD=GET>
City ?
<INPUT TYPE =text NAME =city size=20>

<INPUT TYPE =HIDDEN NAME =session VALUE="6345789">

<BR>
<INPUT TYPE=SUBMIT VALUE="Go ">
<INPUT TYPE=RESET>
</FORM>
```

URL REWRITING

A similar method to passing information as hidden form variables is explicitly rewriting URLs to include session information. With hidden variables the information will be passed as the query part of the URL with the GET method or passed via stdin with the POST method. The session information could be added directly as a parameter so that the form action includes the session information and a form contain no hidden values. This is illustrated in the variant of the previous example. We still ask for a city but the session information is written into the form action now, rather than the form itself.

```
<FORM ACTION= "city.cgi?session=6345789" METHOD=GET>
City ?
<INPUT TYPE =text NAME =city size=20>

<BR>
<INPUT TYPE=SUBMIT VALUE="Go ">
<INPUT TYPE=RESET>
</FORM>
```

Other forms of URL rewriting can add extra path information to the URL rather than parameters, as above. In this case the path information will have to be extracted by the CGI application. If session information is exposed as part of a URL there may be problems if the URL is bookmarked. This can be overcome, but will need building into an application to stop old invalid sessions being re-used.

COOKIES

The cookie mechanism allows a small piece of information to be stored on the client computer. This is supplied by an application and is only usable by applications coming from the same domain. This is intended to be strictly limited access to the computer and should not present a security risk. Nonetheless there have been problems in the past and not all users will have cookies turned on.

It is possible to use cookies to store a session id that can then be read by the different parts of an application to track a user. Languages used for Web programming all have facilities for reading and writing cookies which can be integrated into applications. It is then simple to write a new session id into a cookie at the start of an application and read that cookie to identify the session at each interaction. A simple id may be stored or more complex or changing information, but since cookies are limited in size (to 4K) smaller ids are often best. The following Set-Cookie header would be sent as part of an HTTP header to set the same session id as used above, the path makes the cookie accessible to all URLs in the domain and the life of the cookie will be for the current session only.

```
Set-Cookie: session=6345789; path=/;
```

USER AUTHENTICATION

In some circumstances a user will be asked to identify themselves, for example, by logging on. This will occur at the start of their interaction with a system. It may then be possible to use that information to provide session information. For many applications that allow a user to "browse" this will not be possible. It may be more appropriate in intranet applications where the users are known, than World Wide Web applications where the users are largely unknown.

SESSION TRACKING TECHNIQUES—SUMMARY

All the above techniques can be used by any Web application, not just a database one. Database applications may have an advantage in that we already have a database and this can be used as a repository for the session related information too. One of the problems with passing information can be the amount of data. Cookies are limited in size; forms and URLs with too many parameters can be cumbersome. A database can be used to generate session ids and store information, like names and addresses, with those ids. Then only the session id needs passing through the application, other information is always accessible on the Web server.

If the information to be passed can be minimised to a single id, what are the advantages and disadvantages of the different methods?
- Forms and URL rewriting have the big advantage of not requiring the user's cooperation.
- Users must permit cookies but not all will allow them.
- URL rewriting may cause bookmarking problems.

Cookies have one different advantage, that is the possibility of longer term tracking. We have considered them as a way of tracking a user in a single session. Cookies can remain beyond the life of a single session. This is done by setting an additional parameter, expires, to those shown above. This means that on a subsequent session an application can read an old cookie and re-use its information. If that was only a session id it may be that only the fact that the user has visited before may be usable. However, it may be possible to use the old session id to link to other information about the user from a previous session. This is commonly done with systems to target adverts. The danger here is that the cookie is stored on the computer but the user on the computer may be different.

For example, revealing a previous user's personal details to the next customer at an Internet Café is not a good idea.

It may be possible to use some techniques in combination. For example cookies can be used to detect that a user has visited a site before but hidden fields can then be utilised for the session itself.

In all cases a mechanism needs to be in place to ensure the validity of session information, that is, making sure that unique ids are created so that sessions do not get mixed. Since many interactions on the Web may end abruptly it will also be necessary to have a way to expire old sessions. Users may get disconnected, decide they want to go elsewhere, etc. In all cases a way of tidying up sessions is needed especially if database resources are tied up with a session.

In general, facilities for maintaining the validity of sessions in a conventional database are well supported by the DBMS itself. However, in the Web environment mechanisms for maintaining the validity of sessions, particularly when connections or systems fail, must be specified on an application by application basis.

6.8 SECURITY, PRIVACY AND IDENTITY

Key questions that users of a Web application will ask if the application involves the transmission of sensitive data, such as credit card numbers, are "How secure is the system? How private is my transaction?" The viability of Web-based commerce, for example, is wholly dependent on the trust users have in the security and privacy of the system. These issues are reviewed in the section.

Security issues can be broken into two areas, those connected with the Web and network aspects of Web database systems and those associated with the database side. We will examine these in turn.

Why do we need security? It is necessary to ensure the integrity of the database as a whole. We need to protect it as a whole system so that it keeps working. We may also need to ensure the security of information from those who should not have access to it. This is the privacy aspect, if a database holds personal information, from credit card information through to medical details, there is a moral if not legal responsibility to maintain that information securely. Associated with these issues is how we identify who has the right to access what information.

WEB SECURITY

There are a number of security issues associated with transmitting data over networks. These can be broken into three main areas.

- Can we guarantee the identities of those involved?
- Can we guarantee that no one else can access the data?
- Can we guarantee that no one can tamper with the data?

These are all issues for many Web systems; not just database connected ones. Simple HTTP authentication is built into the HTTP protocol but this is not adequate for many applications which require a higher level of security. Real security is built using digital certificates based on public key cryptography.

Simple HTTP authentication is based on the Web server requesting usernames and passwords to protect certain resources. This level of protection may be adequate for some applications but we can see also how it may not satisfy the needs identified above. Since with HTTP authentication the usernames and passwords may be stored as plain text on the server and sent in an easily decoded form, it may be possible to compromise security by accessing the files on the server or monitoring the network traffic. Beyond the usernames and passwords themselves other data might be monitored in transit.

A high level of security can be obtained by encrypting all data transfers. Public key cryptography is the method used to secure the data. This is based on pairs, one public one private, of keys that are used to encode and decode data. These keys which are generated by security software (such as PGP) are then stored as Digital Certificates and can be used by servers and browsers.

The Secure Socket Layer (SSL) is a protocol that implements public key cryptography to encode data transmission between client and server. Version 2.0 concentrates on server authentication and version 3.0 adds client authentication. Servers using SSL can be identified by URLs starting https instead of http because of the additional protocol in use.

CLIENT SECURITY

Systems that undertake client processing should ensure that the client itself cannot be compromised. In a client-based processing situation programs provided by the server are run on the client computer. In traditional client-server situations there is a level of confidence in the server that may not be present in Web systems. Web-based systems that involve client processing are running programs from a possibly unknown and untrusted source. The server is simply the computer identified within the URL. This computer may be run by a multinational corporation, a government, or your next-door neighbour, all of whom may be untrustworthy. Is the client safe from the processing done by the code coming from the server? It should be possible to limit what can be done by limiting the resources that can be used. This can be done by the client browser not permitting the downloaded page and any associated code to have unlimited access to the client. What limits should be placed on the code? In general we require the browser to operate in what is sometimes called a sandbox, where it cannot reach or reveal anything about the system beyond. For example, we do not want programs from a server to be able to access the file system on the client. If they could, they would be able to damage the system in a number of ways, obvious ones such as deleting files or more surreptitious ones such as replacing files or sending information from the files back to the server.

Programs run by the browser should also not disrupt the client by excessive demands on the client's resources. This implies that the source of the browser is itself trusted. Java was designed with a security model that adheres to these limitations and despite some concerns does not seem to have caused problems in this area. It is also possible to increase the access given to individual Java applets and servlets if they are trusted.

JavaScript and the use of ActiveX components from VBScript have a much poorer history in terms of security leaks, although work has been done to fix many of the early problems. This is often put forward as a good reason for upgrading to more recent versions of browsers, since they should have security problems fixed; however, they might also have new problems of course. These problems are one reason why many users do not use all the facilities available on their browsers and hence why it can be a problem to rely on features like Java and JavaScript when building a system. These issues are common to many Web systems and do not have a specific database element.

One exception to the limitation on access to the client file system is that for cookies. The implementation of cookies by a browser should give only a strictly limited opportunity for a Web system to write to the client's file system. Cookies are limited in size, number and accessibility by other servers and to a single cookie file. Nonetheless, as with Java and JavaScript, some users may limit cookies' use and so building systems that rely on them can again be problematic.

DATABASE SECURITY

Many issues of Web database security are the same as the issues of securing any database application. We must ensure that the integrity of the database is maintained. To do this we can restrict access to the database itself, to particular parts of the database and to particular operations on the database. The mechanisms provided by different DBMS may differ but similar facilities are available in most systems.

Systems have a means of authorising which users can use a database. The Ingres DBMS for example allows databases to be set up as public, accessible by all users, or private, accessible by authorised users. The lists of authorised users are contained within another database iidbdb maintained by the system's DBA. Once inside a database, SQL permits restrict which tables users can access and which operations (select, insert, update, and delete) can be performed on them. Further restrictions may be possible by limiting access to views rather than tables in some cases. It may also be possible to restrict users by only allowing them to access a table via a database procedure. Limiting users to views or procedures may mean that they can, for example, update a table but in a more limited way than if they had an update permit on the underlying table. Many DBMS also include auditing and logging features so that changes in the database can be tracked. These security considerations should have been identified at the system design stage of application development.

The area in which security becomes more complex with Web database systems is in identifying users. A number of different strategies may be used. For example, it may be possible to use a login and password system. This may operate on a number of levels.

For a low level of security it may be possible to password protect the database application with passwords applied via the Web server. This might be appropriate as a means of limiting access on an intranet to one group of staff who might have a common password. Here the particular identity of the user is not significant.

Logins and passwords can be built into the database application itself. In this case this information could be entered onto a form with other information used in the application. The issue here may be whether that information needs to be carried throughout the application. In some cases an initial login may be all that is needed. After that the user's identity may not need to be maintained at all stages. If identity must be kept it might be passed by one of the mechanisms for maintaining state discussed above.

There may be problems then of exposing the login and password across the network. It may also be possible to reverse the logic of an initial login and only request identifying information at a final confirmatory stage of an application. This will not be the case where information of a restricted or personal nature is retrieved in the course of the application but may be appropriate for an essentially data entry application.

With some ways of connecting to a database from a Web page the user and password can be established as parameters. These can be requested on the Web page via an HTML form. An example of this is the JDBC getConnection method in the form

```
DriverManager.getConnection
  ("driver_info:db_info","login","password")
```

If the interaction takes place in an applet, the database connection and state may be maintained. In other technologies the database connection may be broken and the link will need re-establishing. In such a case a way needs to be found to keep the user information securely so that it can be re-used.

For many operations, however, a login may not be appropriate. It should be possible to run general queries on a system without trying to force users to identify themselves. In the Eagleley examples we would like to make it easy for the casual enquirer to use the system and we do not want to put any barriers in their way. One solution to this may be to have two databases or a partition between parts of one, so that general queries can run in an unrestricted fashion on one set of tables. Bookings that need identification could then run on another set of tables. This may have some consequences for the issues of maintaining state. If a user sees that there are vacancies, shown from a read only table, can they then make a booking in a separate updateable table? What happens if another user has also seen the vacancy and just booked it? In a traditional database or transaction processing system, seeing the vacancy would have established a read lock which stops another user from updating that data till the first user's transaction is complete.

In many situations a login is not appropriate because the user is not known to the database system. Unlike many traditional database applications where the users are essentially known, the workers in an office for example, with Web applications the users are unknown. Because of this most Web database applications will have to access the database as a pseudo user. This user may have to be given a name and is often called "www" or "nobody". CGI programs and connections to the database are then made as this pseudo user. The rights of this user, the great unknown public, are then set at an appropriate level. Individual users may identify themselves uniquely with, for example, a credit card number, but they will not access the database as a particular user.

Relatively unrestricted access to a database opens up many possible problems. If we allow anyone to add information to a database, how then can we stop it becoming corrupted? One solution is to add information to temporary tables and validate it in some way before it is actually added to the database. This sort of procedure may be undertaken for non-Web-based database systems as well of course.

Many of the above security measures are illustrated in Example 6.9.

EXAMPLE 6.9

The Eagleley Group.wants to enable users to register with it so that they can be sent out brochures and online bulletins. Users are invited to fill in an HTML form with their details: postal address for brochures and email address for online bulletins. This information is added to the database when the user submits the form. The table that the data is added to is not used directly. Eagleley wants to check whether the names are already in their database and confirm that the email address is valid. There are a number of operations run on the database on a regular basis. Duplicates from the list are removed, these occur when for example a user submits the form twice in error. There would be no key on the table data is put into since we cannot be sure of a unique identifier. Postal addresses are checked against the real mailing list table and only added if not already present. Email addresses are checked against the real online bulletin list table. Eagleley does not want people being added to the email list maliciously by others. A test message is sent to ask the user to confirm that they wish to be added to the email list. When that confirmation is received the details are added to the real online bulletin list table. In this way the Web element of the system is backed up by a number of standard procedures.

MALICIOUS CODE

There are a number of ways in which a Web database system may be exposed to malicious code. These are similar to the general problems that Web administrators have with issues of unexpected input via CGI scripts (see [Gundavarum 96 p 180] for a simple example) but concentrate on SQL problems. It might be expected that problems could arise if a system offered unrestricted SQL access to its database. A form with a text entry box inviting users to write SQL and then executing this would be asking for trouble. However, more restricted applications may also pose security risks. An example of a more restricted application is to offer a form where a user selects from a list of cities. This can be specified as a parameter which is added onto

```
SELECT HotelName FROM Bookings WHERE City = "
```

Finally, the closing quote is added and the statement executed. In this case the statement cannot be modified. If we have a more flexible form that allows user input we open the situation to allowing the SQL statement to be modified. In cases where the user input is quoted the possibilities are limited. A user could add wildcard characters to broaden a query. This might result in much larger query results and could form part of a denial of service attack. More serious problems can occur when a numeric search condition is used since this is not quoted. Code expecting to delete a single row might need a numeric id to complete the following code

```
DELETE FROM some_table WHERE id =
```

Instead of a single value converting this to

```
DELETE FROM some_table WHERE id = 123
```

user input of "123 or id > 0" instead of "123" would result in code of

```
DELETE FROM some_table WHERE id = 123 OR id > 0
```

which could have quite a different effect.

In addition to modifying SQL statements there is a danger of additional statements being added. This is a problem because most DBMS will accept a comma separated sequence of SQL statements where a single statement is expected. Consider the situation where a numeric value was expected to complete the following

```
SELECT * FROM Booking WHERE Id =
```

If a user instead of entering just a numeric value types

```
123; DELETE FROM Booking,
```

then the following valid SQL will be created

```
SELECT * FROM Booking WHERE Id =123;
DELETE FROM Booking
```

The result of the above SQL may be to display the expected results and then remove all rows from the table!

In addition to malicious SQL code, there is a danger of system calls. This area is similar to the general problems of CGI mentioned above. Just as an escape from a Perl script to a shell can be a danger, a similar call to a shell from within SQL can be a problem. Many DBMS support a system call from SQL, so in addition to situations above, we need to avoid the possibility of sequence of SQL statements, such as

```
SELECT * FROM Cities;
SYSTEM(rm -rf *);
```

In addition to the danger of additional entry via forms there is also a potential problem with SQL written into URLs. If the output of a form contains a complete piece of SQL in the URL such as

```
bad.cgi?code=select+*+from+cities
```

then a malicious user could enter a similar URL but with a modified piece of code

```
bad.cgi?code=delete+from+cities
```

There are a number of steps that system builders can take to ensure the safety of their SQL code. One measure is to ensure that the correct permissions exist on the tables. In the example above only select permission might be granted on the cities table. Some DBMS allow limits to be put on the number of rows retrieved by queries. The code can also be parsed in a number of ways before being executed. For example, code containing semicolons or the word system could be rejected. Values that should be only numeric can be tested and rejected if non-numeric characters or a value out of the expected range is found.

EFFICIENCY VS SECURITY
There are situations where the demands of efficiency and security may be in conflict. The increases in efficiency that can be gained by building PHP, mod_perl, or other server APIs into the Web server have a cost. A consequence is that processes now run with the same permissions and rights as the Web server. This may not be a problem. For example, in a situation like the Eagleley example where the Web server is essentially a

dedicated process and likely to only connect to a single database this would not be problem. In situations where the Web server is more general purpose it may be an advantage to have CGI processes running with the rights of individual users. An example of this would be for an ISP that offered CGI facilities. The ISP would not want CGI processes to have rights beyond those of the individual users. In a situation like this there could be a number of entirely separate processes connecting to different databases all with different rights and permits. It is only possible to configure this sort of situation if each CGI process is spawned individually with its individual set of permissions.

6.9 A WEB SITE IN A DATABASE

Finally, we briefly focus on an alternative use of databases within the context of Web systems. Up to now we have concentrated on using a database to manage dynamic content for a Web system. It may be that some systems need a database to manage the volume of content rather than change in content. In this situation, the database acts as a document management system for the Web pages.

If we have a large Web site a database may be useful tool to manage it as an alternative to a large number of separate files. A database can offer logging and auditing of changes to documents. It can also offer a way of making large changes to the appearance of the Web site. Documents can be stored as complete HTML documents or fragments that are then built into complete Web pages. Graphics, photos, etc. may also be stored if the database can support that type of object. In a situation like this, changes to a database may be infrequent. That is, the data is not changing minute by minute, unlike, for example, a stock level. If data changes, for example once a week, the overhead of always fetching it from the database may be unnecessary, since Web pages could then be built automatically by writing reports from the database overnight or at a weekend, for example, unix systems provide a "cron" facility for running jobs at fixed intervals.

Keeping all the Web site's contents in a database make it possible to identify and change all documents with, for example, a URL that needs changing.

There are likely to be advantages in storing components of Web pages rather than entire Web pages in the database. If we have standard parts of Web pages, "boilerplate" as it is sometimes called, kept separate then a single update to this will change the appearance of all the pages that use this boilerplate. New pages can be created by adding new content to the database and this is then extracted with the boilerplate to give a consistent look. If entire pages are stored then standard content will have to be copied into any new documents and larger scale updates made to effect site wide changes.

If a standard header includes the HTML DTD it is possible to upgrade the whole site with one change in the database. This would not of course make all the pages produced compliant with the new DTD. One way global changes could be made is by referencing one style sheet across many pages. Changes to the style sheet will then affect all pages. It is also possible to control the style sheet via the database. In this example we have a style table in the database with a number of named styles. Selecting all the rows corresponding to one style and writing these out to a ".css" style sheet file allows us to swap or update styles across multiple documents. This facility is illustrated in Example 6.10.

EXAMPLE 6.10

Consider the situation where a relational database is used to store a number of different style sheets that can be applied to a range of Web pages.

The style table in Figure 6.13 shows the result of a query,

```
SELECT * FROM style WHERE style ='house'
```

The result table shows a definition for all types of header body and three different types of paragraph. These are, an announcement type (ANN) using a monospaced type style, a normal, literary style with a leading indent, and a reversed style (REV) which swaps the colours used elsewhere. This can be written out using

```
select tag_selector,property_value
from style where style ='house'
```

giving the following style sheet

```
BODY    {color: navy; background-color:lightblue;}
H1      {color: blue;font-family:sans-serif;}
H2      {color: blue;font-family:sans-serif;}
H3      {color: blue;font-family:sans-serif;}
H4      {color: blue;font-family:sans-serif;}
H5      {color: blue;font-family:sans-serif;}
H6      {color: blue;font-family:sans-serif;}
P.ANN   {margin-left: 10em;margin-right:10em;
        font-family:monospace;}
P.LIT   {text-indent: 2em; font-family:serif;}
P.REV   {color: lightblue;background-color: navy;
        font-family:serif;}
```

which can then be used by all, or selected sets of, pages on a Web site.

style	tag_selector	Property_value
house	H1	{color: blue;font-family: sans-serif;}
house	H2	{color: blue;font-family: sans-serif;}
house	H3	{color: blue;font-family: sans-serif;}
house	H4	{color: blue;font-family: sans-serif;}
house	H5	{color: blue;font-family: sans-serif;}
house	H6	{color: blue;font-family: sans-serif;}
house	BODY	{color: navy; background-color: lightblue;}
house	P.LIT	{text-indent: 2em; font-family: serif;}
house	P.ANN	{margin-left: 10em;margin-right: 10em; font family:monospaced;}
house	P.REV	{color: lightblue; background-color: navy; font-family:serif;}

Figure 6.13 Example Relational Table of Style Information for a Web site

The above use of databases is becoming increasing important as the size and complexity of Web sites increase.

6.10 SUMMARY

This chapter has overviewed ways in which Web database systems are implemented. The two aspects covered are physical design of the database and the implementation of the connection between Web pages and the database.

Physical database design is the phase in the design process in which storage structures and access methods that will be used to implement the logical database design are specified. Aims are an acceptable compromise between performance, use of resources and resilience to failure. The design is based on quantities and volatility of the data to be stored, ways in which the data will be used, i.e. characteristics of the applications and transactions, and costs associated with the resources used. Typically, the design is iteratively refined on the basis of analysis of its performance. Logical structures are implemented as files. These are positioned to achieve a balanced use of resources, and partitioning to provide resilience to failure.

Heap files (or **serial files**) are the simplest structure. Using a heap file, new records are added to the end of the file and records are located by searching, one record at a time, from beginning to end. Advantages are fast insertion of new records and economic use of store. Disadvantages are slow retrieval speed, and the need to reorganise to re-claim space occupied by deleted records. Heap files are used for batched insertion of records, small files, and when all records are accessed. They are not suitable when records must be retrieved from large data sets.

Access keys are the fields on which retrieval is based. Tight access keys are those whose values correspond to only a few records in a file. The values of a loose access key corresponds to many records. Tight access keys are most useful, since these can be used to reduce the number of records that must be accessed when searching a file. Retrieval of records can be improved by storing them in a **sorted file**. By maintaining a file in access key sequence, a **binary search**, whereby the file is repeatedly halved, can then be used to locate a record with a specific access key value. A problem is that of maintaining the sequence when new records are inserted. Fast access on access keys can also be provided by organising a file as a **hash** (or **random**) **file**. The home address of a record is computed from an access key value using a **hashing function** both to determine where a new record is to be stored and also to locate that record at a later time. When the home address is full (or does not contained the required record) **overflow techniques** are use to store (or search for) the record elsewhere. Overflow techniques used include progressive overflow, the use of overflow areas, and re-hashing. The DBA must reorganise a hash file when search times increase because of excessive overflow. Hash files are used when access is always on the basis of a single access key, but are not appropriate when retrieval is based on pattern matching, value ranges, or part of a key value. **Indexes** can also be used to provide fast access on access keys. Indexes can provide access to sequences of records and can be used to implement multiple access keys. **Multilevel indexes** comprising a hierarchy of indexes, eventually leading to the data records, are used for large files. The **indexed sequential access method (ISAM)** provides an index to a sequential file, thus allowing both direct access on the basis of the access key value and also sequential processing. Alternatively, **B-trees** can be used. The advantages of these are that they are self-organising and maintain a balanced hierarchy of indexes so that all searches take approximately the same time.

Clustering can improve retrieval speed by storing records that are associated in some way physically close together. This can reduce the number of page accesses when processing related records.

Finally, **denormalising** can be used to improve performance. This modifies the logical design of a relational database so as to combine data that is always accessed together, thus deliberately violating the principles of normalisation.

The second part of this chapter concerns **Web database connectivity**. That is, mechanisms by which Web pages are connected to a database system. The processing that connects the database can be executed in the client **(client side)** or server **(server side)**. The processes may be implemented specially for an application, or alternatively **middleware** software can be used.

Two client side approaches are **browser extensions** and **external applications**. The former is implemented through the use of **scripting languages**, such as **JavaScript**, the use of **bytecode interpreters**, for example the **JVM** to interpret **Java applets**, and through access to operating system resources, such as **Dynamic Link Libraries (DLL)**. The External applications are useful to connect legacy systems to the Web.

Server side approaches include the use of **HTML pre-processors,** (including **ASP, JSP, PHP, Server side JavaScript, SSI,** and **ColdFusion.** and **server API applications**), and **CGI scripts.** The choice of client or server side processing is not straightforward, but generally client side has the advantages of distributing processing, providing fast feedback and increasing the functionality of Web pages. Disadvantages include dependency on the browser used, lack of security, the overhead of downloading the code from the server, and programming limitations imposed by the client. Advantages of server side processing include independence from the browsers used, greater security, no download time overhead, and fewer programming limitation. Disadvantages include the complexity of developing server side processes and the lack of direct control over user interfaces.

Server side processing can be implemented by embedding code in the HTML using scripting, or by embedding the HTML in the program, for example, using CGI. Server side scripting systems allow fragments of code to be inserted into HTML or its variants, which are then processed by the server. CGI is an interface which allows programs written in many programming languages to be executed as Web resources. **Perl** is one language widely used for CGI programming. There are also proprietary systems for generating CGI for specific DBMS, e.g. Ingres-ICE and O2-O2WEB. Significant problems with CGI are efficiency, and security and identity issues. An alternative to CGI is to extend the server functionality using an **API.** Examples are mod_Perl and "Fast CGI".

The **Java** object-oriented programming language can be used in a number of different ways to implement Web database processing. **Java applets** can be used for client side processing. On the server side processes can be implemented with Java Server Pages (JSP), as **Java Servlets,** or as Java CGI programs. Java can access relational database systems using various APIs, including **JDBC** and **SQLJ.** Object databases can be accessed using the **ODMG Java Binding.**

Issues that the developer must consider, are provision for **graceful degradation,** and avoidance of **feature bloat. Browser detection** can be used to determine facilities available for processing, but has limitations. In general, the designer's control over the user interface to a Web database system is limited. Therefore, the focus should be on the logical structure and features, rather than the exact appearance. Similar considerations hold for intranet interface design.

Transaction management is necessary to ensure the correct execution of transactions in the presence of failures and without interference from other transactions. Database transaction management typically enforces the **ACID** properties by using the **two phase locking protocols**, applying **read locks** to prohibit update of data being accessed, and **write locks** to prohibit data that is being updated from being read. **Deadlock** is avoided either pessimistically by requiring all data accessed to be locked at the start of the transactions, or pessimistically by sacrificing and restarting transaction(s) when deadlock occurs. Multidatabase transactions are managed globally using the **two-phase commit protocol**.

With Web database systems, transaction management at the Web level is currently *ad hoc*. Application specific control is built in the Web processes in the client and/or the server. An additional complexity that must also be managed at the Web level is that of supporting multi-connection sessions within the stateless HTTP protocol. This can be done using **hidden variables** in forms, **URL rewriting, cookies,** or **user authentication**.

A further issue when building Web database systems is maintaining the security, privacy and identity of the system. Security issues relate to Web and network aspects. Web security concerns the establishing of the identity of users, and restricting access to applications and data. Simple **HTTP authentication** is built into HTTP, which uses usernames and passwords. For a high level of security, **key encryption** provides a way of encoding data and data transfers. This can be implemented by the **secure socket layer (SSL)**. Traditional database notions of users may not apply for many Web databases systems where most users are unknown. One particular problem for which safeguards are required is that of **malicious code**.

In contrast to the previous discussion which is mostly concerned with the dynamic content of Web pages, the management of the Web pages themselves is also a problem for large and complex Web sites. A further use of database systems is therefore to store and manage Web pages, i.e. to organise the Web site itself.

EXERCISES

(6.1)   What is the purpose of physical database design?

(6.2)   What are the inputs and outputs of the physical database design process?

(6.3)   What properties will a good physical database design have?

(6.4)   Identify four factors which will influence the physical design of a table in a relational database.

(6.3)   Identify the stages of the physical database design process.

(6.4)   What is the difference between a logical and a physical data structure?

(6.5)   What is the relationship between an RDBMS and the operating system file manager?

(6.6)   How can a table be represented as a file?

(6.7)   Draw a diagram to show how the EmployeeTelephone table may be represented:

    i) as a heap file;

    ii) as a sorted file (sorted on EmpNo);

    iii) as a hash file (hashed on EmpNo);

    iv) as an ISAM file (indexed on EmpNo);

    v) as a B+-Tree file (indexed on EmpNo).

Assume pages may each store two records, or three index entries.

(6.8)   Under what circumstances would you choose i), ii), iii), iv) or v) in 6.7.

(6.9)   Use your sorted file diagram   (in 6.7 (ii)) to illustrate a binary search for employee E9's row. Contrast this with the equivalent search of the heap file (in 6.7 (i)).

(6.10)   Why is the physical positioning of files important in an implementation of a relational database?

(6.11)   How are new records inserted and deleted from a heap file? Illustrate our answer by inserting <E99, R20, 555> into the heap file in your answer to (6.7) (i), and deleting <E7,R35,123>.

(6.12)   What is an access key? Illustrate your answer by considering an application that retrieves employees from the Figure 6.14 table, who can be contacted by specified telephone numbers and/or room number.

EmployeeTelephone

EmpNo	Office	Extension
E1	R101	811
E1	R102	813
E2	R10	111
E3	R35	123
E5	R35	123
E6	R35	123
E7	R35	123
E8	R35	123
E9	R35	123
E10	R35	123

Figure 6.14

(6.13) The Figure 6.14 table can be accessed by employee number, room number or telephone number. Which of these is the tightest and which is the loosest access key?

(6.14) Give example applications for which it would be advantageous to represent the table in Figure 6.14 as a file sorted on telephone number. When would this representation be a disadvantage?

(6.15) Describe and illustrate the use of a binary search to locate a record in the Figure 6.14 table if its representation is sorted on employee number.

(6.16) How is a record stored and located in a hash file?

(6.17) What is meant by the term overflow record, within the context of a hash file? Describe three ways of handling overflow records.

(6.18) Why is it necessary for a DBA to monitor the performance of a hash file, and possibly to recreate it?

(6.19) What are the strengths and limitations of using a hash file? Give two examples of applications in which one would be used, and two examples of when one would not.

(6.20) What is an index, within the context of a representation of a relational table?

(6.21) Identify two advantages that using indexes have over using a hash file.

(6.22) Indexes are used in ISAM files and also B-trees. What is the difference between these two structures? What are their relative advantages and disadvantages?

(6.23) What is clustering, within the context of physical database design? An application retrieves details of all employees in a department by joining a Department and Employee table. Explain how clustering could improve the performance of this application.

(6.24) What is meant by the term denormalisation? When should this technique be used?

(6.25) Give two examples, within a Web database system for hotel bookings, when you would use a heap file. When, in this application, would you not use a heap file?

(6.26) Demonstrate the way in which an ISAM deteriorates with update by inserting the three rows in 6.10 into the ISAM file (in 6.7).

(6.12) What is meant by the term Web database connectivity?

(6.13) The Web architecture provides a number of options for implementing the processing of a Web database system. Identify three.

(6.14) What are the two general approaches to client side processing?

(6.15) What are the two general approaches to server side processing?

(6.16) What is meant by the term middleware, within the context of Web database systems? What are the advantages of using a middleware solution?

(6.17) Client side processing can be implemented using legacy systems. Give an example of when this approach would be appropriate.

(6.18) Describe the general operations that a server side process must execute.

(6.19) Outline and contrast three general approaches to server side processing in a Web database system.

(6.20) Consider the case of a Web database application for entering details of forthcoming conferences into a database. Discuss how the associated processing could be distributed between the client and server.

(6.21) Discuss the complexities of validating the postcode or zip code part of an address on the client of a Web database system.

(6.22)   Write a short report for the technical director of an e-commerce business, outlining the pros and cons of server side or client side processing for their online cosmetics selling application.

(6.23)   Explain three ways in which a browser can be extended to implement client side processing.

(6.24)   Describe and contrast side processing using server side scripting and CGI.

(6.25)   Describe how VBScript is used with ASP to retrieve records from a product table, as part of a cosmetics selling Web database application.

(6.26)   Two ASP built-in objects are Response and Active X Data objects. Explain their functions within server processing.

(6.27)   What are the limitations of ASP?

(6.28)   JSP provides an alternative to ASP for server processing. Contrast the two approaches.

(6.29)   What is PHP, and how does it differ from ASP and JSP?

(6.30)   Using PHP, what impact is it likely to make if the relational DBMS used is changed, for example, from Ingres to Oracle?

(6.31)   Are Java and JavaScript based on the same language? What are the origins of these two languages?

(6.32)   What are the advantages and disadvantages of using JavaScript?

(6.33)   What is SSI? Outline limitations of using SSI for server processing in a Web database system.

(6.34)   What is ColdFusion? What is CFML?

(6.35)   CFML includes the following tags, <CFQUERY>, <CFOUTPUT>, <CFINSERT> and <CFUPDATE>. Explain the use of each of these.

(6.36)   Identify three ways in which ColdFusion can connect to databases? What are the similarities in approach between ASP, JSP, PHP, SSI, JavaScript and ColdFusion? Which factors are likely to influence the choice to use one rather than the others?

(6.37)   What is CGI, and how does its approach differ to that of server side scripting, e.g. using ASP.

(6.38)   Many programming languages can be used to code a CGI program. Identify some of the languages that could be used, and discuss factors which would influence the choice.

(6.39)   Give three reasons why Perl has become dominant as a CGI programming language.

(6.40)   Part of the power of Perl stems from the availability of pre-existing modules. These include CGI.pm, DBD and DBI. Explain what each of these is and how they are used in Web database systems.

(6.41)   INGRES-ICE is an example of a proprietary system for creating applications for a specific DBMS. Describe the facilities for development of Web database applications supported by the DBMS that you currently use.

(6.42)   In what way does a system, such as INGRES-ICE, simplify the development of CGI programs for Web database systems?

(6.43)   Identify and outline ways in which an O2 database can connect to the Web.

(6.44)   What is "o2web-gateway" and how is it used to construct a Web database application?

(6.45)   Explain the efficiency problem associated with CGI programs.

(6.46)   What are "FastCGI" and "mod_perl"? What approaches do they take to solving the efficiency problem associated with CGI programs?

(6.47)   What is an API? How can an API be use to extend the functionality of a server?

(6.48)   What is ISAPI and how is it used?

(6.49)   Describe how IDC provides generic database connectivity services, using ".idc" and "htx" files.

(6.50)   Why is Java so important as a language for Web database applications?

(6.51)   Describe two ways in which Java can be used for client side processing.

(6.52)   Describe two ways in which Java can be used for server side processing.

(6.53)   What are the features of the Java programming language that give it advantages over other object-oriented programming languages for Web database programming?

(6.54)   What advantage does the JVM provide for Web database application programming?

(6.55)   What is JDBC? What is it used for?

(6.56)   What effect does the Java instruction, "input java.sql.*;" have?

(6.57)   What is a Java Applet? What is it used for?

(6.58)   How can a Java applet connect to a database?

(6.59) How can SQL be executed by a Java applet, and how are the results accessed?

(6.60) What is a Java Servlet and how does it differ from an Applet?

(6.61) How is a database connected to, and how is SQL executed and the results accessed by a Java Servlet?

(6.62) What is a Java CGI, and how does it differ from a Java Applet or Servlet?

(6.63) How is a database connected to, and how is SQL executed and the results accessed by a Java CGI program?

(6.64) What is metadata, and why is it advantageous that JDBC can access metadata? Give an example Web database application where this facility would be useful.

(6.65) Why is JDBC called a low level API. Give an example of a high level API for Java programs.

(6.66) Describe how Java code can be generalised, such that it can run as an Applet, Servlet or CGI program.

(6.67) What is SQLJ and what is it used for?

(6.68) Identify advantages that SQLJ has over JDBC.

(6.69) What is the ODMG Java binding? What is it used for, and what are the limitations of using it to implement a Web database system?

(6.70) The director of an e-commerce company requires advice on whether to adopt Java or JavaScript for implementation. One consideration is that the appearance of the Web pages is very important, as is the widest possible distribution to Web users. Write a short report weighing out the pros and cons.

(6.71) Contrast the facilities for connecting to a database supported by Java and JavaScript.

(6.72) Contrast the facilities for data validation supported by Java and JavaScript.

(6.73) What is graceful degradation, with respect to Web database systems, and why is it important? What strategies can be used to ensure that a system has this property?

(6.74) Browser detection is one technique for establishing how a Web database application will be handled by specific clients. Explain how this is done, and what the limitations of this technique are.

(6.75) What is meant by "feature bloat" in the context of Web database systems. Why is it a bad thing and how can it be avoided?

(6.76)   Identify nine factors which may influence the look of a Web database application.

(6.77)   Explain the different factors that influence the design of a Web database system interface for the Internet and for an intranet.

(6.78)   Users can be given control of the appearance of Web database systems using style sheets. Explain how this mechanism works.

(6.79)   Why are "cascading style sheets" so called?

(6.80)   What is a transaction?

(6.81)   What is the ACID test for correct execution of a transaction?

(6.82)   What effect does a COMMIT instruction have?

(6.83)   What effect does a ROLLBACK or ABORT instruction have?

(6.84)   Give an example of how an update may be lost when two updates occur simultaneously.

(6.85)   Give an example of how concurrent transactions can:
         a) cause inconsistent data to be retrieved;
         b) consistent but incorrect data to be retrieved.

(6.86)   Show how, using read and write locks, the problems that are illustrated in (6.85) could be avoided.

(6.87)   Why is "two-phase locking" so called, and how does it ensure serialisability?

(6.88)   What is "two-phase commit" and how does it operate in conjunction with "two-phase locking" to ensure correct execution of transactions involving multiple databases?

(6.89)   How are Web database transactions managed?

(6.90)   Locking strategies can cause deadlock. What is deadlock, and give an example of how it can occur.

(6.91)   How can deadlock be avoided?

(6.92)   How can a deadlock be resolved, without the database user knowing anything about it?

(6.93)   Why is session tracking sometimes necessary when using HTTP? Describe the following techniques for session tracking:
         (i)   Hidden variables
         (ii)   URL rewriting
         (iii)   Cookies
         (iii)   User authentication.

(6.94)   Identify three general Web security issues that must be addressed by the security system for a Web database system.

(6.95)   Client processing can be initiated for a Web database system by anonymous untrusted users. How then can the system safeguard the security of the system?

(6.96)   What security facilities are built into HTML? Why then are more sophisticated mechanisms often required?

(6.97)   What roles does encryption play in Web database systems? Give examples of where encryption for each role identified would be desirable.

(6.98)   What is PGP? What is it used for?

(6.99)   What is SSL? What is it used for?

(6.100) What are the security risks that a DBA must safeguard against. Identify the facilities typically supported by a DBMS which allow the DBA to take these safeguards.

(6.101) What is meant by the term "sandbox" with respect to client side security of a Web database system?

(6.102) What security risks do cookies pose to Web database systems, and how can these risks be minimised?

(6.103) Identify the ways in which ensuring security for a Web database system is more complex than for a conventional database system.

(6.104) How can JDBC enforce username and password security for a database?

(6.105) In which situations is username and password security inappropriate for a Web database system? Give an example and suggest an alternative approach to enforcing security.

(6.106) If a Web database system provides anonymous users with open access, how then can security be ensured?

(6.107) What is encryption, and what is it used for?

(6.108) What is meant by the term "malicious code"?

(6.109) A Web database application allows users to enter the name of a product. This text is then appended to the following SQL,

```
SELECT * FROM Products WHERE ProductName = "
```

Explain the risks of malicious code that the above application poses. Describe precautions that could be taken to avoid these.

(6.110) The director has heard that an e-commerce organisation has been alarmed by comments she has heard to the effect that the security of their Web site may be compromised if efficiency is increased by building APIs into the Web server. Write a short report explaining the basis for these comments, with recommendations on how best to safeguard security in this situation.

(6.111) An e-commerce organisation has evolved rapidly, and now finds the size and complexity of their Web site is proving hard to manage using conventional file-based techniques for storing the Web pages, etc. Write a short report for the directors of this company, outlining the advantage of using a database system to store and manage the Web site. In your report you should focus both on the content of the Web site and also its appearance.

————————EPILOGUE————————

Preceding chapters have studied two technologies, those of databases and the Web. The former is mature and well established, whereas Web technology is still in its infancy and rapidly developing. The main part of the book then examined the ways in which these technologies can be combined to create Web database systems. We have attempted to cover the main technologies currently in use. What does the future hold? Speculating is difficult given the current rapid state of progress. Information and Communications technology, and the Web in particular, is currently bringing about dramatic changes in all walks of life and given its volatile state and the still untapped potential, it is likely to cause further dramatic but unexpected changes. There are however two trends that seem to be significant at present for the immediate future. These are changes associated with SQL:1999 and XML.

The dominant type of database at present is the relational database. Previous models, i.e. hierarchical and network, are still in use in legacy systems, and object database systems have only so far found a small niche market. Deductive systems technology, in which database technology and artificial intelligence are combined to give a database capabilities to representing knowledge and to reasoning, is perhaps the sleeping giant of the coming century. However deductive databases remain largely limited to research.

Although, as we have said above, the basic technologies are well established, relational systems are undergoing a rapid evolution into object-relational systems and the direction and nature of this change can be seen in the SQL:1999 standard. The standard includes a number of features, such as the multimedia ones in SQL/MM, which are significant for use in Web applications. Also, to be included are facilities for data warehousing and mining, which will become increasingly important as the potential of the Web for interconnecting data sources is exploited. The extent to which database system vendors adopt all or parts of SQL:1999 remains an open question.

XML began in the Web community and provided a framework in which HTML could be formalised and stabilised and within which other languages such as MathML and related initiatives such as the metadata work on RDF could be built. It is hard to measure the influence of XML on the Web at present but it is also clear that its influence is spreading beyond the Web itself. XML is a generalised markup language, and like its parent SGML, can be applied to data of any sort. This is clearly starting to happen in a number of areas. For example, the use of XML by products such as Microsoft Word is one indicator of this. As XML becomes widely adopted, one area in which it will be used is that of databases. The newest products from database vendors, such as Oracle 8i, are now including features for handling XML. Whether XML, and its derivatives such as xhtml, become a dominant format for storing data or simply for transferring it remains another open question.

We therefore conclude this book with a question mark. We look forward to seeing what future development will emerge, and whether the unexpected will happen again, as it did with the extraordinarily rapid penetration and impact of Web technology that has taken place over the last decade!

BIBLIOGRAPHY

INTRODUCTION

Since this is a rapidly changing area many resources are available on the Web as well as in print. In many cases the Web resources may be more up-to-date. References to Web resources are given thus: [Name] with no date since the contents of many sites change on a day to day basis. For this reason we have also generally given references to the top level of a site rather than particular pages since these often change. Print resources are referenced thus: [Name Date].

DATABASE STANDARDS

In recent years while the new SQL standards have been under discussion drafts of parts of SQL3/SQL:1999 were freely available on the Web. As the parts of the standard have appeared officially those drafts are no longer available. SQL:1999 is available on the Web for purchase from [ANSI] or [NCITS]. Up-to-date information on the state of SQL can be found in the [Sigmod Record] online. Information and drafts of ODMG standard material can be found at [ODMG] and the newest version of the standard is available only in printed form [Cattell 00]. Most DBMS come with large amounts of documentation, either printed or online and users should check this for details of particular implementations of the standards including extensions and other non-standard features.

WEB STANDARDS

The starting point for Web standards is the World Wide Web Consortium's site [W3C]. In addition to the specifications for HTML, CSS, DOM, etc. the site contains a large number of drafts, etc. Since many Web standards are *de facto* and other bodies may work to different standards it may well be worth checking the sites for [Netscape] and [Internet Explorer]. The Internet Engineering Task Force [IETF] site was the original source for RFCs but these may be found more easily at [RFC Editor]. The specification of JavaScript can be found at [ECMAScript].

WEB RESOURCES

[ANSI] http://webstore.ansi.org

[Any Browser] http://www.anybrowser.org/campaign/

[ASP] http://msdn.microsoft.com/workshop/server/default.asp

[Bobby] http://www.cast.org/bobby/

[Browserwatch] http://www.browserwatch.com/

[Chilisoft] http://www.chilisoft.com/

[ColdFusion] http://www.allaire.com

[CGI spec] http://hoohoo.ncsa.uiuc.edu/cgi/interface.html

[CGI.pm] http://stein.cshl.org/WWW/software/CGI/cgi_docs.html

[Cookie Central] http://www.cookiecentral.com

[Cookies] http://home.netscape.com/newsref/std/cookie_spec.html

[CSS Pointers Group] http://css.nu/

[DBI] http://www.symbolstone.org/technology/perl/DBI/index.html

[ECMAScript] http://www.ecma.ch/stand/ecma-262.htm

[IETF] http://www.ietf.org

[Internet Explorer] http://www.microsoft.com/windows/ie/

[Java] http://java.sun.com/

[Java Servlets] http://java.sun.com/products/servlet/

[JDBC] http://java.sun.com/products/jdbc

[JSP] http://java.sun.com/products/jsp/

[JavaScript] http://developer.netscape.com/docs/manuals/javascript.html

[JScript] http://msdn.microsoft.com/scripting/

[Mozilla] http://www.mozilla.org

[NCITS] http://www.cssinfo.com/ncits.html

[Netscape] http://home.netscape.com/

[ODMG] http://www.odmg.org

[OMG] http://www.omg.org

[Perl] http://www.perl.com

[PHP] http://www.php.net

[Rational] http://www.rational.com

[RFC Editor] http://www.rfc-editor.org/

[Search Engine Watch] http://www.searchenginewatch.com/

[Sigmod Record] http://www.acm.org/sigmod/record/

[SQLJ] http://www.sqlj.org

[W3C] http://www.w3.org

[WDG] http://www.htmlhelp.com

[Xanadu] http://www.xanadu.com

[XML Cover Pages] http://www.oasis-open.org/cover/sgml-xml.html

PRINT RESOURCES

[Atkinson 90] Atkinson, M. et al., The Object-Oriented Database System Manifesto, in Kim, W., Nicolas, J-M. and Nishio, S. eds., Deductive and Object-Oriented Databases, pp 223–239, Elsevier, 1990

[Atkinson 96] Atkinson, M.P., Jordan, M.J., Daynes, L. and Spence, S. Design Issues for Persistent Java: a type-safe, object-oriented, orthogonally persistent system, Proceedings of the 7th International Workshop on Persistent Object Systems (POS7), 1996

[Atzeni 99] Atzeni, P. and Ceri, S., Database Systems: Concepts, Languages, Architectures, McGraw-Hill, New York, 1999

[Batini 91] Conceptual Database Design: An Entity-Relationship Approach, Batini, C., Ceri, S., Navathe, S., Addison-Wesley, Reading 1991

[Berners-Lee 94] Berners-Lee,T. et al., The World-Wide Web, Communications of the ACM, 37(8), pp 77–82, 1994

[Berners-Lee 99] Berners-Lee, T., Weaving the Web, Orion Business Books, London, 1999

[Booch 94] Booch, G., Object-Oriented Analysis and Design with Applications, Second edition, Benjamin/Cummings, Redwood City, 1994

[Booch 99] Booch, G., Rumbaugh, J. and Jacobson, I., The Unified Modeling Language User Guide, Addison-Wesley, Reading, 1999

[Bush 45] Bush, V., As We May Think, The Atlantic Monthly, 1945

[Cattell 97] Cattel, R.G.C. and Barry, D.K. eds., The Object Database Standard: ODMG 2.0, Morgan Kaufman, San Francisco, 1997

[Cattell 00] Cattel, R.G.C. et al. eds., The Object Database Standard: ODMG 3.0, Morgan Kaufman, San Francisco, 2000

[Chen 76] Chen, P., The Entity-Relationship Model—Towards a Unified View of Data, ACM Transactions on Database Systems, 1(1), 1976

[Codd 70] Codd, E.F., A Relational Model for Large Shared Data Banks, Communications of the ACM, 13(6), pp 377–387, 1970

[Codd 74] Codd, E.F., Recent Investigations into Relational Data Base Systems, Procs IFIP Congress, 1974

[Comer 00] Comer, D., Internetworking with TCP/IP Vol. 1, Prentice Hall, 2000

[Eaglestone 91] Eaglestone, B., Relational Databases, Stanley Thornes, Leckhampton, 1991

[Eaglestone 98] Eaglestone, B. and Ridley, M., Object Databases: An Introduction, McGraw-Hill, Maidenhead, 1998

[Fagin 77] Fagin, R. Multivalued Dependencies and a New Normal Form for Relational Databases, ACM TODS 2:3, September 1977.

[Fagin 79] Fagin, R. Normal Forms and Relational Database Operators, Proc 1979 ACM SIGMOD International Conference on Management of Data, Boston, Mass (May/June 1997).

[Flanagan 98] Flanagan, D., JavaScript: The Definitive Guide 3rd ed., O'Reilly, Sebastopol, 1998

[Goldfarb 91] Goldfarb, C.F., The SGML Handbook, OUP, London, 1991

[Gundavaram 96] Gundavaram, S., CGI Programming on the World Wide Web, O'Reilly, Sebastopol, 1996

[Hamilton 97] Hamilton, G., Cattell, R. and Fisher, M., JDBC Database Access with Java, Addison-Wesley, Reading, 1997

[Hilton 00] Hilton, C. and Willis, J., Building Database Applications on the Web Using PHP3, Addison-Wesley, Reading, 2000

[Hunter 98] Hunter, J., with Crawford, W., Java Servlet Programming, O'Reilly, Sebastopol, 1998

[Jacobson 92] Jacobson, I.M., Object-Oriented Software Engineering, Addison-Wesley, Reading, 1992

[Jacobson 99] Jacobson, I., Booch, G. and Rumbaugh, J., The Unified Software Development Process, Addison-Wesley, Reading, 1999

[Kent 83] Kent, W., A Simple Guide to Five Normal Forms in Relational Database Theory, Communications of the ACM 26(2), Feb. 1983, pp.120-125.

[Labrinidis 00] Labrinidis, A. and Roussopoulos, N., Generating Dynamic Content at Database-Backed Web Servers: cgi-bin vs. mod_perl, ACM Sigmod Record 29(1), pp. 26-31, March 2000

[Leung 93] Leung, T.W., Mitchell, B., Subramanian, B., Vance, S.L., Vandenberg, S.L. and Zdonik, S.B., The AQUA Data Model and Algebra, Proceedings DBPL (1993), pp. 157-175, 1993

[Musciano 97] Musciano, C. and Kennedy, B., HTML: The Definitive Guide 2nd ed., O'Reilly, Sebastopol, 1997

[Nelson 91] Nelson, M.L., An Object-Oriented Tower of Babel, OOPS Messenger, 2(3), July 1991

[Nelson 95] Nelson, T. H., The Heart of a Connection: Hypermedia Unified by Transclusion, Communications of the ACM, 38(8), pp 31-33, 1995

[Nielsen 00] Nielsen, J., Designing Web Usability, New Riders, 2000

[OMG 91] Object Management Group, The Common Object Request Broker: Architecture and Specification, Revision 1.1, OMG Document No 91.12.1

[OMG 97] Object Management Group, Corbaservices: Common Object Service Specification, Nov. 1997

[Paton 99] Paton, N.W. and Diaz, O., Active Database Systems, ACM Computing Surveys, 31(1), pp 63–105, 1999

[Rumbaugh 91] Rumbaugh, J., Premerlani, W., Eddy, F. and Lorenson, W., Object-Oriented Modeling and Design, Prentice–Hall, Englewood Cliffs, 1991

[Rumbaugh 99] Rumbaugh, J., Jacobson, I. and Booch, G., The Unified Modeling Language Reference Manual, Addison-Wesley, Reading, 1999

[Sheth 90] Sheth, A.P., and Larson, J.A., Federated Database Systems for Managing Distributed, Heterogeneous, and Autonomous Databases, ACM Computing Surveys, 22(3), pp 183–236, 1990

[Yang 98] Yang, J., and Kaiser, G.E., JpernLite: An Extensible Transaction Server for the World Wide Web, IEEE Transactions on Knowledge and Data Engineering, 1998

INDEX

>, in OQL, 151, 152
    in SQL, 72, 87
>=, in OQL, 151,152
    in SQL, 72, 87
<, in OQL, 151, 152
    in SQL, 72, 87
<=, in OQL, 151, 152
    in SQL, 72, 87
=, in OQL, 151, 152
    in SQL, 72, 87
||, in OQL, 156
!=, in OQL, 151
    in SQL, 72, 87
*, in OQL, 149
    in SQL, 69, 77-78
**, in SQL, 77-78
_, in SQL, 74-76
%, in SQL, 74-76
[...],in OQL, 156
    in SQL, 74-76
_, in SQL, 74-76
+, in OQL, 153, 156
    in SQL, 77-78
-, in SQL, 77-78
/, in SQL, 77-78
->. in OQL, 150

<!--, in HTML, 230
<!--#exec...>, in SSI, 365-366
<!--#include ...>, in SSI, 366
<%...>, 361
<?....>, 361
<A...>, in HTML, 219-220, 223
<ADDRESS>, in HTML, 229
<BASE>, in HTML, 221
<BODY>, in HTML, 214-215, 218
<BOLD> or <B>, in HTML, 228-229

, in HTML, 230
<CITE>, in HTML, 229
<CODE>, in HTML, 229
<DIV ...>, in HTML, 230
<FORM>, in HTML, 226-227
<H1>, <H2>, ..., in HTML, 217-218, 229
<HEAD>, in HTML, 214-215, 217-219,
    237

<HR>, in HTML, 230
<IMG>, in HTML, 226
<INPUT>, in HTML, 227
<LINK...>, in HTML, 223, 233
<LI>, in HTML, 223-224
<OL>, in HTML, 223
<P>, in HTML, 218
<SCRIPT>, in HTML, 242
<SERVLET>, in SSI, 368-369
<STRONG>, in HTML, 228-229
<TABLE ...>, in HTML, 225
<TD>, in HTML, 225
<TH>, in HTML, 225
<TR>, in HTML, 225
<UL>, in HTML, 223

1NF (see First Normal Form)
2NF (see Second Normal Form)
2PC (see Two-phase commit)
2PL (see Two-phase locking)
3NF (see Third Normal Form)
4GL, 48, 399
5NF (see Fifth Normal Form)

Abandoned transactions, 405-406
Abort, a transaction, 406
absolute links, in HTML, 220-221
Abstract type in ODL, 133
Abstract Windows Toolkit (see AWT)
access.conf (see Apache, NCSA
    server)
Access keys, of a database file, 334-
    335
ACID test, for transactions, 405
ActiveX object,
    in ASP, 362
    controls, 351
    security, 421
Activities,
    of an organisation, 7
    Information activities, 7, 21
Actor function, in SQL:1999, 174
Adding content, to HTML, 217-226
Addition of lists (or arrays), in OQL, 153
Add-on, client side, 349, 351

Address, of Web document, 26
ADO (see ActiveX object)
ADT (see Abstract data type, in SQL)
Advanced features, of HTML, 229-231
Aggregating functions, in SQL (see
    Summarising functions, in SQL)
Aliases (see Alternative names, on
    Internet name server)
Aliasing (see virtual directory)
ALL, in OQL, 151
    in SQL, 86
Alternate key (See Key, in the relational
    data model)
Alternative names, on Internet name
    servers, 197
ALTER TABLE, in SQL, 57-58
Anchor tag, in HTML, 219-220
AND, in SQL, 70-72
ANY, in OQL, 151
    in SQL, 87
ANSI (see Standards)
Apache, NCSA server, 209-210, 365,
    381
Appearance, of Web pages, 397-398
API, 349, 351
    Server extensions, 382-384, 427
Applet, client side, 241349, 351, 384,
    386-388, 397, 398, 421
Application layer, of protocol stack, 194
Application Program Interface, (see
    API)
Applications, 11
AQUA, object algebra, 140
Architecture, of database system (see
    Database, architecture)
Architecture, of the Web (see Web,
    architecture)
Arithmetic, in SQL (see Computations,
    in SQL)
ARPANET, 208
array, 137-138
    in OQL (see also Type Generator)
    137-138, 158
Array-object type, (see array)
AS, in SQL, 83-84, 99-100
ASP, 349, 352, 360, 362-363
Assertions, in SQL, 97
Assignment, in SQL:1999, 175
Association, between entities, 119, 267

Authorisations, in database systems,
    422
ATM, 195
Atomicity, of transactions, 405
Attribute,
    in data analysis, 267, 282-283
    in ER modelling, 271
    in the object data model, 119
    in relational data model, 49
    in ODL, 135-136, 139
    in UML, 126
Atomic literal types, 139
Atomic object, 139
AVG, in SQL, 78
AWT, 398

bag, 137-138
    in ODL (see also Type generator),
    137-138
    in OQL, 145, 158
Base URL, in HTML, 221
BCNF (see Boyce Codd Normal Form)
Behaviour, of an object, 118, 122, 133,
    136
Behavioural semantics, 113
Berners-Lee, Tim, 206
BETWEEN, in SQL, 73
Bidirectional iterator object (see also
    Collection–object type),
Binary large objects (see BLOB)
Binary search, of sorted files, 336-337
Binding, ODL/OML, 115, 140
Binding, of object languages and
    SQL:1999, 163
BLOB, in SQL:1999, 164-165
Block structure, in ODL, 132
Boilerplate, 429
Booch, design method, 117
Boolean conditions, in SQL (see
    WHERE, in SQL)
Boolean, literal type, in ODL, 139
Bottom up database analysis, 272-279
Boyce Codd Normal Form, 300-301
Browser, 30, 198-200, 349, 214, 397
    Cache, 235-236
    Extensions, 349, 351
Browser detection, 401
Browser sniffing, 401
BSI (see Standards)

B-tree, in Physical design, 342-345
    Comparison with ISAM, 344-345
Built–in properties and operations, in
    OQL, 127
Built–in object types, 139
Bush, Vannevar, 207

C++ (see Object–oriented programming
    languages)
C++ ODL/OML (see ODL/OML binding),
CALL, in SQL:1999, 175
Candidate key (see Key, in the
    relational data model)
Cardinality, of a relationship, 268-270,
    274-275
Cartesian product, in relational algebra,
    61, 66
CASCADE, in SQL, 95-97
Cascading style sheets, in HTML (see
    Style sheet, in HTML)
Caching (see Web Caching)
CAST, in SQL:1999, 173
CERN, 206
CFML, 369-370
CGI, 30, 238-240, 242, 349, 351,360,
    371-384, 391-394
    Efficiency of CGI, 381
    Problem with CGI, 381-382
CGI.pm module, in Perl, 373
CGI script, 352, 360
Chained progressive overflow, in Hash
    files, 338
Chamberlin, D, 47
Changing schema contents, in a
    relational database, 57-58
Changing logical database design, in
    Physical design, 346
CHAR, in SQL, 56
Char, literal type, in ODL, 139
Character large objects (see CLOB)
Changing values, in SQL, 90-93
CHECK, in SQL, 97
Class (see also Implementation class),
    in UML, 125
Class definition, in ODL, 132, 134
Class indicator, in OQL, 157-158
Client, on the Web, (see Web, client)
Client security, 421-422
Client-server architecture, 34, 193

Client side, processing, 240, 349, 350-
    351, 358-359, 397-400
    Or server side, 352
CLOB, in SQL:1999, 164-165
Clustering, in Physical design, 345-346
Codd,E.F., 47, 109
Codd's twelve rules, of relational
    databases, 109-110
Coercion, in SQL:1999, 176
ColdFusion, 360, 369-370
Coldfusion Markup Language (see
    CFML)
Collection object types,
    in ODL, 137-138
    in OQL, 145, 151, 156-158
Collection–oriented queries, 144
Collisions, (see Hash file, in Physical
    design)
Column, in the relational data model, 49
COM (see Component Object Model)
Combining data models, in data
    analysis, 278-279, 283-284
Comments, in HTML, 230
Commit, a transaction, 406
Common Gateway Interface (see CGI)
Common Request Broker Architecture
    (see CORBA)
Communications protocols, 22-24
Comparison operators, in SQL, 72-76
    in SQL:1999, 173
Completeness rules, for Web data
    extraction, 291-293
Complex behaviour, 110-111
Complex object, 127, 139, 145
    in OQL, 150
Complex structures, 110-111, 127
    Of Web pages, 312
Component Object Model, 363
Compound statement, in SQL:1999,
    174-175
Computations, in OQL, 155
    in SQL, 77-78
Computer network (see Network, of
    computers)
Computer Supported Cooperative Work
    (see CSCW)
Concept box, in Web data analysis,
    286, 314
Conceptual model, 262, 266

Conceptual Web data model, 263-264,
  284-295, 314
Conditions, in SQL (see WHERE, in
  SQL)
Connection, to the Internet, 24
Connection, to databases, 398-399
Connectivity, between Web pages, 262
Consistency, of transactions, 405
Constant declaration,
  in ODL, 132
  representation of (see Literals)
const, in ODL, 132
Constraints (see Integrity constraints)
Constructor operations,
  in OQL, 159,
  in SQL:1999, 173, 175
Conversion, of object type, in OQL, 160
  in SQL:1999, 173
Cookies, 2, 400, 413, 417, 422
CORBA, 117
Corporate database, 5
Correlation names, in SQL, 82-84
COUNT, in SQL, 78
Costs, of the database approach, 17
CREATE ASSERTION, in SQL, 97
CREATE DOMAIN, in SQL2, 57
CREATE TABLE, in SQL, 55-56, 92,
  94-97
  in SQL:1999, 170
CREATE TRIGGER, in SQL:1999, 165
CREATE OBJECT TYPE, in SQL:1999,
  171-172
CREATE TYPE, in SQL:1999, 167-170
CREATE TYPE TEMPLATE,
  in SQL:1999, 177
CREATE VIEW, in SQL, 99-100
Creating an HTML document, 213-214
Creating a relational database, 55-56
CSCW, 32
Cut operations, in relational algebra, 59-
  60

Data, 9
Data aggregation (see Bottom-up data
  analysis)
Data analysis, 266-284,
  Methods, 271-284
Data design, 295-310
Data dictionary, 55
Data files, 10

Data independence, 14-16
Data manipulation language (see DML)
Data model, 17, 45-47
  evolution, 114
  roles, 46
Database,
  architecture, 14-15, 54-55
  basics, 3-4
  definition, 4
  embedded, 6, 13
Database administrator, 13-14, 16-17,
  338-339, 342, 412, 422
Database approach, 2, 10-14, 51
  objective, 12
  vs. file–oriented approach, 10-12
Database driver module (See DBD
  modules, in Perl)
Database enhancement of Web
  systems (see also Web
  databases), 35-36
Database management system, 3-4, 10,
  14-19
Database schema, 129
Database technology, 3-19
Data communications, 20
Data analysis, 262
Data association, in Web page design,
  262
Data design, 262
Database interface module (see DBI
  modules, in Perl)
Data items,
  Identifying in data analysis, 273
Data model, 45-47, 261
Data redundancy, and Normalisation,
  300
Data representation, in Web page
  design, 262
Data source administrator, 362
Data structure (see also Logical data
  structure, Physical data structure),
  11,14
Data types,
  in data analysis, 266-268
  in SQL, 56-57
Data validation, 399-400
Date,
  literal type, 139
DB2, 47
DBA (see Database administrator)

DBD modules in Perl, 373
DBI modules, in Perl, 373-375
DBMS, (see Database management system)
DBTG (see CODASYL Database Task Group)
DCOM (see Distributed Component Object Model)
Deadlock, 410-412
DECIMAL, in SQL, 56
Deep equality (see Equality of objects)
default.html (see Home page)
Default style, in O2-O2WEB, 380
Default values, in SQL, 56, 57
DEFAULT, in SQL, 57, 96
    in SQL:1999, 173
define...as..., in OQL, 162-163
Definition, of domains in SQL, 56-57
deftype, in ODL, 132, 138-139
DELETE, in SQL, 90, 93
    in SQL:1999, 173
Delete operation (see built–in object types)
Denormalisation, in Physical design, 346
Dereferencing, in OQL, 149
Design methods, for databases, 259-327
DESTRUCTOR function, in SQL:1999, 173-175
DESTROY, in SQL:1999, 175
Dictionary, in ODL (see also Type generator), 137-138
Difference, in relational algebra, 64-65, 88-90
Digital certificates, for Web security, 420
Directional relationships, in Web data analysis, 287-288
Disc cache (see Browser cache)
DISTINCT, in OQL, 160
    in SQL, 68
Distinct UDT, in SQL:1999, 167-168
Distributed Component Object Model, 363
Distributed database system, 6, 34, 109
Distributed object-oriented environment, 117
Distributed Transaction Processing (see DTP)

DLL, 382
DML, of SQL, 48, 65-93
    Basic statement structure, 65-66
DNS, 196
Document Object Model (see DOM)
Document request, in HTTP, 204
Document type definition (see DTD, in HTML)
DOM, 234-235, 242
Domain, in the relational data model, 52
    Definition in SQL, 56-57
Domain Name System (see DNS)
DOUBLE PRECISION, in SQL, 56
DROP TABLE, in SQL, 57
DTD, in HTML, 216-217, 231, 429
DTP, 350
Duplicate elimination in OQL, 160
Durability, of transactions, 405
Dynamic hashing, in Hash files, 338
Dynamic Link libraries (see DLL)
Dynamic Web pages, 237-244, 312

ECMAScript (see also JavaScript), 242
E-commerce, 32
Efficiency, vs. security of Web systems, 427-428
Electronic commerce (see E-commerce)
Electronic mail, (see Email)
element, in HTML, 218
    in OQL, 160
Email, 24, 193, 208, 222
Embedded database system, 6,13
Embedded database languages, 48, 144
Embedded Web systems, 33
Encapsulation, 122-123
    in SQL:1999, 172-173
Encryption, 420
Entity, 10, 18
    With complex structure, 18
    in bottom-up data analysis, 272, 275-278
    in data analysis, 267
    in data design, 296-297
    in top-down data analysis, 279-281
    Relational representation, 51
Entity integrity, in the relational data model, 93-94

Entity relationship analysis / modelling, 268-271
Entity relationship model, 266, 268-271
Extensions for Web database design, 285-288
Entry SQL (see also SQL), 49
Entity types, 268
Enumeration, literal type (see also Type generator), 139
Environment variable, in CGI program, 239
Equality, of objects, 121
EQUAL, in SQL:1999, 173
Equi-join, in relational algebra (see Theta-join, in relational algebra)
Error code, in HTTP, 205
ESCAPE, in SQL, 76
Ethernet, 195
Evaluation, of Boolean expressions, in SQL, 70-72
Evolution, of database system, 16
EXCEPT, in SQL, 89
Exception, in SQL:1999, 175
in ODL, 132, 136
Exercises, 38-42, 101-105, 180-186, 235-240, 320-327, 425-443
Existential quantifier, in OQL, 151
EXISTS, in OQL 151
in SQL, 88
Extender type (see EXTENDS, inheritance relationship), 135
Extensible Markup Language (see XML)
Extensible Transaction Services for WWW, 350
Extension, 14
Extent, of an object type, 125
in ODL, 134
External application, server side, 349, 351
External function definition, in SQL:1999, 175
External level (see External model)
External model, 14-15, 54
Extranet, 24

FastCGI, 381, 382
Feature bloat, 401-402
Fifth Normal Form, 301
File–oriented systems, 10-12
File transfer protocol (see FTP)

First generation, of databases, 112, 113
first, in OQL, 153
First normal form, of the relational data model, 52, 300, 302
flatten, in OQL, 160
Float, literal type, 139
FLOAT, in SQL, 56
for all, in OQL, 151
Formal Information flow (see also Information flow), 8, 22
Forms, in HTML, 226-227, 376
Fourth Generation Language (see 4GL)
Fourth Normal Form, 301
Fragment, of a hypertext document, 203, 221
FROM, in OQL, 154
in SQL, 81-84
FTP protocol, 193, 194, 208, 222
Full outer join, in relational algebra, 63, 83
Full SQL (See also SQL), 49
Function, in SQL:1999, 173
Functional dependency, 302-304
Fuzzy string matching, in SQL (see String matching, in SQL)

Gateways, 30, 195
Generalisation / specialisation, in ER modelling, 271
in SQL:1999, 166, 176
Generalisation–specialisation relationships, (see Subtype/supertype relationship)
GET, Web document method, 204-206, 238-239, 377, 416
Global schema, in distributed database,
Gopher server, 193, 194, 222
Graceful degradation, 400-401
Graphical notation, for Web Page Schemas, 313
Group activities, on the Web, 32
GROUP BY, in OQL, 146
in SQL, 79
in SQL:1999, 165

Hashing (see Hash file, in Physical design)

Hash key (see Hash file, in Physical design)
Hash file, in Physical design, 336-339
Header information, in HTTP, 204-205, 237, 375
Headings, in HTML, 217-219
Heap file, 332-337
Hidden variables, in HTML, 376, 413, 415-416
History, of data models,
    Of the Web, 206-208
Home address (see Hash file, in Physical design)
Home directory (see Root directory)
Home page, 211
Host, in the Internet, 193
HTML, 2, 26-29, 211, 212-213, 349, 360
    Common errors, 215-216
    Element, 218
    Extension file, 382
    Form, 226-227, 351
    html_footer, 379
    html_header, 379
    html_report, 380
    Heading, 217-219
    Images, 226, 400
    Links, 219-233
    Lists, 223-224
    Meta tags, 237
    Paragraph, 217-219
    Preprocessor, 351
    Programmatic interface, 235
    Tables, 225-226
    tags, 29, 214
    tutorial, 213-232
    unknown tags, 217
    validity, 216-217, 231-232
HREF, in HTML, 220
HTTP, World Wide Web protocol, 29-30, 204-206, 350, 413
    Authentication, 420
    Security, 420
httpd, 209
httpd.conf (see Apache, NCSA server)
http daemon (see httpd)
hyperlinks, 212-213,
    in Web data analysis, 285
Hypermedia, 25-26, 207
Hypermedia document, 29-30

Hyper-Text Mark-up Language (see HTML)
Hypertext systems, 207
Hypertext Theory, 207
Hyper-Text Transfer Protocol, (see HTTP)

ICE, 370, 376-379
IDC, 382
IDE, 396
IDENTITY, in SQL:1999, 177
Identity, of an object,118, 120-121, 124, 127-128
    in SQL:1999, 166, 170-171
IDL (see also Object Management Group), 117, 235
ii_procedure, in ICE, 376
ii_query_statement, in ICE, 376
ii_success_message, in ICE, 376
ii_report, in ICE, 376
ii_success_variable, in ICE, 376
Images, as data (see Multimedia)
    in HTML, 226-227
Implementation class, 125
Implementation, of an object type, 137
Implicit closing tags, in HTML, 219
Immutable object (see Literal)
IN,
    in OQL, 151
    in SQL, 73, 85-88
Inclusion,
    in OQL, 152
    in SQL:1999, 176
Incomplete transactions, 405-406
Independence, of transactions, 405
Index, in Physical design, 339-341
Indexed Sequential Access Method, 341
    Comparison with B-tree, 344-345
InetPup (see Root directory)
INGRES-ICE, 360, 376-379
INGRES/STAR, distributed database,
Informix, 364
Informal information flow (see also Information Flow), 8, 22
Information, 9
    Stored on the Web, 208-213
Information activities (see Activities)
Information flow, within an information system, 7-9, 22
Information system, 7-9, 21

Inheritance (see also Subtype/supertype relationships), 128
  in ODL, 134-135
Inner join, in relational algebra, 83
inout, in ODL, 136
INSERT, in SQL, 90-92
  in SQL:1999, 173
Instance, of an object type, 125
Instance operations (see Operations, of an object)
Instance properties (see Properties, of an object)
Integer, literal type, 139
Integrated Development Environment (see IDE)
Integrity constraints, 16, 93-97, 109, 111
Integrity features, in SQL, 94-97
Integrity part, of a data model, 46
Integrity part, of the relational data model, 93-94
Intension, 14
Interface definition language, (see IDL)
Interface definition, in ODL, 132, 133, 134
Interface design, in Web page design, 262
Interface, of an object, 122
Interference, between transactions, 406-409
Intermediate SQL (See also SQL), 49
Internal level (see Internal model)
Internal model, 14-15, 54
Internet, 20-31, 192-197
  Client, 193
  Server, 193
Internet Commerce Enabled (see ICE)
Internet Database Connector (see IDC)
Internet Explorer, 351, 198, 200
Internet layer of protocol stack, 194
Internet protocol, (see IP)
Internet Server Application Program Interface (see ISAPI)
Internet Service Provider (see ISP)
INTERSECT, in SQL, 89
Intersection, in relational algebra, 64, 88-90
INTERVAL, in SQL, 56
Interval literal type, 139
Intranet, 24

Inverse relationships, 120
Investment,
  in collecting data, 12, 16
  in developing applications, 12, 16
IP, 192
  address, 23, 195-197
  packet, 194
  Protocol, 194
    Symbolic address, 196
IS NULL, in SQL, 76-77
is_a relationships (see Subtype/supertype relationship)
ISAM (see Indexed Sequential Access Method)
ISAPI, 382
ISO (see Standards)
ISP, 198

Jacobson, design method, 117
Java (see also Object–oriented programming languages), 2, 240-242, 351, 352, 359, 363, 384-397, 397-400
Java applets (see Applets)
Java CGI, 391-394
Java binding (see also ODL/OML binding), 379, 396-397
Java database connectivity (see JDBC)
JavaScript, 242-244, 351, 360, 362, 365, 397-400, 421
Java Server Pages (see JSP)
Java Virtual Machine, 240-242, 384
JDBC, 352, 363, 379, 385, 396
  Alternative to JDBC, 394-395
JOIN, in SQL2, 83-84
Join, in relational algebra, 61-63, 80-84
JSP, 352, 360, 363
JVM (see Java Virtual Machine)

Keys, in ER modelling, 271, 283
Key, of a relational table, 52-53, 302-303
Key, of an object, 119, 122
  in ODL, 134
Knowledge, representation, 111

Large objects, in SQL:1999, 164-165
last, in OQL, 153
Late binding,
  in OQL, 157-158

in SQL:1999, 176, 198
LEAVE, in SQL:1999, 175
LEFT JOIN, in SQL2, 83-84
Left outer join, in relational algebra, 63, 83
Legacy systems, 351, 378
LESS THAN, in SQL:1999, 173
LIKE, in SQL, 73-76
Limitations, of relational database technology, 19, 108-112
Linking, C++ ODL/OML,
Links, in HTML, 219-223
to email, 222
Links, between Web pages, 312
Lists, 137-138
in HTML, 223-224
in ODL (see also Type generator) 137-138
in OQL, 158, 160
LIST_OF, in Web Page Schemas, 313
listtoset, in OQL, 160
Lite, 370
Literals, 124
atomic, 139
structured, 139
in ODL, 139
Locators, in SQL:1999, 165
Locking protocol, 409-412
Logic (see Mathematical logic)
Logical data structures, 14
Logical database design, 261-262
Logical level (see Logical model)
Logical mapping, between Web pages, 262, 288
Logical model, 14-15, 54, 262
Logical Web data analysis, 265
Logical Web data model, 263
Logical Web page schema, 311-318
LOOP, in SQL:1999, 175
Loose access key (see Access key, of database file)
Lynx, 200, 400

Mail server (see email)
Malicious code, 425-427
mailto, 222
Manifesto (see Third generation database manifesto, and Object-oriented database manifesto)
Manipulative part, of a data model, 46

of the relational data model, 58-94
SQL implementation, 65-93
of the Object Data Model, 140-162
Many–to–many relationship,
in data design, 295-296
in ER modelling, 269
in bottom-up data analysis, 277-278
Many-to-one relationships (see One-to-many relationships)
Mark-up language (see also HTML), 29, 212-213
Mathematical logic, 70
MAX, in SQL, 78
Membership testing, in SQL, 73
Memex, 207
Memory cache (see Browser cache)
Meta-language, 212-213
Metadata, 115, 399
Methods, of an object, 118, 137, 143
of Web documents, 204
Microsoft,
Internet Explorer, 30
JScript (see also JavaScript), 242, 362
Word, 213
Middleware, 349-350
Migration, computer room to workplace, 20-21
MIME, 210, 213, 222, 380
Mime types (see Apache, NCSA server)
MIN, in SQL, 78
Minority browser, 198
MINUS, in SQL, 89-90
Minus (see Difference, in Relational algebra)
Mobile browsers, 228
mod_perl, 381, 382, 427
Modification, of objects, in C++ OML, –
Module, in ODL, 132
Multidatabases, 6, 34
Multilevel indexes, 341-345
Multimedia, 6, 19, 112, 164, 191
Multiple inheritance, 129, 171-172
Mutable object, 124
in OQL, 149, 159
Multipurpose Internet Mail Extension (see MIME)
MySQL, 363, 370

Name, of an attribute (see Attribute)
Name, of an object (see Object name)
Name, of a query, 162
Name resolution (see Operation name resolution)
Name server, on the Internet, 197
Natural join, in relational algebra, 61-62, 83
Natural keys, in bottom-up data analysis, 272
   in Normalisation, 303
Natural representation, of information as data, 12, 14
Navigational access, 144, 146
Nelson, Ted, 207
Nested lists, in HTML, 224
Nested selects, in SQL, 84-88
Nested tables, in HTML, 225
Netscape Navigator, 30, 200, 351
Network aware language, 384
Network data model (See First Generation Data Model)
Network Information Centre (see NIC)
Network Interface Layer, of ProtocolStack, 195
Network, of computers, 20, 21-22
New, object creation operation,
   in OQL, 159
   in SQL:1999, 175
news server, 193, 222
NF data model (see Nested– relationional data model)
NIC, 195-196
Non-cachable Web pages, 237
Normalisations, in relational database design, 300-310
NOT, in SQL, 70-72
NOT EXISTS, in SQL, 88
NOT NULL, in SQL, 56, 95-97
n-tuple, in the relational data model, 49
NULL, in SQL, 76-77
Null value, 53, 76-77, 109
NUMERIC, in SQL, 56

O2, 379
   epilog method, 380
   prolog method, 380
O2-O2WEB, 360, 379-381
O2ODBC, 379
O2WEB, 379

o2web_gateway, 379
Oak, 240
Occurrences, in data analysis, 267-268
Opera, 200
Object algebra, 140
Object databases, 19, 108, 111, 112-163
   Example, 141
   Manipulations, 142-143
   O2-O2WEB, 379
Object database entity (see Database entity)
Object database design, 126
Object Database Management System, 19,115-116,144,396
Object Data Management Group, 2, 113-117, 143, 396
Object data model,
   manipulative part, 140-143
   structural part, 118-139
Object diagram, in UML, 119
Object Definition Language (see ODL)
Object identifiers (see Identity, of an object)
Object intensive applications, 110
Object key (see Key, of an object)
Object Management Group, 117, 117
Object Manipulation Language, (see OML)
Object name , 122
Object–Oriented Database Manifesto, 114
Object–oriented data models (see Object data model)
Object–oriented programming language, 19, 113
Object-oriented features, in SQL:1999, 165-173
Object Query Language (see OQL)
Object–relational databases, 19, 108, 111, 163-179
Object-Relational Database Management System, 19
Object request broker, 117
Object Transaction Service (see OTS)
Object type, 124-126, 132
   Name, 133, 134, 159
   Characteristics, 133
   in UML, 125
Octet, literal type, 139

ODBC, 352, 362, 364, 379
ODBMS (see Object Database
  Management System)
ODL, 115, 129-139
  Example schema, 129-132
  Schema, 129
ODL/OML, 116, 140
ODMG (see Object Data Management
  Group)
OID (see Identity, of an object)
OIF (see Object Interchange Format)
OLAP, in SQL:1999, 163
OMG (see Object Management Group)
One-to-one relationships, in ER
  modelling, 268-269
  in bottom-up data analysis, 275-
  276, 277-278
ON, in SQL2 (see JOIN, in SQL2)
ON DELETE, in SQL, 95-97
ON UPDATE, in SQL, 95-97
One–to–many relationship,
  in data design, 297-298
Open Ingres, 376
Operating system, relationship with
  DBMS, 331-332
Operation name resolution (see Late
  binding)
Operation overloading, in SQL:1999
  (see also Late binding), 176
Operations, of an object, 118, 122
  in ODL, 136
  in OQL, 154
  Operation type, 136
Operations, on a relational database, 18
Operations on a UDT, in SQL:1999,
  168-169, 173-175
Operator composition, in OQL, 161-163
Optimistic locking protocols, 411-412
OR, in SQL, 70-72
ORDER BY, in OQL, 146
  in SQL, 79-80
  in SQL:1999, 165
Ordered collection objects, in OQL (see
  also List, in OQL and Array, in
  OQL), 153
Ordered lists, in HTML, 223
Organisation, 4-9
  boundaries within and between,
  33

OQL, 115, 140, 143-163, 396
  in O2-O2WEB, 379-380
  SQL-like syntax, 145
  pick and mix operations, 149-151
Oracle, 323, 364, 373, 396, 399
O-RDBMS (see Object-Relational
  Database Management System)
Orthogonality, of OQL, 148, 151, 161
OTS, 350
Outer join, in relational algebra, 63, 83
Overflow, in Hash files, 337-338
Overflow, in ISAM, 341
Overlapping tag pairs, in HTML, 215-
  216
Overloading, (see Operation
  overloading)
Override, late binding, 157-158

Packet switching, 195
Page, of a file, 331
PAGE-SCHEMA, in a Web page
  schema, 313
Parameterised types, in SQL:1999, 177
Partial functional dependency, 304-307
Partial links, in HTML, 220-221
Paste operations, in relational algebra,
  61-63
Path, of a relationship,
  in OQL, 150
Pattern definition, in SQL, 74-76
Perl, 352, 360, 372-376, 381
PerlScript, 363, 374-375
Persistent programming languages, 179
Pessimistic locking protocols, 411-412
PHP, 360, 361, 363-365, 381, 427
Physical database design, 328-348
  objectives, 328-329
  inputs to, 329-329
  methodology, 330-331
Physical data structure, 14
Physical mapping, between Web pages,
  263
Physical Web data design, 265-266
Physical Web data model, 263
Platform independence, 350
Polymorphism (see also Late binding),
  in SQL:1999, 175-176
Port number, 203
Positioning, of database files, 332
PostgresSQL, 363, 364

POST, Web document method, 204-
206, 238, 377, 416
Pre-processors, 352, 360
Presentation, of HTML documents, 228-
231, 232-234
Primary key (see Key, in the relational
data model)
PRIMARY KEY, in SQL, 56, 95-97
Private computer networks (see
Network, of computers)
PRIVATE, in SQL:1999, 172
Procedural programming language (see
Imperative programming
language)
Processing objects, in OQL, 154-160
Processing, of Web pages, 232-237
Progressive overflow, in Hash files, 338
Project, in relational algebra, 59-60, 66-
76
Project / Join Normal Form (See Fifth
Normal Form)
PROTECTED, in SQL:1999, 172-173
Protocol stack (see also TCP/IP), 194
Prototyping (see Rapid prototyping)
Proxy cache, 236-237
Pseudo users, 424
Public computer networks (see Network,
of computers)
PUBLIC, in SQL:1999, 172-173
Public key cryptography (see
Encryption)
PUT, Web document method, 239

Query program, in OQL, 163
QUERY_STRING, CGI environment
variable, 239

Random file (see Hash file, in Physical
design)
Range testing, in SQL, 73
Rapid prototyping, 378, 379
RDBMS (see Relational Database
Management System)
Read lock, 410
readonly, in ODL, 136
REAL, in SQL, 56
Recommendations for Comment, 2
Redundancy (see Data redundancy)
REFERENCE, in SQL, 95-97

Referential integrity, in the relational
data model, 93-94
Rehashing, in Hash files, 338
Relation, in a relational model (see
Tables, in relational databases)
Relational algebra (see Relational
database, relational algebra)
Relational data model (see also
Relational databases), 17
Representational weaknesses,
111
Structural part, 49-58
Relational database, 17, 47-100
Advantages, 47, 108
Gap between theory and
implementation, 108
Inappropriate applications, 110
Limitations, 19, 108-112
Relational algebra, 58-65
Relationships, 10-11
Between objects, 119-120, 128
in ER Modelling, 268
Relational representation, 51
Between data items, in data
analysis, 273-275
Between entities, in top-down
data analysis, 281-282
Between ODL and other
programming languages, 115
Between ODL and the schema
and applications, 116
in bottom-up data analysis, 272
in data analysis, 267
in ODL, 136
in UML, 126-127
Relative links, in html, 220-221, 222
Remote connection to Web databases,
34
Remote Database Access, language
(see RDA)
Repeated singular tags, in HTML, 216
REQUEST_METHOD, CGI environment
variable, 239
Requirements analysis, in database
design, 260-261
Resolution (see Object name resolution)
Response object, in ASP, 362
Restrict, in relational algebra, 58, 66-67
Retrieval operations, on an object, 123
RETURN, in SQL:1999, 175

Reuse, of types, 129
RFC (see Recommendations for Comment)
Right outer join, in relational algebra, 63, 83
RM/2, 110
Rollback, of transactions, 406
Root directory, 210- 211
Row, in the relational data model, 49
Row identifier, in SQL:1999, 166, 177
Row type, in SQL:1999, 178
Rule intensive applications, 111
Rumbaugh, design method, 117

Sandbox, 421
Schema (see also Database schema), 14, 54
Schema definition language (see SDL)
Scope, within an ODL schema, 132
Scoped names, within an ODL schema, 132
Script, 198
Scripting languages, 242, 352
Scripts, client side, 349
Scripts, server side, 349
SDL, of SQL, 48, 54-58
Second generation, of databases, (see Relational database), 112, 113
Second Normal Form, 300-301, 304-307
Secure Socket Layer (see SSL)
Security, in database systems, 16, 422-425, 427-428
Security mode, in Java, 384, 421
Security software, 420
SELECT...FROM...WHERE,
    in OQL, 149
    in SQL, 65-67
    Removing duplicate values, 68
    Retrieval from more than one table, 80-84
    Retrieval of columns from a single table, 67-69
    Retrieval of rows from a single table, 68-76
Search component, of a URL, 203-204
Search engine, 200-201
Semantic data model, 266
Semantic features, of relational data model, 111

Semantic gap, 110
Semantics, of an operation,
Sequence, in ODL (see Array, in OQL)
Serialisability, of transactions, 409, 410
Serial search (see Heap file, in Physical design)
Server, on the Web (see Web server)
Server configuration files (see Apache, NCSA server)
Server side JavaScript, 365
Server side inclusion (see SSI)
Server side, processing, 349, 351-358
    or client side, 352-381
Server side scripting, 360, 360-371
Servlets, in Java, 242, 384, 389-391, 421
    in SSI, 368-369
Session Identification URI, 413
Session tracking, 414
SET, in OQL, 158, 160
    in SQL, (see UPDATE, in SQL; Integrity features, in SQL)
Set inclusion, in OQL (see also Type generator), 137-138
Set operations, in relational algebra, 64-65, 88-90
Sets, in ODL, 137-138
SGML, 213, 231
Shallow equality (see Equality, of objects)
Side effects, of operations, 123, 155
Signature, of a type, in SQL:1999, 166
Singular tags, in HTML, 216
SMALLINT, in SQL, 56
Smalltalk (see Object–oriented programming languages)
Smalltalk binding (see ODL/OL binding)
SOME, in OQL, 151
    in SQL, 87
Sort keys, in OQL (see Order by, in OQL)
Sounds, as data (see Multimedia)
Sorted files, in Physical design, 335-336
Sorting rows, in SQL (see ORDER BY, in SQL)
Speaking browsers, 228
Spiders, 200-201, 228
SQL, 47-100,
    in ASP, 362-363
    in Java applets, 388

in ICE, 376
using JDBC, 394
in Perl, 373-375
Malicious code, 425-427
OQL compatibility, 144-145
Permits, 422
SQL1 (see also SQL), 48
SQL2 (see also SQL), 48, 57, 83-84, 88
SQL-89 (see SQL1)
SQL-92 (see SQL2)
SQL:1999 (see also SQL), 2,49, 163-173, 396
SQL3 (See SQL:1999)
SQL/DS, 47
SQLJ, 395-396
SQL*STAR, distributed database,
srm.conf (see Apache, NCSA server)
SSI, 360, 365-369
SSL, 420
Stand–alone database language, 48, 144
Standard Generalised Markup
Language (see SGML)
Standards, 2
Communication protocols, 22-24, 192
ECMA-262 (see also JavaScript), 242, 365
ODMG, 113-117
SQL, 48-49, 108
RDA, 108
UML, 117-118
Statelessness, of HTTP, 350, 199, 412-419
State, of an object, 118-119
in ODL, 135-136
Static hashing, in Hash files, 338
Storage schema, 54
Storage structures, in physical database design, 331-346
String literal type, in ODL, 139
in OQL, 156
String matching, in SQL, 73-76
Struct, in ODL (see also Type generator), 137
in OQL, 158
Structural part, of data model, 46, 49-58
Structural semantics, 112

Structured object types,
in ODL, 137-138
in OQL, 158-160
Structure of HTML documents, 228-231
Structured literal type (see Structures)
Structured UDT, in SQL:1999, 168-169
Structures, in OQL, 158
Structure, of a Web site, 210-212
Structured Query Language (see SQL)
Style sheet, in HTML, 219, 228, 232-234, 400, 401,403-404 429-430
Sub-schema, 54
Subtable/supertable relationship, in
Subtype, (see Subtype/supertype relationship)
Supertype (see Subtype/supertype relationship)
Subtype/supertype relationship,
Between objects, 128-129
in C++ ODL/OML, –
in ER modelling, 271
in ODL, 133
in OQL, 157-158
in SQL:1999, 171-172
in UML, 126-127
SUM, in SQL, 78
Summarising functions, in SQL, 78
Sybase, 323, 364
Synthesis (see Bottom-up data analysis)
System catalogue (see Data dictionary)
System R, 47

Tables, in Relational databases, 17-18, 49-52
Tables,
in HTML, 224-226
in SQL:1999, 177-179
Tags, in HTML (see HTML, tags)
TCP/IP, 23, 192, 193-195, 208
Telnet, 194
Templates, in SQL:1999, 177
Temporal database, 7
Text only browsers, 400
Tight, access keys (see Access key, of database file)
Theoretical model, of databases, 46
Theta-join, in relational algebra, 62-63, 81
The Web (see Web)

Third generation, of databases, 112
Third Normal Form, 300-301, 307-309
Three level database architecture (see
    Database architecture)
Time, as data (see Temporal
    Databases)
Time, literal type, 139
    in ODL,
Timestamp, literal type, 139
    in ODL,
Times operator, in relational algebra, 61
Top down data analysis, 279-284
Transactions, in databases, 404-412
    Inconsistent data, 407-409
    Lost operations, 406-407
Transactions, in Web database
    systems, 404-419
Transactions, in HTTP, 206
Transitive functional dependency, 307-
    309
Transmission Control Protocol / Internet
    Protocol (see TCP/IP)
Transport layer, of protocol stack, 194
Triggers, in SQL:1999, 165
Tuning, of database system, 15-16
Tuple, in relational data model, 49
Tuple, object type (see Structures)
Twelve rules, of relational databases,
    109-110
Two-phase commit, 412
Two-phase locking, 410
Type conversion operators, in OQL,
    160
Type declarations, in ODL, 133, 138-
    139
Type, of an object, (see Object type)
Type diagram, 125-126
Type generator, (see also Enumeration,
    Sets, Bags, Lists, Arrays,
    Structures), 137-138
Type properties, 134-135
Type system, 113

UDT, in SQL:1999, 165-173
    Advantages, 166-167
    Definition, 166
UML (see Unified Modeling Language)
UNDER, in SQL:1999, 171, 177
Unified Modeling Language,117-118,
    119, 125, 266

Uniform Resource Locator, (see URL)
union, in relational algebra, 58, 64, 88-
    90
unique, in OQL, 151
UNIQUE, in SQL, 56
Unique Web pages, 311
Universal quantifier, in OQL, 151
UNION, in SQL, 88-90
Unix,
    .cshrc files, 375
    cron facility, 428
Untrusted source, 421
UPDATE, in SQL, 90-91
Update anomalies, and Normalisation,
    300
Update operation, in SQL (see
    Changing values, in SQL)
Update operations, on an object, 123,
    154
Upgrade lock, 410
URL, 29-30, 201-204
URL rewriting, 413, 416-417
User-Agent header, in HTTP, 204
User authentication, 413, 418, 420
User defined types, in SQL:1999 (see
    UDT, in SQL:1999)
User interfaces,
    to Web database systems, 402
    to Intranet systems, 402-403
    and control of Web systems, 403-
    404

Validation, of Web Page Schemas, 314
Validation, of data, 399-400
Validity, of HTML, 216-217, 231-232
Validator, HTML, 231-232
VALUES, in SQL (see INSERT, in SQL)
Value-based model, 54
VBScript, 352, 361, 362, 421
Verification, of Web Page Schemas,
    314
Video, as data (see Multimedia)
Views, in relational databases, 97-100,
    109
Virtual directory, 211

W3C, 2, 231, 234, 413
WAIS, 222
Web, 24-31, 189-255
    architecture, 349

address, 26
applications, 31-33
basic concepts, 190-208
caching, 235-237
client, 29, 193, 349, 197-198
differences between Web data
and databases, 35
database implementation, 397-404
document file, 198
Internet application, 197-201
page, 210-211
security, 420
server, 30, 349, 193, 197-198, 209-210, 382-384
site, 197, 210-213
storing information, 208-213
usability, 404
Web application-specific concepts, 285-286, 288
Web data analysis, 264, 284, 288-295
Web database connectivity, 348-
Web database connectivity analysis, 293-295
Web data extraction, 289-293
Web database design, 259-327, 262-266
Web database systems, 31-36, 108
Introduction 1-42
Web documents, 191
Webmaster, 209
Web enhanced database systems, 33-34
Web page design, 262
Web page schema (see Logical Web page schema)
Web publication, 31-32
WebShare (see Root directory)
Web site, in a database, 428-430
WHERE, in SQL, 69-76
Wildcard characters, in OQL (see Strings)
WITH IDENTITY, in SQL:1999
Wizard, 48
Workflow management systems, 32
World Wide Web (see Web)
WWWRoot (see Root directory)
Write lock, 410
WWW (see Web)

X.25, 195
Xanadu, 207
XML, 213, 235
X/Open, 350

Zero-or-one-to-many relationships,
in data design, 298-300
in ER modelling, 270
in bottom-up data analysis, 276-278